A PRESCRIPTION FOR DIGNITY

A Prescription for Dignity
Rethinking Criminal Justice and Mental Disability Law

MICHAEL L. PERLIN
New York Law School, USA

ASHGATE

Published by

Ashgate Publishing Limited
Wey Court East
Union Road
Farnham
Surrey, GU9 7PT
England

Ashgate Publishing Company
110 Cherry Street
Suite 3-1
Burlington, VT 05401-3818
USA

www.ashgate.com

British Library Cataloguing in Publication Data
Perlin, Michael L., 1946–
A prescription for dignity: rethinking criminal justice and mental disability law.
1. Mentally ill offenders–Legal status, laws, etc. 2. Criminal justice, Administration of.
I. Title
364.3’8-dc23

The Library of Congress has cataloged the printed edition as follows:
Perlin, Michael L., 1946–
A prescription for dignity : rethinking criminal justice and mental disability law / by Michael L. Perlin.
pages cm
Includes bibliographical references and index.
ISBN 978-0-7546-7724-6 (hardback : alk. paper) — ISBN 978-0-7546-9440-3 (ebook) — ISBN 978-1-4724-0170-0 (epub) 1. Mental health laws. 2. People with mental disabilities—Civil rights. 3. Respect for persons—Law and legislation. 4. Mental health courts. 5. Insanity (Law) 6. Human rights. I. Title.
K640.P49 2013
345’.03–dc23

2012044665

ISBN 9780754677246 (hbk)
ISBN 9780754694403 (ebk – PDF)
ISBN 9781472401700 (ebk – ePUB)

MIX
Paper from responsible sources
FSC
www.fsc.org
FSC® C013056

Printed and bound in Great Britain by
TJ International Ltd, Padstow, Cornwall

Contents

Preface

I was a Public Defender (PD) for just three years, some 40 years ago, but, in many ways, those were the years that defined the rest of my career, both structurally and philosophically. After that job, I became the first director of the NJ Public Advocate's Division of Mental Health Advocacy, a statewide, state-funded law office that represented individuals with psychiatric disabilities in individual and law reform actions. I then became a professor at New York Law School, where I have been teaching mental disability law since 1985, and where I now supervise 13 separate courses in the school's online mental disability law program, and where I also direct the International Mental Disability Law Reform Project in the law school's Justice Action Center. I lecture and write frequently about all aspects of mental disability law, often with respect to questions of criminal law and procedure. My PD experiences have informed and guided all of this work, and they are never far from my mind.

One of my primary responsibilities as a PD was the representation of persons in New Jersey's Vroom Building, the "maximum security facility for the criminally insane" (persons awaiting incompetency-to-stand-trial evaluations, persons found incompetent to stand trial, and persons who had been found not guilty by reason of insanity). I represented these individuals on their applications for writs of *habeas corpus*, and, as I have written previously, "the cases were—to be charitable—charades."[1] With the bravado of the 27 year-old lawyer that I was, I filed suit on their behalf to seek enforcement of the Supreme Court's mandate, in *Jackson v. Indiana*,[2] that had held that a person who was not likely to regain his competency to stand trial could not be detained indefinitely in such a facility. The publicity that followed that case[3] is what led directly to the creation of the NJ Division of Mental Health Advocacy, and inexorably guided the rest of my career.

---

1 Michael L. Perlin, *"Half-Wracked Prejudice Leaped Forth": Sanism, Pretextuality, and Why and How Mental Disability Law Developed As It Did*, 10 J. Contemp. Leg. Iss. 3, 7 (1999).

2 406 U.S.715 (1972).

3 *See* Dixon v. Cahill, No. L30977/y-71 P.W. (N.J. Super. Ct. Law Div. 1973), reprinted in 5 Michael L. Perlin, Mental Disability Law: Civil and Criminal § 14-7, at 119–21 (2d ed. 2002) (mandating *Jackson* hearings for all Vroom Building residents). After the entry of the consent decree in *Dixon*, the trial judge appointed me to individually represent each member of the class. Approximately 215 of the class members had previously been found incompetent to stand trial. *See* Michael L. Perlin, *"For the Misdemeanor Outlaw": The Impact of the ADA on the Institutionalization of Criminal Defendants with Mental Disabilities*, 52 Alabama L. Rev. 193, 207 n.94 (2000).

I discuss how my friend and mentor, Dr. Robert Sadoff, inspired me to file this suit in Michael L. Perlin, *"May He Stay Forever Young": Robert Sadoff and the History of Mental*

But there is more to my PD days. I have also written about my experiences in court representing my clients, when "I had grown accustomed to asides, snickers and comments from judges, to 'eyerolling' from my adversaries, to running monologue commentaries by bailiffs and court clerks (all about my clients' 'oddness')."[4] It was clear to me that, as far as many prosecutors and some judges went, when a defendant with a serious mental disability appeared in court—whether or not there was a question as to the incompetency status or the insanity defense—the courtroom became (and these are the words of a former research assistant describing a like court in NYC in the late 2000s), a "due process-free zone." Most often (there were important exceptions, of course), no one took the case, my client, or the disposition of the matter seriously.[5] After all, my client was seen as "crazy," "a nut case," "bonkers," "touched," or other similarly pejorative descriptive adjectives. The attitude was "why go through all the bother of making believe that the process really mattered?" when, no matter how the case was ultimately resolved, my client would ultimately wind up for life in a psychiatric institution (either civil or criminal).

I recall vividly—and this was more than 35 years ago—when I prepared to conduct a *voir dire* of a state's expert witness (someone who had testified previously in hundreds of cases) and brought in to court a stack of treatises in order to challenge his credentials. The trial judge was floored. "Mr. Perlin, what in the world do you think you are doing?" Reluctantly, he let me do the cross-examination.[6]

This, as I have written before, all illuminated to me the way that the legal system was riddled with *sanism* and with *pretextuality*.[7] And these insights have informed the bulk of my scholarly work for over 20 years.[8] But it was much more than that. These experiences clarified to me a reality that is at the heart of this book: that persons with mental disabilities were, by and large, robbed of their dignity when they entered the criminal justice system.[9]

Health Law, 33 J. AMER. ACAD. PSYCHIATRY & L. 236, 236–37 (2005). For this and for so much else, I am forever indebted to Bob.

4 Perlin, *supra* note 1, at 9.

5 *See* Michael L. Perlin, *"You Have Discussed Lepers and Crooks": Sanism in Clinical Teaching*, 9 CLINICAL L. REV. 683, 695 (2003) (discussing how some lawyers "take less seriously case outcomes that are adverse to their clients [with mental disabilities]").

6 The judge allowed the witness to testify, of course, but there was no question in my mind that, down the road, he evaluated the witness's testimony much more carefully than had I never launched this challenge.

7 *See generally* MICHAEL L. PERLIN, THE HIDDEN PREJUDICE: MENTAL DISABILITY ON TRIAL (2000). I discuss these concepts extensively *infra* Chapter 2.

8 For my first articles on these concepts, see Michael L. Perlin, *Morality and Pretextuality, Psychiatry and Law: Of Ordinary Common Sense, Heuristic Reasoning, and Cognitive Dissonance*, 19 BULL. AM. ACAD. PSYCHIATRY & L. 131 (1991); Michael L. Perlin, *On Sanism*, 46 SMU L. REV. 373 (1992); Michael L. Perlin, *Pretexts and Mental Disability Law: The Case of Competency*, 47 U. MIAMI L. REV. 625 (1993).

9 *See infra* Chapter 7. "There is perhaps no more solid foundation for human rights than a widespread awakening to the human dignity that resides in every one of us." Soka Gakkai

I was not naïve. I knew from the start that a white-collar corporate criminal defendant or a politician defendant would often be treated much more civilly (sometimes, even deferentially) than the defendants that made up the bulk of my "regular" PD caseload: economically impoverished, inner city youth. But in comparing how *those* clients of mine were treated to the ways that my clients with mental disabilities were treated, the contrasts jumped out. The latter were mostly treated with no dignity at all.

Since I became a professor, I have regularly taught courses in Criminal Law and Criminal Procedure, and have supervised students in judicial externships and in placements in PD and District Attorneys' offices. I talk to my students about their work, and with some important exceptions,[10] very little has changed in the four decades since I first entered an appearance in a criminal case. That, of course, saddens me deeply.

I thus decided to write this book about the need for dignity in the criminal trial process in cases involving defendants with mental disabilities. Although, for reasons of space, I have limited my substantive topics to three aspects of criminal law and procedure —insanity,[11] incompetency[12] and sentencing[13]—I believe that my findings, conclusions and recommendations will also apply to all other aspects of this process as it relates to this population.[14] I say this because I believe that the perspectives that I have chosen to focus upon are of universal significance to this population. In this work, I write about *counsel*,[15] about *international human rights law*,[16] about *mental health courts*,[17] and about *alternative jurisprudences*.[18] I believe that careful examinations of each of these gives us building blocks that will allow us to reconstruct our criminal justice system in a way in which dignity is privileged, not subordinated.

- The quality of counsel afforded this population is often shamelessly subpar; and what is even more of a shame is that courts often do not care.[19] If a defendant's lawyer is sanist,[20] why should we expect much more from other

---

International, Buddhism and Human Dignity (accessible at http://www.sgi.org/buddhism/buddhist-concepts/buddhism-and-human-dignity.html, last accessed, October 9, 2012).

10 Those who work in mental health courts, see *infra* Chapter 5, come back with very different stories.

11 *See infra* Chapter 8.

12 *See infra* Chapter 9.

13 *See infra* Chapter 10.

14 I write about this separately in connection with defendants with mental disabilities who face the death penalty in Michael L. Perlin, Mental Disability and the Death Penalty: The Shame of the States (2013).

15 *See infra* Chapter 3.

16 *See infra* Chapter 4.

17 *See infra* Chapter 5.

18 *See infra* Chapter 6.

19 In one of my last cases before I became a professor, I "second sat" the case of Strickland v. Washington, 466 U.S. 668, 668 (1984) (establishing effectiveness of counsel standards).

20 *See generally* Perlin, *supra* note 3.

players in the system?[21] Only an overhaul—a complete overhaul—of our expectations of counsel representing this population will allow a system of dignity to flourish.

- I travel the world doing human rights work on behalf of persons institutionalized because of mental disabilities. If I go to Finland, if I go to Israel, if I go to Uganda, if I go to Taiwan, if I go to Uruguay, if I go to Indonesia, most of my audience is familiar with the United Nations Convention on the Rights of Persons with Disabilities.[22] When I speak in the US (to rooms of lawyers, of forensic mental health professionals, of citizens generally concerned about world issues) and I raise the topic of the Convention, I am met mostly with blank stares. This Convention is a blueprint for the creation of a dignified system; we ignore it with impunity.[23]
- In 1997, I received a phone call from a woman I did not know. "Hi, Professor Perlin," she said. "My name is Ginger Lerner-Wren, and I am a judge in Fort Lauderdale. I've just been asked by my assignment judge to head a new mental health court, and I want to make sure that it promotes therapeutic jurisprudence, honors defendants' civil liberties, and values human rights protections. Can I chat with you for a while?" We talked (and subsequently have become good friends), and Judge Lerner-Wren has gone on to preside over what is arguably the best mental health court in the nation.[24] There are now more than 300 of these courts with varying mandates and varying jurisdictional limitations. But I believe, when they are modeled after Judge Lerner-Wren's court (and the courts of several

21 *See, e.g.*, Michael L. Perlin, *"I Might Need a Good Lawyer, Could Be Your Funeral, My Trial": A Global Perspective on the Right to Counsel in Civil Commitment Cases, and Its Implications for Clinical Legal Education*, 28 Wash. U. J. L. & Soc'l Pol'y 241 (2008).

22 *See, e.g.*, Michael L. Perlin, International Human Rights And Mental Disability Law: When The Silenced Are Heard (2011); Michael L. Perlin, *"A Change Is Gonna Come": The Implications of the United Nations Convention on the Rights of Persons with Disabilities for the Domestic Practice of Constitutional Mental Disability Law*, 29 No. Ill. U. L. Rev. 483 (2009).

23 President Obama signed the CRPD three years ago, *see* Michelle Diament, *Obama Urges Senate To Ratify Disability Treaty* (May 18, 2012), accessible at http://www.disabilityscoop.Com/2012/05/18/Obama-Urges-Senate-Treaty/15654/, but the Senate failed to ratify on December 4, 2012 for lack of a "super majority" of votes. The Democratic leadership has promised to bring the Convention up again for ratification in 2013. See http://usicd.org/index.cfm/crpdupdates. Although the United States has not ratified the CRPD, "a state's obligations under it are controlled by the Vienna Convention of the Law of Treaties[,] which requires signatories 'to refrain from acts which would defeat [the Disability Convention's] object and purpose.'" See Henry Dlugacz & Christopher Wimmer, *The Ethics of Representing Clients with Limited Competency in Guardianship Proceedings*, 4 St. Louis U. J. Health L. & Pol'y 331, 362-63 (2011).

24 For her views, see Ginger Lerner-Wren, *Mental Health Courts: Serving Justice and Promoting Recovery*, 19 Annals Health L. 577 (2010).

other trailblazers in this area),[25] such courts offer the best opportunity for insuring meaningful dignity for the population in question.[26]

- My good friends, David Wexler and the late Bruce Winick, conceived of the idea of therapeutic jurisprudence (TJ) as an alternative way of thinking about the law and the legal system, envisioning the law as a potential "therapeutic agent."[27] I quickly became a "fellow traveler," and, in 1993, ran a TJ conference at New York Law School that led to the first law journal symposium ever on this topic.[28] TJ has blossomed and expanded since that times in ways that I don't think David and Bruce could have imagined when they first articulated TJ's principles, and, with each expansion, its role as a dignity-promoter grows. Similarly, the insights of procedural justice (PJ) and of restorative justice (RJ) (many flowing from the research and papers of Tom Tyler[29] and John Braithwaite)[30] showed us that individuals with mental disabilities, like all other citizens, are affected by such process values as participation, dignity, and trust, and that there were ways that the legal system could be restructured to avoid stigma, the heart of sanism. I believe that the insights of TJ, PJ and RJ all must be taken seriously if we are to find new and creative ways to enhance dignity.

So, I have written this book in an effort to underscore what can be done and what needs to be done if we are to create a system that provides the sort of dignity that recognizes that people "possess an intrinsic worth that should be recognized and respected."[31] In 1995, I wrote an article about the Colin Ferguson trial[32] and

---

25 *See infra* Chapter 5.

26 In a recent email, Judge Lerner-Wren characterized the objective of her court in this manner: "To bring persons with mental disabilities in the criminal law system out from the shadows and into a place of judicial prominence." (email from Ginger Lerner-Wren to Michael Perlin, October 8, 2012, on file with author).

27 *See, e.g.*, Therapeutic Jurisprudence: The Law as a Therapeutic Agent (David B. Wexler ed., 1990). For a description of the thought processes that led Professors Wexler and Winick to develop this idea, see David Wexler & Bruce Winick, *Preface*, in Essays in therapeutic Jurisprudence i, ix–xiv (David B. Wexler & Bruce Winick eds, 1991), describing the preliminary conversations in the development of TJ that took place on the beach, at law professors' meetings in cafes, and during morning jogs.

28 *See* Michael L. Perlin, *What Is Therapeutic Jurisprudence?*, 10 N.Y.L. Sch. J. Hum. Rts. 623, 623 n. a (1993).

29 *See, e.g.*, Tom Tyler, *The Psychological Consequences of Judicial Procedures: Implications for Civil Commitment Hearings*, 46 SMU L. Rev, 433 (1992).

30 *See, e.g.*, John Braithwaite, Restorative Justice & Responsive Regulation (2002).

31 Carol Sanger, *Decisional Dignity: Teenage Abortion, Bypass Hearings, and the Misuse of Law*, 18 Colum. J. Gender & L. 409, 415 (2009).

32 Ferguson was a criminal defendant with serious mental illness who was charged with, and ultimately convicted of, multiple murders on a commuter railroad trail on Long Island, NY, in 1993, and who represented himself *pro se* at his trial. *See* Michael L. Perlin,

titled it, in part, "Dignity Was the First to Leave."[33] There was no dignity in Ferguson's trial, and there have been many other less famous and less politically consequential cases that, similarly, have been without dignity. But all of these cases matter—to the defendants before the court, to their victims (alleged and actual), to the judicial system and, necessarily, to all of us. And that is why I have written this book.

There are many thanks to offer: to David Wexler for inspiring me to follow the TJ path,[34] to Ginger Lerner-Wren for creating the court that she did, to Eva Szeli for showing me exactly how important international human rights were to this entire inquiry, to Evelin Lindner and Linda Hartling—the core of the Human Dignity and Humiliation Studies Network (on whose Global Advisory Board I have sat for several years)—who have taught me so much about the meaning and importance of dignity, and have been such an inspiration for all I have done in this area of law and policy, and to my colleagues teaching in the NYLS online mental disability law program (especially, Eva, Heather Ellis Cucolo, Pam Cohen, Rick Friedman, Patrick Reilly, Henry Dlugacz and Debbie Dorfman) for their encouragement and support. I want to especially acknowledge my research assistant, Alison Lynch, for her outstanding work, her good humor and her helpful insights into all of the topics I cover here. She has done a brilliant job and I am in her debt. Anna Blaine, a lawyer-librarian in the New York Law School library, has done an outstanding job of finding me whatever I needed, seemingly in minutes. I also want to thank my current and former Deans and Associate Deans at New York Law School—Rick Matasar, Carol Buckler, Steve Ellmann, Jethro Lieberman, Anthony Crowell and Deborah Archer—for supporting the sabbatical that has given me the opportunity and the time to write this book.

I dedicate this book to my wife Linda and my children, Julie and Alex. They are my joy, my heart, my soul, my life. Two years ago, Alex started his legal career as a Public Defender in Trenton, NJ, where I began my career 41 years ago. Six months ago, he relocated to Brooklyn and joined the staff of the Brooklyn Defender Service. My hopes are that the judges in the courtrooms in which he represents his clients provide them—and, again, all of us—with the dignity to which they are entitled.

Michael L. Perlin
New York City
March 16, 2013

"Dignity Was the First to Leave": Godinez v. Moran, Colin Ferguson, and the Trial of Mentally Disabled Criminal Defendants, 14 BEHAV. SCI. & L. 61 (1996).

33 The title comes from Bob Dylan's song "Dignity." *See* Michael L. Perlin, *Tangled Up In Law : The Jurisprudence of Bob Dylan*, 38 FORD. URB. L.J. 1395, 1397 (2011), explaining the thought process that led me to use this as the article title.

34 I so regret that Bruce Winick is no longer with us for me to thank here.

Chapter 1
Introduction

The relationship between mental disability and the criminal justice system is complex, and it serves as a screen upon which society projects bundles of attitudes, emotions and feelings about responsibility, free will, autonomy, choice, public safety and the meaning and purpose of punishment.[1] Too often, it serves as an escape valve through which society's prejudices and stereotypes overwhelm our commitment to fairness and justice.[2] Too often, it creates an atmosphere in which society winks its collective eye at known-to-be-false expert testimony, teleologically offered to meet an approved social end.[3] Twenty-five years ago, I characterized the relationship between the judicial process and persons with mental disabilities as a "doctrinal abyss";[4] the reality is that all too little has changed in the intervening two and a half decades.[5]

---

1 *See* Virgin Islands v. Fredericks, 578 F.2d 927, 937 (3d Cir.1978) (Adams, J., dissenting) ("the insanity defense [is] a screen upon which the community … project[s] its visions of criminal justice.").

2 *Cf.* Michael L. Perlin, *Unpacking the Myths: The Symbolism Mythology of Insanity Defense Jurisprudence*, 40 Case W. Res. L. Rev. 599, 628–29 (1989–90) ("punishment is clearly a socially sanctioned safety valve through which we express community condemnation of wrongdoers, especially the wrongdoers we fear the most").

3 *See, e.g.,* Michael L. Perlin, *Pretexts and Mental Disability Law: The Case of Competency*, 47 U. Miami L. Rev. 625, 653–58 (1993) (Perlin, *Pretexts)* (on how the desire for specific social ends "animate[s] the entire incompetency to stand trial system"). On the teleology of decisonmakers in cases involving the application of the death penalty to persons with mental disabilities, see Michael L. Perlin, *The Sanist Lives of Jurors in Death Penalty Cases: The Puzzling Role of Mitigating Mental Disability Evidence,* 8 Notre Dame J. L., Ethics & Pub. Pol. 239, 262–65 (1994) (Perlin, *Sanist Jurors).*

4 *See* Michael L. Perlin, *The Supreme Court, the Mentally Disabled Criminal Defendant, and Symbolic Values: Random Decisions, Hidden Rationales, or Doctrinal Abyss*? 29 Ariz. L. Rev. 1 (1987).

5 I spent 13 years as a lawyer representing persons with mental disabilities (3 years as the Deputy Public Defender in charge of the Mercer County (Trenton) NJ Office of the Public Defender, 8 years as the director of the NJ Division of Mental Health Advocacy, and 2 years as Special Counsel to the NJ Public Advocate), and have taught mental disability law and criminal law and procedure courses at New York Law School since 1984. I expect that I am the only law professor in the nation (and most likely, the world) who teaches and/or supervises *thirteen* different courses in the mental disability law subject matter area. *See e,g.*, Michael L. Perlin, *"They Keep It All Hid": The Ghettoization of Mental Disability Law and Its Implications for Legal Education*, 54 St. Louis U. L. J. 857 (2010).

I have written about these issues before, in a series of law review articles and in full-length books on (1) the insanity defense,[6] (2) the ways that what I call "sanism" and "pretextuality" permeate and infect the entire legal process,[7] (3) the relationship between international human rights and mental disability law,[8] and (4) the relationship between mental disability law and the death penalty.[9] Here, I widen my range to include the entire criminal justice system as it affects persons with mental disabilities.

Sanism is an irrational prejudice of the same quality and character of other irrational prejudices that cause (and are reflected in) prevailing social attitudes of racism, sexism, homophobia, and ethnic bigotry. It permeates all aspects of mental disability law and affects all participants in the mental disability law system: litigants, fact finders, counsel, expert and lay witnesses. Its corrosive effects have warped mental disability law jurisprudence in involuntary civil commitment law, institutional law, tort law and all aspects of the criminal process.[10]

Pretextuality defines the ways in which courts accept testimonial dishonesty (either implicitly or explicitly) and engage similarly in dishonest (and frequently meretricious) decision-making. It is especially poisonous where witnesses, especially expert witnesses, show a "high propensity to purposely distort their testimony in order to achieve desired ends."[11] This pretextuality infects all participants in the judicial system, breeds cynicism and disrespect for the law, demeans participants, and reinforces shoddy lawyering, blasé judging, and, at times, perjurious and/or corrupt testifying.[12] It continues to this day.[13]

In this volume, I am broadening my substantive focus to consider multiple substantive criminal law topics, and my theoretical focus to move beyond the

6 Michael L. Perlin, The Jurisprudence of the Insanity Defense (1994).

7 *See* Michael L. Perlin, The Hidden Prejudice: Mental Disability on Trial (2000).

8 Michael L. Perlin, International Human Rights and Mental Disability Law: When the Silenced Are Heard (2011).

9 Michael L. Perlin, Mental Disability and the Death Penalty: The Shame of the States (2013).

10 *See, e.g.*, Michael L. Perlin, *"You Have Discussed Lepers and Crooks": Sanism in Clinical Teaching*, 9 Clinical L. Rev. 683, 684 (2003) (Perlin, *Lepers)*; Perlin, *supra* note 7, at 21–58; *see infra* Chapter 2.

11 Michael L. Perlin, *Morality and Pretextuality, Psychiatry and Law: Of "Ordinary Common Sense," Heuristic Reasoning, and Cognitive Dissonance*, 19 Bull. Am. Acad. Psychiatry & L. 131, 135 (1991).

12 *See generally*, Perlin, *supra* note 7.

13 *See, e.g.*, William H. Fisher & Thomas Grisso, *Commentary: Civil Commitment Statutes—40 Years of Circumvention*, 38 J, Am. Acad. Psychiatry & L. 365, 368 (2010) (discussing how trial judges have regularly "stretched and circumvented" civil commitment law). On how these laws are applied differentially in cases involving individuals simply facing civil commitment and those facing civil commitment following a finding of incompetency to stand trial, see Gwen Levitt et al., *Civil Commitment Outcomes of Incompetent Defendants*, 38 J. Am. Acad. Psychiatry & L. 349 (2010).

attitudinal factors that I have already discussed extensively.[14] I have chosen to do this because my teaching, my writing, and my involvement in the public sector over the past 25 years have led me to focus on several additional principles that, I think, require greater scrutiny.

- It is meaningless (perhaps fatuous) to engage in any sort of serious discussion of these issues without looking carefully at issues of adequacy

14 I have, by way of example, explored the relationships between sanism and pretextuality in matters involving, inter alia, competency to stand trial, *e.g.*, Michael L. Perlin, *"Everything's a Little Upside Down, As a Matter of Fact the Wheels Have Stopped": The Fraudulence of the Incompetency Evaluation Process,* 4 HOUSTON J. HEALTH L. & POL'Y 239 (2004) (Perlin, *Evaluation Process*); Perlin, *Pretexts, supra* note 3; sexual autonomy, *e.g.,* Michael L. Perlin, *Hospitalized Patients and the Right to Sexual Interaction: Beyond the Last Frontier?*, 20 NYU REV. L. & SOC'L CHANGE 302 (1993–94); Michael L. Perlin, *"Everybody Is Making Love/Or Else Expecting Rain": Considering the Sexual Autonomy Rights of Persons Institutionalized Because of Mental Disability in Forensic Hospitals and in Asia*, 83 U. WASH. L. REV. 481 (2008); the right to refuse treatment, *e.g.*, Michael L. Perlin, *"And My Best Friend, My Doctor / Won't Even Say What It Is I've Got": The Role and Significance of Counsel in Right to Refuse Treatment Cases*, 42 SAN DIEGO L. REV. 735 (2005) (Perlin, *Role and Significance of Counsel*); Michael L. Perlin & Deborah A. Dorfman, *"Is It More Than Dodging Lions and Wastin' Time?": Adequacy of Counsel, Questions of Competence, and the Judicial Process in Individual Right to Refuse Treatment Cases*, 2 PSYCHOLOGY, PUB. POL'Y & L.114 (1996); "autonomous decision-making," *e.g.*, Michael L. Perlin, *"Make Promises by the Hour": Sex, Drugs, the ADA, and Psychiatric Hospitalization*, 46 DEPAUL L. REV. 947 (1997); the Americans with Disabilities Act, *e.g.*, Michael L. Perlin, *The ADA and Persons with Mental Disabilities: Can Sanist Attitudes Be Undone?*, 8 J. L. & HEALTH 15 (1993–94); competency to plead guilty or waive counsel, *e.g.*, Michael L. Perlin, *"Dignity Was the First to Leave":* Godinez v. Moran, *Colin Ferguson, and the Trial of Mentally Disabled Criminal Defendants*, 14 BEHAV. SCI. & L. 61 (1996)(Perlin, *Dignity*); jury decision-making in death penalty cases, *e.g.*, Perlin, *Sanist Jurors, supra* note 3; special education, *e.g.*, Michael L. Perlin, *"Simplify You, Classify You": Stigma, Stereotypes and Civil Rights in Disability Classification Systems*, 25 GA. ST. U. L. REV. 607 (2009); international human rights law, *e.g.*, Michael L. Perlin, *Promoting Social Change in Asia and the Pacific: The Need for a Disability Rights Tribunal to Give Life to the UN Convention On The Rights Of Persons With Disabilities*, 44 GEO. WASH. INT'L L. REV. 1 (2012) (Perlin, *Promoting Social Change*); forensic ethics, *e.g.,* Michael L Perlin, *"They're An Illusion To Me Now": Forensic Ethics, Sanism and Pretextuality*, in PSYCHOLOGY, CRIME AND LAW: BRIDGING THE GAP 239 (David Canter & Rita Zukauskien eds, 2008); the use of neuroimaging evidence in the criminal trial process, *e.g.*, Michael L. Perlin, *"His Brain Has Been Mismanaged with Great Skill": How Will Jurors Respond to Neuroimaging Testimony in Insanity Defense Cases?*, 42 AKRON L. REV. 885 (2009); *"Good and Bad, I Defined These Terms, Quite Clear No Doubt Somehow": Neuroimaging and Competency to be Executed after Panetti*, 28 BEHAV. SCI. & L. 621 (2010); and the bar's attitude towards *counsel* with mental disabilities, *e.g.,* Michael L. Perlin, *"Baby, Look Inside Your Mirror": The Legal Profession's Willful and Sanist Blindness to Lawyers with Mental Disabilities*, 69 U. PITT. L. REV. 589 (2008) (Perlin, *Mirror).*

of counsel in the specific context of the representation of persons with mental disabilities.[15]

- It is essential that we begin to think seriously about the impact of international human rights law, specifically, the recently ratified United Nations Convention on the Rights of Persons with Disabilities (CRPD),[16] on the issues in question.[17]

15 *See, e.g.*, Michael L. Perlin & Robert L. Sadoff, *Ethical Issues in the Representation of Individuals in the Commitment Process*, 45 LAW & CONTEMP. PROBS. 161 (Summer 1982); Michael L. Perlin, *Fatal Assumption: A Critical Evaluation of the Role of Counsel in Mental Disability Cases*, 16 LAW & HUM. BEHAV. 39 (1992); Perlin, *Lepers*, *supra* note 10; Perlin, *Role and Significance of Counsel*, *supra* note 12; Perlin, *Promoting Social Change, supra* note 14; Perlin, *Mirror*, *supra* note 14; Michael L. Perlin, *"Too Stubborn To Ever Be Governed By Enforced Insanity": Some Therapeutic Jurisprudence Dilemmas in the Representation of Criminal Defendants in Incompetency and Insanity Cases* (Perlin, *Too Stubborn*) 33 INT'L J. L. & PSYCHIATRY 475 (2010). On counsel issues in the context of defendants with mental disabilities facing the death penalty, see PERLIN, *supra* note 9, at 123–38. On counsel issues in the civil commitment context in an international perspective, see Michael L. Perlin, *"I Might Need a Good Lawyer, Could Be Your Funeral, My Trial": A Global Perspective on the Right to Counsel in Civil Commitment Cases, and Its Implications for Clinical Legal Education*, 28 WASH. U. J. L. & SOC'L POL'Y 241 (2008) (Perlin, *Your Funeral, My Trial*).

16 G.A. Res. A/61/611 (2006).

17 *See generally*, PERLIN, *supra* note 8; MICHAEL L. PERLIN ET AL., INTERNATIONAL HUMAN RIGHTS AND COMPARATIVE MENTAL DISABILITY LAW: CASES AND MATERIALS (2006); *see also*, *e.g.*, Perlin, *Promoting Social Change*, *supra* note 14; Michael L. Perlin, *International Human Rights Law and Comparative Mental Disability Law: The Universal Factors*, 34 SYRACUSE J. INT'L L. & COMMERCE 333 (2007) (Perlin, *Universal Factors*); Perlin, *Your Funeral, My Trial*, *supra*, note 13; Michael L. Perlin & Eva Szeli, *Mental Health Law and Human Rights: Evolution and Contemporary Challenges*, in MENTAL HEALTH AND HUMAN RIGHTS: VISION, PRAXIS, AND COURAGE 98 (Michael Dudley ed., 2012); Michael L. Perlin, *"Through the Wild Cathedral Evening": Barriers, Attitudes, Participatory Democracy, Professor tenBroek, and the Rights of Persons with Mental Disabilities*, 13 TEX. J. ON CIV. LIBS. & CIV. RTS. 413 (2008); Michael L. Perlin & Valerie McClain, *"Where Souls Are Forgotten": Cultural Competencies, Forensic Evaluations and International Human Rights*, 15 PSYCHOL., PUB. POL'Y & L. 257 (2009); Michael L. Perlin & Henry A. Dlugacz, *"It's Doom Alone That Counts": Can International Human Rights Law Be An Effective Source of Rights in Correctional Conditions Litigation?*, 27 BEHAV. SCI. & L. 675 (2009); Astrid Birgden & Michael L. Perlin, "*Tolling for the Luckless, the Abandoned and Forsaked": Community Safety, Therapeutic Jurisprudence and International Human Rights Law As Applied to Prisoners and Detainees*, 13 LEG. & CRIMINOL. PSYCHOLOGY 231 (2008) (Birgden & Perlin, *Tolling*); Astrid Birgden & Michael L. Perlin, *"Where The Home In The Valley Meets The Damp Dirty Prison": A Human Rights Perspective On Therapeutic Jurisprudence And The Role Of Forensic Psychologists In Correctional Settings*, 14 AGGRESSION & VIOLENT BEHAVIOR 256 (2009) (Birgden & Perlin, *Home in the Valley*).

- It is time to restructure the dialogue about mental health courts,[18] and to begin to (1) consider whether the development of such courts will finally allow us to move away from society's predominantly currently-held position that mental illness reflects "a defect of morality or will,"[19] and (2) take seriously the potential ameliorative impact of such courts on the ultimate disposition of all cases involving criminal defendants with mental disabilities.[20]
- It is necessary to consider the impact of therapeutic jurisprudence,[21]

---

18 *See, e.g.*, Michael L. Perlin, "*There Are No Trials Inside the Gates of Eden": Mental Health Courts, the Convention on the Rights of Persons with Disabilities, Dignity, and the Promise of Therapeutic Jurisprudence*, in COERCIVE CARE: LAW AND POLICY (Bernadette McSherry & Ian Freckelton, eds, 2013) (in press) (Perlin, *Gates)*; Michael L. Perlin, *"John Brown Went Off to War": Considering Veterans' Courts as Problem-Solving Courts*, – NOVA L. REV. – (2013) (in press) ; Michael L. Perlin, *"The Judge, He Cast His Robe Aside": Mental Health Courts, Dignity and Due Process,* – J. MENT. HEALTH L. & POL'Y – (2013) (in press); MICHAEL L. PERLIN & HEATHER ELLIS CUCOLO, MENTAL DISABILITY LAW: CIVIL AND CRIMINAL, §1-2.4, at 11–12 n.254.2 (2012 Cum. Supp.); Allison D. Redlich et al., *The Second Generation of Mental Health Courts*, 11 PSYCHOL. PUB. POL'Y & L. 527 (2005); Matthew J. D'Emic, *The Promise of Mental Health Courts*, 22 CRIM. JUST. 24 (Fall 2007); Gregory L. Acquaviva, *Mental Health Courts: No Longer Experimental*, 36 SETON HALL L. REV. 971 (2006); Carol Fisler, *Building Trust And Managing Risk: A Look At A Felony Mental Health Court*, 11 PSYCHOL., PUB. POL'Y, & L. 587 (2005).

19 Amanda C. Pustilnik, *Prisons of the Mind: Social Value and Economic Inefficiency in the Criminal Justice Response to Mental Illness*, 96 J. CRIM. L. & CRIMINOLOGY 217, 263 (2005).

20 *See, e.g.*, Bruce Winick & Susan Stefan, *A Dialogue on Mental Health Courts*, 11 PSYCHOL. PUB. POL'Y & L. 507, 516 (2005) (on how mental health courts can give litigants a "sense of voice and validation"). On the significance of "voice and validation" in this inquiry in general, *See, e.g.*, Bruce J. Winick & David B. Wexler, *The Use of Therapeutic Jurisprudence in Law School Clinical Education: Transforming the Criminal Law Clinic*, 13 CLIN. L. REV. 605, 619 (2006); Amy Ronner, *Songs Of Validation, Voice, And Voluntary Participation: Therapeutic Jurisprudence, Miranda And Juveniles*, 71 U. CIN. L. REV. 89 (2002).

21 *See generally*, THERAPEUTIC JURISPRUDENCE: THE LAW AS A THERAPEUTIC AGENT (David B. Wexler ed., 1990); ESSAYS IN THERAPEUTIC JURISPRUDENCE (David B. Wexler & Bruce J. Winick eds, 1991); LAW IN A THERAPEUTIC KEY: RECENT DEVELOPMENTS IN THERAPEUTIC JURISPRUDENCE (David B. Wexler & Bruce J. Winick eds, 1996); THERAPEUTIC JURISPRUDENCE APPLIED: ESSAYS ON MENTAL HEALTH LAW (Bruce B. Winick ed., 1998). I have considered TJ frequently in my articles and book chapters as well. *See, e.g.*, PERLIN, *supra* note 6, at 417–38; PERLIN, *supra* note 7, at 261–72; PERLIN, *supra* note 8, at 203–19; PERLIN, *supra* note 8, Chapter 2; Perlin, *Too Stubborn*, *supra* note 15; Birgden & Perlin, *Tolling*, *supra* note 17; Birgden & Perlin, *Home in the Valley*, *supra* note 17; Perlin, *Gates, supra* note 18; Michael L. Perlin, *Considering Pathological Altruism in the Law from Therapeutic Jurisprudence and Neuroscience Perspectives*, in PATHOLOGICAL ALTRUISM 156 (Barbara Oakley et al. eds, 2011); Michael L. Perlin, *Therapeutic Jurisprudence and Outpatient Commitment: Kendra's Law as Case Study*, 9 PSYCHOL. PUB. POL'Y & L. 183 (2003); Keri K. Gould & Michael L. Perlin *"Johnny's in the Basement/Mixing Up His Medicine": Therapeutic Jurisprudence and Clinical Teaching*, 24 SEATTLE U. L. REV. 339 (2000);

> procedural justice[22] and restorative justice[23] (what I will call "alternative jurisprudences")[24] on these issues.[25]

This is emphatically *not* to say that I am abandoning my focus on the impact of sanism and pretextuality (or my collateral considerations of the impact of false "ordinary common sense" (OCS)[26] and the use of cognitive-simplifying heuristic devices[27] on this body of the law) in our thinking about these issues. On the contrary, I think it is essential that we take these concepts even more seriously than ever. Rather, I am suggesting that we must add new perspectives to our inquiry: a counsel-adequacy-based perspective, an international human rights-

---

Michael L. Perlin, *Therapeutic Jurisprudence: Understanding the Sanist and Pretextual Bases of Mental Disability Law*, 20 N. Eng. J. Crim. & Civ. Confinement 369 (1994); Michael L. Perlin, Keri Gould & Deborah A. Dorfman, *Therapeutic Jurisprudence and the Civil Rights of Institutionalized Mentally Disabled Persons: Hopeless Oxymoron or Path to Redemption*?, 1 Psychology, Pub. Pol'y & L. 80 (1995); Michael L. Perlin, *What Is Therapeutic Jurisprudence?*, 10 N.Y.L. Sch. J. Hum. Rts. 623 (1993); Michael L. Perlin, *Therapeutic Jurisprudence: A Multi-Professional Perspective*, in Mental Health Law and Practice Through the Life Cycle 76 (Simon Verdun-Jones ed., 1994).

22 *See generally*, E. Allen Lind & Tom R. Tyler, The Social Psychology of Procedural Justice 61–92 (1988); Amy Ronner, *The Crucible, Harvard's Secret Court, and Homophobic Witch Hunts*, 73 Brook. L. Rev. 217, 238–40 (2007).

23 *See, e.g.*, Mark S. Umbreit, *Holding Juvenile Offenders Accountable: A Restorative Justice Perspective*, 46 Juv. & Fam. Ct. J. 31 (1995); John Braithwaite, Restorative Justice & Responsive Regulation (2002); Restorative Justice & Criminal Justice: Competing or Reconcilable Paradigms (Andrew von Hirsch et al. eds, 2003).

24 For a discussion of other additional and related jurisprudential perspectives whose common goal is "a more comprehensive, humane and psychologically optimal way of handling legal matters," see Ian Freckleton, *Therapeutic Jurisprudence Misunderstood and Misrepresented: the Price and Risks of Influence*, 30 T. Jefferson L. Rev. 575, 578 (2008), quoting Judging in a Therapeutic Key: Therapeutic Jurisprudence and the Courts 106 (Bruce J. Winick & David B. Wexler eds, 2003); *see also*, Susan Daicoff, *Growing Pains: The Integration vs. Specialization Question for Therapeutic Jurisprudence and Other Comprehensive Law Approaches*, 30 T. Jefferson L. Rev. 551, 552–53 (2008): Susan Daicoff, *Law as a Healing Profession: The "Comprehensive Law Movement,"* 6 Pepp. Disp. Resol. L.J. 1, 1–3 (2006).

25 *See* Perlin, *supra* note 7, at 259–304; Perlin, *Too Stubborn*, *supra* note 15; Birgden & Perlin, *Tolling*, *supra* note 14; Birgden & Perlin, *Home in the Valley*, *supra* note 14.

26 *See, e.g.*, Michael L. Perlin, *"She Breaks Just Like a Little Girl": Neonaticide, The Insanity Defense, and the Irrelevance of Ordinary Common Sense*, 10 Wm. & Mary J. Women & L. 1, 26–28 (2003) (Perlin, *Neonaticide*); Michael L. Perlin, *Psychodynamics and the Insanity Defense: Ordinary Common Sense and Heuristic Reasoning*, 69 Neb. L. Rev. 3 (1990) (Perlin, *Psychodynamics*).

27 *See, e.g.*, Perlin, *supra* note 7, at 21–58; Perlin, *Lepers*, *supra* note 8, at 710–11.

based perspective, a mental health courts-based perspective and a comprehensive "alternative jurisprudences"-based perspective.[28]

It is also essential that we consider the importance of *dignity* to this entire area of law and policy. Human rights are necessary for all individuals—human rights violations occur when persons are treated as objects or as a means to others' ends.[29] All citizens—including ones who are institutionalized, whether in jails, prisons, facilities for persons with intellectual disabilities, or psychiatric facilities—have enforceable human rights.[30] Professor Aaron Dhir has written, "Degrading living conditions, coerced 'treatment,' scientific experimentation, seclusion, restraints—the list of violations to the dignity and autonomy of those diagnosed with mental disabilities is both long and egregious."[31] So are a failure to provide adequate and effective counsel and honor human rights an affront to the dignity that must be the bedrock of our legal system.[32] Importantly, perceptions of systemic fairness are driven, in large part, by "the degree to which people judge that they are treated with dignity and respect."[33] The words of a federal district court judge from nearly 40 years ago still ring true: "[i]f there is to be the reality of a fair trial, both in fact and in appearance, it must be conducted in an atmosphere of respect, order, decorum and dignity befitting its importance both to the prosecution and the defense."[34] Each of the chapters in this book must be read through this lens of dignity.

I hope that, by adding these perspectives to this project, I will offer a blueprint for policy development, further scholarly inquiries, and, optimally, social change. I hope

---

28 Professor David Wexler, one of the founders of the "therapeutic jurisprudence" (TJ) school, has recently published a major work on the relationship between TJ and criminal law; *see* David B. Wexler, Rehabilitating Lawyers: Principles of Therapeutic Jurisprudence for Criminal Law Practice (2008); *see also,* David B. Wexler, *Therapeutic Jurisprudence and the Rehabilitative Role of the Criminal Defense Lawyer*, 17 St. Thomas L. Rev. 743 (2005). The late Professor Bruce Winick, TJ's *other* founder, has written extensively about these issues as well; *see, e.g.*, Bruce Winick, *Redefining the Role of the Criminal Defense Lawyer at Plea Bargaining and Sentencing: A Therapeutic Jurisprudence/Preventive Law Model*, 5 Psychol. Pub. Pol'y & L. 1034 (1999); Winick & Wexler, *supra* note 17; Bruce Winick, *Psychotropic Medication in the Criminal Trial Process: The Constitutional and Therapeutic Implications of Riggins v. Nevada*, 10 N.Y.L. Sch. J. Hum. Rts. 637 (1993).

29 Tony Ward & Astrid Birgden, *Accountability And Dignity: Ethical Issues In Forensic And Correctional Practice*, 14 Aggression & Violent Behav. 227 (2009); Perlin, *supra* note 8; Perlin, *supra* note 9.

30 Perlin & Dlugacz, *supra* note 14; Birgden & Perlin, T*olling*, *supra* note 14; Birgden & Perlin, *Home in the Valley*, *supra* note 14.

31 Aaron A. Dhir, *Human Rights Treaty Drafting Through the Lens of Mental Disability: The Proposed International Convention on Protection and Promotion of the Rights and Dignity of Persons with Disabilities*, 41 Stan. J Int'l L. 181, 182 (2005).

32 *See* Perlin, *Evaluation Process*, *supra* note 14, at 251.

33 Michael L. Perlin, *A Law of Healing*, 68 U Cin. L. Rev. 407, 415 (2000), quoting Tom R. Tyler, *The Psychological Consequences of Judicial Procedures: Implications for Civil Commitment Hearings*, 46 SMU L. Rev. 433, 442 (1992).

34 In re Cohen, 370 F. Supp. 1166, 1174 (S.D.N.Y, 1973).

that by focusing on counsel issues, and stressing that, in many areas (using that term both in its geographic and its substantive sense), we have not shown any incremental improvement in the 38 years since Judge David Bazelon charged that lawyers in his court representing criminal defendants with mental disabilities were "walking violations of the Sixth Amendment,"[35] this book will encourage law schools, bar associations, and other lawyers' "trade groups" to take this issue more seriously.

I hope that, by focusing on international human rights issues in the specific context of the criminal trial process, a focus almost entirely absent from the otherwise-robust debate about interpretation and implementation of the CRPD,[36] this book will encourage policymakers in criminal justice, and international human rights activists and scholars, to, again, take this issue more seriously.[37]

I hope that, by looking at mental health courts in this context, we will begin to change public attitudes towards persons with mental disabilities,[38] to begin to decrease the attendant stigma,[39] and to consider more seriously the ways that such

35 David L. Bazelon, *The Defective Assistance of Counsel*, 42 U. Cin. L. Rev. 1, 2 (1973). *See also*, Fred Cohen, *Law, Lawyers, and Poverty*, 43 Tex. L. Rev. 1072, 1086 (1965) ("Providing warm bodies with law degrees is one thing—assuring competent representation is quite another").

36 *See, e.g.*, Dhir, *supra* note 28; Michael Ashley Stein, *Disability Human Rights*, 95 Cal. L. Rev. 75 (2007); Tara Melish, *The UN Disability Convention: Historic Process, Strong Prospects, and Why the U.S. Should Ratify*, 14 Hum. Rts. Brief 37, 44 (Winter 2007); Kathryn DeMarco, *Disabled by Solitude: The Convention On The Rights Of Persons With Disabilities and its Impact on the Use of Supermax Solitary Confinement*, 66 U. Miami L. Rev. 523 (2012). I consider this issue briefly in Perlin & McClain, *supra* note 14, at 270: "The ratification of the Convention underscores the international human rights principle of equal access to justice for all persons with disabilities, whether the 'justice' in question relates to the civil or the criminal legal process." *See also*, Perlin & Dlugacz, *supra* note 14; Birgden & Perlin, *Tolling*, *supra* note 14; Birgden & Perlin, *Home in the Valley*, *supra* note 14.

37 I have discussed previously the relationship between international human rights law and individuals institutionalized in forensic psychiatric facilities; *see* Perlin, *Universal Factors*, *supra* note 13, at 354–55 (considering the core "failure to provide humane services" to such patients); Perlin, *supra* note 8, at 100–01; Michael L. Perlin et al., International Human Rights and Comparative Mental Disability Law 881–87 (2006). In this book, however, I extend the scope of my attention to *all* individuals with mental disabilities in the criminal process.

38 Research suggests that increased contact with persons with mental illness is positively associated with improved attitudes. *See, e.g.*, Monika E. Kolodziej & Blair T. Johnson, *Interpersonal Contact and Acceptance of Persons with Psychiatric Disorders: A Research Synthesis*, 64 J. Consulting & Clinical Psychol. 1387 (1996).

39 *See, e.g.*, John Parry & Eric Drogin, Criminal Law Handbook on Psychiatric and Psychological Evidence and Testimony 5 (2000):

> Stigma affects the law in at least two ways: (1) the negative effect on the liberty interests of the person with a mental disability who is the subject of a legal proceeding and (2) potential bias due to sanism that judges and other courtroom participants may demonstrate towards that person.

courts can bring additional dignity, respect and fairness to the criminal justice system.[40]

Finally, I hope that, by focusing on the therapeutic jurisprudence/procedural justice/restorative justice implications of all that takes place when a person with a mental disability is involved in the criminal trial process, a focus that builds on the insights of and expands on the groundbreaking work of Profs. Wexler and Winick, this book will encourage those who practice criminal law (prosecutors *as well as* defense lawyers), who judge criminal law cases, and who write about *other* "alternative jurisprudence" -related matters to, once more, take this issue seriously.

This book will proceed in this manner: I will first briefly discuss the core issues of sanism and pretextuality, and of OCS and heuristics, concepts that I have explored in depth in other works.[41] Next, I will consider the four perspectives that are at the core of this work: adequacy of counsel, the application of international human rights law, the growth of mental health courts, and the redemptive power of "alternative jurisprudences"[42]—and then will look more carefully and comprehensively at the role of dignity in this area of law and social policy.[43] Then, I will move into a substantive topic-by-topic consideration of three of the discrete subject matter issues that we need to consider:[44]

---

40 *See, e.g.*, Norman J. Poythress et al., *Perceived Coercion and Procedural Justice in the Broward Mental Health Court*, 25 Int'l J.L. & Psychiatry 517 (2002) (reporting on the Broward County (Ft. Lauderdale, FL) mental health court (finding "high levels of procedural justice," and concluding that defendants in that court "do not perceive the way they are dealt with in mental health court as being as coercive as other types of criminal processing"), as discussed in Winick & Stefan, *supra* note 17, at 516–17). Judge Ginger Lerner-Wren, the creator and presiding judge of the Broward Court has described her vision in this way: "We view the Mental Health Court as a 'strategy' to bring fairness to the administration of justice for persons being arrested on minor offenses who suffer from major mental disability." *See* Shauhin Talesh, *Mental Health Court Judges as Dynamic Risk Managers: a New Conceptualization of the Role of Judges*, 57 DePaul L. Rev. 93, 126 n. 206 (2007), and *see generally*, Perlin, *supra* note 18

41 *See infra* Chapter 2.

42 *See infra* Chapters 3–6.

43 *See infra* Chapter 7.

44 I have recently dealt with these issues in a full-length book on the death penalty—*see* Perlin, *supra* note 9—and am thus largely omitting death penalty issues from this work. I am also omitting, for reasons of space, discussion of other trial process issues (*e.g.*, confessions law) and collateral issues regarding the right of forensic patients to refuse the involuntary imposition of antipsychotic medications. I deal with these in 4 Michael L. Perlin, Mental Disability Law: Civil and Criminal, §§ 8A-4.2 to 4.2d, at 51–60, and §§ 10-3 to 10-3.3d, at 397–421,(2d ed. 2002), in Perlin & Cucolo, *supra* note 19, § 8A-4.2c(1), at 18–27, and in a series of articles. *See*, e.g., Michael L. Perlin, "*And My Best Friend, My Doctor/ Won't Even Say What It Is I've Got": The Role and Significance of Counsel in Right to Refuse Treatment Cases*, 42 San Diego L. Rev. 735 (2005); Michael L. Perlin, *"Salvation" or a "Lethal Dose"? Attitudes and Advocacy in Right to Refuse*

- the range of criminal incompetency issues (including, competency to stand trial, and competency to waive counsel/self-represent, with some consideration of the question of when a death row defendant is deemed to be competent to be executed);[45]
- the insanity defense;[46] and
- sentencing.[47]

I will conclude with a series of recommendations for future action.[48]

This book calls attention to a cluster of issues that, sadly, still remain "under the radar" (or, perhaps, more pessimistically-but-accurately, "*off* the radar") for almost all participants in the criminal justice system. My hope is that, eventually, it will lead to invigorated thinking and ameliorative action in all of these areas of the law.

I have chosen to title this book "*A Prescription for Dignity*" because I believe that dignity *must* be at the core of the entire criminal justice system, and that its absence is even more jarring in cases involving defendants with mental disabilities.

Treatment Cases, 4 J. Prof'l Psychol. Pract. 51 (2004); Michael L. Perlin & Deborah A. Dorfman, "*Is It More Than Dodging Lions and Wastin' Time"? Adequacy of Counsel, Questions of Competence, and the Judicial Process in Individual Right to Refuse Treatment Cases*, 2 Psychology, Pub. Pol'y & L.114 (1996); Michael L. Perlin, *Decoding Right to Refuse Treatment Law*, 16 Int'l J. L. & Psychiatry 151 (1993); Michael L. Perlin, *Reading the Supreme Court's Tea Leaves: Predicting Judicial Behavior in Civil and Criminal Right to Refuse Treatment Cases*, 12 Am. J. Forens. Psychiatry 37 (1991); Michael L. Perlin, *"I'll Give You Shelter From The Storm": Privilege, Confidentiality, and Confessions of Crime*, 29 Loyola L.A. L. Rev. 1699 (1996); Michael L. Perlin, *Criminal Confessions and the Mentally Disabled:* Colorado v. Connelly *and the Future of Free Will*, in 5 Critical Issues in Law and Psychiatry 157 (Richard Rosner & Ronnie Harmon eds, 1988).

45 *See infra* Chapter 8. *See, e.g.*, Perlin, *Evaluation Process*, *supra* note 14; Perlin, *Dignity*, *supra* note 11; Michael L. Perlin, *Beyond Dusky and Godinez: Competency Before and After Trial*, 21 Behav. Sci. & L. 297 (2003); Michael L. Perlin et al., Competence in the Law: From Legal Theory to Clinical Application 25–133 (2008); 4 Perlin, *supra* note 44, chapter 8.

46 *See infra* Chapter 9. *See, e.g.*, Perlin, *supra* note 2; Perlin, *supra* note 6; Perlin, *Neonaticide*, *supra* note 26; Perlin, *Psychodynamics*, *supra* note 26; Michael L. Perlin, *Myths, Realities, and the Political World: The Anthropology of Insanity Defense Attitudes*, 24 Bull. Am. Acad. Psychiatry & L. 5 (1996); Michael L. Perlin, *"The Borderline Which Separated You From Me": The Insanity Defense, the Authoritarian Spirit, the Fear of Faking, and the Culture of Punishment*, 82 Iowa L. Rev. 1375 (1997); 4 Perlin, *supra* note 44, chapter 9.

47 *See infra* Chapter 10. *See, e.g.*, Michael L. Perlin & Keri K. Gould, *Rashomon and the Criminal Law: Mental Disability and the Federal Sentencing Guidelines*, 22 Am. J. Crim. L. 431 (1995); Michael Perlin, *Recent Criminal Legal Decisions: Implications for Forensic Mental Health Experts*, in Forensic Psychology: Advanced Topics 333, 353–55 (Alan Goldstein ed., 2006); 4 Perlin, *supra* note 44, chapter 11.

48 *See infra* Chapter 11.

I also believe that serious consideration of the perspectives that I focus on in this work—counsel, international human rights, mental health courts, and alternative jurisprudences—will serve as a means of infusing more dignity into this process. It is only then, I think, that we will be able to think seriously about what needs to be done to "transform the criminal-justice system into a dignity-affirming institution."[49]

49 Anthony V. Alfieri, *Jim Crow Ethics and the Defense of the Jena Six*, 94 Iowa L. Rev. 1651, 1689 (2009), discussing David Luban, Legal Ethics and Human Dignity 118 (2007).

PART I
The Four Factors

Chapter 2
The Four Factors: Sanism, Pretextuality, Heuristics and "Ordinary Common Sense"

I. Introduction: Why the Critical Factors?

It is impossible to make any conceptual sense of the relationship between mental disability and the criminal trial process without an understanding of four critical factors that dominate—and control—this relationship. What is most vexing is that they often exercise this domination in an invisible manner.[1] I have been writing about these factors—sanism, pretextuality, heuristics and "ordinary common sense"—in different guises for over two decades,[2] and I continue to write about them in different contexts to this date.[3]

There is no question in my mind, however, that in no area is the impact of these factors more pernicious than in the criminal trial process.[4] I believe that

1 *See, e.g.*, MICHAEL L. PERLIN, THE HIDDEN PREJUDICE: MENTAL DISABILITY ON TRIAL (2000).

2 *See, e.g.*, Michael L. Perlin, *On "Sanism,"* 46 SMU L. REV. 373 (1992) (Perlin, *Sanism*); Michael L. Perlin, *Morality and Pretextuality, Psychiatry and Law: of "Ordinary Common Sense," Heuristic Reasoning, and Cognitive Dissonance*, 19 BULL. AM. ACAD. PSYCHIATRY & L. 131 (1991) (Perlin, *Morality*): Michael L. Perlin, *Psychodynamics and the Insanity Defense: "Ordinary Common Sense" and Heuristic Reasoning*, 69 NEB. L. REV. 3 (1990) (Perlin, *Heuristic Reasoning*). This is not to say that these are the *only* factors that "matter" in this context. *See, e.g.*, Paul Secunda, *Cultural Cognition at Work,* 38 FLA. ST. U. L. REV. 107, 107 (2010) ("[Cultural cognition theory] suggests that values act as a subconscious influence on cognition rather than as a self-conscious motive of decision-making".)

3 *See, e.g.*, MICHAEL L. PERLIN, INTERNATIONAL HUMAN RIGHTS AND MENTAL DISABILITY LAW: WHEN THE SILENCED ARE HEARD (2011); Michael L. Perlin & Deborah A. Dorfman, *"The Sources of This Hidden Pain": Why a Class in Race, Gender, Class and Mental Disability*, in VULNERABLE POPULATIONS & TRANSFORMATIVE LAW TEACHING 313 (Hazel Weiser ed., 2011); Michael L. Perlin, *Online, Distance Legal Education as an Agent of Social Change*, 24 PAC. MCGEORGE GLOBAL BUS. & DEV. L.J. 95. (2011); Michael L. Perlin, *"They Keep It All Hid": The Ghettoization of Mental Disability Law and Its Implications for Legal Education,* 54 ST. LOUIS U. L. J. 857 (2010) (Perlin, *Ghettoization*); Michael L. Perlin, *"Simplify You, Classify You": Stigma, Stereotypes and Civil Rights in Disability Classification Systems*, 25 GA. ST. U. L. REV. 607 (2009) (Perlin, *Simplify You*).

4 As I discuss subsequently, *see infra* Chapter 4, the ways that international human rights standards are regularly violated in the treatment of persons with mental disabilities are equally pernicious. *See, e.g.*, PERLIN, *supra,* note 3*;* Michael L. Perlin, *"A Change Is Gonna Come": The Implications of the United Nations Convention on the Rights of Persons*

unless and until we fully understand the malignancy of sanism and pretextuality, and the ways that heuristic reasoning and false "ordinary common sense" cause us to make and reinforce biased and irrational judgments, we are doomed to repeat the errors that we continue to make. Writing 12 years ago about the insanity defense, I said, "sanism, pretextuality, [and the] shaky underpinnings of heuristic reasoning and a false OCS (ordinary common sense) … may ultimately doom to failure any attempt to reconstitute insanity defense policy."[5] I believe that this thought applies to the criminal trial process as a whole. As I will discuss at length in a later chapter, I also believe it will be impossible to infuse this process with a needed measure of dignity unless and until we come to grips with these issues.[6]

---

with Disabilities for the Domestic Practice of Constitutional Mental Disability Law, 29 No. Ill. U. L. Rev. 483 (2009); Michael L. Perlin, *"Everybody Is Making Love/Or Else Expecting Rain": Considering the Sexual Autonomy Rights of Persons Institutionalized Because of Mental Disability in Forensic Hospitals and in Asia*, 83 U. Wash. L. Rev. 481 (2008) (Perlin, *Expecting Rain*); Michael L. Perlin, *"Through the Wild Cathedral Evening": Barriers, Attitudes, Participatory Democracy, Professor tenBroek, and the Rights of Persons with Mental Disabilities*, 13 Tex. J. on Civ. Libs. & Civ. Rts. 413 (2008); Michael L. Perlin, *International Human Rights Law and Comparative Mental Disability Law: The Universal Factors*, 34 Syracuse J. Int'l L. & Commerce 333 (2007); Michael L. Perlin & Eva Szeli, *Mental Health Law and Human Rights: Evolution and Contemporary Challenges*, in Mental Health and Human Rights: Vision, Praxis, and Courage 98 (Michael Dudley et al. eds, 2012).

5 Michael L. Perlin, *"For the Misdemeanor Outlaw": The Impact of the ADA on the Institutionalization of Criminal Defendants with Mental Disabilities*, 52 Alabama L. Rev. 193, 209 n.103 (2000).

6 *See infra* Chapter 7. I have discussed this previously, inter alia, in the context of the right to refuse treatment in *civil* mental disability law. *See, e.g.*, Michael L. Perlin, *A Law of Healing*, 68 U. Cin. L. Rev. 407, 420–21 (2000):

> Sanist thinking allows judges to avoid difficult choices in mental disability law cases; their reliance on non-reflective, self-referential alleged "ordinary common sense" contributes further to the pretextuality that underlies much of this area of the law. Such reliance makes it even less likely that judicial decisions in right to refuse treatment cases reflect the sort of "dignity" values essential for a fair hearing.

See also, Symposium, *International Human Rights Law and the Institutional Treatment of Persons with Mental Disabilities: The Case of Hungary*, 21 N.Y.L. Sch. J. Int'l & Comp. L. 361, 386–87 (2002) (remarks of Jean Bliss):

> If each advocate dedicates themselves to the idea of turning up the volume in a concerted and cohesive effort, educating those who still may stand under the shadows of sanism, all the while stressing the concepts of dignity, liberty and self determination, that is what I would call an ideal form of advocacy.

II. The Factors

A. Sanism[7]

"Sanism" is an irrational prejudice of the same quality and character of other irrational prejudices that cause (and are reflected in) prevailing social attitudes of racism, sexism, homophobia, and ethnic bigotry.[8] It infects both our jurisprudence and our lawyering practices.[9] Sanism is largely invisible and largely socially acceptable. It is based predominantly upon stereotype, myth, superstition and deindividualization, and is sustained and perpetuated by our use of alleged "ordinary common sense" (OCS) and heuristic reasoning in an unconscious response to events both in everyday life and in the legal process.[10] Discrimination pervades the lives of people with psychiatric diagnosis.[11]

In a series of papers, I have explored the roots of the assumptions that are made by the legal system about persons with mental disabilities[12]—who they are,

---

7 *See generally* 1 Michael L. Perlin, Mental Disability Law: Civil and Criminal § 2D-2, at 523–28 (2d ed. 1998) (Perlin, Mental Disability Law); Michael L. Perlin, Mental Disability and the Death Penalty: The Shame of the States (2013) (Perlin, Death Penalty).

8 The classic treatment is Gordon W. Allport, The Nature of Prejudice (1954). For an important alternative perspective, see Elizabeth Young-Bruehl, The Anatomy of Prejudices (1996). See Perlin, *Sanism, supra* note 2.

9 The phrase "sanism" was most likely coined by Dr. Morton Birnbaum. Morton Birnbaum, *The Right to Treatment: Some Comments on its Development*, in Medical, Moral and Legal Issues in Health Care 97, 106–07 (Frank J. Ayd ed., 1974). I discuss his insights in this context in Michael L. Perlin, *Competency, Deinstitutionalization, and Homelessness,* 28 Hous. L. Rev. 63, 92–93 (1991); see also, Perlin, *Simplify You, supra* note 3, at 620 n.60.

10 See *infra* text accompanying notes 62–108. Deindividualization comes about because we see persons with mental disabilities as alienated from mainstream society, and as, in Sander Gilman's phrase, "the Other." *See infra* Chapter 6, note 75, discussing Michael L. Perlin, *"Where the Winds Hit Heavy on the Borderline": Mental Disability Law, Theory and Practice, Us and Them*, 31 Loyola L.A. L. Rev. 775, 787 (1998), in this context.

11 Susan Stefan, Unequal Rights: Discrimination Against People with Mental Disabilities and the Americans with Disabilities Act 4 (2001).

12 *See, e.g.,* Perlin, *Morality, supra* note 2; Perlin, *Sanism, supra* note 2; Michael L. Perlin, *Pretexts and Mental Disability Law: The Case of Competency*, 47 U. Miami L. Rev. 625 (1993) (Perlin, *Pretexts*); Michael L. Perlin & Deborah A. Dorfman, *Sanism, Social Science, and the Development of Mental Disability Law Jurisprudence*, 11 Behav. Sci. & L. 47 (1993); Michael L. Perlin, *"They're An Illusion To Me Now": Forensic Ethics, Sanism and Pretextuality*, in Psychology, Crime and Law: Bridging the Gap 239 (David Canter & Rita Zukauskien eds, 2008). On how such individuals are seen as "The Other," *see* Christopher Harding & Richard W. Ireland, Punishment: Rhetoric, Rule, and Practice 105 (1989), and Sander L. Gilman, Difference and Pathology: Stereotypes of Sexuality, Race and Madness 130 (1985).

how they got that way, what makes them different, what there is about them that lets society treat them differently, and whether their condition is immutable.[13] These assumptions—which reflect societal fears and apprehensions about mental disability, persons with mental disabilities, and the possibility that any individual may become mentally disabled—ignore the most important question of all: why do we feel the way we do about people with mental disabilities?[14] Just as importantly, perhaps *more* importantly, we rarely even ask this question.[15] Have we learned anything in the nearly 20 years since Carmel Rogers wrote, "Because the preserve of psychiatry is populated by 'the mad' and 'the loonies', we do not really want to look at it too closely—it is too frightening and maybe contaminated"?[16]

Significantly, we tend to ignore, subordinate, or trivialize behavioral research in this area, especially when acknowledging that such research would be cognitively dissonant with our intuitive (albeit empirically flawed) views.[17] "Sensational media portrayals of mental illness"[18] exacerbate the underlying tensions. We believe that "[m]ental illness can be easily identified by lay persons and matches up closely to popular media depictions."[19] It is commonly assumed that persons with mental

---

13 *See generally* Martha Minow, Making All the Difference: Inclusion, Exclusion, and American Law (1990); Sander Gilman, Difference and Pathology: Stereotypes of Sexuality, Race and Madness (1985). *See also*, *e.g.*, Katherine B. O'Keefe, *Protecting the Homeless Under Vulnerable Victim Sentencing Guidelines: An Alternative to Inclusion in Hate Crime Laws*, 52 Wm. & Mary L. Rev. 301, 314 (2010), citing Tami Iwamoto, *Adding Insult to Injury: Criminalization of Homelessness in Los Angeles*, 29 Whittier L. Rev. 515, 521 (2007) ("Mental illness is not a choice, and even if it can be treated, it is an immutable characteristic of a person's being").

14 *See*, *e.g.*, Michael L. Perlin, *"You Have Discussed Lepers and Crooks": Sanism in Clinical Teaching*, 9 Clinical L. Rev. 683, 688 (2003).

15 *See* Michael L. Perlin, *"Half-Wracked Prejudice Leaped Forth": Sanism, Pretextuality, and Why and How Mental Disability Law Developed As It Did*, 10 J. Contemp. Legal Issues 3, 20 (1999).

16 Carmel Rogers, *Proceedings Under the Mental Health Act 1992: The Legalisation of Psychiatry*, 1994 N.Z. L.J. 404, 408.

17 *See generally* J. Alexander Tanford, *The Limits of a Scientific Jurisprudence: The Supreme Court and Psychology*, 66 Ind. L.J. 137 (1990). On the dangers of teleological decision-making in this context, *see* Michael L. Perlin, *"Baby, Look Inside Your Mirror": The Legal Profession's Willful and Sanist Blindness to Lawyers with Mental Disabilities*, 69 U. Pitt. L. Rev. 589, 599–600 (2008).

18 Bruce Winick, *The Supreme Court's Evolving Death Penalty Jurisprudence: Severe Mental Illness as the Next Frontier*, 50 B.C. L. Rev. 785, 847 (2009). *See also*, John R. Cutcliffe & Ben Hannigan, *Mass Media, "Monsters," and Mental Health Clients: The Need for Increased Lobbying*, 8 J. Psychiatric & Mental Health Nursing 315 (2001).

19 Perlin, *Sanism*, *supra* note 2, at 395. See Sarah J. Bredemeier, *Hollow Verdict: Not Guilty by Reason of Insanity Provokes Animus-Based Discrimination in the Social Security Act*, 31 St. Mary's L.J. 697, 736 n.184 (2000), quoting, inter alia, Fred S. Berlin & H. Martin Malin, *Media Distortion of the Public's Perception of Recidivism and Psychiatric Rehabilitation*, 148 Am. J. Psychiatry 1572, 1573 (1991) (stressing the media's influence on

illness cannot be trusted.[20] Common stereotypes about people with mental illness include the beliefs that they are dangerous, unreliable, lazy, responsible for their illness or otherwise blameworthy, faking or exaggerating their condition, or childlike and in need of supervision or care."[21] Evidence that, by way of example, persons with mental illness document information in advance directive documents that are "consistent with community practice standards"[22] is counterintuitive to a sanist public.

Social science research confirms that mental illness is "one of the most—if not the most—stigmatized of social conditions."[23] Historically, individuals with psycho-social disabilities "have been among the most excluded members of society. Research firmly establishes that people with mental disabilities are subjected to greater prejudice than are people with physical disabilities."[24] One

---

the idea that treatment of persons with mental illness is often ineffective and unsuccessful); Steven E. Hyler et al., *Homicidal Maniacs and Narcissistic Parasites: Stigmatization of Mentally Ill Persons in the Movies*, 42 Hosp. & Commun. Psychiatry 1044, 1045–46 (1991) (bemoaning the distorted depiction of persons with mental illness in films). On the collateral influence of the media on attitudes towards criminal sentencing, see Jared Rosenberger & Valerie Callahan, *The Influence of Media on Penal Attitudes*, 36 Crim. Just. Rev. 435 (2011).

20 E. Lea Johnston, *Representational Competence: Defining the Limits of the Right to Self-Representation at Trial*, 86 Notre Dame L. Rev. 523, 536 (2011). On the basic "sanist myths," *see* Perlin, *Sanism, supra* note 2, at 393–97.

21 Elizabeth F. Emens, *The Sympathetic Discriminator: Mental Illness, Hedonic Costs, and the ADA*, 94 Geo. L.J. 399, 416 (2006). *See also, e.g.*, Jude T. Pannell, *Unaccommodated: Parents with Mental Disabilities In Iowa's Child Welfare System and the Americans With Disabilities Act*, 59 Drake L. Rev. 1165, 1181–82 (2011) ("[Sanism] most commonly manifests itself in the belief that, despite the lack of supporting evidence, people with mental disabilities are inherently incompetent, deviant, dangerous, or violent"); Johnston, *supra* note 20, at 536 ("'Sanism' may manifest in a general tendency to distrust decisions of persons with mental illness and in assumptions that individuals who exercise their right to counsel are 'crazy' and incapable of sufficiently autonomous decisionmaking.") (discussing sanism in the context of criminal defendants who seek to represent themselves at trial). On the ways that these stereotypes can interact with stereotypes of gender and race, *see*, *e.g.*, Ryan Elias Newby, *Evil Women and Innocent Victims: The Effect of Gender on California Sentences for Domestic Homicide*, 22 Hastings Women's L.J. 113, 132–33 (2011).

22 Eric Elbogen et al., *Effectively Implementing Psychiatric Advance Directives to Promote Self-Determination of Treatment among People with Mental Illness*, 13 Psychol. Pub. Pol'y & L. 273, 283 (2007).

23 Stefan, *supra* note 11, at 5, as quoted in Deirdre M. Smith, *The Disordered and Discredited Plaintiff: Psychiatric Evidence in Civil Litigation*, 31 Cardozo L. Rev. 749, 809 n.328 (2010). *See* Michael L. Perlin, *The ADA and Persons with Mental Disabilities: Can Sanist Attitudes Be Undone?*, 8 J. L. & Health 15, 26 (1993-94) ("mental disabilities are the most negatively perceived of all disabilitites").

24 Michael E. Waterstone & Michael Ashley Stein, *Disabling Prejudice*, 102 Nw. U. L. Rev. 1351, 1363–64 (2008), as quoted in Smith, *supra* note 23, at 809 n.329. See also Christopher C. Ligatti, *No Training Required: The Availability of Emotional Support*

might optimistically expect, though, that this gloomy picture should be subject to change because of a renewed interest in the integration of social science and law, and greater public awareness of defendants with mental disabilities. One might also expect that litigation and legislation in these areas would draw on social science data in attempting to answer such questions as the actual impact that deinstitutionalization has had on homelessness, or whether experts can knowledgeably testify about criminal responsibility in so-called "volitional prong" insanity cases.[25]

What are some reasons for this expectation? First, scholars such as John Monahan and Laurens Walker have constructed a jurisprudence of "social science in law,"[26] articulating coherent theories about the role of social science data and research in the trial process and outlining specific proposals for obtaining, evaluating, and establishing the findings of such research.[27] Second, a series of social and political developments (primarily, the public awareness of psychiatric hospital deinstitutionalization and its purported link to homelessness,[28] and a series of sensational criminal trials in which mental status defenses have been raised)[29]

Animals as a Component of Equal Access for the Psychiatrically Disabled under the Fair Housing Act, 35 T. Marshall L. Rev. 139, 140 (2010) ("The stigma of psychiatric disability in society is great"); Smith, *supra* note 23, at 810 n.329 (discussing legal scholarship on the impact of stigma on persons with mental illness).

25 *See, e.g.*, Norman Finkel, *The Insanity Defense: A Comparison of Verdict Schemas*, 15 Law & Hum. Behav. 533, 535 (1991); Richard Rogers, *APA's Position on the Insanity Defense: Empiricism Versus Emotionalism*, 42 Am. Psychologist 840 (1987); Richard Rogers, *Assessment of Criminal Responsibility: Empirical Advances and Unanswered Questions*, 17 J. Psychiatry & L. 73 (1987).

26 *See generally* John Monahan & Laurens Walker, *Twenty Five Years of Social Science in Law*, 35 Law & Hum. Behav. 72 (2010).

27 John Monahan & Laurens Walker, *Social Authority: Obtaining, Evaluating, and Establishing Social Science in Law*, 134 U. Pa. L. Rev. 477 (1986); Laurens Walker & John Monahan, *Social Facts: Scientific Methodology as Legal Precedent*, 76 Cal. L. Rev. 877 (1988); John Monahan & Laurens Walker, *Judicial Use of Social Science Research*, 15 Law & Hum. Behav. 571 (1991). Similarly illuminating are Gary Melton's and Michael Saks' insights into "psychological jurisprudence" (the study of community and cultural norms through structures that create or sustain social behavior consistent with values that promote human welfare), *see, e.g.*, Gary Melton & Michael Saks, *The Law as an Instrument of Socialization and Social Structure*, in 33 Nebraska Symposium on Motivation: The Law as a Behavioral Instrument 235 (Gary Melton ed., 1985); Michael Saks, *Judicial Attention to the Way the World Works*, 75 Iowa L. Rev. 1011 (1990); Gary Melton, *Law, Science, and Humanity: The Normative Foundation of Social Science in Law*, 14 Law & Hum. Behav. 315 (1990).

28 *See generally* 2 Perlin, Mental Disability Law, *supra* note 7, §§ 4B-1 *et seq.*(2d ed. 1999)

29 *See generally* 4 *id.*, §§ 9C-1 to 9C-7 (2d ed. 2002). During the time that I was writing this manuscript, 12 people were killed and 50 injured in a Colorado movie theater (the so-called "Batman murders"). *See* http://www.nytimes.com/2012/07/21/us/shooting-at-colorado-theater-showing-batman-movie.html?pagewanted=all (accessed August 28,

has resulted in significantly increased visibility of some persons with mentally disabilities in predominantly negative ways.[30]

And yet, any attempt to place mental disability law jurisprudence in context results in confrontation with a discordant reality: social science is rarely a coherent influence on mental disability law doctrine.[31] Rather, the legal system selectively—teleologically[32]—either accepts or rejects social science data depending on whether or not the use of that data meets the *a priori* needs of the legal system.[33] In other

---

2012). Within days, I received at least a half-dozen phone calls asking if I thought the defendant was going to plead the insanity defense since, per my callers, "they always do to get off in this kind of case." That, of course, assumes a fact nowhere in evidence. The reality is that the last mass murderer or serial killer successfully to plead the insanity defense in an American court did so over 100 years ago. See. Lisa L. Dahm, *Regulation of Nurses: Should the NPDB Be Expanded?*, 11 MICH. ST. U. J. MED. & L. 33, 41 (2007); *see generally* Anne S. Gresham, *The Insanity Plea: A Futile Defense for Serial Killers*, 17 LAW & PSYCHOL. REV. 193, 205–06 (1993) (footnotes omitted):

> Serial killers are rarely found not guilty by reason of insanity because society, and therefore the jury, does not want to bear the risk that violent offenders, including serial killers, will be released prematurely and again be a threat to the community. Ralph Slovenko, of the Wayne State Law School, may have said it best: "No serial killer is [found to be insane]."

30 Perlin, *supra* note 9, at 106–08; Perlin, *Sanism*, *supra* note 2, at 398–400; Robert Burt, *Constitutional Law and the Teaching of the Parables*, 93 YALE L.J. 455, 462 (1984). *See also*, Jennifer L. Skeem & Stephen L. Golding, *Describing Jurors' Personal Conceptions of Insanity and Their Relationship to Case Judgments*, 7 PSYCHOL. PUB. POL'Y & L. 561, 594 (2001) (86% of newspaper stories that involved psychiatric patients focused on the commission of a violent crime, usually murder or mass murder). This data has been consistently found for decades. *See, e.g.*, Henry, Steadman & Joseph Cocozza, *Selective Reporting and the Public's Misconceptions of the Criminally Insane*, 41 PUB.OPINION Q. 523 (1978).

31 *See, e.g.*, Jodi English, *The Light Between Twilight and Dark: Federal Criminal Law and the Volitional Insanity Defense*, 40 HASTINGS L.J. 1, 20 (1988); Michael L. Perlin, *Unpacking the Myths: The Symbolism Mythology of Insanity Defense Jurisprudence*, 40 CASE W. RES. L. REV. 599, 658 n.256 (1989–90) (federal legislators ignored empirical evidence about the insanity defense in the debate leading to the passage of the Insanity Defense Reform Act of 1984); *see generally* 4 PERLIN, MENTAL DISABILITY LAW, *supra* note 7, § 9C-5.

32 That is, the ways that the judicial system either accepts or rejects social science evidence depending on whether or not the use of that data meets the system's *a priori* needs. *See, e.g.*, Paul Appelbaum, *The Empirical Jurisprudence of the United States Supreme Court*, 13 AM. J.L. & MED. 335, 341–42 (1987); Perlin, *supra* note 15, at 29.

33 See Perlin, *Heuristic Reasoning*, *supra* note 2, at 60–61; Perlin, *Pretexts*, *supra* note 12, at 668; Appelbaum, *supra* note 32, at 341–42; David Faigman, *"Normative Constitutional Fact-Finding": Exploring the Empirical Component of Constitutional Interpretation*, 139 U. PA. L. REV. 541, 577 (1991); *see also*, for an excellent and provocative consideration, Ansar Haroun & Grant Morris, *Weaving a Tangled Web: The Deceptions of Psychiatrists*, 10 J. CONTEMP. LEG. ISS. 227 (1999).

words, social science data is privileged when it supports the conclusion the fact finder wishes to reach, but it is subordinated when it questions such a conclusion.[34]

These ends are sanist.[35] In other words, decision-making in mental disability law cases is inspired by (and reflects) the same kinds of irrational, unconscious, bias-driven stereotypes and prejudices that are exhibited in racist, sexist, homophobic, and religiously and ethnically bigoted decision-making.[36] Sanist decision-making infects all branches of mental disability law, and distorts mental disability jurisprudence.[37] Paradoxically, while sanist decisions are frequently justified as being therapeutically based, sanism customarily results in anti-therapeutic outcomes.[38]

---

34 Perlin, *supra* note 17, at 599–600, discussing JOHN Q. LA FOND & MARY L. DURHAM, BACK TO THE ASYLUM: THE FUTURE OF MENTAL HEALTH LAW AND POLICY IN THE UNITED STATES 156 (1992):

> Judges' refusals to consider the meaning and realities of mental illness cause them to act in what appears, at first blush, to be contradictory and inconsistent ways and, teleologically, to privilege (where that privileging serves what they perceive as a socially-beneficial value) and subordinate (where that subordination serves what they perceive as a similar value) evidence of mental illness.

See also Tanford, *supra* note 17, at 157; Faigman, *supra* note 33, at 581; Donald Bersoff, *Autonomy for Vulnerable Populations: The Supreme Court's Reckless Disregard for Self-Determination and Social Science*, 37 VILL. L. REV. 1569 (1992); compare JOHN MONAHAN & LAURENS WALKER, SOCIAL SCIENCE IN LAW: CASES AND MATERIALS 28–29 (1985) (discussing critical legal studies scholars' criticisms of social science in law for privileging empirical findings that are the "product of a closed capitalistic cultural system"); Tanford, *supra* note 17, at 151 (discussing criticism that social science "will be used instrumentally … to hide the true political/ideological bases for [judicial] decisions").

35 *See generally* Perlin, *Sanism*, *supra* note 2. *See also*, *e.g.*, Bruce Winick, *The Side Effects of Incompetency Labeling and the Implications for Mental Health Law*, 1 PSYCHOL., PUB. POL'Y & L. 6, 33 n.155 (1995); Christopher Slobogin, *Therapeutic Jurisprudence: Five Dilemmas to Ponder*, 1 PSYCHOL, PUB. POL'Y & L. 193, 199–200 n.35 (1995) (both discussing sanism in a therapeutic jurisprudence context). For a thoughtful, relatively recent consideration of these issues, *see* Michael Waterstone & Michael Stein, *Disabling Prejudice*, 102 NW. U. L. REV. 1351 (2008).

36 Perlin, *Sanism*, *supra* note 2, at 373–77. On the phobic base of these fears, *see generally* Perlin & Dorfman, *supra* note 12

37 On the ways that judges derogatorily conceptualize mental disability professionals in forensic testimonial contexts, see Douglas Mossman, *"Hired Guns," "Whores," and "Prostitutes": Case Law References to Clinicians of Ill Repute*, 27 J. AM. ACAD. PSYCHIATRY & L. 414 (1999); John F. Edens et al., *"Hired Guns," "Charlatans," and Their "Voodoo Psychobabble": Case Law References to Various Forms of Perceived Bias Among Mental Health Expert Witnesses*, 9 PSYCHOL. SERVS. 259 (2012).

38 *See*, *e.g.*, David Wexler, *Justice, Mental Health, and Therapeutic Jurisprudence*, 40 CLEV. ST. L. REV. 517 (1992); THERAPEUTIC JURISPRUDENCE: THE LAW AS A THERAPEUTIC AGENT (David Wexler ed., 1990). *See generally infra* Chapter 6.

Judges are not immune from sanism. "[E]mbedded in the cultural presuppositions that engulf us all,"[39] judges also take deeper refuge in heuristic thinking[40] and flawed, non-reflective "ordinary common sense".[41] They reflect and project the conventional morality of the community, and judicial decisions in all areas of civil and criminal mental disability law continue to reflect and perpetuate sanist stereotypes.[42] This applies whether the question involves involuntary civil commitment,[43] the criminal trial process[44] or other areas of the law, such as the child welfare system,[45] guardianship[46] or family protection.[47]

Judges are not the only sanist actors. Lawyers, legislators, jurors and witnesses (both lay and expert) all exhibit sanist traits and characteristics.[48] Until system

---

39 Anthony D'Amato, *Harmful Speech and the Culture of Indeterminacy*, 32 Wm. & Mary L. Rev. 329, 332 (1991).

40 See *infra* Chapter 2, II. C.

41 See *infra* Chapter 2, II. D.

42 Perlin, *Sanism*, *supra* note 2, at 400–04.

43 *See, e.g.*, Perlin, *Pretexts*, *supra* note 12.

44 *See, e.g.*, Michael L. Perlin, *"Everything's a Little Upside Down, As a Matter of Fact the Wheels Have Stopped": The Fraudulence of the Incompetency Evaluation Process*, 4 Houston J. Health L. & Pol'y 239 (2004). On the specific issues related to sanism in the imposition of the death penalty, see John Parry, *The Death Penalty and Persons with Mental Disabilities: A Lethal Dose of Stigma, Sanism, Fear of Violence, and Faulty Predictions of Dangerousness*, 29 Mental & Physical Disability L. Rep. 667 (2005); *see generally* Perlin, Death Penalty, *supra* note 7.

45 *See, e.g.*, Theresa Glennon, *Walking with Them: Advocating for Parents with Mental Illnesses in the Child Welfare System*, 12 Temp. Pol. & Civ. Rts. L. Rev. 273, 292 (2003). *See also* Pannell, *supra* note 21, at 1183 ("On a system-wide level, some caseworkers fail to make the necessary efforts to preserve and reunite families because sanism leads them to believe any efforts they make are futile and mentally disabled parents cannot become capable of parenting").

46 *See* Henry A. Dlugacz & Christopher Wimmer, *The Ethics of Representing Clients with Limited Competency in Guardianship Proceedings*, 4 St. Louis U. J. Health L. & Pol'y 331, (2011).

47 *See* Pamela R. Champine, *A Sanist Will?*, 22 N.Y.L. Sch. J. Int'l & Comp. L. 177 (2003).

48 Perlin, *Sanism*, *supra* note 2, at 398–406; Keri K. Gould & Michael L. Perlin, *"Johnny's in the Basement/Mixing Up His Medicine": Therapeutic Jurisprudence and Clinical Teaching*, 24 Seattle U. L. Rev. 339, 345 n.35 (2000); see *also* Michael L. Perlin, *Fatal Assumption: A Critical Evaluation of the Role of Counsel in Mental Disability Cases*, 16 Law & Hum. Behav. 39, 45–52 (1992), and Perlin, *supra* note 14, at 684: "Sanist myths exert especially great power over lawyers who represent persons with mental disabilities."Sanism and the improper use of heuristics (*see infra* II.C; *see generally* Perlin, *Heuristic Reasoning*, *supra* note 2) often overlap here. Thus, legislators in one state estimated that, during a specified time period, 4,400 defendants pled insanity and 1,800 of those pleas were successful; in reality, only 102 defendants asserted the defense, and just one was successful. *See* 4 Perlin, Mental Disability Law, *supra* note 7, § 9C-3.1, at 331 n.34, discussing findings reported in Richard Pasewark & Mark Pantle, *Insanity Plea: Legislators' View,* 136 Am. J. Psychiatry

"players" confront the ways that sanist biases (selectively incorporating or misincorporating social science data) inspire such pretextual decision-making, mental disability jurisprudence will remain incoherent. Behaviorists, social scientists and legal scholars must begin to develop research agendas so as to (1) determine and assess the ultimate impact of sanism, (2) better understand how social science data is manipulated to serve sanist ends, and (3) formulate normative and instrumental strategies that can be used to rebut sanist pretextuality in the legal system. Practicing lawyers need to articulate the existence and dominance of sanism and of pretextual legal behavior in their briefs and oral arguments so as to sensitize judges to the underlying issues.[49]

B. Pretextuality

Sanist attitudes also lead to pretextual decisions. "Pretextuality" means that courts regularly accept (either implicitly or explicitly) testimonial dishonesty, countenance liberty deprivations in disingenuous ways that bear little or no relationship to case law or to statutes, and engage similarly in dishonest (and frequently meretricious) decision-making, specifically where witnesses, especially expert witnesses, show a "high propensity to purposely distort their testimony in order to achieve desired ends."[50] This pretextuality is poisonous; it infects all participants in the judicial system, breeds cynicism and disrespect for the law, demeans participants, and reinforces shoddy lawyering, blasé judging, and, at times, perjurious and/or corrupt testifying.[51]

222–23 (1979). The defense is raised in one percent of all cases, and is successful just about one-fourth of the time. *See* Lisa Callahan et al., *The Volume and Characteristics of Insanity Defense Pleas: An Eight-State Study,* 19 BULL. AM. ACAD. PSYCHIATRY & L. 331 (1991). On the *public's* misunderstanding of insanity defense use and success, *see generally* Valerie Hans, *An Analysis of Public Attitudes Toward the Insanity Defense,* 24 CRIMINOLOGY 393 (1986).

49 See PERLIN, DEATH PENALTY, *supra* note 7, at 11-18.

50 Perlin, *Morality*, *supra* note 12, at 133; *see also*, Charles Sevilla, *The Exclusionary Rule and Police Perjury*, 11 SAN DIEGO L. REV. 839, 840 (1974) (discussing fabricated police testimony). On pretextuality in the civil commitment system, *see, e.g.*, Ian Freckelton, *Ideological Divarication in Civil Commitment Decision-making*, 10 PSYCHIATRY, PSYCHOL. & L. 390, 395 (2003); Erica Grundell, *Psychiatrists' Perceptions of Administrative Review,* 12 PSYCHIATRY, PSYCHOL. & L. 68, 86 n.41 (2005). On pretextuality in the sex offender civil commitment system, *see e.g.*, Michael L. Perlin, *"There's No Success like Failure/and Failure's No Success at All": Exposing the Pretextuality of* Kansas v. Hendricks, 92 NW. U. L. REV. 1247 (1998); Jeslyn A. Miller, *Sex Offender Civil Commitment: The Treatment Paradox,* 98 CAL. L. REV. 2093 (2010); Jason A. Cantone, *Rational Enough to Punish, But Too Irrational to Release: The Integrity of Sex Offender Civil Commitment,* 57 DRAKE L. REV. 693 (2009). On the problem of *diagnostic* pretextuality in sex offender cases, see Karen Franklin, *Hebephilia: Quintessence of Diagnostic Pretextuality*, 28 BEHAV. SCI. & L. 751 (2010).

51 Michael L. Perlin, *"She Breaks Just Like a Little Girl": Neonaticide, the Insanity Defense, and the Irrelevance of "Ordinary Common Sense,"* 10 WM. & MARY J. WOMEN & L. 1, 25 (2003).

Pretextual devices such as condoning perjured testimony, distorting appellate readings of trial testimony, subordinating statistically significant social science data, and enacting purportedly prophylactic civil rights laws that have little or no "real world" impact dominate the mental disability law landscape.[52] Judges in mental disability law cases often take relevant literature out of context,[53] misconstrue the data or evidence being offered,[54] and/or read such data selectively,[55] and/or inconsistently.[56] Other times, courts choose to flatly reject this data or ignore its existence.[57]

In other circumstances, courts simply "rewrite" factual records so as to avoid having to deal with social science data that is cognitively dissonant with their view of how the world "ought to be."[58] Even when courts do acknowledge the existence and possible validity of studies that take a contrary position from their decisions,

---

52 See PERLIN, *supra* note 1, at 67.

53 Faigman, *supra* note 33, at 577.

54 *Id.* at 581. *See also*, William Brooks, *The Tail Still Wags the Dog: The Pervasive and Inappropriate Influence by the Psychiatric Profession on the Civil Commitment Process*, 86 N.D. L. REV. 259, 299 (2010) ("The use of structured clinical decision-making can help eliminate pretextual assessments of danger").

55 Katheryn Katz, *Majoritarian Morality and Parental Rights*, 52 ALB. L. REV. 405, 461 (1988) (on court's reading of impact of parents' homosexuality in child custody decisions); Tanford, *supra* note 17, at 153–54. *See, e.g.*, Holbrook v. Flynn, 475 U.S. 560, 571 n.4 (1986) (defendant's right to fair trial not denied where uniformed state troopers sat in front of spectator section in courtroom; court rejected contrary empirical study, and based decision on its own "experience and common sense").

56 *See, e.g.*, Thomas Hafemeister & Gary Melton, *The Impact of Social Science Research on the Judiciary*, in REFORMING THE LAW: IMPACT OF CHILD DEVELOPMENT RESEARCH 27 (Gary Melton ed., 1987); Peter W. Sperlich, *The Evidence on Evidence: Science and Law in Conflict and Cooperation*, in THE PSYCHOLOGY OF EVIDENCE AND TRIAL PROCEDURE 325 (Saul Kassin & Lawrence S. Wrightsman eds, 1985); Craig Haney, *Data and Decisions: Judicial Reform and the Use of Social Science*, in THE ANALYSIS OF JUDICIAL REFORM 43 (Philip L. Du Bois ed., 1982).

57 *See, e.g.*, Barefoot v. Estelle, 463 U.S. 880, 897–902 (1983), *discussed extensively* in PERLIN, DEATH PENALTY, *supra* note 7, at 19–28; Faigman, *supra* note 33, at 584 (discussing Parham v. J.R., 442 U.S. 584 (1979)); *see also* Watkins v. Sowders, 449 U.S. 341 (1981) (refusal of courts to acknowledge social science research on ways that jurors evaluate and misevaluate eyewitness testimony).

58 On "empirical pretextuality," see Perlin, *Pretexts*, *supra* note 12, at 635. The classic example in a mental disability law context is Chief Justice Burger's opinion for the court in *Parham*, 442 U.S. at 605–10 (approving more relaxed involuntary civil commitment procedures for juveniles than for adults). *See, e.g.*, Gail Perry & Gary Melton, *Precedential Value of Judicial Notice of Social Facts: Parham as an Example*, 22 J. FAM. L. 633 (1984):

> The *Parham* case is an example of the Supreme Court's taking advantage of the free rein on social facts to promulgate a dozen or so of its own by employing one tentacle of the judicial notice doctrine. The Court's opinion is filled with social facts of questionable veracity, accompanied by the authority

this acknowledgement is frequently little more than mere "lip service."[59] Although courts are beginning to examine to examine to examine decision-making for evidence of pretextuality, that is being done—mostly but not exclusively[60]—in the context of employment questions.[61]

> to propel these facts into subsequent case law and, therefore, a spiral of less than rational legal policy making.

Id. at 645; *see also* Winsor Schmidt, *Considerations of Social Science in a Reconsideration of Parham v. J.R. and the Commitment of Children to Public Mental Institutions*, 13 J. Psychiatry & L. 339 (1985) (same). On the Supreme Court's special propensity in mental health cases to base opinions on "simply unsupportable" factual assumptions, see Stephen Morse, *Treating Crazy People Less Specially*, 90 W. Va. L. Rev. 353, 382 n.64 (1987). Compare Secunda, *supra* note 2, at 107 ("Judges, in many instances, are not fighting over ideology, but over legally consequential facts").

59 *See, e.g.*, Washington v. Harper, 494 U.S. 210, 229-30 (1990) (prisoners retain limited liberty interest in right to refuse forcible administration of antipsychotic medications), in which the majority acknowledges, and emphasizes in response to the dissent, the harmful, and perhaps fatal, side-effects of the drugs. The court also stressed the "deference that is owed to medical professionals ... who possess ... the requisite knowledge and expertise to determine whether the drugs should be used." *Id.* at 230 n.12. *Cf. id.* at 247–49 (Stevens, J., concurring in part & dissenting in part) (suggesting that the majority's side effects acknowledgement is largely illusory), discussed in 2 Perlin, Mental Disability Law, *supra* note 7, § 3B-8.2 (2d ed. 1999). *See generally* Michael L. Perlin, *The Sanist Lives of Jurors in Death Penalty Cases: The Puzzling Role of Mitigating Mental Disability Evidence*, 8 Notre Dame J. L., Ethics & Pub. Pol. 239, 264–65 (1994).

60 See Monaco v. Hogan, 576 F.Supp.2d 335, 351 n.32 (E.D.N.Y. 2008) (rejecting plaintiffs' arguments that pretextuality of some certifications of dangerousness supported a conclusion that the psychiatrists in question acted with deliberate indifference). On the pretextuality of the dangerousness certifications in Monaco, see Brooks, *supra* note 54, at 282 n.126, and *see id.* at 299 (recommending the use of structured clinical decision-making as a way to "help eliminate pretextual assessments of danger.")

61 *See, e.g.*, Milanes v. Holder, 2011 WL 1261576 (D.P.R. Mar. 31, 2011); Rosado v. Am. Airlines, 2010 WL 4015789 (D.P.R. Oct. 14, 2010); Modaffare v. Owens-Brockway Glass Container, 643 F. Supp. 2d 697 (E.D. Pa. 2009); LaGatta v. Pa. Cyber Charter Sch., 2010 WL 2633915 (W.D. Pa. June 30, 2010); Drwal v. Borough of West View, Pennsylvania, 617 F. Supp. 2d 397 (W.D. Pa. 2009). *See also* Oti Kaga, Inc. v. S.D. Hous. Dev. Auth., 342 F.3d 871 (8th Cir. 2003) (on question of pretextuality in case involving service animals under federal housing regulations); Schroer v. Billington, 577 F. Supp. 2d 293 (D.D.C. 2008) (termination of transgendered employee was pretextual); the pretextuality of the administrative decision in that case is discussed specifically in Sharon McGowan, *Working with Clients to Develop Compatible Visions of What It Means to "Win" a Case: Reflections on Schroer v. Billington*, 45 Harv. C.R.-C.L. L. Rev. 205, 221 n. 56 (2010). On the court's pretextuality in its failure to appropriately consider the defendant's mental illness in the sentencing decision in United States v. Irey, 612 F. 3d 1160 (11th Cir. 2010), see Adam Shajnfeld, *The Eleventh Circuit's Selective Assault on Sentencing Discretion*, 65 U. Miami L. Rev. 1133, 1153 (2011). On pretextuality in the assessment of mental disability under the Federal Sentencing Guidelines in general, see Michael L. Perlin & Keri K. Gould, *Rashomon*

C. Heuristics[62]

"Heuristics" is a cognitive psychology construct that refers to the implicit thinking devices that individuals use to simplify complex, information-processing tasks,[63] the use of which frequently leads to distorted and systematically erroneous decisions,[64] and causes decision-makers to "ignore or misuse items of rationally useful information."[65] One single vivid, memorable case overwhelms mountains of abstract, colorless data upon which rational choices should be made.[66] Empirical

---

and the Criminal Law: Mental Disability and the Federal Sentencing Guidelines, 22 AM. J. CRIM. L. 431, 453-55 (1995). On sentencing issues in general, see *infra* Chapter 10.

62 This section is largely adapted from 1 MICHAEL L. PERLIN & HEATHER ELLIS CUCOLO, MENTAL DISABILITY LAW: CIVIL AND CRIMINAL, § 2.4 (3d ed.) (in press).

63 *See, e.g.*, Perlin, *Heuristic Reasoning*, *supra* note 2, at 12–17 (1990); *see generally* Michael Saks & Robert Kidd, *Human Information Processing and Adjudication: Trial by Heuristics*, 15 LAW & SOC'Y REV. 123 (1980–81); Robert Scott, *Error and Rationality in Individual Decisionmaking: An Essay on the Relationship Between Cognitive Illusions and the Management of Choices*, 59 S. CAL. L. REV. 329 (1986); Wim De Neys, Sofie Cromheeke & Magda Osman, *Biased but in Doubt: Conflict and Decision Confidence*. PLoS ONE 6(1): e15954. doi:10.1371/journal.pone.0015954 (2011).

64 *See, e.g.*, Saks & Kidd, *supra* note 63; Michael L. Perlin, *Are Courts Competent to Decide Questions of Competency? Stripping the Façade From United States v. Charters*, 38 U. KAN. L. REV. 957 (1990) (Perlin, *Façade*); Michael L. Perlin, *Tarasoff and the Dilemma of the Dangerous Patient: New Directions for the 1990s*, 16 LAW & PSYCHOL. REV. 29, 52–54 (1992) (Perlin, *Dilemma*); John Carroll & John W. Payne, *The Psychology of the Parole Decision Process: A Joint Application of Attribution Theory and Information-Processing Psychology*, in COGNITION AND SOCIAL BEHAVIOR 13, 21 (John Carroll & John Payne eds, 1976); Norman Poythress, *Procedural Preferences, Perceptions of Fairness, and Compliance with Outcomes*, 18 LAW & HUM. BEHAV. 361 (1994); John Coverdale et al., *A Legal Opinion's Consequences for Stigmatisation of the Mentally Ill; Case Analysis*, 7 PSYCHIATRY, PSYCHOLOGY & L. 192 (2000).

65 *See* Perlin, *Façade*, *supra* note 64, at 966 n.46 (quoting Carroll & Payne, *supra* note 64, at 21); Michael L. Perlin, *"The Borderline Which Separated You From Me": The Insanity Defense, the Authoritarian Spirit, the Fear of Faking, and the Culture of Punishment*, 82 IOWA L. REV. 1375, 1417 (1997) (Perlin, *Borderline*) (same); Douglas Mossman, *Dangerousness Decisions: An Essay on the Mathematics of Clinical Violence Prediction and Involuntary Hospitalization*, 2 U. CHI. L. SCH. ROUNDTABLE 95, 100 n.32 (1995) (quoting Perlin, *Pretexts*, *supra* note 12, at 660). *See also*, Perlin, *supra* note 49, at 57 n.115 ("Heuristics are cognitive-simplifying devices that frequently lead to systematically erroneous decisions through ignoring or misusing rationally useful information"). For a comprehensive overview, see Donald Bersoff, *Judicial Deference to Nonlegal Decisionmakers: Imposing Simplistic Solutions on Problems of Cognitive Complexity in Mental Disability Law*, 46 SMU L. REV. 329 (1992); *see also* Philip Gould & Patricia Murrell, *Therapeutic Jurisprudence and Cognitive Complexity: An Overview*, 29 FORDHAM URB. L. J. 2117 (2002).

66 *See* Michael L. Perlin, *"His Brain Has Been Mismanaged with Great Skill": How Will Jurors Respond to Neuroimaging Testimony in Insanity Defense Cases?*, 42 AKRON L.

studies reveal jurors' susceptibility to the use of these devices.[67] Similarly, legal scholars are notoriously slow to understand the way that the use of these devices affects the way individuals think.[68] The use of heuristics "allows us to willfully blind ourselves to the 'gray areas' of human behavior,"[69] and predispose "people to beliefs that accord with, or are heavily influenced by, their prior experiences."[70]

Elsewhere, I have argued:

> [T]estimony [in mental disability law cases] is further warped by a heuristic bias. Expert witnesses—like the rest of us—succumb to the seductive allure of simplifying cognitive devices in their thinking and employ such heuristic gambits as the vividness effect or attribution theory in their testimony. This testimony is then weighed and evaluated by frequently sanist fact-finders. Judges and jurors, both consciously and unconsciously, often rely on reductionist, prejudice-driven stereotypes in their decision-making, thus subordinating statutory and case law standards as well as the legitimate interests of the mentally disabled persons who are the subject of the litigation. Judges' predispositions to employ the same sorts of heuristics as do expert witnesses further contaminate the process.[71]

Rev. 885, 892 (2009). *See generally* David Rosenhan, *Psychological Realities and Judicial Policy*, 19 Stan. Law. 10, 13 (1984). President Reagan's famous "welfare queen" anecdote is thus a textbook example of heuristic behavior. *See, e.g.*, Perlin, *Heuristic Reasoning*, *supra* note 2, at 16 n.59, 20. On the failures of the vividness heuristic as a cognitive device, *see* Amitai Aviram, *The Placebo Effect of Law: Law's Role in Manipulating Perceptions*, 75 Geo. Wash. L. Rev. 54, 74–75 (2006–07).

67 *See, e.g.*, Jonathan Koehler & Daniel Shaviro, *Veridical Verdicts: Increasing Verdict Accuracy Through the Use of Overtly Probabilistic Evidence and Methods*, 75 Cornell L. Rev. 247, 264–65 (1990); Perlin, *Heuristic Reasoning*, *supra* note 2, at 39–53; Morrison Torrey, *When Will We Be Believed? Rape Myths and the Idea of a Fair Trial in Rape Prosecutions*, 24 U.C. Davis L. Rev. 1013, 1050 (1991); Joel Lieberman & Daniel Krauss, *The Effects of Labeling, Expert Testimony, and Information Processing Mode on Juror Decisions in SVP Civil Commitment Trials*, 6 J. Investigative Psychol. & Offender Profiling 25 (2009); *see also* Caton Roberts & Stephen Golding, *The Social Construction of Criminal Responsibility and Insanity*, 15 Law & Hum. Behav. 349, 372 (1991) (jurors' pre-existing attitudes toward insanity defense strongest predictor of individual verdicts).

68 Thomas Tomlinson, *Pattern-Based Memory and the Writing Used to Refresh*, 73 Tex. L. Rev. 1461, 1461–62 (1995), citing Perlin, *supra* note 31, at 611–12. *But see* Stephen Ellmann, *What Are We Learning*, 56 N.Y.L. Sch. L. Rev. 171, 196–97 (2011/2012), quoting Brook K. Baker, *Practice-Based Learning: Emphasizing Practice and Offering Critical Perspectives on the Dangers of "Co-Op"tation*, 56 N.Y.L. Sch. L. Rev. 619, 627 (2011–12) (on how "learning in the workplace promotes confrontation of ineffective heuristics and their replacement with genuine understanding").

69 Perlin, *supra* note 51, at 27.

70 Russell Covey, *Criminal Madness: Cultural Iconography and Insanity*, 61 Stan. L. Rev. 1375, 1381 (2009).

71 Perlin, *Pretexts*, *supra* note 17, at 602–03: Perlin, *Ghettoization*, *supra* note 3, at 874–75.

Thus, through the "availability" heuristic, we judge the probability or frequency of an event based upon the ease with which we recall it.[72] Through the "typification" heuristic, we characterize a current experience via reference to past stereotypic behavior;[73] through the "attribution" heuristic, we interpret a wide variety of additional information to reinforce pre-existing stereotypes.[74] Through the heuristic of the "hindsight bias," we exaggerate how easily we could have predicted an event beforehand.[75] Through the heuristic of "outcome bias," we base our evaluation of a decision on our evaluation of an outcome.[76] Through the "representative heuristic," we extrapolate overconfidently based upon a

72 Perlin, *Borderline*, *supra* note 65, at 1417; see also, M. Gregg Bloche, *The Invention of Health Law*, 91 Cal. L. Rev. 247, 278 n.107 (2003), discussed in Covey, *supra* note 70, at 1381 n.24.

73 Michael L. Perlin, *Power Imbalances in Therapeutic and Forensic Relationships*, 9 Behav. Sci. & L. 111, 125 (1991) (use of the typification heuristic by which treating doctors slot "patients into certain categories, and prescribes a similar regimen for all.").

74 See Perlin, *supra* note 66, at 892. *See generally* Laura Stephens Khoshbin & Shahram Khoshbin, *Imaging the Mind, Minding the Image: An Historical Introduction to Brain Imaging and the Law*, 33 Am. J.L. & Med. 171, 182 (2007). (discussing how we attribute human behavior "to a physical source in the head").

75 Perlin, *supra* note 59, at 255.

76 *Id. See generally* Sharon S. Brehm & Jack W. Brehm, Psychological Reactance: A Theory of Freedom and Control (1981); Judgment Under Uncertainty: Heuristics and Biases (Daniel Kahneman et al. eds, 1982) (Judgment); Richard E. Nisbett & Lee Ross, Human Inference: Strategies and Shortcomings of Social Judgment (1980) (all discussing heuristics in general); Hal R. Arkes, *Principles in Judgment/Decision Making Research Pertinent to Legal Proceedings*, 7 Behav. Sci. & L. 429 (1989) (hindsight and outcome biases); Neal V. Dawson, et al., *Hindsight Bias: An Impediment to Accurate Probability Estimation in Clinicopathologic Conferences*, 8 Med. Decision Making 259 (1988) (hindsight bias); Anthony N. Doob & Julian V. Roberts, *Social Psychology, Social Attitudes and Attitudes Toward Sentencing*, 16 Can. J. Behav. Sci. 269 (1984) (vividness effect); Shari S. Diamond & Loretta J. Stalans, *The Myth of Judicial Leniency in Sentencing*, 7 Behav. Sci. & L. 73 (1989) (same) Baruch Fischhoff, *Hindsight, Foresight: The Effect of Outcome Knowledge on Judgment Under Uncertainty*, 104 J. Experimental Psychol.: Hum. Perception & Performance 288 (1975) (both biases); Harold Kelley, *The Process of Causal Attribution*, 28 Am. Psychologist 107 (1973) (attribution); Dan Russell, *The Causal Dimension Scale: A Measure of How Individuals Perceive Causes*, 42 J. Personality & Soc. Psychol. 1137 (1982) (same); Saks & Kidd, *supra* note 63 (availability); David Van Zandt, *Common Sense Reasoning, Social Change, and the Law*, 81 Nw. U. L. Rev. 894 (1987) (typification). In mental health contexts, *see, e.g.*, Harold Bursztajn et al., *"Magical Thinking," Suicide, and Malpractice Litigation*, 16 Bull. Am. Acad. Psychiatry & L. 369 (1988); David B. Wexler & Robert F. Schopp, *How and When to Correct for Juror Hindsight Bias in Mental Health Malpractice Litigation: Some Preliminary Observations*, 7 Behav. Sci. & L. 485 (1989). On the relationship between cultural cognition and biased judicial decision-making, see Secunda, *supra* note 2.

small sample size of which they happen to be aware.[77] Through the heuristic of "confirmation bias," people tend to favor "information that confirms their theory over disconfirming information."[78]

Research confirms that heuristic thinking dominates all aspects of the mental disability law process whether involuntary civil commitment law,[79] violence assessment,[80] medication refusal,[81] questions of diagnostic accuracy,[82] the insanity defense,[83] incompetency to stand trial procedures,[84] the relationship between homelessness and deinstitutionalization,[85] or the scope of a therapist's duty to protect a third party from a tortious act by the therapist's patient or client (the so-

---

77 *See, e.g.*, Amos Tversky & Daniel Kahneman, *Belief in the Law of Small Numbers*, in JUDGMENT, *supra* note 76, at 23, 24–25, as discussed in Perlin, *supra* note 66, at 898 n.89.

78 Alafair S. Burke, *Improving Prosecutorial Decision Making: Some Lessons of Cognitive Science*, 47 WM. & MARY L. REV. 1587, 1594 (2006), as discussed in Covey, *supra* note 70, at 1381 n.22.

79 Virginia A. Hiday & Lynn Newhart Smith, *Effects of the Dangerousness Standard in Civil Commitment*, 15 J. PSYCHIATRY & L. 433, 449 (1987) (aberrant behavior by small number of patients in sample studied "distort[ed] outcome perceptions"; mental health professionals significantly overstate percentage of involuntary civil commitment cases that began as police referrals and that jeopardized staff safety); *accord* Henry J. Steadman et al., *Psychiatric Evaluations of Police Referrals in a General Hospital Emergency Room*, 8 INT'L J.L. & PSYCHIATRY 39 (1986); R. Michael Bagby & Leslie Atkinson, *The Effects of Legislative Reform on Civil Commitment Admissions Rates: A Critical Analysis*, 6 BEHAV. SCI. & L. 45, 46 (1988).

80 Jennifer Murray & Mary E. Thomson, *Applying Decision Making Theory to Clinical Judgments in Violence Risk Assessment*, 2 EUR. J. PSYCHOL. 150 (2010).

81 *See* Perlin, *supra* note 73, at 125 (discussing Watkins v. United States, 589 F.2d 214 (5th Cir. 1979) (doctor prescribed 50-day supply of Valium without taking medical history or checking patient's medical records), Hale v. Portsmouth Receiving Hosp., 338 N.E.2d 371 (Ohio Ct. Cl. 1975) (doctor failed to change prescription following his observation of side-effects and onset of self-destructive behavior on patient's part), and Rosenfeld v. Coleman, 19 Pa. D. & C. 635 (C.P. 1959) (doctor prescribed addictive drugs so as to help patient see nature of his addictive personality)). *See generally* 3 PERLIN, MENTAL DISABILITY LAW, *supra* note 7, § 7A-6.4a (2d ed. 2000).

82 *See also* Arkes, *supra* note 76; David Faust, *Data Integration in Legal Evaluations: Can Clinicians Deliver on Their Premises?*, 7 BEHAV. SCI. & L. 469, 480 (1989) (discussing results found in Robyn Dawes et al., *Clinical Versus Actuarial Judgment*, 243 SCIENCE 1668 (1989); Baruch Fischhoff, *Debiasing*, in JUDGMENT, *supra* note 76, at 442; Sarah Lichtenstein et al., *Calibration of Probabilities: The State of the Art*, in JUDGMENT, *supra* note 77, at 305); Michael Saks, *Expert Witnesses, Nonexpert Witnesses, and Nonwitness Experts*, 14 LAW & HUM. BEHAV. 291, 294 (1990).

83 MICHAEL L. PERLIN, THE JURISPRUDENCE OF THE INSANITY DEFENSE 263–331 (1995); Perlin, *Borderline*, *supra* note 67.

84 Perlin, *Façade*, *supra* note 64; Perlin, *Pretexts*, *supra* note 12.

85 Perlin, *supra* note 9.

called *Tarasoff* obligation).[86] Most recently, I have, by way of example, questioned the "potential heuristic power" of neuroimaging evidence in the criminal trial process.[87]

D. "Ordinary Common Sense"[88]

"Ordinary common sense" (OCS) is a "powerful unconscious animator of legal decision making."[89] It is a psychological construct that reflects the level of the disparity between perception and reality that regularly pervades the judiciary in deciding cases involving individuals with mental disabilities.[90] OCS is self-referential and non-reflective: "I see it that way, therefore everyone sees it that way; I see it that way, therefore that's the way it is."[91] It is supported by our reliance on a series of heuristics-cognitive-simplifying devices that distort our abilities to consider information rationally.[92]

The positions frequently taken by former Chief Justice Rehnquist, Justice Scalia and Justice Thomas in criminal procedure cases[93] best highlight the power of OCS as an unconscious animator of legal decision-making. Such positions frequently

---

86 Perlin, *Dilemma*, *supra* note 64; see also, Michael L. Perlin, *"You Got No Secrets to Conceal": Considering the Application of the Tarasoff Doctrine Abroad*, 75 U. Cin. L. Rev. 611 (2006).

87 Michael L. Perlin, *"And I See Through Your Brain": Access to Experts, Competency to Consent, and the Impact of Antipsychotic Medications in Neuroimaging Cases in the Criminal Trial*, 2009 Stan. Tech. L. Rev. 4, *5.

88 This section is largely adapted from 1. Perlin & Cucolo, *supra* note 62, § 2.5.

89 Perlin, *supra* note 51, at 25.

90 See Perlin, *Borderline*, *supra* note 65, at 1417.

91 Perlin, *supra* note 87, at *24 n.84. Professors are not immune from succumbing to OCS. See Perlin, *Pretexts*, *supra* note 12, at 667 n. 210:

> Law professors are not necessarily any better. A visiting professor presented a paper about pornography and the first amendment at a recent faculty development seminar. I asked him if he was familiar with recent empirical studies raising some important questions about his basic thesis, for example, Joseph E. Scott, *What Is Obscene? Social Science and the Contemporary Community Standard Test of Obscenity,* 14 Int'l J.L. & Psychiatry 29 (1991); Berl Kutchinsky, *Pornography and Rape: Theory and Practice?,* 14 Int'l J.L. & Psychiatry 47 (1991); Judith Becker & Robert M. Stein, *Is Sexual Erotica Associated with Sexual Deviance in Adolescent Males?,* 14 Int'l J.L. & Psychiatry 85 (1991). He responded, "Well, I don't tend to think very much of empirical arguments." Most of those present grinned and nodded. No one challenged or commented on his answer.

92 Perlin, *supra* note 6, at 421–23.

93 *See, e.g.*, Michael L. Perlin, *"Life Is In Mirrors, Death Disappears": Giving Life to Atkins*, 33 N. Mex. L. Rev. 315, 329–30 (2003), discussing, in this context, Justice Scalia's dissent in Atkins v. Virginia, 536 U.S. 304 (2002) (death penalty unconstitutional as applied to persons with mental retardation).

demonstrate a total lack of awareness of the underlying psychological issues and focus on such superficial issues as whether a putatively mentally disabled criminal defendant bears a "normal appearance."[94]

These are not the first jurists to exhibit this sort of closed-mindedness. Trial judges will typically say, "he (the defendant) doesn't look sick to me," or, even more revealingly, "he is as healthy as you or me."[95] In short, advocates of OCS believe that simply by using their OCS, jurists can determine whether defendants conform to "popular images of 'craziness'".[96] If they do not, the notion of a handicapping mental disability condition is flatly, and unthinkingly, rejected.[97] Such views—reflecting a false OCS—are made even more pernicious by the fact that we "believe most easily what [we] most fear and most desire."[98] Thus, OCS presupposes two "self-evident" truths: "First, everyone knows how to assess an individual's behavior. Second, everyone knows when to blame someone for doing wrong."[99]

Reliance on OCS is one of the keys to an understanding of why and how, by way of example, insanity defense jurisprudence has developed.[100] Not only is it pre-reflexive and self-evident, it is also susceptible to precisely the type of idiosyncratic, reactive decision making that has traditionally typified insanity defense legislation and litigation.[101] Paradoxically, the insanity defense is

94 *See, e.g.*, State Farm Fire & Cas. Ltd. v. Wicka, 474 N.W.2d 324, 327 (Minn. 1991) (stating that both law and society are always more skeptical about a putatively mentally ill person who has a "normal appearance" or "doesn't look sick"), cited in Perlin, *Borderline*, *supra* note 65, at 1418 n.280.

95 Michael Perlin, *Psychiatric Testimony in a Criminal Setting*, 3 BULL. AM. ACAD. PSYCHIATRY & L. 143, 147 (1975). On how some propositions simply appear to be (falsely) common sense, see Covey, *supra* note 70, at 1381.

96 Harold Lasswell, *Foreword* to RICHARD ARENS, THE INSANITY DEFENSE xi (1974).

97 Lasswell, *supra* note 96, at xi. On courts' "continued reliance" on OCS, see Arlie Loughan, *"In a Kind of Mad Way": A Historical Perspective on Evidence and Proof of Mental Incapacity*, 35 MELB. U. L. REV. 1049, 1070 n.103 (2011).

98 PERLIN, *supra* note 1, at 18, quoting Thomas D. Barton, *Violence and the Collapse of Imagination*, 81 IOWA L. REV. 1249, 1249 (1996) (book review of WENDY KAMINER, IT'S ALL THE RAGE: CRIME AND CULTURE (1995)).

99 Richard Sherwin, *Dialects and Dominance: A Study of Rhetorical Fields in the Law of Confessions*, 136 U. PA. L. REV. 729, 738 (1988).

100 *See generally* PERLIN, *supra* note 83.

101 On the role of false OCS in the perpetuation of false beliefs in police and criminal psychology, see Michael G. Aamodt, *Reducing Misconceptions and False Beliefs in Police and Criminal Psychology*, 35 CRIM. JUST. & BEHAV. 1231 (2008); *see also*, Arthur J. Lurigio, *Examining Prevailing Beliefs about People with Serious Mental Illness in the Criminal Justice System*, 75 FED. PROBATION 11 (June 2011); on the relationship between such OCS and attitudes towards law enforcement in general, see David Flagel & Paul Gendreau, *Sense, Common Sense, and Nonsense*, 35 CRIM. JUST. & BEHAV. 1354 (2008). Professor Jennifer Mnookin captures this phenomenon perfectly—in the context of forensic science—in her story about a conversation she had with her seatmate on a recent airline flight:

necessary precisely because it rebuts "common-sense everyday inferences about the meaning of conduct."[102]

Empirical investigations corroborate the inappropriate application of OCS to insanity defense decision-making.[103] Judges "unconsciously express public feelings .... reflect[ing] community attitudes and biases because they are 'close' to the community."[104] Virtually no members of the public can actually articulate what the substantive insanity defense test is.[105] The public is seriously misinformed about both the "extensiveness and consequences" of an insanity defense plea.[106] And the public explicitly and consistently rejects any such defense substantively broader than the "wild beast" test.[107]

Elsewhere, in discussing the insanity defense, I have stated,

---

> On a recent flight, the person next to me on the crowded airplane began to chat with me. When I told her about what I researched and studied, she looked at me with a big grin. "I LOVE forensic science," she said. "I watch CSI whenever I can. They can do such amazing things. It's all so high tech—and incredibly accurate! It's almost like magic, isn't it?" She leaned in a bit closer and looked at me intently. "Tell me, is it like that in real life?" I looked at her for a moment before answering. I felt a bit like the older child on the playground about to reveal to her younger friend that Santa Claus doesn't really exist. I shook my head. "No, I wouldn't say that CSI's depiction is entirely realistic. In the real world, forensic science isn't nearly so glossy. It isn't nearly so speedy. And most important, it isn't nearly so foolproof, either." "Really? That's too bad," she told me. She looked at me directly for a brief moment, shook her head, and then looked away. "Well, to tell you the truth, I think I'd rather just keep believing in the television version." Figuring that reality was not going to be any match for CSI, I shrugged, and went back to the book I was reading.

Jennifer Mnookin, *The Courts, the NAS, and the Future of Forensic Science*, 75 BROOK. L. REV. 1209, 1209 (2010).

102 Benjamin Sendor, *Crime as Communication: An Interpretative Theory of the Insanity Defense and the Mental Elements of Crime*, 74 GEO. L.J. 1371, 1372 (1986).

103 *See* Tarika Daftary-Kapur et al., *Measuring Knowledge of the Insanity Defense: Scale Construction and Validation*, 29 BEHAV. SCI,. & L. 40 (2011).

104 Richard Arens & Jackwell Susman, *Jury Charges and Insanity*, 12 HOW. L.J. 1, 34 n. 23 (1966); A.L. Bloechl et al., *An Empirical Investigation of Insanity Defense Attitudes: Exploring Factors Related to Bias*, 30 INT'L J. L. & PSYCHIAT. 153 (2007).

105 Valerie Hans & Dan Slater, *"Plain Crazy": Lay Definitions for Legal Insanity*, 7 INT'L J.L. & PSYCHIAT. 105, 105–06 (1984).

106 Valerie Hans, *An Analysis of Public Attitudes Toward the Insanity Defense*, 24 CRIMINOLOGY 393 (1986).

107 Caton Roberts et al., *Implicit Theories of Criminal Responsibility: Decision Making and the Insanity Defense*, 11 LAW & HUM. BEHAV. 207, 226 (1987). *See generally* Perlin, *Borderline*, *supra* note 65, at 1420; Perlin, *supra* note 1, at 18–19.

> [Insanity defense decicionmaking] also ignores our rich, cultural, heterogenic fabric that makes futile any attempt to establish a unitary level of OCS to govern decisionmaking in an area where we have traditionally been willing to base substantive criminal law doctrine on medieval conceptions of sin, redemption, and religiosity.[108]

III. Conclusion

In short, it is impossible to make any coherent sense out of our incoherent criminal justice policies[109] unless we take seriously the pernicious power of sanism, pretextuality, heuristics, and OCS.[110] In subsequent chapters, I will demonstrate how these factors contaminate every aspect of the criminal justice process that has an impact on persons with mental disabilities.[111]

I turn now to the perspectives that must be considered before any turn to substantive criminal procedure law—the role of counsel, the significance of international human rights developments, the ascendance of mental health courts, the potential application of "alternative jurisprudences" (including therapeutic jurisprudence, procedural justice, and restorative justice)[112]—and also to the centrality of dignity to any investigation of the subject areas in question.[113]

---

108 Perlin, *Heuristic Reasoning*, *supra* note 2, at 29.

109 *See* PERLIN, *supra* note 83, at 1 ("(o)ur insanity defense jurisprudence is incoherent.").

110 *See*, *e.g.*, Perlin, *supra* note 15, at 26 (on sanism and pretextuality); Perlin, *supra* note 4, at 492 (heuristics); Perlin, *supra* note 17, at 592 (sanism).

111 *See infra* Chapters 8–10.

112 *See infra* Chapters 3–6.

113 *See infra* Chapter 7.

PART II
The Five Perspectives

Chapter 3
Counsel

I. Introduction[1]

It is impossible to approach the issues dealt with in this book without first considering the quality of counsel made available to criminal defendants with mental disabilities. Nearly 35 years ago, when surveying the availability of counsel to mentally disabled litigants, President Carter's Commission on Mental Health noted the frequently substandard level of representation made available to mentally disabled criminal defendants.[2] Nothing that has happened in the intervening decades has been a palliative for this problem; if anything, it is confounded by the myth that adequate counsel is available to represent both criminal defendants in general and mentally disabled litigants in particular.[3]

---

1 Portions of this section of this subchapter are adapted from MICHAEL L. PERLIN, MENTAL DISABILITY AND THE DEATH PENALTY: THE SHAME OF THE STATES 123–38 (2013).

2 *See Mental Health and Human Rights: Report of the Task Panel on Legal and Ethical Issues*, 20 Ariz. L. Rev. 49, 62 (1978), discussed in Michael L. Perlin, *Unpacking the Myths: The Symbolism Mythology of Insanity Defense Jurisprudence,* 40 CASE W. RES. L. REV. 599, 654 (1989–90). On the special competencies needed by defense counsel in *all* cases involving defendants with mental disabilities, *see, e.g.*, Danielle Laberge & Daphne Morin, *Evaluating the Case, Evaluating the Cost: Criteria for Constructing the Defense Strategy of Persons Suffering From Mental Illness*, 7 SOC'L DISTRESS & THE HOMELESS 189 (1988).

3 *See e.g.*, Melody Martin, *Defending the Mentally Ill Client in Criminal Matters: Ethics, Advocacy, and Responsibility*, 52 U. TORONTO FAC. L. REV. 73 (1993) (discussing ethical issues facing counsel in cases involving mentally disabled criminal defendants); Kenneth B. Nunn, *The Trial as Text: Allegory, Myth, and Symbols in the Adversarial Criminal Process: A Critique of the Role of the Public Defender and a Proposal for Reform*, 32 AM. CRIM. L. REV. 743 (1995) (discussing myth in criminal cases); Michael L. Perlin, *Fatal Assumption: A Critical Evaluation of the Role of Counsel in Mental Disability Cases,* 16 LAW & HUM. BEHAV. 39 (1992) (discussing myth in mental disability cases); *see generally* Douglas W. Vick, *Poorhouse Justice: Underfunded Indigent Defense Services and Arbitrary Death Sentences*, 43 BUFF. L. REV. 329 (1995) (discussing myth in criminal cases). For a numbing account of criminal justice defense services provided in many states, see AMY BACH, ORDINARY INJUSTICE—HOW AMERICA HOLDS COURT (2009). For an analysis in one state, see Justine Finney Guyer, *Saving Missouri's Public Defender System: A Call for Adequate Legislative Funding*, 74 MO. L. REV. 335, 360 (2009) ("Missouri's public defender system is being crushed by the weight of excessive caseloads"); Stephanie Saul, *When Death Is the Penalty: Attorneys for Poor Defendants Often Lack Experience and Skill*, N.Y. NEWSDAY, Nov. 25, 1991, at 8. On how lawyers' self-image may be negatively affected by their representation of persons with mental disabilities, see Laberge & Morin, *supra* note 2, at 203–05.

And what is worse, since 1983, when the Supreme Court established a pallid, nearly-impossible-to-violate adequacy standard in *Strickland v. Washington*[4] (requiring simply that counsel's efforts be "reasonable" under the circumstances), courts have become less and less interested in the question at hand, and little evidence disputes the failure of *Strickland* to insure that such defendants truly receive adequate assistance of counsel.[5]

II. The *Strickland* Case

Per *Strickland*,[6] the benchmark for judging an ineffectiveness claim is "whether counsel's conduct so undermined the proper function of the adversarial process that the trial court cannot be relied on as having produced a just result."[7] To determine whether counsels' assistance was "so defective as to require reversal,"[8] the Court established a two-part test:

> First, the defendant must show that counsel's performance was deficient. This requires showing that counsel made errors so serious that counsel was not functioning as the "counsel" guaranteed the defendant by the Sixth Amendment. Second, the defendant must show that the deficient performance prejudiced the defense. This requires showing that counsel's errors were so serious as to deprive the defendant of a fair trial, a trial whose result is reliable. Unless a defendant makes both showings, it cannot be said that the conviction or death sentence resulted from a breakdown in the adversary process that renders the result unreliable.[9]

4 466 U.S. 668, 668 (1984).

5 *See generally,* 4 Michael L. Perlin, Mental Disability Law: Civil and Criminal, § 12-3.6, at 177–88 (2002) (2d ed.); Michael L. Perlin & Heather E. Cucolo, Mental Disability Law: Civil and Criminal, § 12-3.6, at 137–40 (2012 Cum. Supp.); *see also, e.g.*, Ivan K. Fong, *Ineffective Assistance of Counsel at Capital Sentencing*, 39 Stan. L. Rev. 461, 461–62 (1987); William S. Geimer, *A Decade of Strickland's Tin Horn: Doctrinal and Practical Undermining of the Right to Counsel*, 4 Wm. & Mary Bill of Rts. J. 91, 93 (1995). Although there have been multiple cases in which *Strickland* violations have been found—*see* Perlin, *supra* note 1, at 123-38—there is no dispute that the "sterile and perfunctory" standard, established in *Strickland* (see Michael L. Perlin, *Fatal Assumption: A Critical Evaluation of the Role of Counsel in Mental Disability Cases,* 16 Law & Hum. Behav. 39, 53 (1992)), has made such reversals relatively rare. See Michael L. Perlin & Valerie McClain, *"Where Souls Are Forgotten": Cultural Competencies, Forensic Evaluations and International Human Rights,* 15 Psychol., Pub. Pol'y & L. 257, 260 (2009).

6 Text accompanying footnotes 7–19 is largely adapted from 2 Perlin, *supra* note 5, § 2B-11.2, at 261–67 (2d ed. 1998).

7 *Strickland*, 466 U.S. at 686.

8 *Id.* at 687.

9 *Id.* at 688.

The Court adopted an "objective," "reasonably effective assistance" standard, to be measured by "simple reasonableness under prevailing professional norms."[10] In assessing claims, the Court will "indulge a strong presumption that counsel's conduct falls within the wide range of reasonable professional assistance."[11]

In looking at the case before it, the Court found that counsel had a duty to "make reasonable investigations or to make a reasonable decision that makes particular investigations unnecessary."[12] However, even a "professionally unreasonable"[13] error will not result in reversal if it "had no effect on the judgment."[14] Prejudice—measured by showing of "a reasonable probability that, but for counsel's unprofessional errors, the result… would have been different"[15]—must be shown.[16]

In a sharply worded dissent,[17] Justice Marshall criticized the majority opinion of adoption of a performance standard "that is so malleable that, in practice, it will either have no grip at all or will yield excessive variation in the manner in which the Sixth Amendment is interpreted."[18] By the vagueness of its holding, he charged, the Court has "not only abdicated its own responsibility to interpret the Constitution, but also impaired the ability of the lower courts to exercise theirs."[19]

---

10 *Id.* at 687–88.

11 *Id.* at 689.

12 *Id.* at 691.

13 *Id.* at 693.

14 *Id.*

15 *Id.* at 694.

16 Applying these principles to the case before the Court was "not difficult." It found that respondent's trial counsel's conduct "cannot be found unreasonable," and that, even assuming unreasonableness, "respondent suffered insufficient prejudice to warrant setting aside his death sentence." The Court characterized trial counsel as having made a "strategic choice," with nothing in the record showing that his "sense of hopelessness distorted his professional judgment, and the decision not to seek more character or psychological evidence than was already in hand was likewise reasonable." In short, "[f]ailure to make the required showing of either deficient performance or sufficient prejudice defeats the ineffectiveness of the claim." "More generally," the Court concluded, "respondent has made no showing that the justice of his sentence was rendered unreliable by a breakdown in the adversary process caused by deficiencies in counsel's assistance"; thus, "the sentencing proceeding was not fundamentally unfair." *Id.* at 698–700. See Michael L. Perlin, The Jurisprudence of the Insanity Defense 148–54 (1995).

17 *Strickland*, 466 U.S. at 706.

18 *Id.* at 707.

19 *Id.* at 708. Justice Marshall characterized the standard as suffering from a "debilitating ambiguity," *id.*, which will likely "stunt the development of Constitutional doctrine in this area," *id.* at 709. Justice Brennan filed a separate opinion, concurring in part and dissenting in part. *Id.* at 701. *Compare* Jones v. Barnes, 463 U.S. 745, 759, 763 (1983) (Brennan, J., dissenting), noting that the Sixth Amendment right to counsel:

> is predicated on the view that the function of counsel under the Sixth Amendment is to protect the dignity and autonomy of a person on trial by assisting him in making choices that are his to make, not to make choices

III. Post-*Strickland* Developments

Individual post-*Strickland* cases are striking. In one case, counsel was found to be effective even though he had failed to introduce ballistics evidence showing that the gun taken from the defendant was not the murder weapon.[20] In another case, an attorney was found constitutionally adequate to provide representation to a death-eligible defendant notwithstanding the fact that he had been admitted to the bar for only six months and had never tried a jury case.[21] Another lawyer was found constitutionally adequate even where during the middle of the trial he appeared in court intoxicated and spent a night in jail.[22] In a pre-*Strickland* case, defense counsel was not even aware that separate sentencing proceedings were to be held in death penalty cases.[23] There is little evidence to contradict Welsh White's conclusion that "[l]ower courts' application of *Strickland* has produced appalling results."[24]

The first comprehensive analysis of *Strickland*—written by the chairperson of the Competency Committee of the ABA Section on Criminal Justice—called

---

> for him, although counsel may be better able to decide which tactics will be most effective for the defendant [and recognizing] the values of individual autonomy and dignity central to many constitutional rights, especially those Fifth and Sixth Amendment rights that come into play in the criminal process.

Jones is discussed in this context in Erin Daly, *Human Dignity in the Roberts Court: A Story of Inchoate Institutions, Autonomous Individuals, and the Reluctant Recognition of a Right*, 37 Ohio N.U. L. Rev. 381, 401 n. 112 (2011).

20 See Graham v. Collins, 829 F. Supp. 204, 209 (S.D. Tex. 1993).

21 See Paradis v. Arave, 954 F.2d 1483, 1490–92 (9th Cir. 1992).

22 See Haney v. State, 603 So. 2d 368, 377–78 (Ala. Crim. App. 1991).

23 See Young v. Zant, 677 F.2d 792, 797 (11th Cir. 1982).

24 Welsh S. White, *Capital Punishment's Future*, 91 Mich. L. Rev. 1429, 1436 (1993) (reviewing Raymond Paternoster, Capital Punishment in America (1991)). See Michael L. Perlin, *The Supreme Court, the Mentally Disabled Criminal Defendant, Psychiatric Testimony in Death Penalty Cases, and the Power of Symbolism: Dulling the* Ake *in* Barefoot's *Achilles Heel*, 3 N.Y. L. Sch. Human Rts. Ann. 91, 169 (1985), characterizing *Strickland* as providing a "nearly-standardless, seemingly-impossible-to-fail test"). For other examples, see Stephen Bright, *The Death Penalty as the Answer to Crime: Costly, Counterproductive, and Corrupting,* 31 Santa Clara L. Rev. 1068, 1078–84 (1996); Christine Wisermen, *Representing the Condemned: A Critique of Capital Punishment*, 79 Marq. L. Rev. 731, 742–44 (1996); *see also, e.g.*, Meredith J. Duncan, *The (So-Called) Liability of Criminal Defense Attorneys: A System in Need of Reform,* 2002 B.Y.U.L. Rev. 1, 18–20 (2002) (noting that "[t]he unfortunate aftermath of *Strickland* is that a criminally accused's right to the effective assistance of counsel does not have much substance to it at all" and that "even though the Court professed to fashion a test that would lead to the just review of ineffective assistance of counsel claims, it is doubtful whether ineffective assistance of counsel claims are currently justly reviewed"). The Supreme Court has also construed *Strickland* narrowly in other contexts. *See, e.g.*, Smith v. Spisak, 130 S. Ct. 676 (2010) (defendant not prejudiced by inadequate closing argument at penalty phase).

it "unfortunate and misguided," charging that it "failed to meet is obligation to help ensure that criminal defendants receive competent representation,"[25] and that it was drafted "to ensure that the review test will produce the same results as the old farce and mockery due process test."[26] By its own terms, the test's application to *Strickland*'s facts "underscores this return to the status quo ante."[27] *Strickland* is thus viewed as "a clear signal that [the Supreme Court] is not at all disturbed with inadequate performance by criminal defense lawyers";[28] its message is that "the problem of competency, at least in criminal cases, should be taken off the agenda."[29] Professor Heather Baxter asks, "Will any warm body [in the role of counsel] do?",[30] and sadly, the answer all too often is, "yes." *Strickland* "has been

---

25 William J. Genego, *The Future of Effective Assistance of Counsel: Performance Standards and Competent Representation*, 22 Am. Crim. L. Rev . 181, 182 (1984).

26 *Id.* at 196. *See*, for a comprehensive set of specific performance standards embodying an "efficient and functional assistance test," Note, *The Standard for Effective Assistance of Counsel in Pennsylvania – An Effective Method of Ensuring Competent Defense Representation*, 89 *Dickinson L. Rev*. 41, 69–71 (1985). For excellent early reviews of all relevant issues, see Richard Klein, *The Relationship of the Court and Defense Counsel: The Impact of Competent Representation and Proposals for Reform*, 29 B.C.L. Rev. 531 (1988); Martin, *supra* note 3; Geimer, *supra* note 5; Jeffrey Kirchmeier, *Drink, Drugs, and Drowsiness: The Constitutional Right to Effective Assistance of Counsel and the Strickland Prejudice Requirement*, 75 Neb. L. Rev. 425 (1996). For more recent reconsiderations of *Strickland, see, e.g.*, Eve Brensike Primus, *Structural Reform in Criminal Defense: Relocating Ineffective Assistance of Counsel Claims*, 92 Cornell L. Rev. 679 (2007); Robert R. Rigg, *The T-Rex Without Teeth: Evolving Strickland v. Washington and the Test for Ineffective Assistance of Counsel*, 35 Pepp. L. Rev. 77 (2007); Tigran W. Eldred, *The Psychology of Conflicts of Interests in Criminal Cases*, 58 U. Kan. L. Rev. 43 (2009).

27 Perlin, *supra* note 16, at 16, citing Genego, *supra* note 25, at 196–98, 209–11. See also Note, *The Ineffective Assistance of Counsel Quandary: The Debate Continues*, 18 Akron L. Rev. 325, 334 (1984) (*Strickland's* seemingly "objective" test is "poisoned with obtrusive subjectivity"); Note, 14 U.Balt. L. Rev. 335, 344, 345 (1985) (*Strickland* court's analysis of ineffective counsel claims "self-defeating"; case's result "very well may be the expeditious disposal, if not the outright discouragement, of ineffective assistance allegations, rather than the protection of the fundamental fairness of the proceedings in such claims"). *But cf.* State v. Nash, 694 P.2d 222, 228 (Ariz. 1985) (*Strickland*'s "objective standard provides better guidance to lawyers and judges" than would a "more subjective" test).

28 Genego, *supra* note 25, at 202.

29 *Id.* For a pre-*Strickland* analysis of the economic, psychological, and social factors contributing to counsel's ineffectiveness, concluding that, "unless courts are willing to police the attorney, they should candidly admit that the call for 'effective representation' is simply rhetoric," see Peter Tague, *The Attempt to Improve Criminal Defense Representation*, 15 Am. Crim. L. Rev. 109, 165 (1977).

30 Heather Baxter, *Gideon's Ghost: Providing the Sixth Amendment Right to Counsel in Times of Budgetary Crisis*, 2010 Mich. St. L. Rev. 341, 346. The use of the "warm body" phrase dates back 47 years. See Fred Cohen, *Law, Lawyers, and Poverty*, 43 Tex. L. Rev. 1072, 1086 (1965) ("Providing warm bodies with law degrees is one thing–assuring competent representation is quite another").

interpreted by some courts as essentially a shield for counsel's behavior against judicial scrutiny."[31]

The effectiveness of counsel also, in large measure, may depend on a lawyer's *cultural* competency. As I noted in an earlier article, discussing *Strickland*, "If ... defendants are also from other cultures, the obligations on the defense team are even greater and the stakes are even higher."[32] Of special significance to this issue, there are now multiple *Strickland* cases on the question of ineffectiveness in the context of failure to obtain expert testimony,[33] an issue of even greater importance in cases involving cultural difference.[34]

I believe that it is meaningless (perhaps fatuous) to engage in any sort of serious discussion of these issues without looking carefully at issues of adequacy of counsel in the specific context of the representation of persons with mental

---

31 Carissa Byrne Hessick, *Ineffective Assistance at Sentencing*, 50 B.C. L. Rev. 1069, 1075 (2009), and *see id.* listing examples of cases in which counsel was not held to be ineffective under *Strickland* (footnotes omitted):

> Seemingly egregious examples of substandard representation—including counsel's concession of her client's guilt, counsel's decision to remain essentially silent at trial rather than conducting any real defense, counsel's failure to make any closing argument, counsel sleeping during the trial, counsel referring to client by a racial slur,]counsel representing the defendant while drunk, counsel hinting that death is the appropriate punishment for the defendant in closing arguments, and counsel representing the defendant while under the influence of drugs or mentally ill—have been labeled effective assistance by some courts.

For a recent example, see Muniz v. Smith, 647 F. 3d 619 (6th Cir.2011) (defense counsel napping during cross-examination of defendant did not clearly violate the Sixth Amendment).

32 Perlin & McClain *supra* note 5, at 261. *See also* Nicola Browne et al., C*apital Punishment and Mental Health Issues: Global Examples*, 25 St. Louis U. Pub. L. Rev. 383, 385 (2006) (case examples from other nations provide "strong example of how important it is in any country work to grasp fully the complex socio-cultural and socio-legal background before developing any penal policy strategies").

33 *See* Paul Gianelli, *Ineffective Assistance of Counsel and Expert Testimony*, 26 Crim. Just. 49 (2012). Although the cases Professor Gianelli discusses mostly involve expertise in matters involving blood spatter and arson, the issues are also present in cases involving psychiatric and psychological testimony. *See, e.g.*, People v. Lavoie, 733 N.Y.S.2d 799 (A.D. 2001); Lattrell v. Conway 430 F.Supp.2d 116 (W.D.N.Y. 2006); Halvorsen v. Com. 258 S.W.3d 1 (Ky. 2007); US ex rel. Sams v. Chrans, 165 F.Supp.2d 756 (N.D. Ill. 2001); Link v. Luebbers, 469 F.3d 1197 (8th Cir. 2006); Com. v. Alvarez, 740 N.E.2d 610 (Mass. 2000); State v. Barnes, 724 N.W.2d 807 (Neb. 2006).

34 *See, e.g.*, Morales v. Mitchell, 507 F.3d 916, 935 (6th Cir. 2007) ("the available information that Morales's trial counsel failed to discover and present to the jury included many specific details about his tumultuous life, continued and uncontrolled alcohol and drug abuse, dysfunctional family history, potential mental health problems, and detailed cultural background"); *see generally*, Perlin & McClain, *supra* note 5.

disabilities.[35] Cases continue to reflect a stunningly abysmal level of counsel performance in multiple cases in this cohort.[36]

An examination of an array of reported post-*Strickland* decisions involving findings of deficiency in death penalty cases,[37] in which defendants' history of serious mental disability was ignored by counsel, clearly calls into question one of the core assumptions of the *Strickland* case: that counsel does exercise substantial professional judgment in providing representation.[38] This is especially critical in cases where counsel completely "misses" what might be seen as mitigating evidence.[39] Consider these cases in which counsel was found to be deficient:

- In *Douglas v. Woodford*,[40] defense counsel performed deficiently, in particular by failing to discover reports from a psychologist that found defendant might have been incompetent to stand trial, possible brain damage and head injuries.
- In *Summerlin v. Schriro*,[41] defense counsel failed to investigate defendant's social or mental health background, and failed to find reports determining

35 Subsequently, see *infra* Chapter 4, I discuss the international human rights implications of the issues that are at the core of this book. On the question of whether failure to raise international human rights argument in the context of a death penalty case amounts to ineffective assistance of counsel, see Cribbs v. State, 2009 WL 1905454, *31 (Tenn. Crim. App. 2009), rejecting that argument outright.

36 *See, e.g.*, Cotto v. State, 89 So. 3d 1025 (Fla. App. 2012) (remanded for evidentiary hearing after trial court denial of defendant's assertion of ineffective assistance for counsel's failure to investigate mental health issues); *see generally* Rigg, *supra* note 26, at 86–87.

37 See generally, Perlin, *supra* note, 1, chapter 10.

38 See Hessick, *supra* note 31, at 1076 (*Strickland* is "a shield for counsel's behavior against judicial scrutiny").

39 *See generally*, Valerie McClain, Elliot Atkins & Michael L. Perlin, *"Oh, Stop That Cursed Jury": The Role of the Forensic Psychologist in the Mitigation Phase of the Death Penalty Trial*, in Handbook on Forensic Psychology (Mark Goldstein, ed. 2013) (in press); see also, Leona D. Jochnowitz, *Missed Mitigation: Counsel's Evolving Duty to Assess and Present Mitigation at Death Penalty Sentencing*, 43 Crim. L. Bull. 3 (2007). There are multiple other examples of courts declining to find Strickland violations in cases involving other sorts of errors related to the trials of defendants with mental disabilities. *See, e.g.*, People v. Haynes, 737 N.E. 2d 169 (Ill. 2000) (counsel's failure to advise defendant of his right to remain silent during examinations by state's psychiatric expert did not prejudice defendant). ABA Guidelines have also considered other similar potential violations. See Eric M. Freedman, *Re-stating the Standard of Practice of Death Penalty Counsel: The Supplementary Guidelines for the Mitigation Function of Defense Teams in Death Penalty Cases*, 36 Hofstra L. Rev. 663, 672 (2008), discussing ABA Guideline 4.1, Commentary: "It is simply ineffective assistance for counsel to permit a mental health assessment of the client to occur before having made a reasoned decision about the purpose of the examination and having provided the examiner with the data necessary to reach a professionally competent conclusion respecting the question presented."

40 316 F.3d 1079 (9th Cir. 2003).

41 427 F.3d 623 (9th Cir. 2005).

defendant to be mentally retarded, and disclosing defendant's diagnosis of paranoid schizophrenia.

- In *Daniels v. Woodford*,[42] defense counsel performed deficiently by relying on one sole, inexperienced psychologist who after only a cursory evaluation of defendant, failed to follow up when that evaluation suggested that the defendant was mentally ill, failed to investigate a family history that presented a detailed picture of serious mental illness, and failed to investigate whether the medications prescribed to the defendant or the illegal substances he was taking at the time of crime had any effect on his mental state, either separately or as combined.[43]
- In *Hovey v. Ayers*,[44] counsel failed to give an expert witness documentation about defendant's mental illness and evidence of defendant's conduct at the time of the crime.
- In *Frierson v. Woodford*,[45] counsel failed to read the record of defendant's prior trials and thus failed to learn that defendant potentially suffered from brain damage (and then when made aware, failed to consult a neurologist), and failed to sufficiently investigate defendant's background so as to learn of his very low IQ scores.
- In *Correll v. Ryan*,[46] counsel failed to investigate and present mitigating evidence about defendant's potential brain damage and his heavy drug use, and
- In *Lambright v. Schriro*,[47] the sentence was reversed after court held that counsel failed to conduct basic investigation of mitigating factors including suicide attempts, psychiatric hospitalization, traumatic experiences in Vietnam war, diagnosis of personality disorder, and a history of major drug problems.

In short, the pallid *Strickland* standard corrupts all of criminal procedure, but it is especially damning in cases involving this subset of criminal defendants. Courts are, to be charitable, clueless[48] when it comes to construing it in the context of

42 428 F.3d 1181 (9th Cir. 2005).

43 *Compare* Godinez v. Moran, 509 U.S. 389, 410–11 (1993) (Blackmun, J., dissenting) (criticizing trial judge for failure to have made sufficient inquiry to discover that defendant, at the time of his guilty plea in a death penalty case, was being administered simultaneously four different prescription drugs—phenobarbital, dilantin, inderal, and vistaril—that in combination had a "numbing effect" on the defendant, who later stated, "I guess I really didn't care about anything ... I wasn't very concerned about anything that was going on … as far as the proceedings and everything were going)." See *infra* Chapter 8 for an extended consideration of *Godinez v. Moran*.

44 458 F.3d 892 (9th Cir. 2006).

45 463 F.3d 982 (9th Cir. 2006).

46 465 F.3d 1006 (9th Cir. 2006).

47 490 F.3d 1103 (9th Cir. 2007).

48 On cluelessness in a *Strickland* context, see Vanessa Merton, *What Do You Do When You Meet a "Walking Violation of the Sixth Amendment" if You're Trying to Put*

cases of persons with mental disabilities.[49] The extant case law has little to do with the reality that the representation of persons with mental disabilities requires skills above and beyond those involved in the representation of other criminal defendants.[50] In cases in which such defendants have pled guilty, the results may be even more problematic, since there is, in such cases, rarely even a record to be reviewed on appeal.[51]

That Lawyer's Client in Jail?, 69 FORDHAM L. REV. 997, 1026 (2000) (discussing the "the drunk, senile, or clueless defender"). Some 39 years ago, Judge David Bazelon charged that lawyers in his court representing criminal defendants with mental disabilities were "walking violations of the Sixth Amendment." David L. Bazelon, *The Defective Assistance of Counsel*, 42 U. CIN. L. REV. 1, 2 (1973), discussed *supra* Chapter 1, text accompanying note 35. *Compare* Tom Zimpleman, *The Ineffective Assistance of Counsel Era*, 63 S.C. L. REV. 425, 451 (2011) ("the right to counsel is meaningless if the supposed counsel was merely 'a warm body with a legal pedigree',"), quoting David L. Bazelon, *The Realities of Gideon and Argersinger*, 64 GEO. L.J. 811, 818–19 (1976). Commentators argue persuasively that little has changed. *See* Richard Klein, *The Constitutionalization of Ineffective Assistance of Counsel*, 58 MD. L. REV. 1433, 1446 (1999) ("[T]he *Strickland* Court interpreted the requirements of the Sixth Amendment's right to effective assistance of counsel in such an ultimately meaningless manner as to require little more than a warm body with a law degree standing next to the defendant."); *see generally* David Cole, *Gideon v. Wainwright & Strickland v. Washington,* in CRIMINAL PROCEDURE STORIES 101, 101–03 (Carol S. Steiker ed., 2006) ("in actuality as long as the state provides a warm body with a law degree and a bar admission, little else matters"); *see generally* Baxter, *supra* note 30.

49 See *supra* text accompanying notes 37–47, and see cases cited in Sharon Dolovich, *Legitimate Punishment in Liberal Democracy*, 7 BUFF. CRIM L. REV. 307, 436 n.291 (2004), and Anne Bowen Poulin, *Strengthening the Criminal Defendant's Right to Counsel*, 28 CARDOZO L. REV. 1213, 1241–42, n.117 (2006). According to Professor Laurence Benner, in the past decade there have been over 2,500 published and unpublished appellate court decisions in which the issue of ineffective assistance of counsel was raised. See Laurence Benner, *The Presumption of Guilt, Systemic Factors that Contribute to Ineffective Assistance of Counsel in California*, 45 CAL. W. LAW REV. 263, 276–77 (2009).

50 On the impact of reduced state budgets on this problem, *see, e.g.*, Guyer, *supra* note 2, at 360; *see generally* Alissa Pollitz Worden, Andrew Lucas Blaize Davies & Elizabeth K. Brown, *A Patchwork of Policies: Justice, Due Process, and Public Defense Across American States*, 74 ALB. L. REV. 1423 (2010–11).

51 Hill v. Lockhart, 474 U.S. 52, 56–59 (1985), extended the *Strickland* standard to the context of plea bargains. On this issue in general, *see* Erin A. Conway, *Ineffective Assistance of Counsel: How Illinois Has Used the "Prejudice" Prong of Strickland to Lower The Floor on Performance When Defendants Plead Guilty,* 105 NW. U. L. REV. 1707 (2011); Ana Maria Gutierrez, *The Sixth Amendment: The Operation of Plea Bargaining in Contemporary Criminal Procedure*, 87 DENV. U. L. REV. 695 (2010). I discuss Conway's article in the context of procedural justice issues *infra* Chapter 6.

IV. The Potential Power of the *K.G.F.* Case

The case that has best captured this reality is the Montana state civil commitment case of *In re K.G.F.*[52] K.G.F. was a voluntary patient at a community hospital in Montana whose expressed desire to leave the facility prompted a State petition alleging her need for commitment. Counsel was appointed, and a commitment hearing was scheduled for the next day.[53] The State's expert recommended commitment; patient's counsel presented the testimony of the plaintiff herself and a mental health professional who recommended that the patient be kept in the hospital a few days so that a community-based treatment plan could be arranged nearer to her home.[54] The court ordered commitment.[55] K.G.F.'s appeal was premised, in part, on allegations of ineffective assistance of counsel.[56]

In a thoughtful and scholarly opinion, the Montana Supreme Court relied on state statutory and constitutional sources to find that "the right to counsel … provides an individual subject to an involuntary commitment proceeding the right to effective assistance of counsel. In turn, this right affords the individual with the right to raise the allegation of ineffective assistance of counsel in challenging a commitment order."[57] In assessing what constitutes "effectiveness," the court—startlingly, to my mind—eschewed the *Strickland* standard as insufficiently protective of the "liberty interests of individuals such as K.G.F., who may or may not have broken any law, but who, upon the expiration of a ninety-day commitment, must indefinitely bear the badge of inferiority of a once 'involuntarily committed' person with a proven mental disorder."[58] Interestingly, one of the key reasons why *Strickland* was seen as lacking was the court's conclusion that "reasonable professional assistance"[59]—the linchpin of the *Strickland* decision—"cannot be presumed in a proceeding that routinely accepts—and even requires—an unreasonably low standard of legal assistance and generally disdains zealous, adversarial confrontation."[60]

In assessing the contours of effective assistance of counsel, the court emphasized that it was not limiting its inquiry to courtroom performance; even more

52 29 P.3d 485 (Mont. 2001). *See generally* Michael L. Perlin, *"I Might Need a Good Lawyer, Could Be Your Funeral, My Trial": A Global Perspective on the Right to Counsel in Civil Commitment Cases, and Its Implications for Clinical Legal Education*, 28 Wash. U. J. L. & Soc'l Pol'y 241, 246–49 (2008).

53 *K.G.F.* 29 P. 3d at 488.

54 *Id.*

55 *Id,*

56 *Id.*

57 *Id.* at 491.

58 *Id.*

59 *Strickland,* 466 U.S. at 689.

60 *K.G.F.*, 29 P. 3d at 492, citing Perlin, *supra* note 3, at 53–54 ("identifying the *Strickland* standard as 'sterile and perfunctory' where 'reasonably effective assistance' is objectively measured by the 'prevailing professional norms'").

important was counsel's "failure to fully investigate and comprehend a patient's circumstances prior to an involuntary civil commitment hearing or trial, which may, in turn, lead to critical decision-making between counsel and client as to how best to proceed."[61] Such pre-hearing matters, the court continued, "clearly involve effective preparation prior to a hearing or trial."[62] The court further emphasized the role of state laws guaranteeing the patient's "dignity and personal integrity"[63] and "privacy and dignity"[64] in its decision: "'[q]uality counsel provides the most likely way—perhaps the only likely way—to ensure the due process protection of dignity and privacy interests in cases such as the one at bar."[65]

The court continued in the same vein, underscoring counsel's responsibilities "as an advocate and adversary."[66] The lawyer must "represent the perspective of the [patient] and … serve as a vigorous advocate for the [patient's] wishes,"[67] engaging in "all aspects of advocacy and vigorously argu[ing] to the best of his or her ability for the ends desired by the client,"[68] and operating on the "presumption that a client wishes to not be involuntarily committed."[69] Thus, "evidence that counsel independently advocated or otherwise acquiesced to an involuntary commitment—in the absence of any evidence of a voluntary and knowing consent by the patient-respondent—will establish the presumption that counsel was ineffective."[70] In conclusion, the court stated:

> [I]t is not only counsel for the patient-respondent, but also courts, that are charged with the duty of safeguarding the due process rights of individuals involved at every stage of the proceedings, and must therefore rigorously adhere to the standards expressed herein, as well as those mandated under [state statute].[71]

On one hand, *K.G.F.* provides an "easily transferable blueprint for courts that want to grapple with adequacy of counsel issues";[72] on the other, no other state court has adopted its reasoning in a civil commitment context since it was

---

61 *K.G.F.*, 29 P. 3d at 492.

62 *Id.*

63 *Id.* at 493 (quoting Mont. Code Ann. § 53-21-101(1)).

64 *K.G.F.*, 29 P.3d at 493 (quoting Mont. Code Ann. § 53-21-142(1)). See also Mont. Const. art. II, § 4 ("The dignity of the human being is inviolable."). *See generally* Michael L. Perlin, *"Dignity Was the First to Leave": Godinez v. Moran, Colin Ferguson, and the Trial of Mentally Disabled Criminal Defendants*, 14 Behav. Sci. & L. 61 (1996), and *infra* Chapter 7.

65 *K.G.F.*, 29 P.3d at 494 (citing Perlin, *supra* note 3, at 47).

66 K.G.F., 29 P.3d at 500.

67 *Id.* (internal quotations omitted).

68 *Id.* (internal quotations omitted).

69 *Id.*

70 *Id.*

71 *Id.* at 501.

72 2 Perlin & Cucolo, *supra* note 5, § 2B-11.3, at 96–99.

decided.[73] Its rationale was rejected by the Washington Supreme Court in an opinion that concluded, with no supporting empirical or other statistical evidence:

> We do not share the Montana Supreme Court's dim view of the quality of civil commitment proceedings, or their adversarial nature, in the state of Washington. The *Strickland* standard appears to be sufficient to protect the right to the effective assistance of counsel for a civil commitment respondent in this state.[74]

The question is joined: If *K.G.F.* were the prevailing standard in criminal cases, what impact would that have on the quality of counsel in such cases globally, and, especially, in cases involving defendants with mental disabilities?[75] A Canadian appellate court "got" this issue over 20 years ago: "Mentally ill persons are not to be stigmatized because of the nature of their illness or disability; nor should they be treated as persons of lesser status or dignity. Their right to personal autonomy and self-determination is no less significant, and is entitled to no less protection … ."[76] If we are to afford persons with mental disabilities the dignity to which they are entitled in the criminal process, it is essential that we acknowledge that the *Strickland* doctrine has failed miserably, and that we seriously consider how it can be restructured.

V. Conclusion

The issue of quality of counsel is, in many ways, the most important that the criminal justice system, as an entity, faces.[77]And this issue is magnified—many

---

73 Although the Kansas Supreme Court has declined to apply the reasoning of *K.G.F.* to a case involving sexually violent predator proceedings (nominally "civil" cases, see Kansas v. Hendricks, 521 U.S. 346 (1997)), it did apply *Strickland* in that context. *See In re Ontiberos*, 287 P.3d 855 (Kan. 2012).

74 *In re* Detention of T.A. H.-L., 97 P.3d 767, 771–72 (Wash. Ct. App. 2004). *See also In re* Daryll C., 930 N.E.2d 1048 (Ill. App. 2010) (declining to adopt the Montana court's approach because it was grounded in Montana constitutional and statutory law); *In re* L.G., 2006 WL 2780157, at *8 (Ohio App.2006) (unpublished opinion) (rejecting the Montana Supreme Court's approach and applying the *Strickland* standard).

75 See *infra* Chapters 8–10 (discussing this issue in the context of questions of competency, insanity and sentencing).

76 Fleming v. Reid, 4 O.R. 3d 74, 86–87 (C.A.) (1991). *See generally* Aaron Dhir, *Relationships of Force: Reflections on Law, Psychiatry, and Human Rights*, 25 Windsor Rev. L. & Soc'l Iss. 103, 109 (2008), discussing *Fleming, supra.* On how the *K.G.F.* court relied on dignitarian values in its rejection of the *Strickland* standard, see Elaine M. Dahl, *Taking Liberties: Analysis of In re Mental Health of K.G.F.*, 64 Mont. L. Rev. 295, 296 (2003); Perlin, *supra* note 52.

77 *See, e.g.*, Stephen Bright, *Death by Lottery—Procedural Bar of Constitutional Claims in Capital Cases Due to Inadequate Representation of Indigent Defendants*, 92

times over—in cases involving defendants with mental disabilities. If there is to be any significant change in the way that such individuals are treated in this system—and if dignity values are to be privileged rather than subordinated—it is essential, as a first step, that the shame of shoddy, unprepared, unprofessional counsel be remediated.

W. Va. L. Rev. 679, 695 (1990) ("[t]he death penalty will too often be punishment not for committing the worst crime, but for being assigned the worst lawyer").

Chapter 4
International Human Rights Law

I. Introduction[1]

It is essential that we begin to think seriously about the impact of international human rights law, specifically, the recently ratified United Nations Convention on the Rights of Persons with Disabilities (CRPD),[2] on the issues in question.[3] The CRPD is the most important international human rights document—ever—that recognizes the rights of persons with disabilities. In late 2001, the United Nations General Assembly established an Ad Hoc Committee "to consider proposals for a comprehensive and integral international convention to promote and protect the rights and dignity of persons with disabilities ... ."[4] The Ad Hoc Committee

---

1 Portions of this chapter are adapted from MICHAEL L. PERLIN, INTERNATIONAL HUMAN RIGHTS AND MENTAL DISABILITY LAW: WHEN THE SILENCED ARE HEARD (2011) (PERLIN, SILENCED), and MICHAEL L. PERLIN, MENTAL DISABILITY AND THE DEATH PENALTY: THE SHAME OF THE STATES (2013) (PERLIN, DEATH PENALTY).

2 On the singular role of this convention, *see, e.g.*, PERLIN, SILENCED, *supra* note 1, at 143–58; Frédéric Mégret, *The Disabilities Convention: Toward a Holistic Concept of Rights*, 12 INT'L J. HUM. RTS. 261 (2008); Frédéric Mégret, *The Disabilities Convention: Human Rights of Persons with Disabilities or Disability Rights?*, 30 HUM. RIGHTS 494 (2008) (Mégret, *Disability Rights*); Michael L. Perlin & Eva Szeli, *Mental Health Law and Human Rights: Evolution And Contemporary Challenges*, in MENTAL HEALTH AND HUMAN RIGHTS: VISION, PRAXIS, AND COURAGE 98 (Michael Dudley et al, eds, 2012) (Perlin & Szeli, *Evolution And Contemporary Challenges*); Michael L. Perlin & Eva Szeli, *Mental Health Law and Human Rights: Evolution, Challenges and the Promise of the New Convention*, in UNITED NATIONS CONVENTION ON THE RIGHTS OF PERSONS WITH DISABILITIES: MULTIDISCIPLINARY PERSPECTIVES 241 (Jukka Kumpuvuori & Martin Scheninen, eds, 2010) (Perlin & Szeli, *Promise*). On of the impact of UN human rights treaties on domestic law in general, see Christof Heyns & Frans Viljoen, *The Impact of the United Nations Human Rights Treaties on the Domestic Level*, 23 HUM. RTS. Q. 483 (2001).

3 There are comparative law issues as well, especially with regards to questions of advocacy of counsel. *See generally* CRIMINAL PROCEDURE: A WORLDWIDE STUDY (Craig Bradley ed., 2d ed. 2007), discussing adequacy standards—or, in some cases, *lack* of standards—in other nations, including, *e.g.*, Argentina (*id.* at 52–53), Canada (*id.* at 87), Egypt (*id.* at 143–44), England and Wales (*id.* at 195), France (*id.* at 237–38), Israel (*id.* at 301), Italy (*id.* at 348), Mexico (*id.* at 391), and Russia (*id.* at 467).

4 G.A. Res. 56/168 (2001). On the role of dignity in international human rights law in general, see Christopher McCrudden, *Human Dignity and the Judicial Interpretation of Human Rights*, 19 EUR. J. INT'L L. 655 (2008). *See infra* Chapter 7 on the role of dignity in the context of the topics discussed in this book.

drafted a document over the course of five years and eight sessions, and the new CRPD was adopted in December 2006 and opened for signature in March 2007.[5] It entered into force—thus becoming legally binding on States parties—on May 3, 2008, thirty days after the 20th ratification.[6] One of the hallmarks of the process that led to the publication of the UN Convention was the participation of persons with disabilities and the clarion cry, "Nothing about us, without us."[7] This has led commentators to conclude that the Convention "is regarded as having finally empowered the 'world's largest minority' to claim their rights, and to participate in international and national affairs on an equal basis with others who have achieved specific treaty recognition and protection."[8]

II. The CRPD

This Convention is the most revolutionary international human rights document ever created that applies to persons with disabilities.[9] The Disability Convention

5 G.A. Res. A/61/611 (2006); G.A. Res. A/61/106 (2006).

6 *See* www.Un.Org/News/Press/Docs/2008/Hr4941.Doc.htm. *See generally* Tara Melish, *The UN Disability Convention: Historic Process, Strong Prospects, and Why the U.S. Should Ratify*, 14 Hum. Rts. Brief 37, 44 (Winter 2007); Michael Ashley Stein & Penelope J.S. Stein, *Beyond Disability Civil Rights*, 58 Hastings L. J. 1203 (2007). On the status of the Convention in the United States, see *infra* note 54.

7 *See, e.g.*, Rosemary Kayess & Phillip French, *Out of Darkness into Light? Introducing the Convention on the Rights of Persons with Disabilities*, 8 Hum. Rts. L. Rev. 1, 4 n.15 (2008). *See*, for example, statement by Hon. Ruth Dyson, Minister for Disability Issues, New Zealand mission to the UN, for formal ceremony at the signing of the convention on the rights of persons with disability, 30 March 2007: "Just as the convention itself is the product of a remarkable partnership between governments and civil society, effective implementation will require a continuation of that partnership." The negotiating slogan "nothing about us without us" was adopted by the international disability caucus, available at: http://www.un.org/esa/socdev/enable/documents/stat_conv/nzam.doc [last accessed, August 23, 2011].

8 *Id.*, n.17 (See, for example, statements made by the High Commissioner For Human Rights, Louise Arbour, and the permanent representative of New Zealand and chair of the ad hoc committee on a Comprehensive and Integral International Convention on the Protection and Promotion of the Rights and Dignity of Persons with Disabilities, Ambassador Don Mackay, at a special event on the Convention on the Rights of Persons with Disabilities, convened by the UN Human Rights Council, 26 March 2007, available at: http://www.Unog.Ch/80256EDD006B9C2E/(httpnewsbyyear_En)/7444B2E219117CE8C12572AA004C5701?Opendocument [August 23, 2011].

9 Perlin & Szeli, *Evolution and Contemporary Challenges*, *supra* note 2; Perlin, Silenced, *supra* note 1, at 3–21; *See generally*, Michael L. Perlin, *"A Change Is Gonna Come": The Implications of the United Nations Convention on the Rights of Persons with Disabilities for the Domestic Practice of Constitutional Mental Disability Law*, 29 No. Ill. U. L. Rev. 483 (2009) (Perlin, *Change*); Michael L. Perlin, *"Striking for the Guardians and*

furthers the human rights approach to disability and recognizes the right of people with disabilities to equality in most every aspect of life.[10] It firmly endorses a social model of disability—a clear and direct repudiation of the medical model that traditionally was part-and-parcel of mental disability law.[11] By so situating disability within a social model framework[12] and sketching the "full range of human rights that apply to all human beings, all with a particular application to the lives of persons with disabilities,"[13] the Convention provides a framework for insuring that mental health laws "fully recognize the rights of those with mental illness."[14]

The CRPD categorically affirms the social model of disability[15] by describing it as a condition arising from "interaction with various barriers [that] may hinder their full and effective participation in society on an equal basis with others," instead of inherent limitations,[16] reconceptualizes mental health rights as disability

---

Protectors of the Mind": The Convention on the Rights of Persons with Mental Disabilities and the Future of Guardianship Law, – PENN ST. L. REV. – (2013) (in press).

10 *See, e.g.*, Aaron Dhir, *Human Rights Treaty Drafting Through the Lens of Mental Disability: The Proposed International Convention on Protection and Promotion of the Rights and Dignity of Persons with Disabilities*, 41 STAN. J. INT'L L. 181 (2005).

11 *See generally* Michael L. Perlin, *"Abandoned Love": The Impact of Wyatt v. Stickney on the Intersection between International Human Rights and Domestic Mental Disability Law*, 35 LAW & PSYCHOL. REV. 121 (2011).

12 *See, e.g.*, Janet E. Lord, David Suozzi & Allyn L. Taylor, *Lessons From the Experience of U.N. Convention on the Rights of Persons with Disabilities: Addressing the Democratic Deficit in Global Health Governance*, 38 J.L. MED. & ETHICS 564 (2010); H. Archibald Kaiser, *Canadian Mental Health Law: The Slow Process of Redirecting the Ship of State*, 17 HEALTH L.J. 139 (2009).

13 Janet E. Lord & Michael A. Stein, *Social Rights and the Relational Value of the Rights to Participate in Sport, Recreation, and Play*, 27 B.U. INT'L L. J. 249, 256 (2009); *See also* Ronald McCallum, *The United Nations Convention on the Rights of Persons with Disabilities: Some Reflections*. Accessible at http://ssrn.com/abstract=1563883 (2010).

14 Bernadette McSherry, *International Trends in Mental Health Laws: Introduction*, 26 LAW IN CONTEXT 1, 8 (2008).

15 See Lord, Suozzi & Taylor, *supra* note 12, at 568; Kaiser, *supra* note 12; Michael L. Perlin, *"There's Voices in the Night Trying to Be Heard": The Potential Impact of the Convention on the Rights of Persons with Disabilities on Domestic Mental Disability Law*, In EVOLVING ISSUES IN DISCRIMINATION: SOCIAL SCIENCE AND LEGAL PERSPECTIVES (Richard Wiener et al eds, 2013) (in press); Michael L. Perlin, *"There Must Be Some Way Out Of Here": Why the Convention on the Rights of Persons with Disabilities Is Potentially the Best Weapon in the Fight against Sanism* (paper presented to conference at Deakin University, Melbourne, Australia, co-sponsored by the Australasian Society for Intellectual Disability, June 2011) (on file with author); Michael L. Perlin, *"There Are No Trials Inside the Gates of Eden": Mental Health Courts, the Convention on the Rights of Persons with Disabilities, Dignity, and the Promise of Therapeutic Jurisprudence*, in COERCIVE CARE: LAW AND POLICY (Bernadette McSherry & Ian Freckelton eds,. 2013) (in press).

16 CRPD, Art. 1 And Pmbl., Para. E.

rights,[17] and extends existing human rights to take into account the specific rights experiences of persons with disabilities.[18] To this end, it calls for "respect for inherent dignity"[19] and "non-discrimination."[20] Subsequent articles declare "freedom from torture or cruel, inhuman or degrading treatment or punishment,"[21] "freedom from exploitation, violence and abuse,"[22] and a right to protection of the "integrity of the person."[23]

The CRPD is unique because it is the first legally binding instrument devoted to the comprehensive protection of the rights of persons with disabilities. It not only clarifies that States should not discriminate against persons with disabilities, but also sets out explicitly the many steps that States must take to create an enabling environment so that persons with disabilities can enjoy authentic equality in society.[24] One of the most critical issues in seeking to bring life to international human rights law in a mental disability law context is the right to adequate and dedicated counsel. The CRPD mandates that "States Parties shall take appropriate measures to provide access by persons with disabilities to the support they may require in exercising their legal capacity"[25] Elsewhere, the convention commands:

> States Parties shall ensure effective access to justice for persons with disabilities on an equal basis with others, including through the provision of procedural and age appropriate accommodations, in order to facilitate their effective role as

17 Phillip Fennel, *Human Rights, Bioethics, and Mental Disorder*, 27 Med. & L. 95 (2008).

18 Mégret, *Disability Rights*, *supra* note 2; See Perlin, Silenced, *supra* note 1, at 143–58.

19 CRPD, Article 3(A).

20 *Id.*, Article 3(B).

21 *Id.*, Article 15.

22 *Id.*, Article 16.

23 *Id.*, Article 17.

24 On the changes that ratifying states need to make in their domestic involuntary civil commitment laws to comply with Convention mandates, see Bryan Y. Lee, *The U.N. Convention on the Rights of Persons with Disabilities and Its Impact upon Involuntary Civil Commitment of Individuals with Developmental Disabilities*, 44 Colum. J. L. & Soc'l Probs. 393 (2011). See also, István Hoffman & György Kőnczei, *Legal Regulations Related to the Passive and Active Legal Capacity of Persons with Intellectual and Psychosocial Disabilities in Light of the Convention on the Rights of Persons with Disabilities and the Impending Reform of the Hungarian Civil Code*, 33 Loy. L.A. Int'l & Comp. L. Rev. 143 (2010) (on the application of the CRPD to capacity issues); Kathryn D. Demarco, *Disabled by Solitude: The Convention on the Rights of Persons with Disabilities and Its Impact on The Use of Supermax Solitary Confinement*, 66 U. Miami L. Rev. 523 (2012) (on the application of the CRPD to solitary confinement in correctional institutions).

25 *See* Michael L. Perlin, *"I Might Need a Good Lawyer, Could Be Your Funeral, My Trial": A Global Perspective on the Right to Counsel in Civil Commitment Cases, and Its Implications for Clinical Legal Education*, 28 Wash. U. J. L. & Soc'l Pol'y 241, 252–53 (2008), quoting CRPD, Article 12.

> direct and indirect participants, including as witnesses, in all legal proceedings, including at investigative and other preliminary stages.[26]

"The extent to which this Article is honored in signatory nations will have a major impact on the extent to which this entire Convention affects persons with mental disabilities."[27] If and only if, there is a mechanism for the appointment of dedicated counsel,[28] can this dream become a reality.

The ratification of the CRPD marks the most important development yet in institutional human rights law for persons with mental disabilities. The CRPD is detailed, comprehensive, integrated, and the result of a careful drafting process. It seeks to reverse the results of centuries of oppressive behavior and attitudes that have stigmatized persons with disabilities. Its goal is clear: to promote, protect and ensure the full and equal enjoyment of all human rights and fundamental freedoms of all persons with disabilities, and to promote respect for their inherent dignity.[29] Whether this will actually *happen* is still far from a settled matter.

III. The Impact of the CRPD on Domestic Criminal Law Practice

But what are the implications of this Convention for the domestic practice of criminal law? Consider these overlapping issues:

- Courts in the United States have been inconsistent in their enforcement of and adherence to other relevant UN conventions.[30] In *Lareau v. Manson*,[31] a federal district court cited to the United Nations Standard Minimum Rules for the Treatment of Prisoners standards in cases involving the "double bunking" of inmates. On the other hand, in *Flores v. Southern Peru Copper Corp.*,[32] the Second Circuit found that the United Nations' Convention on the Rights of the Child (CRC) did not convey a private right of action to plaintiffs as a matter of law. In at least one case, however, while noting that the non-ratified convention was not binding on US courts, the Massachusetts Supreme Judicial Court

---

26 CRPD, Article 13.

27 Perlin, *supra* note 25, at 253.

28 On the significance of "cause lawyers" in the development of mental disability law in the United States, *see* Michael A. Stein, Michael E. Waterstone & David B. Wilkins, *Book Review: Cause Lawyering for People with Disabilities*, 123 Harv. L. Rev. 1658 (2010). *See generally supra* Chapter 3.

29 CRPD, Article 1.

30 *See generally* Perlin, *Change, supra* note 9, at 494–95; Michael L. Perlin & Henry A. Dlugacz, *"It's Doom Alone That Counts": Can International Human Rights Law Be An Effective Source of Rights in Correctional Conditions Litigation?*, 7 Behav. Sci. & L. 675 (2009).

31 507 F.Supp. 1177, 1187 n.9 (D. Conn. 1980), *aff'd in part, rev'd in part*, 651 F.2d 96 (2d Cir. 1981).

32 414 F.3d 233, 259 (2d Cir. 2003).

"read the entire text of the convention … and conclude[d] that the outcome of the proceedings in this case are completely in accord with principles expressed therein."[33] Most significantly in *Roper v. Simmons*, in the course of striking down the juvenile death penalty, the Supreme Court (per Justice Kennedy) acknowledged that the United States had not ratified the CRC but added,

> It is proper that we acknowledge the overwhelming weight of international opinion against the juvenile death penalty, resting in large part on the understanding that the instability and emotional imbalance of young people may often be a factor in the crime. The opinion of the world community, while not controlling our outcome, does provide respected and significant confirmation for our own conclusions."[34]

- Traditionally, there has been very little focus in international human rights law on the domestic criminal trial process.[35] As Professor Johanna Kalb has noted:

---

33 *In Re* Adoption of Peggy, 767 N.E.2d 29, 38 (Mass. 2002).

34 543 U.S. 551, 578 (2005). See also, Graham v. Florida, 130 S. Ct. 2011 (2010) (life without parole sentence for juveniles for crimes other than homicide unconstitutional); Miller v. Alabama, 132 S. Ct. 2455 (2012) (mandatory life without parole sentence for juveniles for homicide unconstitutional). I discuss the implications of *Roper* and *Graham* extensively in Michael L. Perlin, *"Yonder Stands Your Orphan with His Gun": The International Human Rights and Therapeutic Jurisprudence Implications of Juvenile Punishment Schemes*,– Texas Tech L. Rev. – (2013) (in press).

35 Courts typically dismiss international human rights-based claims. *See, e.g.*, Contreras v. Harrington, 2011 WL 3740850, * 7 (E.D. Cal. 2011):

> Finally, defendant claims we should be guided by the evolving international human rights standards regarding the punishment and treatment of young offenders. "Defining crime and determining punishment are matters uniquely legislative in nature, resting within the legislature's sole discretion.[citation]." (People v. Lewis (1993) 21 Cal.App.4th 243, 251, 25 Cal.Rptr.2d 827.)

Compare Bott v. Deland, 922 P. 2d 732, 740 (Utah 1996), abrogated on other grounds by Spackman Ex. Rel. Spackman V. Bd. of Educ. of Box Elder County Sch. Dist.,16 P.3d 533 (Utah 2000) (provision of Oregon Constitution, prohibiting the treatment of prisoners with "unnecessary rigor," was based on "internationally accepted standards of humane treatment"), and United States v. Bakeas, 987 F. Supp. 44, 46 n. 4 (D. Mass. 1997) (state adoption of policy of assigning aliens to more restrictive conditions of prison confinement solely by reason of their alienage may violate commitments under international law).

Defendants in death penalty cases often raise international human rights claims in the appellate process, and, so far, have been uniformly unsuccessful. *See, e.g.*, Shisinday v. Quarterman, 2007 WL 776680 (S.D. Tex. 2007); Baird v. State, 831 N.E.2d 109 (Ind. 2005); Lagrone v. Cockrell, 2003 WL 22327519 (5th Cir. 2003); Matheney v. State, 833 N.E.2d 454 (Ind. 2005); Buell v. Mitchell, 274 F.3d 337 (6th Cir.2001); *See generally*, Sandra Babcock, *The Limits of International Law: Efforts to Enforce Rulings of the International Court of Justice in U.S. Death Penalty Cases,* 62 Syracuse L. Rev. 183 (2012); on *Strickland v. Washington* (see

Only on rare occasions have United States courts—state, federal or territorial—considered international conceptions of "dignity," even those embodied in the human rights instruments signed and ratified by the United States, when discussing the role that dignitary interests have to play in resolving the claims before them.[36]

- Although scholars argue that "criminal trials should be fully compliant with the due process requirements of international human rights law,"[37] that "international human rights law may prove a useful tool in rights advocacy

---

supra Chapter 3) implications of counsel's failure to raise international human rights law claims, see Cribbs v. State, 2009 WL 1905454 (Tenn. Crim. App. 2009) (rejecting argument).

On the other hand, there has been a robust connection between international human rights law and the movement to abolish the death penalty, both in the Uunited States and in other retentionist nations, and the US Supreme Court has relied on international law in its opinion barring execution of persons with mental retardation, see Atkins v. Virginia, 536 U.S. 304, 316 (2002), and see the discussion of *Atkins* in this context in Kane v. Winn, 319 F. Supp. 2d 162, 201 (D. Mass. 2004). *See generally* PERLIN, DEATH PENALTY, *supra* note 1, at 139–48; David T. Johnson, *American Capital Punishment in Comparative Perspective*, 36 LAW & SOC. INQUIRY 1033 (2011); Ryan Florio, *The [Capital] Punishment Fits the Crime: A Comparative Analysis of the Death Penalty and Proportionality in the United States of America and the People's Republic of China*, 16 U. MIAMI INT'L & COMP. L. REV. 43, 61 (2008); Richard Wilson, *International Law Issues in Death Penalty Defense*, 31 HOFSTRA L. REV. 1195 (2003); William A. Schabas, *International Law, Politics, Diplomacy and the Abolition of The Death Penalty*, 13 WM. & MARY BILL OF RTS. J. 417 (2004); Mark Warren, *Death, Dissent and Diplomacy: The U.S. Death Penalty as an Obstacle to Foreign Relations*, 13 WM. & MARY BILL OF RTS. J. 309, 337 (2004); James H. Wyman, *Vengeance Is Whose?: The Death Penalty and Cultural Relativism in International Law*, 6 J. TRANSNAT'L L. & POL'Y 543, 548 (1997), especially in the context of defendants with mental illness, *see, e.g.*, Liliana Lyra Jubilut, *Death Penalty and Mental Illness: The Challenge of Reconciling Human Rights, Criminal Law, and Psychiatric Standards*, 6 SEATTLE J. SOC. JUST. 353 (2007); Simon H. Fisherow, *Follow the Leader?: Japan Should Formally Abolish the Execution of the Mentally Retarded in the Wake of Atkins v. Virginia*, 14 PAC. RIM L. & POL'Y J. 455, 461 (2005); Nicola Browne et al., *Capital Punishment and Mental Health Issues: Global Examples*, 25 ST. LOUIS U. PUB. L. REV. 383 (2006); Jaw-Perng Wang, *The Current State of Capital Punishment in Taiwan*, 6 Nat'l Taiwan U.L. REV. 143, 158(2011); Andrew Novak, *Constitutional Reform and The Abolition of the Mandatory Death Penalty in Kenya*, 45 SUFFOLK L. REV. 285 (2012). For an international human rights law-based criticism of the death penalty as administered in the United States, *see, e.g.*, Linda A. Malone, *From Breard to Atkins to Malvo: Legal Incompetency and Human Rights Norms on the Fringes of the Death Penalty*, 13 WM. & MARY BILL RTS. J. 363, 397 (2004).

36 Johanna Kalb, *Litigating Dignity: A Human Rights Framework*, 74 ALB. L. REV. 1725, 1726–27 (2010–11).

37 Cindy G. Buys, *Notteboh's Nightmare: Have We Exorcised the Ghosts of WWII Detention Programs or Do They Still Haunt Guantanamo?*, 11 CHI.-KENT J. INT'L & COMP. L. 1, 60 (2011).

at all levels,"[38] and even that criminalization of certain acts in and of itself may be a human rights violation,[39] the universe of domestic criminal cases that cite international human rights conventions and treaties is meager,[40] although scholars have urged a broader use of international human rights law in this context.[41] This is in stark contrast to the *intense* focus on these issues, of course, in the international criminal courts process,[42] as well as to the way that the influence of such law is "widely accepted" in Europe and other parts of the world.[43]

---

38 Johanna Kalb, *Human Rights Treaties in State Courts: The International Prospects of State Constitutionalism after Medellín*, 115 Penn St. L. Rev. 1051, 1060 (2011). *See also* Jordan J. Paust, *Customary International Law and Human Rights Treaties Are Law of the United States*, 20 Mich. J. Int'l L. 301 (1999); Oona Hathaway, Sabria McElroy & Sara Solow, *International Law At Home: Enforcing Treaties in U.S. Courts*, 37 Yale J. Int'l L. 51 (2012).

39 Barbara Frey & Z. Kevin Zhao, *The Criminalization of Immigration and the International Norm of Non-Discrimination: Deportation and Detention in U.S. Immigration Law*, 29 Law & Ineq. 279, 279 (2011).

40 *See, e.g.*, United States v. Superville, 40 F. Supp. 2d 672, 675 (D.V.I. 1999); United States v. Lombera-Camorlinga, 188 F.3d 1177 (9th Cir. 1999); State v. Reyes-Camarena, 7 P.3d 522 (Or. 2000); U.S. ex rel. Madej v. Schomig, 2002 WL 31386480 (N.D.Ill. 2002). *See generally*, Jordan J. Paust, *Medellín, Avena, The Supremacy of Treaties and Relevant Executive Authority*, 31 Suffolk Transnat'l L. Rev. 301, 306–07 N.16 (2008) (Discussing Cases); Kristen D.A. Carpenter, *The International Covenant on Civil and Political Rights: A Toothless Tiger?*, 26 N.C. J. Int'l L. & Com. Reg. 1, 54 (2000) (listing cases).

41 *See, e.g.*, Richard Wilson, *Defending a Criminal Case with International Human Rights Law*, 24 Champion 28 (May 2000); Emmanuel Decaux, *The Place of Human Rights Courts and International Criminal Courts in the International System*, 9 J. Int'l Crim. Just. 597 (2011); Damien Scalia, *Long-Term Sentences in International Criminal Law: Do They Meet the Standards Set Out by the European Court of Human Rights?*, 9 J. Int'l Crim. Just. 669 (2011).

42 *See, e.g.*, Frédéric Mégret, *Beyond "Fairness": Understanding the Determinants of International Criminal Procedure*, 14 UCLA J. Int'l L. & Foreign Aff. 37, 53–59 (2009). On the relationship between international criminal law and international human rights law in general, *see, e.g.*, Robert Cryer et al, An Introduction To International Criminal Law And Procedure 9–11 (2008 reprint); Steven R. Ratner, Jason S. Abrams & James L. Bischoff, Accountability For Human Rights Atrocities In International Law (3rd ed. 2008); Salvatore Zappalà, Human Rights in International Criminal Proceedings (2003); Hari M, Osofsky, *Domesticating International Criminal Law: Bringing Human Rights Violators to Justice*, 107 Yale L. J. 191 (1997); M. Cherif Bassiouni, *Human Rights in the Context of Criminal Justice: Identifying International Procedural Protections and Equivalent Protections in National Constitutions*, 3 Duke J. Comp. & Int'l L. 235 (1993).

43 Richard J. Wilson, *Supporting or Thwarting the Revolution? The Inter-American Human Rights System and Criminal Procedure Reform in Latin America*, 14 Sw. J. L. & Trade Am. 287, 288 (2008), and see *id.*, n.3, citing Stefan Trechsel, Human Rights In Criminal Proceedings (2005); The Right To Fair Trial (David Weissbrodt & Rüdiger Wolfrum eds, 1997); *See also* Javaid Rehman, *The Influence of International Human Rights Law upon Criminal Justice Systems*, 66 J. Crim. L. 510 (2002); in a disability-specific context,

- There is also very little overlap in the academy between scholars who write about international human rights law and those who write about criminal law and procedure,[44] a lack of overlap that has recently been characterized as "increasingly difficult to justify ."[45]
- There has been almost no scholarly inquiry into the relationship between the international criminal court system and the issues under discussion in this volume.[46] Although some scholars have written about the need for the international criminal court apparat to be synergistic with international human rights law,[47] this literature does not generally consider the questions faced here. Although the Restatement on Foreign Relations Law of the United States makes it clear that "torture or other cruel, inhuman, or degrading treatment or punishment" violates international law,[48] there are no references to the issues that are most germane to this volume.[49]

---

see Gerard Quinn & Eilionóir Flynn, *Transatlantic Borrowings: The Past and Future of EU Non-Discrimination Law and Policy on Ground of Disability*, 60 Am. J. Comp. L. 23 (2012).

44 For a recent (and rare) exception, see Christopher Slobogin, *Preventive Detention in Europe and the United States*, accessible *at http://papers.ssrn.som/sol3/papers.cfm?Abstract_Id=2094358*; *see also* Christopher Slobogin, *An Empirically Based Comparison of American and European Regulatory Approaches to Police Regulation*, 22 Mich. J. Int'l L. 423 (2001). Christopher Slobogin, *Comparative Empiricism and Police Investigation Practices*, 37 N.C. J. Int'l L. & Com. Reg. 321 (2011).

45 *See* Mykola Sorochinsky, *Prosecuting Torturers, Protecting "Child Molesters": Toward a Power Balance Model of Criminal Process for International Human Rights Law*, 31 Mich. J. Int'l L. 157, 160 (2009):

> [Herbert] Packer's models and their implications have traditionally been the province of criminal justice academics, while developments in international human rights law have been mostly tracked by international lawyers. Today the continuing separation of criminal justice theory and international human rights law theory is increasingly difficult to justify.

The reference to "Packer's models" relates to Packer's famous two models of criminal process—his "due process" and "crime control" models. *See* Herbert L. Packer, *Two Models Of The Criminal Process*, 113 U. Pa. L. Rev. 1 (1964).

46 *See, e.g.*, Cryer et al., *supra* note 42. The scholarship on the international criminal courts system is, of course, extensive. A simple search of "international criminal courts" in the WESTLAW JLR database reveals 762 documents. (Search conducted October 5, 2012).

47 *See, e.g.*, Robert D. Sloane, *The Evolving "Common Law" of Sentencing of the International Criminal Tribunal for Rwanda*, 5 J. Int'l Crim. Just. 713, 720 n. 37 (2007). On the extent to which international human rights norms "constrain" the development of international criminal justice, see Mégret, *supra* note 42, at 50.

48 Restatement (Third), Foreign Relations Law Of The United States, § 702 (D) (1987).

49 For a rare related caselaw example, see Jama v. U.S. I.N.S., 22 F.Supp.2d 353, 362 (D.N.J. 1998) (mental and physical abuses allegedly inflicted upon plaintiffs violated the international human rights norm of the right to be free from cruel, inhuman, and degrading treatment; alien tort claims act conferred subject matter jurisdiction). On the application of international human rights to forensic facilities, see Astrid Birgden & Michael L. Perlin,

- Much has been written about the new CRPD, but little of it has dealt—either directly or indirectly—with the Convention's application to the criminal trial process, as it relates to:

  a) Appointment of counsel[50]
  b) "Due process" considerations[51]
  c) Determinations of mental status[52]
  d) Case disposition[53]

- The United States has signed but not yet ratified the Convention.[54] However, since it has also ratified the Vienna Convention on the Law of Treaties, it is thus obligated to "refrain from acts which would defeat [the CRPD's] object and purpose."[55]

"Tolling for the Luckless, the Abandoned and Forsaked": Community Safety, Therapeutic Jurisprudence and International Human Rights Law As Applied to Prisoners and Detainees, 13 Leg. & Criminol. Psychology 231 (2008), and Astrid Birgden & Michael L. Perlin, *"Where The Home In The Valley Meets The Damp Dirty Prison": A Human Rights Perspective On Therapeutic Jurisprudence And The Role Of Forensic Psychologists In Correctional Settings,* 14 Aggression & Violent Behavior 256 (2009). On the application of international human rights to correctional settings, see Perlin & Dlugacz; *supra* note 30.

50 See Jennifer L. Aronson, *The Kafkaesque Experience of Immigrants with Mental Disabilities Navigating the Inexplicable Shoals of Immigration Law*, 6 Interdisc. J. Hum. Rts. L. 145, 154–55 (2011–12).

51 *Id*, at 156.

52 I consider the sparse developments around this topic *infra* Chapter 8.

53 *See* Stephanie Ortoleva, *Inaccessible Justice: Human Rights, Persons with Disabilities and the Legal System*, 17 ILSA J. Int'l & Comp. L. 281, 308–09 (2011).

54 *See* Henry Dlugacz & Christopher Wimmer, *The Ethics of Representing Clients with Limited Competency in Guardianship Proceedings*, 4 St. Louis U. J. Health L. & Pol'y 331, 362–63 (2011). President Obama signed the CRPD three years ago, *see* Michelle Diament, *Obama Urges Senate To Ratify Disability Treaty* (May 18, 2012), accessible at http://www.disabilityscoop.Com/2012/05/18/Obama-Urges-Senate-Treaty/15654/, but the Senate failed to ratify on December 4, 2012 for lack of a "super majority" of votes. The Democratic leadership has promised to bring the Convention up again for ratification in 2013. See http://usicd.org/index.cfm/crpdupdates.

55 In The Matter of Mark C.H. 906 N.Y.S. 2d 419 (Sur. 2010), citing Vienna Convention, Art. 18. *See* Kalb, *supra* note 38, at 1060, and *id.* n.49. On the question of making human rights treaties actionable in US courts, see Penny Venetis, *Making Human Rights Treaty Law Actionable in the United States: The Case for Universal Implementing Legislation*, 53 Ala. L. Rev. 97 (2011). On the question of the importance of individual complaint mechanisms within the international human rights law context, see Alexandra Harrington, *Don't Mind The Gap: The Rise of Individual Complaint Mechanisms within International Human Rights Treaties*, 22 Duke L.J. Comp. & Int'l L. 153 (2012).

- The Convention's focus on dignity demands a reconsideration of the ways that persons with mental disabilities are treated in the criminal trial process.[56]

It is this issue that demands the greatest focus.[57] In the introductory chapter of this book, I stressed the importance of dignitarian vales to this inquiry, stressing that the failure to honor human rights is an affront to the dignity that must be the bedrock of our legal system.[58] Criminal trials must be conducted in an atmosphere of respect, order, decorum and dignity befitting its importance both to the prosecution and the defense."[59] As ratified, the Convention calls for "respect for inherent dignity."[60] The Preamble characterizes "discrimination against any person on the basis of disability [as] a violation of the inherent dignity and worth of the human person ... ."[61] And these provisions are consistent with the entire Convention's "rights-based approach focusing on individual dignity,"[62] placing the responsibility on the State "to tackle socially created obstacles in order to ensure full respect for the dignity and equal rights of all persons."[63]

---

56 See Perlin, Silenced, *supra* note 1, at 100–01. On the application of the UN Convention on the Rights of the Child to the right to dignity in the criminal trial process, see McCrudden, *supra* note 3, at 670. On the relationship in this context between dignity, human rights norms and forensic psychology, see Michael L. Perlin, *"With Faces Hidden While The Walls Were Tightening": Applying International Human Rights Standards To Forensic Psychology,* 7 U.S.-China Law Review 1 (2010).

57 See *infra* Chapter 7.

58 See Michael L. Perlin, *"Everything's A Little Upside Down, As A Matter Of Fact The Wheels Have Stopped": The Fraudulence of the Incompetency Evaluation Process*, 4 Houston J. Health L. & Pol'y 239, 251 (2004) .

59 In Re Cohen, 370 F. Supp. 1166, 1174 (S.D.N.Y, 1973).

60 CRPD, Article 3(A).

61 *Id.*, Para. H.

62 Dhir, *supra* note 10, at 195.

63 Gerard Quinn & Teresa Degener, *Human Rights And Disability: The Current Use And Future Potential Of United Nations Human Rights Instruments*, in The Context Of Disability 14 (2002). *See also*, Robert Vischer, *How Do Lawyers Serve Human Dignity?*, 9 St. Thomas L. Rev. 222, 248 (2011) ("A commitment to human dignity requires lawyers to widen their gaze"); Michael Stein, *Disability Human Rights*, 95 Cal. L. Rev. 75, 106 (2007) (A "dignitary perspective compels societies to acknowledge that persons with disabilities are valuable because of their inherent human worth"); Cees Maris, *A ≠ A: Or, Freaky Justice*, 31 Cardozo L. Rev. 1133, 1156 (2010) ("The Convention's object is to ensure disabled persons enjoy all human rights with dignity"); Therese Murphy & Gearoid O Cuinn, *Works In Progress: New Technologies And The European Court On Human Rights*, 10 Hum. Rts. L. Rev. 601, 612 (2010), quoting Pretty v. United Kingdom, 35 EHRR 1, Para. 65 (2002) ("The very essence of the [European Convention On Human Rights] is respect for human dignity and human freedom").

IV. Conclusion

Domestic courts have, in general, paid little attention to international human rights law in criminal trial process matters. Nonetheless, the dignitarian mandates of the CRPD may force a significant sea change in these attitudes in coming years, at least with regards to defendants with mental disabilities. It is essential, I believe, that scholars, policy makers and judges begin to take seriously the relationship between domestic and international law in this area.

Chapter 5
Mental Health Courts[1]

I. Introduction

One of the most important developments in the past two decades in the way that criminal defendants with mental disabilities are treated in the criminal process has been the creation and expansion of mental health courts, one kind of "problem-solving court."[2] There are now, according to the Council of State Governments' Justice Center, over 300 such courts in operation in the United States,[3] some dealing solely with misdemeanors,[4] some solely with non-violent offenders,[5] and some with no such restrictions.[6] There is a wide range of dispositional alternatives available to judges in these cases,[7] and an even wider range of judicial attitudes.[8] And the entire concept of "mental health courts" is certainly not without controversy.[9]

There is no question, however, that these courts offer a new approach—perhaps a *radically* new approach—to the problems at hand. For the purposes of this volume, they become even more significant because of their articulated focus

---

1 *See generally* Michael L. Perlin, *"There Are No Trials Inside the Gates of Eden": Mental Health Courts, the Convention on the Rights of Persons with Disabilities, Dignity, and the Promise of Therapeutic Jurisprudence*, in COERCIVE CARE: LAW AND POLICY (Bernadette McSherry & Ian Freckelton eds, 2013) (in press).

2 *See, e.g.*, Greg Berman & Aubrey Fox, *The Future of Problem-Solving Justice: An International Perspective*, 10 U. MD. L.J. RACE, RELIGION, GENDER & CLASS 1, 3 (2010); Greg Berman & John Feinblatt, *Problem-Solving Courts: A Brief Primer*, 23 LAW & POL'Y, 125, 127 (2001).

3 *See* http://www.consensusproject.org/programs?q=mental+health+court&submit=Go.

4 *See, e.g.*, Ursula Castellano, *Courting Compliance: Case Managers as "Double Agents" in the Mental Health Court*, 36 LAW & SOC. INQUIRY 484, 490 (2011).

5 *See, e.g.*, Julie Grachek, *The Insanity Defense in the Twenty-First Century: How Recent United States Supreme Court Case Law Can Improve the System*, 81 IND. L.J. 1479, 1495 (2006).

6 *See, e.g.*, E. Leah Johnston, *Theorizing Mental Health Courts*, 89 WASH. L. REV. 519, 521 (2012).

7 *See, e.g.*, Henry J. Steadman et al., *From Referral to Disposition: Case Processing in Seven Mental Health Courts*, 23 BEHAV. SCI. & L. 215, 220 (2005).

8 *See, e.g.* Michael S. King, *Should Problem-Solving Courts Be Solution-Focused Courts?* 80 REV. JUR. U.P.R. 1005 (2011).

9 *See, e.g.*, Tammy Seltzer, *A Misguided Attempt to Address the Criminal Justice System's Unfair Treatment of People with Mental Illness*, 11 PSYCHOL. PUB. POL'Y & L. 570, 576 (2005); see generally, Michael L. Perlin, *"The Judge, He Cast His Robe Aside": Mental Health Courts, Dignity and Due Process,* – J. MENT. HEALTH L. & POL'Y – (2013).

on dignity,[10] as well as their embrace of therapeutic jurisprudence, their focus on procedural justice, and their use of the principles of restorative justice.[11]

It is time to restructure the dialogue about mental health courts and begin to (1) consider whether the development of such courts will finally allow us to move away from society's currently predominant position that mental illness reflects "a defect of morality or will," and (2) take seriously the potential ameliorative impact of such courts on the ultimate disposition of all cases involving criminal defendants with mental disabilities.

Mental health courts have come under attack from both the right and the left. Of these attacks, I believe only one, which is relevant to the issues discussed in this book, has merit: that they may provide "false hope" to those who come before them.[12] I believe this is so because our "culture of blame" still infects the entire criminal justice process, and because it continues to demonize persons with mental illness for their status.[13] Until this is remediated, there can be no assurances that mental health courts—or any other such potentially ameliorative alternative—will be ultimately "successful" (however we choose to define that term).

Much of the recent debate on mental health courts has focused either on empirical studies of recidivism or on theorization.[14] All of this discussion, while important and helpful, bypasses the critical issue that is at the heart of this book: do such courts provide additional dignity to the criminal justice process or do they detract from that? Until we refocus our sights on this issue, much of the discourse on this topic remains wholly irrelevant.

In this section, I will first discuss the role of *blame* in the criminal justice process, and then look at the structure of mental health courts. Finally, I will raise two

---

10 On dignity, *see* Ginger Lerner-Wren, *Mental Health Courts: Serving Justice and Promoting Recovery*, 19 Annals Health L. 577, 593 (2010). Note that Judge Lerner-Wren concludes that, to preserve dignity, the "guiding principles and values articulated in the United Nations Convention on the Rights of Persons with Disabilities should be implemented and fully integrated into every mental health court process," *id*; *see supra* Chapter 4, and *infra* Chapter 7.

11 On therapeutic jurisprudence, see Henry J. Steadman et al, *Mental Health Courts: Their Promise and Unanswered Questions*, 52 Law & Psychiatry 457, 457 (2001). On procedural justice, see Thomas L. Hafemeister, Sharon G. Garner & Veronica E. Bath, *Forging Links and Renewing Ties: Applying the Principles of Restorative and Procedural Justice to Better Respond to Criminal Offenders with a Mental Disorder*, 60 Buff. L. Rev. 147, 201–02 (2012). On restorative justice, see *id. See generally infra* Chapter 6.

12 I am also concerned about quality of counsel issues. See *infra* text accompanying notes 70–75.

13 For a consideration of the many obstacles faced by such courts, see Kevin Daly, Chrysanti Leon & Margaret Mahoney, *Delaware Mental Health Courts' Process Evaluation: Progressive Treatment and Systematic Obstacles*, accessible at http://papers.ssrn.com/soL3/papers.cfm?abstract_id=1584835.

14 *See, e.g.*, Richard Wiener et al., *A Testable Theory of Problem Solving Courts: Past Empirical and Legal Failures*, 33 Int'l J. L. & Psychiatry 417 (2010).

concerns about such courts that I believe are of particular relevance: the adequacy of counsel provided to defendants who appear before mental health courts, and the competency of defendants to voluntarily participate in such court proceedings.

II. The Role of Blame[15]

Society has always demonized persons with mental illness. Ever since Prince Ptah-hotep attempted the first classification of mental illness almost five thousand years ago, conceptions of such illness have been inextricably linked to the notion of sin.[16] This linkage appears in the Old Testament, and in other religious volumes throughout the centuries.[17] Similarly, mental illness has been inextricably linked to evil[18]

15 This section is partially adapted from Michael L. Perlin, *"There Was an Evil Messenger": Blame, Mental Illness, Wickedness, the Insanity Defense and the Pretexts of the Justice System* (paper presented at 30th Annual Congress, International Academy of Law and Mental Health, Padua, Italy, June 2007) (on file with author).

16 Michael L. Perlin, The Jurisprudence of the Insanity Defense 37 (1994). *See* Russell Covey, *Criminal Madness: Cultural Iconography and Insanity*, 61 Stan. L. Rev. 1375, 1411 (2009), quoting Robinson v. California, 370 U.S. 660, 669 (1962) (Douglas, J., concurring):

> [T]he idea of basing treatment for disease on purgatorial acts and ordeals is an ancient one in medicine. It may trace back to the Old Testament belief that disease of any kind, whether mental or physical, represented punishment for sin; and thus relief could take the form of a final heroic act of atonement.

17 Deuteronomy 28:15–28 (cursing with madness those who fail to observe all of God's commandments). *See* Michael L. Perlin, *"What's Good Is Bad, What's Bad Is Good, You'll Find out When You Reach the Top, You're on the Bottom": Are the Americans with Disabilities Act (and Olmstead v. L.C.) Anything More than "Idiot Wind"?*, 35 U. Mich. J. L. Ref. 235, 239 n.29 (2001–02), (Perlin, *Olmstead*) citing, inter alia, Michael L. Perlin, *On Sanism*, 46 SMU L. Rev. 373, 388–91 (1992) (Perlin, *Sanism*) (pointing to the deep-rooted misconceptions and hatred toward persons with mental illness throughout history); John Biggs, Jr., The Guilty Mind: Psychiatry and the Law of Homicide 26–27 (1955) (explaining that insanity was tied to sin, and a special class of priests were the only people capable of ridding the sinner of his demonic possession); Wolf Wolfensberger et al., The Principle of Normalization in Human Services 12–25 (1972) (noting that mental retardation has often been regarded as the result of sin and God's punishment).

18 Perlin, *Olmstead*, *supra* note 17, at 239 n.30, citing Walter Bromberg, From Shaman to Psychotherapist: A History of the Treatment of Mental Illness 63–64 (1975) (discussing various historical perspectives of mental illness); Michael S. Moore, Law and Psychiatry: Rethinking the Relationship 64–65 (1984) (examining the American and English tests for insanity—specifically knowing the difference between good and evil—under the theory that humans become somewhat godlike once this distinction is recognized); Judith S. Neaman, Suggestion of the Devil: The Origins of Madness 31, 144 (1975) (addressing the stereotype of persons with mental illness as evil). On how these stereotypes persist in mainstream media imagery, *see, e.g.*, Donald L. Diefenbach, *The Portrayal of Mental Illness on Prime-*

and to the supernatural world.[19] These conflations[20] have profound implications for both the criminal justice and the mental disability law systems, and are, in large

time Television, 25 J. Commun. Psychol. 289 (1997); Raymond Nairn, John Coverdale & Donna Claussen, *What Is the Role of Intertextuality in Media Depictions of Mental Illness? Implications for Forensic Psychiatry*, 13 Psychiatry, Psychol. & L. 243 (2006).

19 *See, e.g.*, Christopher Harding & Richard Ireland, Punishment: Rhetoric, Rule and Practice 153–55 (1989).

20 I have discussed other mental disability law conflations in past papers dealing with a variety of mental disability law topics. *See, e.g.*, Michael L. Perlin, *She Breaks Just Like a Little Girl: Neonaticide, The Insanity Defense, and the Irrelevance of Ordinary Common Sense*, 10 Wm. & Mary J. Women & L. 1, 23 (2003) (conflation of neonaticide and other infanticide cases); Michael L. Perlin, *"Life Is In Mirrors, Death Disappears": Giving Life to Atkins*, 33 N. Mex. L. Rev. 315, 337 (2003) (conflation of mental retardation and mental illness); Michael L. Perlin, *"For the Misdemeanor Outlaw": The Impact of the ADA on the Institutionalization of Criminal Defendants with Mental Disabilities*, 52 Alabama L. Rev. 193, 235 (2000); (conflation of substantive mental status tests); Michael L. Perlin, *Therapeutic Jurisprudence: Understanding the Sanist and Pretextual Bases of Mental Disability Law*, 20 N. Eng. J. Crim. & Civ. Confinement 369, 380 (1994) (same); Michael L. Perlin, *"The Borderline Which Separated You from Me": The Insanity Defense, the Authoritarian Spirit, the Fear of Faking, and the Culture of Punishment*, 82 Iowa L. Rev. 1375, 1422 (1997) (Perlin, *Culture of Punishment*) (same); Michael L. Perlin, *"His Brain Has Been Mismanaged with Great Skill": How Will Jurors Respond to Neuroimaging Testimony in Insanity Defense Cases?*, 42 Akron L. Rev. 885, 892 (2009) (same); Michael L. Perlin, *Pretexts and Mental Disability Law: The Case of Competency*, 47 U. Miami L. Rev. 625, 679–80 (1993) (Perlin, *Pretexts*) (same); Michael L. Perlin, *"There's No Success like Failure/and Failure's No Success at All": Exposing the Pretextuality of Kansas v. Hendricks*, 92 Nw. U. L. Rev. 1247, 1271 (1998) (conflation of civil commitment law and insanity law) (Perlin, *Hendricks*); Michael L. Perlin, *"Where the Winds Hit Heavy on the Borderline" : Mental Disability Law, Theory and Practice, Us and Them*, 31 Loyola L.A. L. Rev. 775, 780 (1998) (Perlin, *Borderline*) (conflation of "deinstitutionalization" and "homelessness"); Michael L. Perlin, *Competency, Deinstitutionalization, and Homelessness: A Story of Marginalization*, 28 Hous. L. Rev. 63, 69 (1991) (Perlin, *Marginalization*) (same); Michael L. Perlin, *"Make Promises by the Hour": Sex, Drugs, the ADA, and Psychiatric Hospitalization*, 46 DePaul L. Rev. 947, 965 (1997) (conflation of taboos and stigma attached to sexual behavior and stereotypes of the meaning of mental disability); Michael L. Perlin & Deborah A. Dorfman, *Is It More Than "Dodging Lions and Wastin' Time"? Adequacy of Counsel, Questions of Competence, and the Judicial Process in Individual Right to Refuse Treatment Cases*, 2 Psychology, Pub. Pol'y & L.114, 120 (1996) (conflation of institutionalization with incompetency); Michael L. Perlin, *Back to the Past: Why Mental Disability Law "Reforms" Don't Reform* (Book Review of John Q La Fond & Mary Durham, Back to the Asylum: The Future of Mental Health Law and Policy in the United States (1992)), 4 Crim. L. Forum 403, 406 (1993) (conflation of expanded insanity defense with higher crime rates); Perlin, *Sanism*, *supra* note 17, at 390–91 (conflation of stereotypes of mental illness with stereotypes of race, sex and ethnicity). On the "blurring" between civil and criminal mental disability law in the context of assisted outpatient commitment and sexually violent predator laws (SVPA), see Michael L. Perlin & Deborah A. Dorfman, *"On Desolation Row": The Blurring of the Borders Between Civil and Criminal Mental Disability Law, and*

part, responsible for our needs to blame individuals with mental disabilities for their mental disabilities, as part of our "culture of punishment."[21]

Thousands of years ago, it was commonly believed that sickness was "a punishment sent by God."[22] The historian Judith Neaman thus has concluded that "demonic possession remains the simplest, the most dramatic, and secretly, the most attractive of all explanations of insanity in the Middle Ages."[23] Society saw madness as a condition "in which a person was 'possessed, controlled, or affected by some supernatural power or being,'"[24] and this connection has remained "extremely resilient in western culture."[25]

Thus, historically, mental illness has been positively associated with "sin, evil, God's punishment, crime, and demons,"[26] or signs of "divine punishment."[27]

What It Means to All of Us (manuscript in progress). On the "blurring" between the insanity defense and SPVA laws, see Covey, *supra* note 16, at 1420.

21 I discuss this concept extensively in PERLIN, *supra* note 16, at 59–69; *see also* Perlin, *Culture of Punishment*, *supra* note 20, at 1392 (describing the "'negative pattern of fear and repression' that once again dominates penology" as the core of the "culture of punishment"). The earliest use I can find of the phrase in an academic context is in Todd Clear, *The Punishment Addiction: Twenty Years of Compulsive Punishment Lifestyle*, in NATIONAL CONFERENCE ON SENTENCING ADVOCACY 55, 56 (1989) ("Our culture suffers from a punishment addiction."). On the concept of "blame" in the criminal justice system, *see, e.g.*, Richard Boldt, *The Construction of Responsibility in the Criminal Law*, 140 U. PA. L. REV. 2245 (1992).

22 BIGGS, *supra* note 17, at 26 (discussing Egyptian Papyrus from 1559 BC, See also NEAMAN, *supra* note 18, at 50 (mental illness was "God's punishment for sin").

23 NEAMAN, *supra* note 18, at 31; *see also*, GEORGE ROSEN, MADNESS IN SOCIETY: CHAPTERS IN THE HISTORICAL SOCIOLOGY OF MENTAL ILLNESS 80–83 (1969 ed.) (attribution of mental illness to supernatural causes).

24 PERLIN, *supra* note 16, at 39, quoting ROSEN, *supra* note 23, at 82.

25 H.C. Erik Midelfort *Madness and Civilization in Early Modern Europe: A Reappraisal of Michel Foucault*, in AFTER THE REFORMATION 247, 254 (Barbara Malament ed., 1980).

26 Perlin, *Sanism*, *supra* note 17, at 388; *see also, e.g.*, Karin A. Guiduli, *Challenges for the Mentally Ill: The "Threat to Safety": Defense Standard and the Use of Psychotropic Medication under Title I of the Americans with Disabilities Act of 1990*, 144 U. PA. L. REV. 1149, 1157 (1996) (same).

27 Barbara Zanotti & Rick Becker, *Marching to the Beat of a Different Drummer: Is Military Law and Mental Health Out-of-Step After Jaffee v. Redmond?*, 41 A.F. L. REV. 1, 64 n.457 (1997). On the question of whether "evil" can be objectively quantified, or even exists as a discrete condition, compare Michael Welner, *Defining Evil: A Depravity Scale for Today's Courts*, 2 THE FORENSIC ECHO 4 (1998), to Robert Simon, *Should Forensic Psychiatrists Testify about Evil?* 31 J. AM. ACAD. PSYCHIATRY & L. 413 (2003), to Michael Welner, *Response to Simon: Legal Relevance Demands That Evil be Defined and Standardized,* 31 J. AM. ACAD. PSYCHIATRY & L. 417 (2003), and James L. Knoll, *The Recurrence of an Illusion: The Concept of "Evil" in Forensic Psychiatry*, 36 J, AM. ACAD, PSYCHIATRY & L. 105 (2007), to, Michael Welner, *The Justice and Therapeutic Promise of Science-Based Research on Criminal Evil*, 37 J, AM. ACAD, PSYCHIATRY & L. 442 (2008).

People with mental illness were considered beasts, or persons possessed by evil spirits;[28] a person who lost his capacity to reason was seen as having lost his claim "to be treated as a human being."[29] In some cases, portions of such persons' skulls were removed "to allow evil spirits to escape."[30] European scholars typically associated psychopathology with demonic possession or with punishment for sin,[31] and researchers conclude that the view "that psychopathology is punishment for sin persists today."[32]

It is thus no wonder that *any* reform of the criminal justice system as it deals with defendants with mental disabilities that promises to be less punitive and less unforgiving faces significant obstacles. If this population is viewed as having a "defect of morality or will,"[33] it is little wonder that our "culture of punishment"[34] stands in the way of meaningful reform.

See also, Tom Mason, Joel Richman & Dave Mercer, *The Influence of Evil 0n Forensic Clinical Practice*, 11 INT'L J. MENTAL HEALTH NURSING 80 (2002).

28 Willis Spaulding et al., *Applications of Therapeutic Jurisprudence in Rehabilitation For People With Severe And Disabling Mental Illness*, 17 T.M. COOLEY L. REV. 135, 140 (2000). In some cultures, this continues to persist. *See* Michael Curran, *Flickering Lamp Beside the Golden Door: Immigration, the Constitution, & Undocumented Aliens in the 1990s*, 30 CASE W. RES. J. INT'L L. 57, 129 n.303 (1998) (discussing Vietnamese immigrant culture).

29 Perlin, *Sanism*, *supra* note 17, at 388–89, quoting Andrew T. Scull, *Moral Treatment Reconsidered: Some Sociological Comments on an Episode in the History of British Psychiatry*, in MADHOUSES, MAD DOCTORS, AND MADMEN: THE SOCIAL HISTORY OF PSYCHIATRY IN THE VICTORIAN ERA 105, 108–09 (Andrew T. Scull ed., 1981).

30 Richard Gardner, *Mind over Matter?: The Historical Search for Meaningful Parity Between Mental and Physical Health Care Coverage*, 49 EMORY L.J. 675, 677 (2000).

31 Jennifer Skeem & Stephen Golding, *Describing Jurors' Personal Conceptions of Insanity and Their Relationship to Case Judgments,* 7 PSYCHOL. PUB. POL'Y & L. 561, 594 (2001), citing ROBERT CARSON, ABNORMAL PSYCHOLOGY AND MODERN LIFE (10th ed. 1998).

32 Skeem & Golding, *supra* note 31, quoting Norman Dain, *Madness and the Stigma of Sin in American Christianity*, in STIGMA AND MENTAL ILLNESS 73, 80 (Paul Fink & Allan Tasman eds, 1992).

33 *See* Amanda Pustilnik, *Prisons of the Mind: Social Value and Economic Inefficiency in the Criminal Justice Response to Mental Illness*, 96 J. CRIM. L. & CRIMINOLOGY 217, 263 (2005).

34 *See* Perlin, *Culture of Punishment*, *supra* note 20.

III. The Structure of Mental Health Courts[35]

Mental health courts—one form of "problem-solving courts"[36]—follow the legal theory of therapeutic jurisprudence in an attempt "to improve justice by considering the therapeutic and antitherapeutic consequences that 'flow from substantive rules, legal procedures, or the behavior of legal actors'."[37]

---

35 *See generally* Bruce Winick, *Outpatient Commitment: A Therapeutic Jurisprudence Analysis*, 9 PSYCHOL. PUB. POL'Y & L. 107 (2003); Susan Stefan & Bruce Winick, *A Dialogue on Mental Health Courts*, 11 PSYCHOL. PUB. POL'Y & L. 507 (2005).These courts are different from and independent of traditional involuntary civil commitment courts, currently operating in many states. For a critique of such courts, see Michael L. Perlin, *A Law of Healing*, 68 U. CIN. L. REV. 407, 425–26 (2000) ("[T]he overwhelming number of cases involving mental disability law issues are 'litigated' in pitch darkness. Involuntary civil commitment cases are routinely disposed of in minutes behind closed courtroom doors."). For a thoughtful reconsideration of such courts in a transnational perspective, see Terry Carney, David Tait & Fleur Beaupert, *Pushing the Boundaries: Realising Rights Through Mental Health Tribunal Processes?*, 30 SYDNEY L. REV. 329, 344 (2008).

36 Problem-solving courts grew out of an interdisciplinary approach to address the underlying problem, not just the symptoms, of substance abuse, domestic violence, child abuse, mental illness, and certain kinds of criminality). *See generally* Bruce J. Winick, *Therapeutic Jurisprudence and Problem Solving Courts*, 30 FORDHAM URB. L.J. 1055, 1060 (2003). For overviews, see Michael Dorf & Jeffrey Fagan, P*roblem-Solving Courts: From Innovation to Institutionalization*, 40 AM. CRIM. L. REV. 1501 (2003); Jeffrey Fagan & Victoria Malkin, *Theorizing Community Justice through Community Courts*, 30 FORDHAM URB. L.J. 897 (2003). Included in this array are mental health courts, drug courts, domestic violence courts, juvenile justice courts, sex offense courts, community courts, truancy courts, veterans courts, and homeless courts. For a full list, see Deborah Chase & Peggy Hora, *The Best Seat in the House: The Court Assignment and Judicial Satisfaction*, 47 FAM. CT. REV. 209, 210 n.8 (2009). For a critical reading on the ways that such courts "redefine" criminal justice, see James L. Nolan, *Redefining Criminal Courts: Problem-Solving and the Meaning of Justice*, 40 AM. CRIM. L. REV. 1541 (2004). For a critical reading of their impact on child welfare cases, see Jane Spinak, *A Conversation About Problem-Solving Courts: Take 2*, 10 U. MD. L.J. RACE, RELIGION, GENDER & CLASS 113 (2010). For a consideration of an evidence-based model in one state, see Melissa Aubin, *The District of Oregon Reentry Court: An Evidence-Based Model*, 27 FED. SENT. R. 39 (2009).

37 Nancy Wolff, *Courts as Therapeutic Agents: Thinking Past the Novelty of Mental Health Courts*, 30 J. AM. ACAD. PSYCHIATRY L. 431, 431 (2002); *see also*, Randal Fritzler, *How One Misdemeanor Mental Health Court Incorporates Therapeutic Jurisprudence, Preventive Law, and Restorative Justice*, in MANAGEMENT AND ADMINISTRATION OF CORRECTIONAL HEALTH CARE: POLICY, PRACTICE, ADMINISTRATION 1, 1 (Jacqueline Moore ed., 2003) ("the fundamental principle underlying therapeutic jurisprudence is the selection of options that promote health and are consistent with the values of the legal system"). This is not a phenomenon limited to the United States. *See, e.g.*, RICHARD D. SCHNEIDER, HY BLOOM & MARK HEEREMA, MENTAL HEALTH COURTS: DECRIMINALIZING THE MENTALLY ILL (2007) (Canada); Sarah Ryan & Darius Whelan, *Diversion of Offenders with Mental Disorders: Mental Health Courts*, 1 WEB J. CURR. LEG. ISSUES (2012), accessible at http://

They are designed to deal holistically[38] with people arrested (usually, but not exclusively, for nonviolent misdemeanors)[39] when mental illness rather than criminality appears to be the precipitating reason for the behavior in question.[40]

---

webjcli.ncl.ac.uk/2012/issue1/ryan1.html (Ireland); James Duffy, *Problem-Solving Courts, Therapeutic Jurisprudence and the Constitution: If Two Is Company, Is Three a Crowd?*, 35 MELB. U. L. REV. 394, 395 (2011). On therapeutic jurisprudence in general in connection with this inquiry, see *infra* Chapter 6, IIA.

38 See Shauhin Talesh, *Mental Health Court Judges as Dynamic Risk Managers: A New Conceptualization of the Role of Judges*, 57 DEPAUL L. REV. 93, 112 (2007).

39 Most mental health courts typically hear only cases of nonviolent offenders, *see* Grachek, *supra* note 5, at 1495, or only misdemeanor cases, *see* Castellano, *supra* note 4, at 490, but some hear felony cases as well, *see* Talesh, *supra* note 38, at 112, and the trend is towards the expansion of predicate case jurisdiction to include felonies, including violent felonies, *see* Johnston, *supra* note 6, at 521. At this time, misdemeanors are accepted by 87% of mental health courts, 77% accept non-violent felonies, and over one-third of the courts accept violent felonies. See Julie B. Raines & Glenn T. Laws, *Mental Health Court Survey*, 45 CRIM. L.BULL. 627, 630 (2009). *See, e.g.*, Andrew Wasicek, *Mental Illness and Crime: Envisioning a Public Health Strategy and Reimaging Mental Health Courts*, 48 CRIM. L. BULL. 106, 135 (2012):

> Mental health courts should accept violent felonies because it is morally unsound to punish criminal behavior that is mainly a product of mental disease. With appropriate eligibility criteria, the new mental health court model would encapsulate persons who are not shielded by the insanity defense—especially persons from post-*Jones v. U.S.*, 463 U.S. 354 …, (1983) [approving stringent statutory measures governing releases of persons found not guilty by reason of insanity, see 4 MICHAEL L. PERLIN, CIVIL AND CRIMINAL § 9B-2.3, at 298 (2d ed. 2002)] era—but should still be held blameless.

40 *See generally* Stefan & Winick, *supra* note 35, relying on, inter alia, Fritzler, *supra* note 37; Arthur Lurigio et al., *Therapeutic Jurisprudence in Action: Specialized Courts for the Mentally Ill*, 84 JUDICATURE 184 (2001); John Petrila et al., *Preliminary Observations from an Evaluation of the Broward County Mental Health Court*, 37 CT. REV. 14 (2002); Ian Freckelton, *Mental Health Review Tribunal Decision-making: A Therapeutic Jurisprudence Lens*, 10 PSYCHIATRY, PSYCHOL. & L. 44 (2003); *see also* BUREAU OF JUSTICE ASSISTANCE, MENTAL HEALTH COURTS: A PRIMER FOR POLICYMAKERS AND PRACTITIONERS (2008). The salient elements of mental health courts are identified in Peggy Fulton Hora, *Courting New Solutions Using Problem-Solving Justice: Key Components, Guiding Principles, Strategies, Responses, Models, Approaches, Blueprints and Tool Kits*, 2 CHAPMAN J. CRIM. JUST. 7, 21–22 (2011), in Allison Redlich et al., *The Second Generation of Mental Health Courts*, 11 PSYCHOL PUB. POL'Y & L. 527, 537 (2005), and in Wasicek, *supra* note 39, at 112, *see generally* PAMELA M. CASEY & DAVID B. ROTTMAN, NAT'L CTR. FOR STATE CTS., PROBLEM-SOLVING COURTS: MODELS AND TRENDS (2003). Positive and negative arguments about mental health courts are collected in Andrea M. Odegaard, *Therapeutic Jurisprudence: The Impact of Mental Health Courts on the Criminal Justice System*, 83 N.D. L. REV. 225, 250–54 (2007); *see generally* LeRoy Kondo, *Advocacy of the Establishment of Mental Health Specialty Courts in the Provision of Therapeutic Justice for Mentally Ill Offenders*, 28 AM. CRIM. L.J. 255 (2001); Arthur J.

The mental health court judge[41] seeks to divert the individual from the criminal court in exchange for an agreement to participate in community treatment,[42] and to "help participants avoid future criminal court involvement."[43]

Mental health courts are premised on team approaches;[44] representatives from justice and treatment agencies assist the judge in screening offenders to determine whether they would present a risk of violence if released to the community, in devising appropriate treatment plans, and in supervising and monitoring the individual's performance in treatment.[45] The mental health court judge functions as part of a mental health team that decides whether the individual has treatment needs and can be safely released to the community.[46] The team formulates a treatment plan, and a court-employed case manager and court monitor track the individual's participation in the treatment program, and submit periodic reports

---

Lurigio & Jessica Snowden, *Putting Therapeutic Jurisprudence into Practice: The Growth, Operations, and Effectiveness of Mental Health Court*, 30 JUST. SYS. J. 196 (2009).

41 Judges are the most common referral source of participants into diversion programs (100% of survey respondents), with mental health personnel (93% of respondents) coming in second, and attorneys (90% of respondents) coming in a close third. For those agencies that chose the "other" category, they indicated that referrals could come from families, service providers, law enforcement personnel, community agencies, and parole officers. Raines & Laws, *supra* note 39, at 632.

42 Marjorie A. Silver, *Lawyering and Its Discontents: Reclaiming Meaning in the Practice of Law*, 19 TOURO L. REV. 773, 803 (2004); *see also* Talesh, *supra* note, 38, at 110; Camille Nelson, *Racializing Disability, Disabling Race: Policing Race and Mental Status*, 15 BERKELEY J. CRIM. L. 1,2 (2010) (on the necessity of diversion); John Cummings, *The Cost of Crazy: How Therapeutic Jurisprudence and Mental Health Courts Lower Incarceration Costs, Reduce Recidivism, and Improve Public Safety*, 56 LOY. L. REV. 279, 306 (2010) (discussing mental health courts' "palpable results"). On the question of whether this diversion is swifter than traditional court processing, *see* Allison Redlich et al., *Is Diversion Swift: Comparing Mental Health Court and Traditional Criminal Justice Processing*, 39 CRIM. JUST. & BEHAV. 420 (2012) (although diversion may not be swifter, that may be less important than the fact of diversion itself).

43 Kirk Kimber, *Mental Health Courts—Idaho's Best Kept Secret*, 45 IDAHO L. REV. 249, 270 (2008); *see also*, Brenda Desmond & Paul Lenz, *Mental Health Courts: An Effective Way of Treating Offenders with Serious Mental Illness*, 34 MENTAL & PHYSICAL DISABILITY L. REP. 525, 526 (2010). On the creation of juvenile mental health courts, see Daniel M. Filler & Austin Smith, *The New Rehabiliation*, 91 IOWA L. REV. 951, 971 n.105 (2006).

44 *See, e.g.*, Lurigio & Snowden, *supra* note 40, at 210; Marlee E. Moore & Virginia A. Hiday, *Mental Health Court Outcomes: A Comparison of Rearrest and Re-arrest Severity Between Mental Health Court and Traditional Court Participants*, 30 LAW & HUM. BEHAV. 659, 660 (2006).

45 Winick, *supra* note 35, at 125–26. On the role of jail as a potential sanction in the cases of non-compliant defendants, see Allison Redlich et al., *Patterns and Practice in Mental Health Courts: A National Survey*, 30 LAW & HUM. BEHAV. 347 (2006).

46 On the often-conflicting roles of case managers in mental health courts, see Castellano, *supra* note 4.

to the judge concerning his or her progress. Participants are required to report to the court periodically so that the judge can monitor treatment compliance, and additional status review hearings are held on an as-needed basis.[47]

To serve effectively in this sort of court setting, the judge needs to develop enhanced interpersonal skills and awareness of a variety of psychological techniques that can help the judge to persuade the individual to accept treatment and motivate him or her to participate effectively in it.[48] She must be able to build trust and manage risk.[49] These skills include the ability to convey empathy and respect, to communicate effectively with the individual, to listen to what the individual has to say, thereby fulfilling the individual's need for voice and validation, to earn the individual's trust and confidence, and to engage in motivational interviewing and various other techniques designed to encourage the individual to accept treatment and comply with it.[50] These courts provide "nuanced" approaches,[51] and may signal a "fundamental shift" in the criminal justice system.[52] According to Judge Randal Fritzler, a successful mental health court thus needs: 1) a therapeutic environment and dedicated team; 2) an environment free from stigmatizing labels; 3) opportunities for deferred sentences and diversion away from the criminal system; 4) the least restrictive alternatives; 5) decision-making that is interdependent; 6) coordinated treatment; and 7) a review process that is meaningful.[53] It is

47 Stefan & Winick, *supra* note 35, at 520–21.

48 Winick, *supra* note 35, at 126, citing Carrie Petrucci, *Respect as a Component in the Judge-Defendant Interaction in a Specialized Domestic Violence Court that Utilizes Therapeutic Jurisprudence*, 38 Crim. L. Bull. 263 (2002). On the "collateral institutional authority of the judge" in mental health courts, see Eric J. Miller, *The Therapeutic Effects of Managerial Re-entry Courts*, 30 Fed'l Sentencing Rep. 127, 128 (2008). On the way that judgmental descriptive language can adversely affect the work of such courts in civil cases, see Ian Freckelton, *Distractors and Distressors in Involuntary Status Decision-making*, 12 Psychiatry, Psychology & L 88 (2005).

49 Carol Fisler, *Building Trust and Managing Risk: A Look at a Felony Mental Health Court*, 11 Psychol. Pub. Pol'y & L. 587 (2005).

50 For a thoughtful critique of mental health courts, see Johnston, *supra* note 6. On the role of the legislature in insuring the success of such courts, see Sheila Moheb, *Jamming the Revolving Door: Legislative Setbacks for Mental Health Court Systems in Virginia*, 14 Rich. J. L. & Pub. Int. 29 (2010).

51 Patricia C. McManus, *A Therapeutic Jurisprudential Approach to Guardianship of Persons with Mild Cognitive Impairment*, 36 Seton Hall L. Rev. 591, 598 (2006).

52 *Developments in the Law—The Law of Mental Illness: Mental Health Courts and the Trend Toward a Rehabilitative Justice System*, 121 Harv. L. Rev. 1168, 1174 (2008) (Harvard Note).

53 Randal B. Fritzler, *10 Key Components of a Criminal Mental Health Court*, reprinted in Judging in a Therapeutic Key: Therapeutic Jurisprudence and the Courts 118, 118 (Bruce J. Winick & David B. Wexler eds, 2003), and Fritzler, *supra* note 37, at 1 ("The [mental health court] must avoid contributing negative stigma to its clients"). *See also* Georgia Lee Sims, *The Criminalization of Mental Illness: How Theoretical Failures*

essential that such courts be free of the "pretextual dishonesty" that is so often the hallmark of judicial proceedings in cases of individuals with mental disabilities.[54]

Some defense attorneys fear that problem-solving courts, in general, "arm twist … [their clients] into diversion with a condition of entry being that they take a plea, and/or that the effective treatment is raised above the least restrictive treatment."[55] By way of example, Cait Clarke and James Neuhard raise this potential dilemma:

> For example, a defense attorney may devote less attention to the desires of the defendant, focusing more on the goals of the "team" (including the defense attorney, prosecutor, judge, and probation officer). An illustration of this would be where the "team" decides the defendant requires in-custody treatment, although the defendant has previously told the defense attorney that she does not want to participate in an in-custody treatment program.[56]

Skeptics argue that MHCs are too dependent on the aura of the charismatic judge.[57] However, we *do* have a database of research on the way that persons whose cases have been heard before one MHC, the one run by Judge Ginger Lerner-Wren in Ft. Lauderdale, FL, and that database is spectacular.[58] Basically, it tells us that defendants before Judge Lerner-Wren report a higher score on a "dignity" scale (and a lower score on a "perceived coercion" scale)[59] than any

---

Create Real Problems in the Criminal Justice System, 62 Vand. L. Rev. 1053, 1079 (2009) (same).

54 *See generally supra* Chapter 2, II.B. *See* Ian Freckelton, *Mental Health Review Tribunal Decision-making: A Therapeutic Jurisprudence Lens*, 10 Psychiatry, Psychol. & L. 44 (2003), citing, Michael L. Perlin, The Hidden Prejudice: Mental Disability on Trial (2000), and Michael L. Perlin, *Preface*, in Involuntary Detention and Therapeutic Jurisprudence: International Perspectives on Civil Commitment xxxiii (Kate Diesfeld & Ian Freckelton eds, 2003), and Ian Freckelton, *Ideological Divarication in Civil Commitment Decision-making*, 10 Psychiatry, Psychol. & L. 390, 395 (2003).

55 Cait Clarke & James Neuhard, *"From Day One": Who's in Control as Problem Solving and Client-Centered Sentencing Take Center Stage?*, 29 N.Y.U. Rev. L. & Soc. Change 11, 29 (2004). *See generally* King, *supra* note 8.

56 Clarke & Neuhard, *supra* note 55, at 29 n.49.

57 A caution on relying on such charisma in the context of other problem solving courts is raised in Jane Spinak, *Romancing the Court*, 46 Fam. Ct. Rev. 258, 269–71 (2008).

58 On the difficulties generally in assessing mental health courts, see Nancy Wolff & Wendy Pogorzelski, *Measuring the Effectiveness of Mental Health Courts*, 11 Psychol. Pub. Pol'y & L. 539 (2005).

59 On the role of therapeutic jurisprudence, see *infra* Chapter 6 II A. On dealing with coercion in the mental health court process, see Bruce Winick, *A Therapeutic Jurisprudence Approach to Dealing with Coercion in the Mental Health System*, 15 Psychiatry, Psychol. & L. 25 (2008). On the significance of the presence of dignity in mental health tribunals in Australia, see David Tait, *The Ritual Environment of the Mental Health Tribunal Hearing: Inquiries and Reflections*, 10 Psychiatry, Psychol. & L. 91 (2003). On dignatiarian issues in general, see *infra* Chapter 7.

group of criminal defendants who have ever been studied.[60] In short, the actual, real-life experiences of the persons before Judge Lerner-Wren demonstrate that one MHC *can* be a non-coercive, dignified experience that provides procedural justice and therapeutic jurisprudence to those before it.[61]

A. Two Concerns

I do have two concerns that have not been the focus of much scholarly attention. It is these two concerns that temper my full enthusiasm for mental health courts, especially in the context of the issues I focus on in this book; but I believe they can be remediated. They are the lack of concern paid to the question of *competency* in the mental health court process,[62] and the lack of concern paid to the question of the quality of *counsel* made available to individuals in the mental health court process.

Dr. Steven Erickson and his colleagues point out what should be obvious: Given the impaired cognition that accompanies many mental disorders, "there is little evidence to suggest that mental health courts ensure that prospective candidates are competent to accept [the] plea bargains [into which many enter], as required by constitutional law."[63] Allison Redlich similarly worries that "the very types of

---

60 *See* Norman G. Poythress et al., *Perceived Coercion and Procedural Justice in the Broward Mental Health Court*, 25 Int'l J.L. & Psychiatry 517 (2002). Judge Lerner-Wren discusses her judicial philosophy in Lerner-Wren, *supra* note 10. On how levels of emotional intelligence correlate with judicial success in problem-solving courts, see James Duffy, *Problem-Solving Courts, Therapeutic Jurisprudence and the Constitution*, 35 Melb. U. L. Rev. 394 (2011); Michael King, *Restorative Justice, Therapeutic Jurisprudence, and the Rise of the Emotionally Intelligent Justice*, 35 Melb. L. Rev. 1096 (2008). On the role of restorative justice, see generally *infra* Chapter 6, IIC, in problem-solving courts, see Megan Stephens, *Lessons from the Front Lines in Canada's Restorative Justice Experiment: The Experience of Sentencing Judges*, 33 Queen's L.J. 19, 63–64 (2007).

61 *See* Judith Kaye, *Lecture*, St. John's L. Rev. 743, 748 (2007) ("mental health courts, which … divert defendants from jail to treatment, reconnect them, where possible, with family and friends who care whether they live or die … restore their greatest loss—their sense of human dignity") (author former Chief Judge of New York Court of Appeals); Hafemeister, Garner & Bath, *supra* note 11, at 201–02 ("procedural justice is a key to the success of mental health courts"). For a less sanguine attitude (based on a visit to a mental health court in Washington, DC), see Allegra M. McLeod, *Decarceration Courts: Possibilities and Perils of a Shifting Criminal Law*, 100 Geo L.J. 1587, 1613–14 (2012) ("actual therapeutic or other effects of this engagement remain uncertain").

62 *See generally* Kathleen Stafford & Dustin Wygant, *The Role of Competency to Stand Trial in Mental Health Courts*, 23 Behav. Sci. & L. 245 (2005) (over three-quarters of potential mental health court defendants in one Ohio court were found to be incompetent).

63 Steven Erickson et al., *Variations in Mental Health Courts: Challenges, Opportunities, and a Call for Caution*, 42 Comm. Mental Health J. 335, 339 (2006), *See also* Stacey M. Faraci, *Slip Slidin' Away? Will Our Nation's Mental Health Court Experiment Diminish the Rights of the Mentally Ill?*, 22 Quinnipiac L. Rev. 811, 828–29

people MHCs were designed for may be the people who do not fully comprehend the purpose, requirements and roles in the courts."[64] In fact, subsequent research done by Redlich and her colleagues reveals that the majority of defendants at two mental courts lacked "nuanced information" about the trial process, and that a minority of defendants had "impairments in legal competence."[65] The researchers concluded, however, that there were some indications that "the clients in the [mental health courts] in this study made knowing, intelligent and voluntary enrollment decisions."[66] Clearly, "a thorough evaluation of the offender's mental competence ... is essential" in the mental health court process.[67] Judge Michael Finkle and several colleagues have recommended that "competency courts" be created as subspeciality courts *within* mental health courts to "improve the competency process and reduce the unnecessary time that mentally ill persons spend in jail,"[68] but there are no signs that this recommendation is being acted upon.

What about counsel? I have written often about the scandalous lack of effective counsel made available to persons with mental disabilities in the civil commitment

(2004) ("[O]ne of the first orders of business is to determine whether the individual is competent ... '[E]ven among those deemed competent to stand trial, serious questions may be raised about the ability of persons to truly understand the choices being presented and the consequences of those choices'"), quoting JOHN S. GOLDKAMP & CHERYL IRONS-GUYNN, BUREAU OF JUSTICE ASSISTANCE, U.S. DEP'T OF JUSTICE, EMERGING JUDICIAL STRATEGIES FOR THE MENTALLY ILL IN THE CRIMINAL CASELOAD: MENTAL HEALTH COURTS IN FORT LAUDERDALE, SEATTLE, SAN BERNARDINO, AND ANCHORAGE xi (Apr. 2000), available at http:// www.ncjrs.org/pdffiles/bja/182504.pdf.

64 Allison Redlich, *Voluntary, But Knowing and Intelligent?*, 11 PSYCHOL. PUB. POL'Y & L. 605, 616 (2005).

65 Allison Redlich et al., *Enrollment in Mental Health Courts: Voluntariness, Knowingness, and Adjudicative Incompetence*, 34 LAW & HUM. BEHAV. 91, 91 (2010).

66 *Id.* at 101. On the other hand, they noted:

> [I]ndividuals making important legal and treatment decisions should have more than a basic knowledge of procedures, requirements, and consequences, particularly given that there are sanctions for non-compliance. Thus, MHCs must now ask: What information do we want MHC participants to have at the time of enrollment? and How can we ensure that the information is meaningfully understood, particularly the complicated nuances?

Id, at 103.

67 Christin E. Keele, *Criminalization of the Mentally Ill: The Challenging Role of the Defense Attorney in the Mental Health Court System*, 71 UMKC L. REV. 193, 202 (2002).

68 Michael J. Finkle et al., *Competency Courts: A Creative Solution for Restoring Competency to the Competency Process*, 27 BEHAV. SCI. & L. 767, 767 (2009). But, with the exception of one student note, see Nicholas Rosinia, *How 'Reasonable' Has Become Unreasonable: A Proposal for Rewriting the Lasting Legacy of Jackson v. Indiana*, 89 WASH. U. L. REV. 673, 693 n.115 (2012); this suggestion has heretofore gone unnoticed in the legal literature.

and criminal justice processes.[69] What is the quality of counsel available to litigants in mental health courts?

Dr. Steven Erickson and his colleagues have expressed concern "as to whether defendants in mental health courts receive adequate representation by their attorneys."[70] Terry Carney characterizes the assumption that adequate counsel will be present at hearings to guarantee liberty values as a "false hope."[71]

Henry Dlugacz and Christopher Wimmer summarize the salient issues:

> It is not reasonable to expect a client to repose trust in an attorney unless she is confident that he is acting in accordance with her wishes. The client with mental illness may already doubt the attorney's loyalty. This risk is exacerbated when the attorney is appointed by the court. The client may wonder whether the attorney has been assigned in order to zealously represent her, or instead to facilitate her processing through the legal system. … There are strong personal disincentives to thorough preparation, even for the committed attorney. There are also institutional pressures: The attorney who depends on the goodwill of others in the system (e.g., judges, state attorneys, or prosecutors) may pull his punches, even unwittingly, in order to retain credibility for future interactions (which he would put to use for his future clients). Judges want cases resolved.[72]

---

69 *See generally* supra Chapter 3; *see* Michael L. Perlin, *"I Might Need a Good Lawyer, Could Be Your Funeral, My Trial": A Global Perspective on the Right to Counsel in Civil Commitment Cases, and Its Implications for Clinical Legal Education*, 28 Wash. U. J. L. & Soc'l Pol'y 241, 241 (2008), 241: "If there has been any constant in modern mental disability law in its thirty-five-year history, it is the near-universal reality that counsel assigned to represent individuals at involuntary civil commitment cases is likely to be ineffective"; *see also,* Michael L. Perlin, *"The Executioner's Face Is Always Well-Hidden": The Role of Counsel and the Courts in Determining Who Dies*, 41 N.Y.L. Sch. L. Rev. 201, 207–08 (1996) ("Nearly twenty years ago, when surveying the availability of counsel to mentally disabled litigants, President Carter's Commission on Mental Health noted the frequently substandard level of representation made available to mentally disabled criminal defendants. Nothing that has happened in the past two decades has been a palliative for this problem"), *discussed supra* Chapter 3, at p. 37. *See generally* Michael L. Perlin, Mental Disability and the Death Penalty: The Shame of the States 123–38 (2013)

70 Erickson et al., *supra* note 63, at 340.

71 Terry Carney, *The Mental Health Service Crisis of Neoliberalism - An Antipodean Perspective*, 31 Int'l J. L. & Psychiatry 101, 111 (2008). *See also* Terry Carney, *Best Interests or Legal Rectitude?; Australian Mental Health Tribunal Stakeholder & Case Flow Implications* (paper presented at Irish Mental Health Commission Conference 'Mental Health Act 2001-Promoting Best Interest, Dublin, November 2009), manuscript at 33 ("The issue of legal advocacy before [mental health tribunals] is a vexed one") (paper of file with author).

72 Henry A. Dlugacz & Christopher Wimmer, *The Ethics of Representing Clients with Limited Competency in Guardianship Proceedings*, 4 St. Louis U. J. Health L. & Pol'y 331, 353–54 (2011). On the need for lawyers taking a TJ approach to view their clients "holistically," see King, *supra* note 60, at 1122.

Some solutions have been offered. Bruce Winick has argued that "lawyers should adequately counsel their clients about the advantages and disadvantages of accepting diversion to mental health court… . As a result, judges and defense counsel in mental health courts should ensure that defendants receive dignity and respect, are given a sense of voice and validation."[73] Turning to the law education clinical context, David Wexler has suggested that "Students might consider the kind of dialogue a lawyer might have with a client about the pros and cons of opting into a [drug treatment court] or mental health court."[74] It is essential that counsel has "a background in mental health issues and in communicating with individuals who may be in crisis."[75]

---

73 Stefan & Winick, *supra* note 35, at 510–11, 520 (comments by Professor Winick).

74 David B. Wexler, *Therapeutic Jurisprudence and the Rehabilitative Role of the Criminal Defense Lawyer*, 17 St. Thomas L. Rev. 743, 750 (2005). On the role of TJ in clinical legal education in general, see Cait Clarke & James Neuhard, *Making the Case: Therapeutic Jurisprudence and Problem Solving Practices Positively Impact Clients, Justice Systems and Communities They Serve*, 17 St. Thomas L. Rev. 781, 807 (2005). I consider dialogues that defense lawyers might have with their clients in incompetency status or insanity defense cases in Michael L. Perlin, *"Too Stubborn To Ever Be Governed By Enforced Insanity": Some Therapeutic Jurisprudence Dilemmas in the Representation of Criminal Defendants in Incompetency and Insanity Cases*, 33 Int'l J. L. & Psychiatry 475 (2010).On the parallel set of issues raised in the context of drug courts, see Clarke & Neuhard, *supra* note 55, at 29 ("In addition to concerns about net-widening, some defense attorneys fear that these courts and the defense attorneys who practice in them are forcing their clients into the drug courts, arm twisting them into diversion with a condition of entry being that they take a plea, and/or that the effective treatment is raised above the least restrictive treatment"); *see generally* Mae C. Quinn, *Whose Team Am I on Anyway: Musings of a Public Defender about Drug Treatment Court Practice*, 26 N.Y.U. Rev. L. & Soc. Change 37 (2001). For an overview of drug courts, see Peggy Hora & Theodore Stalcup, *Drug Treatment Courts in the Twenty-First Century: The Evolution of the Revolution in Problem-Solving Courts*, 42 Ga. L. Rev. 717 (2008). For a recent article by sitting trial judges contrasting mental health courts and drug courts, see Anne Harper & Michael J. Finkle, *Mental Health Courts*, 51 Judges' J. 4 (Spring 2012). For a critique of juvenile drug courts, see Jason Rayne, *An Exposition of the Effectiveness of and the Challenges Plaguing Maine's Juvenile Drug Treatment Court Program*, 62 Me. L. Rev. 649 (2010). For a consideration of family drug courts, see Janet York et al., *Family Drug Treatment Courts and Social Determinants of Health*, 50 Fam. Ct. Rev. 137 (2012). On the question as to whether drug courts should be operated as civil rather than criminal courts, see Alex Kreit, *The Decriminalization Option: Should States Consider Moving from a Criminal to a Civil Drug Court Model?*, 2010 U. Chi. Legal F. 299.

75 Seltzer, *supra* note 9, at 576. *See also*, M. Carmela Epright, *Coercing Future Freedom: Consent and Capacities for Autonomous Choice*, 38 J.L. Med. & Ethics 799, 801 (2010): "Ideally, in mental health courts all courtroom personnel (i.e., judge, prosecutor, defense counsel and other relevant professionals) have experience and training in mental health issues and available community resources."

IV. Conclusion

Mental health courts offer a new way of considering the linkage between mental disability and the criminal justice process. These courts are not without controversy, but the research appears to reveal, in general, a robust relationship between the operation of well-run mental health courts and enhanced dignity. In subsequent chapters, I will return to this topic with an eye on a determination as to whether such courts offer more hope to those who believe, as I do, that the criminal justice system must seriously and systematically rethink the significance of dignity in all aspects of the criminal trial process involving defendants with mental disabilities.

Chapter 6
Alternative Jurisprudences

I. Introduction

It is necessary to consider the impact of therapeutic jurisprudence, procedural justice, and restorative justice (what I will call "alternative jurisprudences")[1] on these issues. In this section, I will discuss each of these separately, and then consider how the criminal justice system must take them all seriously if it is ever to import a needed measure of dignity into proceedings involving defendants with mental disabilities.

II. Alternative Jurisprudences

A. Therapeutic Jurisprudence[2]

One of the most important legal theoretical developments of the past two decades has been the creation and dynamic growth of therapeutic jurisprudence (TJ).[3] Initially employed in cases involving individuals with mental disabilities, but

---

1 *See generally* Susan Daicoff, *Collaborative Law: A New Tool for the Lawyer's Toolkit*, 20 U. Fla. J.L. & Pub. Pol'y 113, 142 n.209 (2009), listing the ten developments in what she terms "collaborative law" as (1) creative problem solving, (2) holistic justice, (3) preventive law, (4) problem-solving courts (including drug treatment courts, unified family courts, mental health courts, and community courts), (5) procedural justice, (6) restorative justice, (7) therapeutic jurisprudence, (8) therapeutically-oriented preventive law, and (9) transformative mediation. *See also* Ian Freckelton, *Therapeutic Jurisprudence Misunderstood and Misrepresented: The Price and Risks of Influence*, 30 T. Jefferson L. Rev. 575, 578–79 (2008) (listing "vectors" of therapeutic jurisprudence movement).

2 *See generally* Michael L. Perlin, *"There Are No Trials Inside the Gates of Eden": Mental Health Courts, the Convention on the Rights of Persons with Disabilities, Dignity, and the Promise of Therapeutic Jurisprudence*, in Coercive Care: Law and Policy (Bernadette McSherry & Ian Freckelton eds, 2013) (in press).

3 *See, e.g.*, David B. Wexler, Therapeutic Jurisprudence: The Law as a Therapeutic Agent (1990); David B. Wexler & Bruce J. Winick, Law in a Therapeutic Key: Recent Developments in Therapeutic Jurisprudence (1996); Bruce J. Winick, Civil Commitment: A Therapeutic Jurisprudence Model (2005); David B. Wexler, *Two Decades of Therapeutic Jurisprudence*, 24 Touro L. Rev. 17 (2008); 1 Michael L. Perlin, Mental Disability Law: Civil and Criminal, § 2D-3, at 534–41 (2d ed. 1998). Wexler first used the term in a paper he presented to the National Institute of Mental Health in 1987. See David B. Wexler,

subsequently expanded far beyond that narrow area, therapeutic jurisprudence presents a new model for assessing the impact of case law and legislation, recognizing that, as a therapeutic agent, the law that can have therapeutic or anti-therapeutic consequences.[4] The ultimate aim of therapeutic jurisprudence is to determine whether legal rules, procedures and lawyer roles can or should be reshaped to enhance their therapeutic potential while not subordinating due process principles.[5] There is an inherent tension in this inquiry, but David Wexler clearly identifies how it must be resolved: "the law's use of "mental health information to improve therapeutic functioning [cannot] impinge upon justice concerns."[6] As I have written elsewhere, "An inquiry into therapeutic outcomes does not mean that therapeutic concerns 'trump' civil rights and civil liberties."[7]

Therapeutic jurisprudence "asks us to look at law as it actually impacts people's lives"[8] and focuses on the law's influence on emotional life and psychological

---

Putting Mental Health into Mental Health Law: Therapeutic Jurisprudence, 16 L. & Hum. Behav. 27, 27, 32–33 (1992).

4 *See* Michael L. Perlin, "*His Brain Has Been Mismanaged with Great Skill": How Will Jurors Respond to Neuroimaging Testimony in Insanity Defense Cases?*, 42 Akron L. Rev. 885, 912 (2009); see Kate Diesfeld & Ian Freckelton, *Mental Health Law and Therapeutic Jurisprudence*, in Disputes and Dilemmas in Health Law 91 (Ian Freckelton & Kate Peterson eds, 2006) (for a transnational perspective).

5 Michael L. Perlin, "*You Have Discussed Lepers and Crooks": Sanism in Clinical Teaching*, 9 Clinical L. Rev., 683–729 (2003) (Perlin, "*Lepers and Crooks*"); Michael L. Perlin, "*And My Best Friend, My Doctor/ Won't Even Say What It Is I've Got": The Role and Significance of Counsel in Right to Refuse Treatment Cases*, 42 San Diego L. Rev. 735 (2005); Michael L. Perlin, "*Everybody Is Making Love/Or Else Expecting Rain": Considering the Sexual Autonomy Rights of Persons Institutionalized Because of Mental Disability in Forensic Hospitals and in Asia*, 83 U. Wash. L. Rev. 481 (2008). On how TJ "might be a redemptive tool in efforts to combat sanism, as a means of 'strip[ping] bare the law's sanist façade'," see Michael L. Perlin, *"Baby, Look Inside Your Mirror": The Legal Profession's Willful and Sanist Blindness to Lawyers with Mental Disabilities*, 69 U. Pitt. L. Rev. 589, 591 (2008), quoting, in part, Michael L. Perlin, The Hidden Prejudice: Mental Disability on Trial 301 (2000). *See also* Bernard P. Perlmutter, *George's Story: Voice and Transformation through the Teaching and Practice of Therapeutic Jurisprudence in a Law School Child Advocacy Clinic*, 17 St. Thomas L. Rev. 561, 599 n.111 (2005) (same); Freckelton, *supra* note 1, at 585–86 (same).

6 David B. Wexler, *Therapeutic Jurisprudence and Changing Concepts of Legal Scholarship*, 11 Behav. Sci. & L. 17, 21 (1993). *See also, e.g.*, David Wexler, *Applying the Law Therapeutically*, 5 Appl. & Prevent. Psychol. 179 (1996).

7 Michael L. Perlin, *A Law of Healing*, 68 U. Cin. L. Rev. 407, 412 (2000) (Perlin, *Healing*); Michael L. Perlin, *"Where the Winds Hit Heavy on the Borderline": Mental Disability Law, Theory and Practice, Us and Them*, 31 Loyola L.A. L. Rev. 775, 782 (1998) (Perlin, *Borderline*).

8 Bruce J. Winick, *Foreword: Therapeutic Jurisprudence Perspectives on Dealing With Victims of Crime*, 33 Nova L. Rev. 535, 535 (2009).

well-being.[9] It suggests that "law should value psychological health, should strive to avoid imposing anti-therapeutic consequences whenever possible, and when consistent with other values served by law should attempt to bring about healing and wellness".[10] TJ understands that, "when attorneys fail to acknowledge their clients' negative emotional reactions to the judicial process, the clients are inclined to regard the lawyer as indifferent and a part of a criminal system bent on punishment."[11] By way of example, therapeutic jurisprudence "aims to offer social science evidence that limits the use of the incompetency label by narrowly defining its use and minimizing its psychological and social disadvantage."[12]

In recent years, scholars have considered a vast range of topics through a therapeutic jurisprudence lens, including, but not limited to, all aspects of mental disability law, domestic relations law, criminal law and procedure, employment law, gay rights law, and tort law.[13] As Ian Freckelton has noted, "it is a tool for gaining a new and distinctive perspective utilizing socio-psychological insights into the law and its applications."[14] It is also part of a growing comprehensive movement in the law towards establishing more humane and psychologically optimal ways of handling legal issues collaboratively, creatively and respectfully.[15] These alternative approaches optimize the psychological well-being of individuals, relationships, and communities dealing with a legal matter, and acknowledge concerns beyond strict legal rights, duties, and obligations. In its aim to use the law to empower individuals, enhance rights, and promote well-being, therapeutic jurisprudence has been described as "… a sea-change in ethical thinking about the role of law… a movement towards a more distinctly relational approach to

---

9 David B. Wexler, *Practicing Therapeutic Jurisprudence: Psychological Soft Spots and Strategies,* in Daniel P. Stolle, David B. Wexler & Bruce J. Winick, Practicing Therapeutc Jurisprudence: Law as a Helping Profession 45 (2000) (Stolle et al.).

10 Bruce Winick, *A Therapeutic Jurisprudence Model for Civil Commitment*, in Involuntary Detention and Therapeutic Jurisprudence: International Perspective on Civil Commitment, 23, 26 (Kate Diesfeld & Ian Freckelton, eds, 2003).

11 Evelyn H. Cruz, *Competent Voices: Noncitizen Defendants and the Right to Know the Immigration Consequences of Plea Agreements*, 13 Harv. Latino L. Rev. 47, 59 (2010).

12 Claire B. Steinberger, *Persistence and Change In The Life Of The Law: Can Therapeutic Jurisprudence Make A Difference?* 27 Law & Psychol. Rev. 55, 65 (2003). The most thoughtful sympathetic critique of TJ remains Christopher Slobogin, *Therapeutic Jurisprudence: Five Dilemmas to Ponder*, 1 Psychol. Pub. Pol'y & L. 193 (1995).

13 Michael L. Perlin, *"Things Have Changed": Looking at Non-institutional Mental Disability Law Through the Sanism Filter*, 46 N.Y.L. Sch. L. Rev. 535 (2002–03).

14 Ian Freckelton, *Therapeutic Jurisprudence Misunderstood and Misrepresented: The Price and Risks of Influence*, 30 T. Jefferson L. Rev. 575, 582 (2008).

15 Susan Daicoff, *The Role of Therapeutic Jurisprudence Within the Comprehensive Law Movement,* in Stolle et al. *supra* note 9, at 365.

the practice of law … which emphasises psychological wellness over adversarial triumphalism".[16] That is, therapeutic jurisprudence supports an ethic of care.[17]

One of the central principles of therapeutic jurisprudence is a commitment to dignity.[18] Professor Amy Ronner describes the "three Vs": voice, validation and voluntariness,[19] arguing:

> What "the three Vs" commend is pretty basic: litigants must have a sense of voice or a chance to tell their story to a decision maker. If that litigant feels that the tribunal has genuinely listened to, heard, and taken seriously the litigant's story, the litigant feels a sense of validation. When litigants emerge from a legal proceeding with a sense of voice and validation, they are more at peace with the outcome. Voice and validation create a sense of voluntary participation, one in which the litigant experiences the proceeding as less coercive. Specifically, the feeling on the part of litigants that they voluntarily partook in the very process that engendered the end result or the very judicial pronunciation that affects their own lives can initiate healing and bring about improved behavior in the future.

---

16 Warren Brookbanks, *Therapeutic Jurisprudence: Conceiving an Ethical Framework*, 8 J.L. & Med. 328, 329–30 (2001); *see also* Bruce J. Winick, *Overcoming Psychological Barriers to Settlement: Challenges for the TJ Lawyer*, in The Affective Assistance of Counsel: Practicing Law as a Healing Profession 342. (Marjorie A. Silver ed., 2007); Bruce J. Winick & David B. Wexler, *The Use of Therapeutic Jurisprudence in Law School Clinical Education: Transforming the Criminal Law Clinic*, 13 Clinical L. Rev. 605, 605–06 (2006). The use of the phrase dates to Carol Gilligan, *In a Different Voice* (1982). On the potential use of therapeutic jurisprudence in all traditional courts, see Michael D. Jones, *Mainstreaming Therapeutic Jurisprudence into the Traditional Courts: Suggestions for Judges and Practitioners*, 5 Phoenix L. Rev. 753 (2012) (Professor Jones is a retired Superior Court judge.) On the potential use of therapeutic jurisprudence in all aspects of the criminal court process, see David B. Wexler, *New Wine in New Bottles: The Need to Sketch a Therapeutic Jurisprudence "Code" of Proposed Criminal Processes and Practices*, in Therapeutic Jurisprudence and Problem-Solving Justice (Jane Donoghue, ed., 2013) (in press).

17 *See, e.g.*, Bruce J. Winick & David B. Wexler, *The Use of Therapeutic Jurisprudence in Law School Clinical Education: Transforming the Criminal Law Clinic*, 13 Clinical L. Rev. 605, 605–07 (2006); David B. Wexler, *Not Such a Party Pooper: An Attempt to Accommodate (Many of) Professor Quinn's Concerns about Therapeutic Jurisprudence Criminal Defense Lawyering*, 48 B.C. L. Rev. 597, 599 (2007); Brookbanks, *supra* note 16; Gregory Baker, *Do You Hear the Knocking at the Door? A "Therapeutic" Approach to Enriching Clinical Legal Education Comes Calling*, 28 Whittier L. Rev. 379, 385 (2006).

18 *See* Bruce J. Winick, Civil Commitment: A Therapeutic Jurisprudence Model 161 (2005).

19 Amy D. Ronner, *The Learned-Helpless Lawyer: Clinical Legal Education and Therapeutic Jurisprudence as Antidotes to Bartleby Syndrome*, 24 Touro L. Rev. 601, 627 (2008). On the importance of "voice," see also, Freckelton, *supra* note 1, at 588.

> In general, human beings prosper when they feel that they are making, or at least participating in, their own decisions.[20]

The question before us is this: does the criminal trial process promote a vision that is consonant with the principles that Professor Ronner sketches out for us in this paragraph, especially in cases of defendants with mental disabilities?[21] Taking as a given the accuracy and importance of Professor Ronner's "three V's," it follows that a litigant must feel that the tribunal has genuinely listened to, heard, and taken seriously his story.[22] To what extent has the criminal trial process *apparat* absorbed TJ values and incorporated them into the daily business of the criminal court system, again, especially in cases involving litigants with mental disabilities?

B. Procedural Justice

"Procedural justice" asserts that "people's evaluations of the resolution of a dispute (including matters resolved by the judicial system) are influenced more by their perception of the fairness of the process employed than by their belief regarding whether the 'right' outcome was reached."[23] The research is consistent:

---

20 Amy D. Ronner, *Songs of Validation, Voice, and Voluntary Participation: Therapeutic Jurisprudence, Miranda and Juveniles*, 71 U. Cin. L. Rev. 89, 94–95 (2002); *See generally* Amy D. Ronner, Law, Literature and Therapeutic Jurisprudence (2010).

21 *See* David B Wexler, Rehabilitating Lawyers: Principles of Therapeutic Jurisprudence for Criminal Law Practice (2008). On the relationship between TJ and the criminal court process in general, see Salmon Shomade, *Case Disposition in the Drug Court: Who Is the Most Central Actor?* 31 Just. Sys. J. 74 (2010); Salmon Shomade, *Judging in Trial Courts: Cross-Fertilization of Therapeutic Jurisprudence Practices from Specialized Courts into Conventional Criminal Courts*, accessible at http://papers.ssrn.com/sol3/papers.cfm?abstract_id=1642379, to be published as Salmon Shomade, *Sentencing Patterns: Drug Court Judges Serving in Conventional Criminal Courts*, Judicature (2012) (in press). On TJ and sentencing, see *infra* Chapter 10, see Bruce J. Winick, *Redefining the Role of the Criminal Defense Lawyer at Plea Bargaining and Sentencing: A Therapeutic Jurisprudence/Preventive law Model*, 5 Psychol Pub. Pol'y & L. 1034, 1041 (1999), *id* at 1065 ("criminal defense lawyers who apply a therapeutic jurisprudence/preventive law model in the plea bargaining and sentencing process therefore have much to offer their clients." and *id.* at 1066 ("conversations about rehabilitation can be an opportunity for empowering the client in ways that can have positive psychological value").

22 A fourth "V" might be "visibility." *See, e.g.*, Bruce Winick, *Therapeutic Jurisprudence and the Civil Commitment Hearing*, 10 J. Contemp. Leg. Issues 37, 58 (1999), discussing involuntary civil commitment hearings ("The patient should not be treated as *invisible* at the hearing") (emphasis added).

23 Thomas L. Hafemeister, Sharon G. Garner & Veronica E. Bath, *Forging Links and Renewing Ties: Applying the Principles of Restorative and Procedural Justice to Better Respond to Criminal Offenders with a Mental Disorder*, 60 Buff. L. Rev. 147, 200 (2012), quoting, in part, Tom R. Tyler, *Procedural Justice and the Courts*, 44 Ct. Rev. 26, 26 (2007); *see also* Freckelton, *supra* note 1, at 585 n.85 (same); Larry Heuer, *What's Just*

"the principal factor shaping [the] reactions [of the general public] is whether law enforcement officials exercise authority in ways that are perceived to be fair."[24] And the fairness of the process used to reach a given outcome is critical to perceptions of legitimacy.[25] The question to be asked is this: does the criminal justice system treat defendants fairly and respectfully regardless of the substantive outcome reached?[26]

About the Criminal Justice System? A Psychological Perspective, 13 J. L. & Pol'y 209, 213 (2005) ("procedural fairness concerns, rather than outcomes, are the best predictors of people's trust and confidence in the courts"). Outcomes are similar in other cultures as well. See Freckelton, *supra* note 1, at 585 n.85 discussing findings reported in Mark Peel, The Lowest Rung: Voices of Australian Poverty 182 (2003) (discussing attitudes of individuals in subsidized housing projects in Australia). *See generally*, Rebecca Hollander-Blumoff, *The Psychology of Procedural Justice in the Federal Courts*, 63 Hastings L.J. 127, 133–34 (2011) (footnotes omitted):

> Procedural justice research has shown that procedural justice effects are present in a wide range of settings. Civil litigants in court care about their treatment by a judge, criminal defendants care about their treatment by judge and jury, disputing parties in arbitration and mediation care about their treatment by an arbitrator or mediator, and even disputing parties in negotiation care about their treatment by the other party. Research outside the legal dispute resolution system has demonstrated that people care about their treatment by other authority figures, such as police officers, work supervisors, and health-care administrators. Beyond both the legal dispute-resolution context and the third party context, research has suggested that individuals care about procedural justice in highly relational settings like the family and even in classic economic settings like markets. Effects are found in field studies, simulations and experimental settings, and in situations with both low and very high stakes.

24 Stephen J. Schulhofer, Tom R. Tyler & Aziz Z. Huq, *American Policing at a Crossroads: Unsustainable Policies and the Procedural Justice Alternative*, 101 J. Crim. L. & Criminology 335, 346 (2011), citing, inter alia, Tom R. Tyler & Yuen J. Huo, Trust in the Law: Encouraging Cooperation With the Police and the Law (2002); Kimberly Belvedere, John L. Worrall & Stephen G. Tibbetts, *Explaining Suspect Resistance in Police-Citizen Encounters*, 30 Crim. Just. Rev. 30 (2005); Ben Bradford, Jonathan Jackson & Elizabeth A. Stanko, *Contact and Confidence: Revisiting the Impact of Public Encounters with the Police*, 19 Policing and Soc'y 20 (2009); Tom R. Tyler, *Procedural Justice, Legitimacy, and the Effective Rule of Law*, 30 Crime & Just. 431 (2003); *see also e.g.*, David B. Rottman, *Procedural Fairness as a Court Reform Agenda*, 44 Ct. Rev. 32 (2007); Victoria Weisz, Twila Wingrove & April Faith-Slaker, *Children and Procedural Justice*, 44 Ct. Rev. 36(2007).

25 David Welsh, *Procedural Justice Post-9/11: The Effects of Procedurally Unfair Treatment of Detainees on Perceptions of Global Legitimacy*, 9 U. N.H. L. Rev. 261, 274 (2011).

26 Erin A. Conway, *Ineffective Assistance of Counsel: How Illinois Has Used the "Prejudice" Prong of Strickland to Lower The Floor on Performance When Defendants Plead Guilty*, 105 Nw. U. L. Rev. 1707, 1732 (2011).

When those affected by decision-making processes perceive the process to be just, "they are much more likely to accept the outcomes of the process, even when the outcomes are adverse."[27] Professor Tom Tyler's groundbreaking research has taught us that individuals with mental disabilities, like all other citizens,[28] are affected by such process values as participation, dignity, and trust, and that experiencing arbitrariness in procedure leads to "social malaise and decreases people's willingness to be integrated into the polity, accepting its authorities, and following its rules."[29]

There is a growing body of research showing that the experience of procedural justice not only enhances evaluations of persons, institutions and specific outcomes, but also leads to greater overall satisfaction with the legal experience and more positive affect with respect to an encounter with the justice system."[30] Perceptions of systemic fairness are driven, in large part, by "the degree to which people judge that they are treated with dignity and respect."[31] And the public's perception of procedural justice—whether the criminal justice system treats defendants fairly

27 Hafemeister, Garner & Bath, *supra* note 23, at 200, quoting, in part, Michael M. O'Hear, *Explaining Sentences*, 36 FLA. ST. U. L. REV. 459, 478 (2009). This applies as well to psychiatric hospital decision-making. See Bruce J. Winick, *A Therapeutic Jurisprudence Approach to Dealing with Coercion in the Mental Health System*, 15 PSYCHIATRY, PSYCHOL. & L. 25, 40 (2008) (discussing importance of "degree of respect" shown to patients by treatment providers).

28 On the application of procedural justice insights to the juvenile court system, see Mark R. Fondacaro, Christopher Slobogin & Tricia Cross, *Reconceptualizing Due Process in Juvenile Justice: Contributions from Law and Social Science*, 57 HASTINGS L.J. 955, 984–89 (2006).

29 Tom Tyler, *The Psychological Consequences of Judicial Procedures: Implications for Civil Commitment Hearings*, 46 SMU L. REV, 433, 443 (1992), as discussed in Michael L. Perlin & Deborah A. Dorfman, "*Is It More Than Dodging Lions and Wastin' Time?" Adequacy of Counsel, Questions of Competence, and the Judicial Process in Individual Right to Refuse Treatment Cases*, 2 PSYCHOLOGY, PUB. POL'Y & L. 114, 119 (1996). *See also* Vidis Donnelly et al., *Working Alliances, Interpersonal Trust and Perceived Coercion in Mental Health Review Hearings*, 5 INT'L J. MENT. HEALTH 29 (2011) (hearings perceived as lacking in procedural justice worsened working alliances between patients and physicians and diminished interpersonal trust) (cases heard in Ireland).

30 E. ALLAN LIND & TOM R. TYLER, THE SOCIAL PSYCHOLOGY OF PROCEDURAL JUSTICE 70 (1988).

31 Tyler, *supra* note 29, at 442, as discussed Perlin, *Healing*, *supra* note 7, at 415. For other important related readings on procedural justice in this context, *see*, *e.g.*, Norman G. Poythress, *Procedural Preferences, Perceptions of Fairness, and Compliance with Outcomes*, 18 LAW & HUM. BEHAV. 361 (1994); P. Christopher Earley & E. Allan Lind, *Procedural Justice and Participation in Task Selection: The Role of Control in Mediating Justice Judgments*, 52 J. PERSONAL. & SOC'L PSYCHOL. 1148 (1987); Tom R. Tyler et al., *Influence of Voice on Satisfaction with Leaders: Exploring the Meaning of Process Control*, 48 J. PERSONAL. & SOC'L PSYCHOL. 72 (1985); Raymond Paternoster et al., *Do Fair Procedures Matter? The Effect of Procedural Justice on Spouse Assault*, 31 LAW & SOC'Y

and respectfully regardless of the substantive outcome reached—determines the public's willingness to engage in and comply with the system.[32]

Importantly, the research demonstrates that participation yields procedural justice results in criminal law contexts, and in the experiences of actual offenders.[33] And it reveals that "the fairness of a process is a separate, independent construct, distinct from how fair or how good an outcome is, and that procedural justice has a separate and independent effect on how people feel about their results, apart from how fair or how good the outcome is."[34] In discussing this phenomenon, Professor Christopher Slobogin argues, correctly, I believe, that a procedure that gives participants a full opportunity to present their version of the facts enhances perceptions of fairness, satisfaction with outcomes, and respect for the process.[35]

It is significant that procedural justice is also a key to the success of mental health courts,[36] in which participants should be actively "engaged in a dialogue with a highly respected authority who speaks to them in a respectful manner," thereby enhancing the likelihood that they will feel positive about and support the outcome of these hearings.[37] This is especially important in light of the reporting of valid and reliable research showing that patients in civil commitment hearings who are provided with procedural justice, treated with dignity and respect, and

---

REV. 163 (1997). *Cf.* James H. Liu & Gerald H. Shure, *Due Process Orientation Does Not Always Mean Political Liberalism*, 17 LAW & HUM. BEHAV. 343 (1993).

32 Conway, *supra* note 26, at 1732, citing Lind & Tyler, *supra* note 30, at 76–81.

33 In criminal law contexts, see Hollander-Blumoff, *supra* note 23, at 135, citing Anne M. Heinz & Wayne A. Kerstetter, *Pretrial Settlement Conference: Evaluation of a Reform in Plea Bargaining*, 13 LAW & SOC'Y REV. 349 (1979); Pauline Houlden, *Impact of Procedural Modifications on Evaluations of Plea Bargaining*, 15 LAW & SOC'Y REV. 267 (1980–81). With regards to the experiences of offenders, see Paternoster, et al., *supra* note 31, at 166. *See also* Irina Elliott, Stuart D.N. Thomas & James R. P. Ogloff, *Procedural Justice in Contacts with the Police: Testing A Relational Model of Authority in a Mixed Methods Study*, 17 PSYCHOL. PUB. POL'Y & L. 592, 594 (2011). ("The most robust and consistent finding to date has been the link between procedural justice judgments based on the relational criteria and perceived police legitimacy.")

34 Rebecca Hollander-Blumoff & Tom R. Tyler, *Procedural Justice and the Rule of Law: Fostering Legitimacy in Alternative Dispute Resolution*, 2011 J. DISP. RESOL. 1, 5.

35 Christopher Slobogin, *The Admissibility of Behavioral Science Information in Criminal Trials From Primitivism to Daubert to Voice*, 5 PSYCHOL. PUB. POL'Y & L. 100, 117 (1999).

36 Hafemeister, Garner & Bath, *supra* note 23, at 201–02, citing Norman G. Poythress et al., *Perceived Coercion and Procedural Justice in the Broward Mental Health Court*, 25 INT'L J.L. & PSYCHIATRY 517, 520 (2002). Note that Judge Ginger Lerner-Wren, the presiding judge of the Broward Court (see *supra* Chapter 5), specifies that the creation of that court was "based upon the application of therapeutic jurisprudence *and* procedural justice," Ginger Lerner-Wren, *Mental Health Courts: Serving Justice and Promoting Recovery*, 19 ANNALS HEALTH L. 577, 587 (2010) (emphasis added).

37 Hafemeister, Garner & Bath, *supra* note 23, at 202, citing Poythress et al., *supra* note 36, at 521.

accorded voice and validation in the civil commitment process, will experience the commitment that they have consented to as voluntary rather than coerced and, as a result, will experience the psychological benefits of choice and avoid the negative benefits of coercion.[38]

Although there has been some literature studying the impact of procedural justice on sentencing cases in general,[39] and as it relates to the plea bargaining process in particular,[40] there has been very limited literature on the question of the interplay between procedural justice and the insanity or incompetency process.[41] It

---

38 Perlmutter, *supra* note 5, at 614 n.155, citing Bruce J. Winick, *Therapeutic Jurisprudence and Problem Solving Courts*, 30 Fordham Urb. L.J. 1055, 1077 (2003), reporting on research by the MacArthur Network on Mental Health and the Law. On TJ and problem-solving courts in this context, *see also* Cait Clarke & James Neuhard, *Making the Case: Therapeutic Jurisprudence and Problem Solving Practices Positively Impact Clients, Justice Systems and Communities They Serve*, 17 St. Thomas L. Rev. 781 (2005).

39 The forerunner of this work is Marvin Frankel, Criminal Sentences: Law Without Order (1973). *See* Jonathan D. Casper et al., *Procedural Justice in Felony Cases*, 22 L. & Soc. Rev. 483, 483 (1988) (procedural justice in felony cases revealed that defendants' evaluations of the judicial system did not depend exclusively on the favorability of sentencing); *see also*, *generally*, Adam Lamparello, *Incorporating the Procedural Justice Model Into Federal Sentencing Jurisprudence in the Aftermath of United States v. Booker: Establishing United States Sentencing Courts*, 4 N.Y.U. J.L. & Liberty 112, 118–19 (2009); Daniel Isaacs, *Baseline Framing in Sentencing*, 121 Yale L.J. 426 (2011); Michael M. O'Hear, *Appellate Review of Sentencing Explanations: Learning from the Wisconsin and Federal Experiences*, 93 Marq. L. Rev. 751 (2009); Edna Erez, *Victim Voice, Impact Statements and Sentencing: Integrating Restorative Justice and Therapeutic Jurisprudence Principles in Adversarial Proceedings*, 40 Crim. L. Bull. 483 (2004).

40 *See, e.g.*, Michael M. O'Hear, *Plea Bargaining and Procedural Justice*, 42 Ga. L. Rev. 407, 420–32 (2008) (arguing that procedural justice should be part of the plea bargaining reform agenda).

41 The only on-point reference I have found in the literature is in an article of LeRoy Kondo's about mental health courts:

> In some states with traditional trial courts, ensuring procedural justice may be more problematic. While the prosecution formerly had the burden of proving the offender was free from mental disorders, in recent years this burden has shifted to the defense. For example, changes in state and federal law have allocated to the defendant the burden of proving an insanity defense. Similarly, some states have upheld decisions placing the burden on the defendant to show incompetence to stand trial under a presumption of competence. Some more radical states have even abolished the insanity defense or permit judges to disregard expert testimony of insanity. Judges in these jurisdictions have the ethical responsibility to uphold therapeutic jurisprudence principles to protect the right to due process and credibility of the judicial process.

LeRoy Kondo, *Advocacy of the Establishment of Mental Health Specialty Courts in the Provision of Therapeutic Justice for Mentally Ill Offenders*, 28 Am. J. Crim. L. 255, 294–95 (2001). *See generally infra* Chapters 8–10. On the relationship between the public's

is necessary in this context to consider the extent to which (a) caselaw reflects an environment that provides these perceptions of fairness and respect for the process, and (b) litigants express satisfaction with the outcomes of the court procedures.[42]

C. Restorative Justice

1. Introduction

What is restorative justice? Professor John Braithwaite defines restorative justice as a means by which to restore victims, restore offenders and restore communities "in a way that all stakeholders can agree is just."[43] Professor Susan Daicoff has characterized it as is "a movement in criminal law in which criminal justice and criminal sentencing are carried out by the community, the victim, and the offender in a collaborative process."[44] Elsewhere, Professor Braithwaite lists the objectives

---

misperceptions about insanity defense outcomes and procedural justice, see Tom R. Tyler & Robert J. Boeckmann, *Three Strikes and You Are Out, but Why? The Psychology of Public Support for Punishing Rule Breakers*, 31 Law & Soc'y Rev. 237 (1997), discussed *infra* Chapter 9.

42 *See, e.g.*, Jose E. Alvarez, *Rush to Closure: Lessons of the Tadic Judgment*, 96 Mich. L. Rev. 2031, 2102 (1998), discussing John W. Thibaut & Laurens Walker, Procedural Justice: A Psychological Analysis 67–116 (1975), in the context of litigants' process satisfaction in international criminal courts.

43 John Braithwaite, *A Future Where Punishment Is Marginalized: Realistic or Utopian?*, 46 UCLA L. Rev. 1727, 1743 (1999). *See also, e.g*, John Braithwaite, Restorative Justice & Responsive Regulation 11 (2002) (Responsive Regulation) ("Restorative justice is a process whereby all the parties with a stake in the offence come together to resolve collectively how to deal with the aftermath of the offence and its implications for the future."). Some scholars criticize the lack of a clear definition of what restorative justice is. *See* Andrew von Hirsch, Andrew Ashworth & Clifford Shearing, *Specifying Aims and Limits for Restorative Justice: A "Making Amends" Model?* in Restorative Justice & Criminal Justice: Competing or Reconcilable Paradigms 21 (Andrew von Hirsch et al. eds, 2003) (Restorative Justice); Paul H. Robinson, Owen D. Jones & Robert Kurzban, *Response, Realism, Punishment, and Reform*, 77 U. Chi. L. Rev. 1611, 1624–25 (2010). On efforts to reconcile restorative justice with retributions, see Antony Dufy, *Restoration and Retribution*, in Restorative Justice, *supra*, at 43.

44 Daicoff, *supra* note 15, in Stolle et al., *supra* note 15, at 476; see also Leonard Riskin et al., Dispute Resolution and Lawyers 537 (3d ed. 2006) (same).

On the synergy between therapeutic jurisprudence and restorative justice, and how "TJ calls for the expansion of the use of RJ [in cases involving] child victims," see Tali Gal & Vered Shidlo-Hezroni, *Restorative Justice as Therapeutic Jurisprudence: The Case of Child Victims*, in Therapeutic Jurisprudence and Victim Participation in Justice, 139, 153 (Edna Erez, Michael Kilchling & Jo-Anne Wemmers eds, 2011). On some key differences between therapeutic jurisprudence and restorative justice, see James L. Nolan, *Redefining Criminal Courts: Problem-Solving and the Meaning of Justice*, 40 Am. Crim. L. Rev. 1541, 1547–48 (2004). Nolan focuses on the emphasis on "reintegrative shaming" that is part of the restorative justice movement—see John Braithwaite, *Restorative Justice and*

of a restorative justice approach as "restoring property loss, restoring injury, restoring a sense of security, restoring dignity, restoring a sense of empowerment, restoring deliberative democracy, restoring harmony based on a feeling that justice has been done, and restoring social support."[45] Tali Gal and Vered Shidlo-Herzoni identify these as the "critical RJ values": participation, reparation, community involvement, "crime as belonging to individuals," deliberation, flexibility of practice, equality, a forward-looking approach, victims' involvement, and, "most important[ly]", respect.[46]

Therapeutic Jurisprudence, 38 CRIM. L. BULL. 244, 257–58 (2002)—but is *not* part of the therapeutic jurisprudence movement, see Nolan, *supra,* at 1548, quoting Bruce Winick ("shame ... throws a lot of people off track").

On how *unacknowledged* shame can lead to violence, see RESPONSIVE REGULATION, *supra* note 43, at 81. On how shame has traits both desirable and undesirable for the restorative justice process, see Raffaele Rodogno, *Shame and Guilt in Restorative Justice,* 14 PSYCHOL PUB. POL'Y & L. 142 (2008). On how it is important to understand the structure of shame in seeking to understand crime patterns, see John Braithwaite, *Shame and Criminal Justice*, 42 CANADIAN J. CRIMINOLOGY & CRIM. JUST. 281 (2000).

45 John Braithwaite, *Restorative Justice: Assessing Optimistic and Pessimistic Accounts,* 25 CRIME & JUST. 1, 6 (1999). See also generally, JOHN DUSSICH & JILL SCHELLENBERG, THE PROMISE OF RESTORATIVE JUSTICE: NEW APPROACHES FOR CRIMINAL JUSTICE AND BEYOND (2010); RESTORATIVE JUSTICE AND CRIMINAL JUSTICE: COMPETING OR RECONCILABLE PARADIGMS (Andrew von Hirsch et al. eds, 2003). On the significance of dignity values in this context, see Kay Pranis, *Restorative Values,* in *Human Rights and Restorative Justice,* in HANDBOOK OF RESTORATIVE JUSTICE 59 (Gerry Johnstone & Daniel W. Van Ness, eds 2007) (HANDBOOK). On concerns about coercion in this context, *see* Lode Walgrave, *Integrating Criminal Justice and Restorative Justice,* in HANDBOOK, *supra*, at 559, 564–66 ; *see also*, Tina S. Ikpa, *Balancing Restorative Justice Principles and Due Process Rights in Order to Reform the Criminal Justice System*, 24 WASH. U. J.L. & POL'Y 301, 315 n.61 (2007), quoting, in part, Christa Obold-Eshleman, *Victims' Rights and the Danger of Domestication of the Restorative Justice Paradigm*, 18 NOTRE DAME J.L. ETHICS & PUB. POL'Y 571, 599 (2004): Even advocates for restorative justice recognize the coercive possibilities of restorative justice:

> [I]n reality there will be a certain level of coercion in most restorative processes, because the looming alternative (and predecessor) will usually be the traditional criminal justice system. It is coercion of the offender by the police that lands her in the criminal justice system, and thus in a restorative justice process such as victim-offender mediation, and it is a much higher level of coercion that probably awaits her as a default if she does not successfully complete such a program. A lesser level of coercion to successfully complete the program exists for the victim if he wishes to play a leading role in the outcome of the process.

For a thoughtful critique, see Chris Cunneen, *The Limits of Restorative Justice*, in CAROLYN HOYLE & CHRIS CUNNEEN, DEBATING RESTORATIVE JUSTICE 101 (2010).

46 Gal & Shidlo-Hezroni, *supra* note 44, at, 148–49.

At the core of restorative justice is a focus on the "restoration of human dignity."[47] Optimally, it involves "the victim, the offender, and the community in a search for solutions which promote repair, reconciliation, and reassurance."[48] It is "a process whereby all the parties with a stake in a particular offense come together to resolve collectively how to deal with the aftermath of the offense and its implications for the future."[49] Its core values are "healing rather than hurting, moral learning, community participation and community caring, respectful dialogue, forgiveness, responsibility, apology, and making amends."[50] Restorative justice scholars have critiqued traditional criminal law's narrow retributive justice model.[51]

2. Restorative justice and the criminal law

In the area of criminal justice, concepts of restorative justice have been steadily growing since the mid-1980s,[52] mostly, though not exclusively, in cases involving post-sentencing victim-offender interaction.[53] RJ seeks to "re-frame the conversation of criminal justice in such a way that the contextual needs of

---

47 Mijha Butcher, *Using Mediation to Remedy Civil Rights Violations When the Defendant is Not an Intentional Perpetrator: The Problems of Unconscious Disparate Treatment and Unjustified Disparate Impacts*, 24 Hamline J. Pub. L. & Pol'y 225, 252 (2003).

48 Howard Zehr, Changing Lenses: A New Focus For Crime and Justice 181 (1990).

49 Responsive Regulation, *supra* note 43, at 11. On process values in restorative justice, see Pranis, *supra* note 44, at 60–63.

50 Braithwaite, *supra* note 45, at 5. Braithwaite acknowledges that international human rights (see *supra* Chapter 4) are a "constraining value" on restorative justice. John Braithwaite, *Principles of Restorative Justice*, in Restorative Justice, *supra* note 43, at 1, 9. Compare Thomas Antowiak, *An Emerging Mandate for International Courts: Victim-Centered Remedies and Restorative Justice,* 47 Stan. J. Int'l L. 279 (2011). On how the restorative justice discourse must be "broaden[ed]" around the issue of international human rights, see Ann Skelton & Makubetse Sekhonyane, *Human Rights and Restorative Justice,* in Handbook, *supra* note 45, at 591–93. From the perspective of an international criminal court judge, see Christine Van den Wyngaert, *Victims Before International Criminal Courts: Some Views and Concerns of an ICC Trial Judge*, 44 Case W. Res. J. Int'l L. 475 (2012).

51 Jonathan Todres, *Moving Upstream: The Merits of a Public Health Law Approach to Human Trafficking*, 89 N.C. L. Rev. 447, 453 n.22 (2011); *see generally* Carrie J. Niebur Eisnaugle, *An International "Truth Commission": Utilizing Restorative Justice as an Alternative to Retribution*, 36 Vand. J. Transnat'l L. 209, 213 (2003).

52 Susan S. Daicoff, Comprehensive Law Practice: Law as a Healing Profession 223 (2011). On restorative justice and healing, see Pranis, *supra* note 44, at 66.

53 Jason R. Holmes, *Share The Road: Why the Current Laws in Arizona Do Not Adequately Protect Cyclists, and a Call To Legislators to Change Those Laws*, 5 Phoenix L. Rev. 591, 598 (2012). *See also* Susan Hadley Duncan, *Restorative Justice and Bullying: A Missing Solution in the Anti-Bullying Laws*, 37 New Eng. J. on Crim. & Civ. Confinement 267, 275 (2011), citing Mark S. Umbreit et al., *Restorative Justice in the Twenty-First Century: A Social Movement Full of Opportunities and Pitfalls*, 89 Marq. L. Rev. 251,

victims are taken more seriously and the nature of crime is understood primarily as a violation of persons and relationships rather than as primarily against the state or an abstract notion of universal justice."[54] Put another way, restorative justice "assumes that a deeper connection exists between the victim of the offense, the offender, and the community than is assumed by the formal criminal justice system."[55] One commonly used mechanism in restorative justice is the sentencing circle,[56] an approach that seeks to "provide a non-adversarial approach that draws on extended family and community members to assist in resolving the dispute

---

254–55 (2005), and Jeffrie G. Murphy, Forgiveness, *Reconciliation and Responding to Evil: A Philosophical Overview*, 27 Fordham Urb. L.J. 1353, 1374 (2000):

> The criminal justice system seeks to determine guilt by identifying who did the act and then impose punishment to make sure offenders get what they deserve. In contrast, the central focus with restorative justice is an effort to find out what the needs are to make things right by encouraging the victims, offenders, and community to work together to determine who is responsible to repair the harm.

54 James W. McCarty III, *Nonviolent Law? Linking Nonviolent Social Change and Truth and Reconciliation Commissions*, 114 W. Va. L. Rev. 969, 990 (2012). On the extent to which judges understand the principles of restorative justice, see Megan Stephens, *Lessons from the Front Lines in Canada's Restorative Justice Experiment: The Experience of Sentencing Judges*, 33 Queen's L.J. 19, 38–40 (2007). *See generally National Justice CEOs Group, National Guidelines or Principles for Restorative Justice Programs and Processes for Criminal Matters*, available at http://www.lawlink.nsw.gov.au/lawlink/SCAG/ll_scag.nsf/vwFiles/Restorative_Justice_National_Guidelines_Discussion_Paper.pdf/$file/Restorative_Justice_National_Guidelines_Discussion_Paper.pdf (last accessed October 9, 2012).

55 Gabriel Hallevy, *Therapeutic Victim-Offender Mediation within the Criminal Justice Process—Sharpening The Evaluation of Personal Potential for Rehabilitation While Righting Wrongs under the ADR Philosophy*, 16 Harv. Negot. L. Rev. 65, 73–74 (2011). *See generally* Walgrave, *supra* note 45.

56 See Christopher D. Lee, *They All Laughed at Christopher Columbus When He Said the World Was Round: The Not-So-Radical and Reasonable Need for a Restorative Justice Model Statute*, 30 St. Louis U. Pub. L. Rev. 523, 550 (2011):

> [Sentencing] circles may resemble a court proceeding and include the judge, attorneys, police, and a court reporter The group members sit in an actual circle, and each member is given an opportunity to speak as they are passed the "talking piece." Each member of the circle who is not an official of the court is encouraged to tell their life story in a personal narrative to help the other members of the circle better understand their situation. The final decision is made by a consensus of the entire circle ensuring that "every participant has a stake in the circle's success." If a decision cannot be made, as with other restorative justice processes, the case can be referred to the traditional criminal justice system.

between the parties."[57] As is the case with procedural justice,[58] offenders perceive restorative justice sessions as "more fair and more just" than the traditional criminal justice process.[59] It clearly has an important rehabilitative component[60] as well as a deterrent one.[61] Research suggests that restorative justice processes have been successful in many states,[62] and there is some evidence that judicial officials are aware of its potential power.[63]

Writing most recently, Braithwaite and a colleague have concluded, "It is never too late to retrieve restorative justice from punitive justice, reconciliation over a

---

57 Sally Goldfarb, *Reconceiving Civil Protection Orders for Domestic Violence: Can Law Help End the Abuse Without Ending the Relationship?* 29 Cardozo L. Rev. 1487, 1518 (2008).

58 *See* Gal & Shidlo-Hezroni, *supra* note 44, at 151, discussing how restorative justice increases "perceptions of fairness."

59 Hafemeister, Garner & Bath, *supra* note 23, at 198, citing, inter alia, Barton Poulson, *A Third Voice: A Review of Empirical Research on the Psychological Outcomes of Restorative Justice*, 2003 Utah L. Rev. 167, 178–98; Responsive Regulation, *supra* note 43, at 78 (same). See also, Mark S. Umbreit et al., *The Impact of Victim-Offender Mediation: Two Decades of Research*, 65 Fed. Probation 29, 30 (2001) (reporting on recent study showing that 80% of victims felt that the process and result was fair in restorative justice cases compared with the 37% who went through the traditional criminal justice system); Leena Kurki, *Evaluating Restorative Justice Practices*, in Restorative Justice, *supra* note 43, at 293, 310 (research reveals "participant satisfaction [and] procedural justice in most restorative justice initiatives"); Mara Schiff, *Models, Challenges and the Promise of Restorative Conferencing Strategies*, in Restorative Justice, *supra* note 43, at 315, 325 (defendants treated through restorative justice mechanisms felt they were treated more fairly than did defendants who had been processed through the courts"). On how the justness of outcomes in the criminal justice system can be insured through the use of restorative justice, see Walgrave, *supra* note 45, at 561. Importantly, some critics of restorative justice argue that this approach "can trample rights because of impoverished articulation of procedural safeguards," see Responsive Regulation, supra note 43, at 164, and see *id.* at 164–66. I discuss the implications of this position for the substantive criminal procedure topics that are the core of this book *infra* Chapters 8–10.

60 *See generally* Lucy Clark Sanders, *Restorative Justice: The Attempt To Rehabilitate Criminal Offenders and Victims*, 2 Charleston L. Rev. 923 (2008).

61 Responsive Regulation, *supra* note 43, at 82, quoting Lawrence Sherman, *Defiance, Deterrrence and Irrelevance: A Theory of the Criminal Sanction,* 30 J. Res. Crime & Delinq. 444, 448–49 (1993); Responsive Regulation, *supra* note 43, at 120–22.

62 David M. Lerman, *Restoring Dignity, Effecting Justice,* 26 Hum. Rts. Q. 20, 20–21 (Fall 1999) (describing successful restorative justice processes in Minnesota, Wisconsin, and Iowa).

63 *See, e.g.*, Chief Justice Elliott Maynard, *State of the Judiciary Address*, 2004 W.Va. Law. 8, 9 (April 2004):

> As we learn more about treatment for mental illness and as our jails and prisons become more crowded, the courts must learn how to use community sentencing alternatives to provide therapeutic and restorative justice.

criminal injustice system (indeed from within its bowels), truth and memory from a history of lies and forgetting."[64] According to Professor David Dolinko:

> Restorative justice involves thinking of crime in a quite different manner from the long-established picture of "a violation of the state, defined by lawbreaking and guilt" and subject to a criminal justice mechanism that "determines blame and administers pain in a contest between the offender and the state directed by systematic rules." Restorative justice instead envisions crime as "a violation of people and relationships" that "creates obligations to make things right" and justice as a process that "involves the victim, the offender, and the community in a search for solutions which promote repair, reconciliation, and reassurance." For restorative justice proponents, "crime is defined by the harm it has caused to victims, and the primary function of the reaction against it is … to repair or compensate for the harm.[65]

Howard Zehr lists four categories of needs that restorative justice addresses: (1) accountability that addresses the resulting harms, that encourages empathy and responsibility, and transforms shame; (2) encouragement to experience personal transformation, including healing for the harms that contributed to their offending behavior, opportunities for treatment for addictions and/or other problems, and enhancement of personal competencies; (3) encouragement and support for integration into the community; and (4), for some, at least temporary restraint.[66]

---

64 John Braithwaite & Ray Nickson, *Timing Truth, Reconciliation, and Justice after War*, 27 Ohio St. J. on Disp. Resol. 443, 473 (2012). *See also* Braithwaite, *supra* note 43.

65 David Dolinko, *Restorative Justice and the Justification of Punishment*, 2003 Utah L. Rev. 319, 320, quoting, in part, Zehr, *supra* note 48, at 181. Compare Lode Walgrave, *Investigating the Potentials of Restorative Justice Practice*, 36 Wash. U. J.L. & Pol'y 91, 137 (2011) ("As restorative justice is mostly being implemented in the context of or mandated by the criminal justice system, more evaluation should address the relation between the restorative justice agencies and the criminal justice institution"). For a discussion of the full array of criminal justice-based restorative justice initiatives, see Lee, *supra* note 56, at 544–58. On the relationship between punishment and restorative justice, see Walgrave, *supra* note 45, at 566–69.

66 Howard Zehr, The Little Book of Restorative Justice 36 (2002), as discussed in Ikpa, *supra* note 45, at 304 n.12. On the relationship, in general, between the due process rights protected by the criminal justice system and restorative justice, see Skelton & Sekhonyane, *supra* note 50, at 580, 581–82. Compare. Lee, *supra* note 56, at 561–62 (footnotes omitted):

> Due process rights are also a key concern in the restorative justice process. Without special protection, restorative justice may become just another form of plea bargaining, a practice which has been questioned by the Supreme Court and debatably leads to the deprivation of certain fundamental rights of the defendant.

3. Restorative justice and defendants with mental disabilities

Is this restoration process even "on the table" in the criminal justice system in cases involving defendants with mental disabilities (or, in the context of the wider restorative justice movement, *victims* with mental disabilities)?[67] Some preliminary work considers the amenability of defendants in mental health courts to restorative justice sessions,[68] and scholars agree that restorative justice "recognizes that a criminal act has many consequences which are not addressed by the traditional model of criminal justice,"[69] but these insights have generally not been applied directly to the cohorts of cases under consideration in this work,[70] at least not in the United States.[71] Importantly, John Braithwaite sees restorative

---

67 For a discussion of the integration of restorative justice in traditional criminal justice, *see* Leena Kurkie, *Incorporating Restorative and Community Justice into American Sentencing and Corrections*, in SENTENCING & CORRECTIONS: ISSUES FOR THE 21ST CENTURY (US Dep't of Justice, Office of Justice Programs, Nat'l Inst. of Justice 1999), SUDOC J 28.24:SE 5/2/NO.3. On the need for training of counsel in restorative justice approaches, *see* Stephens, *supra* note 54, at 53–54. Persons suffering from mental illness are far more likely to be to be victims of violent crime than are members of the general population, *see, e.g.* Brent Teasdale, *Mental Disorder and Violent Victimization*, 36 CRIM. JUST. & BEHAV. 513 (2009), and people with mental illness constitute a vulnerable population much more likely to be the victim of a crime than the perpetrator, *see, e.g.*, Danile Lauber, *A Real LULU: Zoning for Group Homes and Halfway Houses Under the Fair Housing Amendments Act of 1988*, 29 J. MARSHALL L. REV. 369, 377–78 (1996).

68 *See* Hafemeister, Garner & Bath, *supra* note 23, at 221. On the concerns about how restorative justice may "widen the net of social control," see RESPONSIVE REGULATION, *supra* note 44, at 148–50. On the concern that mental health courts, *see supra* Chapter 5, similarly "widen the net," see Heather Barr, *Connecting Litigation to a Grass Roots Movement: Monitoring, Organizing, and Brad H. v. City of New York*, 24 PACE L. REV. 721, 728 (2004).

69 *See, e.g.*, Michael Cobden & Judge Ron Albers, *Beyond the Squabble: Putting the Tenderloin Community Justice Center in Context*, 7 HASTINGS RACE & POVERTY L. J. 53, 56 (2010), citing Gregory Toomey, *Community Courts 101: A Quick Survey Course*, 42 IDAHO L. REV. 383, 391 (2006); *see also* Joanna Shapland, *Restorative Justice and Criminal Justice: Just Responses to Crime?*, in RESTORATIVE JUSTICE, *supra* note 43, at 195, 210 (discussing restorative justice in the context of mental health tribunals in the UK).

70 But *see* Ikpa, *supra* note 45, discussing restorative justice in the insanity defense context, and see, Jeffrey Fagan & Victoria Malkin, *Theorizing Community Justice Through Community Courts,* 30 FORDHAM URB.L.J. 897, 903 (2003) (footnote omitted):

> From the outside, much of the "community justice model" from drug courts and mental health courts to restorative justice and the new "sanctioning circles" can be read as an attempt by the criminal justice system to respond to these challenges.

71 *See, e.g.,* Julian V. Roberts & Kent Roach, *Restorative Justice in Canada: From Sentencing Circles to Sentencing Principles*, in RESTORATIVE JUSTICE, *supra* note 43, at 237; Allison Morris & Gabrielle Maxwell, *Restorative Justice in New Zealand,* in RESTORATIVE JUSTICE, *supra* note 43, at 257.

justice as a means of "dissuad[ing] hasty resort to … stigmatizing response."[72] And there is some evidence that one value of restorative justice practices is to "avoid the detrimental *mental health consequences* victims experience as a result of their contact with the adversarial criminal justice system."[73] But this does not consider the potential impacts on defendants in such cases.[74] Until such time as the criminal justice system takes these issues seriously—in the whole range of cases involving litigants with mental disabilities,[75] *not just* those in which questions such

72 John Braithwaite, *Principles of Restorative Justice, in Restorative Justice*, *supra* note 43 at 1, 1, and *id.* at 17 ("we should abolish … stigma as [a] doctrine[]"); RESPONSIVE REGULATION, *supra* note 43, at 74 ("stigmatization … makes crime worse"). On the relationship between stigma and sanism (*see supra* Chapter 2), *see, e.g.*, Michael L. Perlin, *"What's Good Is Bad, What's Bad Is Good, You'll Find out When You Reach the Top, You're on the Bottom": Are the Americans with Disabilities Act (and Olmstead v. L.C.) Anything More than "Idiot Wind"?*, 35 U. MICH. J. L. REF. 235, 238 (2001–02) ("Underlying sanism's power is the malignancy of stigma").

73 Lorenn Walker & Rebecca Greening, *Huikahi Restorative Circles: A Public Health Approach for Reentry Planning*, 74 FED. PROBATION 43, 44 (June 2010), citing Jim Parsons & Tiffany Bergin, *The Impact of Criminal Justice Involvement on Victims' Mental Health*, 23 J. TRAUMATIC STRESS 182 (2010) (emphasis added). On the potential "zealous" advocacy role for a lawyer in advising her client about the pros and cons of participating in a restorative justice conference, *see* Ikpa, *supra* note 45, at 324 n.109.

74 Compare Skelton & Sekhonyane, *supra* note 50, at 585 ("It is likely that the rights of those who are disempowered, excluded and vulnerable due to [economic, social and racial] inequalities will be at risk in restorative justice practices"), and *id.,* discussing the threat to rights posed by "power imbalances"—"arising from differences such as race, class, culture, age and gender"—in restorative justice programs. Gal and Shidlo-Hezroni acknowledge that the "extreme power imbalance" present in child abuse and domestic violence cases "presents a serious challenge to restorative justice," Gal & Shidlo-Hezroni, *supra* note 45, at 154, but note that RJ has also "empower[ed] young victims to speak up even in front of adults," *id.* On the significance of power imbalances on the mental disability law process, see Michael L. Perlin, *Pretexts and Mental Disability Law: The Case of Competency*, 47 U. MIAMI L. REV. 625, 653 (1993); *see generally* Michael L. Perlin, *Power Imbalances in Therapeutic and Forensic Relationships*, 9 BEHAV. SCI. & L. 111 (1991).

75 On the value of restorative justice in the cases of individuals who are members of minority groups "alienated from the criminal justice system," see Anthony Bottoms, *Some Sociological Reflections on Restorative Justice*, in RESTORATIVE JUSTICE, *supra* note 43, at 79, 105–06. On how persons with mental disabilities are, similarly, often seen as "The Other" and alienated from mainstream society, *see* Perlin, *Borderline*, *supra* note 7, at 787:

> (W)e are doing two things: we are distancing ourselves from mentally disabled persons—the "them"—and we are simultaneously trying to construct an impregnable borderline between "us" and "them," both to protect ourselves and to dehumanize what Sander Gilman calls "the Other." The label of "sickness" reassures us that "the Other"—seen as "both ill and infectious, both damaged and damaging" not like us and further animates our "keen … desire to separate 'us' and 'them'."

as incompetency or insanity are raised—I believe it is unlikely that we will ever truly create a system that comports authentically with dignity.[76]

III. On the Relationship Between These Movements

As noted at the beginning of this subchapter, Professor Susan Daicoff has collected multiple jurisprudential developments (including the three under discussion here), and categorized them as "collaborative law."[77] David Wexler, one of the founders of TJ, has argued forcefully for a "robust relationship" between TJ and PJ,[78] arguing that these principles should lead judges "to strive to change the legal culture in their courts."[79]Professors Brian Sellers and Bruce Arrigo see RJ and TJ, together, as reflecting the "cultivation of an integrity-based society … in which the moral fiber of individuals is more fully embraced and the flourishing prospects for human justice are more completely realized."[80] Natalie Des Rosiers conceives of TJ "as a companion to all the new questions surrounding the

---

On marginalization in this context, *see* Michael L. Perlin & John Douard, *"Equality, I Spoke That Word/As If a Wedding Vow": Mental Disability Law and How We Treat Marginalized Persons*, 53 N.Y.L. Sch. L. Rev. 9 (2008–09); Michael L. Perlin, *Competency, Deinstitutionalization, and Homelessness: A Story of Marginalization*, 28 Hous. L. Rev. 63 (1991).

76 On the relationship between restorative justice and *international* criminal justice (*see generally supra* Chapter 4), see Mark Findlay & Ralph Henham, Transforming International Criminal Justice: Retributive and Restorative Justice in the Trial Process 271–75 (2005); Brianne McGonigle, *Two for the Price of One: Attempts by the Extraordinary Chambers in the Courts of Cambodia to Combine Retributive and Restorative Justice Principles*, 22 Leiden J. Int'l L. 127, 136 (2009); Terri Day & Almir Maljevic, *Teaching and Implementing Restorative Justice and Its Relevance to Criminal Justice in Bosnia-Herzegovina in the 21st Century*, 2 Restorative Directives J. 64 (May 2006); Cynthia Alkon, *The Increased Use of "Reconciliation" in Criminal Cases in Central Asia: A Sign of Restorative Justice, Reform or Cause for Concern?*, 8 Pepp. Disp. Resol. L.J. 41, 59–66 (2007); Paul Roberts, *Restoration and Retribution in International Criminal Justice: An Exploratory Analysis*, in Restorative Justice, *supra* note 43, at 115, 117–23. On its relationship to truth and reconciliation commissions, *see* Braithwaite & Nickson, *supra* note 64.

77 *See* Daicoff, *supra* note 1, at 142 n.209.

78 David Wexler, *Adding Color to the White Paper*, 44 Ct. Rev. 78 (2007).

79 *Id.* at 81.

80 Brian G. Sellers & Bruce A. Arrigo, *Adolescent Transfer, Developmental Maturity, and Adjudicative Competence: An Ethical and Justice Policy Inquiry*, 99 J. Crim. L. & Criminology 435, 439 (2009); *see also* Braithwaite, *supra* note 44, at 246 ("[T]he most solid common ground between Therapeutic Jurisprudence and Restorative Justice is that they are both part of a return to problem-oriented adjudication"); Andrew Cannon, *Therapeutic Jurisprudence in Courts: Some Issues of Practice and Principle*, 16 J. Jud'l Admin. 256, 260 (2007):

re-thinking of the adversarial model and the emergence of a restorative justice, or transformative justice model."[81] Professor Lode Walgrave's discussion of the necessity of *diversion* in the RJ process[82] links with the TJ roots of mental health courts[83] that are premised on the diversion of certain defendants from the criminal justice system.[84]

One potential source of conflict here lies in the attitude of restorative justice proponents towards the role of counsel;[85] Braithwaite has taken the position that,

---

> If we are to be truly therapeutic, we need to ensure they move from the regret that they face imprisonment to sorrow for the harm their actions have caused to those around them. This is the obvious link between therapeutic jurisprudence and restorative justice.

On how TJ "includes concepts" of RJ, see Randal Fritzler, *How One Misdemeanor Mental Health Court Incorporates Therapeutic Jurisprudence, Preventive Law, and Restorative Justice*, in MANAGEMENT AND ADMINISTRATION OF CORRECTIONAL HEALTH CARE: POLICY, PRACTICE, ADMINISTRATION 14-1, 14-7 (Jacqueline Moore ed., 2003) Compare Allegra M. McLeod, *Decarceration Courts: Possibilities and Perils of a Shifting Criminal Law*, 100 GEO L.J. 1587, 1613 (2012) (on how therapeutic jurisprudence is farther reaching than restorative justice). On the significance of the different perspectives on accountability and treatment in RJ, TJ and problem-solving courts, *see* Leslie Paik, *Maybe He's Depressed: Mental Illness as a Mitigating Factor for Drug Offender Accountability*, 34 LAW & SOC. INQUIRY 569, 598 (2009).

81 Nathalie Des Rosiers, *From Québec Veto to Québec Secession: The Evolution of the Supreme Court of Canada on Québec-Canada Disputes*, 13 CAN. J.L. & JURIS. 171 173 n. 18 (2000). *See also* Elena Marchetti, & Kathleen Daly, *Indigenous Sentencing Courts: Towards a Theoretical and Jurisprudential Model*, 29 SYDNEY L. REV. 415, 424 n.31 (2007), discussing how the Navajo justice system is an autonomous system based on traditional beliefs and knowledge, which uses some principles from restorative justice and therapeutic jurisprudence.

82 Walgrave, *supra* note 45, at 573.

83 *See supra* Chapter 5.

84 *See, e.g.*, Allison Redlich et al., *Is Diversion Swift: Comparing Mental Health Court and Traditional Criminal Justice Processing*, 39 CRIM. JUST. & BEHAV. 420 (2012). On the risks of "net widening" in RJ proceedings, *see* Skelton & Sekhonyane, *supra* note 50, at 584–85; compare Cait Clarke & James Neuhard. *"From Day One" : Who's in Control as Problem Solving and Client-Centered Sentencing Take Center Stage?*, 29 N.Y.U. REV. L. & SOC. CHANGE 11, 29 (2004) (discussing "net widening" in the context of problem-solving courts), discussed *supra* Chapter 5.

85 *See* Ikpa, *supra* note 45, at 313 (footnotes omitted):

> Restorative justice, be it pre-adjudication or post-adjudication, also poses a problem for the right to counsel. Critics have acknowledged that restorative justice often leaves lawyers out and diminishes their role in the process. Defense attorneys often see their role in advocating for clients as one of avoiding, or at least limiting, punishment. The primary advice they give to clients is to deny guilt if possible. However, this is difficult to achieve in restorative justice systems when the objective is for the offender to acknowledge responsibility.

as restorative justice is intended to "transcend adversarial legalism," there may be no right to counsel at certain RJ proceedings.[86] Contrarily, Christopher Lee has recently argued that "securing counsel for offenders *before* they agree to be enrolled in a restorative justice program," as well as "educating counsel" about the nature of restorative justice, would help assuage constitutional concerns about restorative justice programs.[87] On balance, it appears that the more experience counsel have with restorative justice, "the more positive they are about its potential in the right contexts."[88]

IV. Conclusion

The time has long passed that criminal court judges and administrators can simply shrug and say, "We've always done it this way." The schools of "alternative jurisprudences" that I have discussed in this chapter make eloquently clear that these are alternative approaches available to the provision of criminal justice services—approaches that will help maximize the level of dignity made available to all participants in the system.

I am convinced that all of these observations merely skim the surface of what is in need of further exploration and investigation: how can we synergistically take what we have learned from all of these movements in such a way as to maximize the presence of dignity in the criminal justice practice as it affects persons with mental disabilities?

86 *See* John Braithwaite, *Standards for Restorative Justice*, 42 Brit. J. Criminol. 563, 566 (2002), as discussed in Skelton & Sekhonyane, *supra* note 50, at 583. I disagree with Professor Braithwaite on this one point. *See supra* Chapter 3; *see* Michael L. Perlin, Mental Disability and the Death Penalty: the Shame of the States 123-38 (2013); Michael L. Perlin, *"I Might Need a Good Lawyer, Could Be Your Funeral, My Trial": A Global Perspective on the Right to Counsel in Civil Commitment Cases, and Its Implications for Clinical Legal Education*, 28 Wash. U. J. L. & Soc'l Pol'y 241 (2008).

87 Lee, *supra* note 55, at 561, citing, with approval, Mary Ellen Reimund, *Is Restorative Justice on a Collision Course with the Constitution*, 3 Appalachian J. L. 1, 30–31 (2004) (emphasis added).

88 Bruce P. Archibald, *Coordinating Canada's Restorative and Inclusionary Models of Criminal Justice: The Legal Profession and the Exercise of Discretion under a Reflexive Rule of Law*, 9 Can. Crim. L. Rev. 215, 249–50 (2005).

Another potential conflict between RJ and TJ is over the issue of voluntariness, some critics questioning whether the RJ process truly is "voluntary" in the full sense of that word. *See, e.g.*, Jennifer Gerarda Brown, *The Use of Mediation to Resolve Criminal Cases: A Procedural Critique*, 43 Emory L.J. 1247, 1264 (1994); Cunneen, *supra* note 45, at 146–47. In discussing this dilemma, Tina Ikpa refers to RJ as a "gentler form of coercion." Ikpa, *supra* note 45, at 315.

Chapter 7
Contextualizing Dignity

I. Introduction

As I noted in the introductory chapter, "Each of the chapters in this book must be read through this lens of dignity."[1] In my discussions of each of the topics covered in this chapter—assignment of counsel, application of international human rights doctrines, role of mental health courts, use of alternative jurisprudential approaches—I have sought to consider the interplay between dignitarian values and the issues in question, focusing on their relationship between mental disability and the criminal trial process. In this chapter, I will seek to further contextualize dignity to "set the table" for the remainder of this book, in which I will apply all these concepts to three substantive aspects of the criminal trial process as it relates to persons with mental disabilities: the incompetency status, the insanity defense and sentencing.

II. On Dignity[2]

Professor Carol Sanger suggests that dignity means that people "possess an intrinsic worth that should be recognized and respected," and that they should not be subjected to treatment by the state that is inconsistent with their intrinsic worth.[3] Treating people with dignity and respect makes them more likely to view procedures as fair and the motives behind law enforcement's actions as well meaning.[4] What individuals want most "is a process that allows them to participate, seeks to merit their trust, and treats them with dignity and respect."[5] All concepts of human rights have their basis in some understanding of human dignity.[6] Dignity

---

1 *See supra*, Chapter 1, text following note 34, and text accompanying notes 29–34.

2 *See* Michael L. Perlin, Mental Disability and the Death Penalty: The Shame of the States 11–18 (2013).

3 Carol Sanger, *Decisional Dignity: Teenage Abortion, Bypass Hearings, and the Misuse of Law*, 18 Colum. J. Gender & L. 409, 415 (2009).

4 Tamar R. Birckhead, *Toward a Theory of Procedural Justice for Juveniles*, 57 Buff. L. Rev. 1447, 1474 (2009).

5 Luther Munford, *The Peacemaker Test: Designing* Legal *Rights to Reduce Legal Warfare*, 12 Harv. Negot. L. Rev. 377, 393 (2007).

6 Soka Gakkai International, *Buddhism and Human Dignity* (accessible at http://www.sgi.org/buddhism/buddhist-concepts/buddhism-and-human-dignity.html, last accessed, October 9, 2012).

has been characterized as one of "those very great political values that defines our constitutional morality."[7]

The legal process upholds human dignity by allowing the litigant—including the criminal defendant—to tell his or her own story.[8] A notion of individual dignity, "generally articulated through concepts of autonomy, respect, equality, and freedom from undue government interference, was at the heart of a jurisprudential and moral outlook that resulted in the reform, not only of criminal procedure, but of the various institutions more or less directly linked with the criminal justice system, including juvenile courts, prisons, and mental institutions."[9] Fair process norms such as the right to counsel "operate as substantive and procedural restraints on state power to ensure that the individual suspect is treated with dignity and respect"[10] Dignity concepts are expansive; a Canadian Supreme Court case has declared that disenfranchisement of incarcerated persons violated their dignity interests.[11] By way of example, "the moral dignity of the criminal process would be frustrated if grossly incompetent defendants were permitted to plead guilty."[12] Perhaps counter-intuitively to much of the lay public, dignity may trump "truth" as a core value of the criminal justice system.[13]

---

7 William A. Parent, *Constitutional Values and Human Dignity*, in THE CONSTITUTION OF RIGHTS: HUMAN DIGNITY AND AMERICAN VALUES 47, 71 (Michael J. Meyer & William A. Parent eds, 1992).

8 Katherine Kruse, *The Human Dignity of Clients*, 93 CORNELL L. REV. 1343, 1353 (2008).

9 Eric Miller, *Embracing Addiction: Drug Courts and the False Promise of Judicial Interventionism*, 65 OHIO ST.L.J. 1479, 1569 n.473 (2004).

10 Peter Arenella, *Rethinking the Functions of Criminal Procedure: The Warren and Burger Courts' Competing Ideologies*, 72 GEO. L.J. 185, 200 (1983).

11 Sauvé v. Canada, [2002] 3 S.C.R. 519, discussed in this context in Michael Pinard, *Collateral Consequences of Criminal Convictions: Confronting Issues of Race and Dignity*, 85 N.Y.U. L. REV. 457, 464 (2010).

12 Bruce J. Winick, *Reforming Incompetency to Stand Trial and Plead Guilty: A Restated Proposal and a Response to Professor Bonnie*, 85 J. CRIM. L. & CRIMINOLOGY 571, 593 (1995); see *infra* Chapter 8. On the specific importance of moral dignity in the death penalty context, see J. Amy Dillard, *Madness Alone Punishes the Madman : The Search for Moral Dignity in the Court's Competency Doctrine as Applied in Capital Cases*, 79 TENN. L. REV. 461 (2012). For a transnational consideration of this issue, see Russell Miller, *The Shared Transatlantic Jurisprudence of Dignity*, 4 GERMAN L.J. 925 (2003) (suggesting that value of dignity may lead to the eradication of the death penalty).

13 Erik Luna & Paul G. Cassell, *Mandatory Minimalism*, 32 CARDOZO L. RV. 1, 52 (2010). On the application of human dignity principles to limit the scope of criminalization of victimless crimes (specifically, drug offenses), see Michal Buchhandler-Raphael, *Drugs, Dignity, and Danger: Human Dignity as a Constitutional Constraint to Limit Overcriminalization*, 80 TENN. L. REV. — (2013) (in press), accessible at http://papers.ssrn.com/sol3/papers.cfm?abstract_id=2128943.

III. Dignity in the Criminal Justice Process

The right to dignity is memorialized in many state constitutions,[14] in multiple international human rights documents,[15] in judicial opinions,[16] and in the

14 *See*, e.g., John D. Castiglione, *Human Dignity under the Fourth Amendment*, 2008 Wis. L. Rev. 655, 690 n.182 (listing provisions).

15 *See* Johanna Kalb, *Litigating Dignity: A Human Rights Framework*, 74 Alb. L. Rev. 1725, 1726 (2010–11) ("the notion of a right to dignity has assumed a prominent role in many international human rights instruments"); *see also*, Michael L. Perlin, International Human Rights and Mental Disability Law: When the Silenced Are Heard 37–41 (2011); Astrid Birgden & Michael L. Perlin, *"Where The Home In The Valley Meets The Damp Dirty Prison": A Human Rights Perspective On Therapeutic Jurisprudence And The Role Of Forensic Psychologists In Correctional Settings*, 14 Aggression & Violent Behavior 256 (2009); Michael L. Perlin & Henry A. Dlugacz, *"It's Doom Alone That Counts": Can International Human Rights Law Be An Effective Source of Rights in Correctional Conditions Litigation?*, 27 Behav. Sci. & L. 675 (2009); Tony Ward & Astrid Birgden, *Human Rights and Clinical Correctional Practice*, 12 Aggression & Viol. Behav. 628 (2007); Neomi Rao, *On the Use and Abuse of Dignity in Constitutional Law*, 14 Colum. J. Eur. L. 201, 216 (2008). On the specific role of human dignity values in an international human rights context, *see* Human Dignity: The Internationalization of Human Rights (Alice Henkin ed., 1979); *see generally* Man Yee Karen Lee, *The Chinese People's Struggle for Democracy and China's Long Quest f*or Dignity, 27 Conn. J. Int'l L. 207, 216 (2012) (since 1948, "dignity has featured prominently in all major international human rights treaties").

16 The United States Supreme Court began to refer to dignity in individual rights cases regularly in the 1940s, *see* Rao, *supra* note 15, at 239–40; although it has "not given human dignity the sort of independent weight found in [other] countries." *Id.* at 239; *see* Erin Daly, *Human Dignity in the Roberts Court: A Story of Inchoate Institutions, Autonomous Individuals, and the Reluctant Recognition of a Right*, 37 Ohio N.U. L. Rev. 381, 381 (2011): *see generally* Judith Resnik & Julie Chi-hye Suk, *Adding Insult to Injury: Questioning the Role of Dignity in Conceptions of Sovereignty*, 55 Stan. L. Rev. 1921 (2003); Buchhandler-Raphael, *supra* note 13, manuscript at 22–25. From the very beginning, the Supreme Court of the United States has recognized that dignity is relevant to the interpretation and application of the Constitution. Indeed, the Court has referred to dignity almost 1,000 times in its 200-plus year history. Most famously, see Schmerber v. California, 384 U.S. 757, 767, 769–70 (1966) ("The interests in human dignity and privacy which the Fourth Amendment protects forbid 'invasive behavior by the state'"); Trop v. Dulles, 356 U.S. 86, 100 (1958) ("[t]he basic concept underlying the Eighth Amendment is nothing less than the dignity of man"), and Irvin v. Dowd, 366 U.S. 717, 721 (1966) ("England, from whom the Western World has largely taken its concepts of individual liberty and of the dignity and worth of every man, has bequeathed to us safeguards for their preservation, the most priceless of which is that of trial by jury"). *See also*, *e.g.*, Marquez v. Collins, 11 F. 3d 1241, 1243 (5th Cir. 1994) ("Solemnity ... and respect for individuals are components of. a fair trial"); Heffernan v. Norris, 48 F. 3d 331, 336 (8th Cir. 1995) (Bright, J., dissenting) ("the forced ingestion of mind-altering drugs not only jeopardizes an accused's right to a fair trial, it also tears away another layer of individual dignity, rendering the criminal trial particularly dehumanizing"); Supt. of Belchertown State School v. Saikewicz, 370 N.E.2d 417, 428 (Mass. 1977) ("Like persons

constitutions of other nations.[17] It is of special significance in the criminal justice process, both at the individual level[18] and at the institutional level.[19] Dignity requires that all individuals be given an opportunity to participate in a political and social community supported by the state.[20] Professor Johanna Kalb concludes: "Even in the absence of an explicit constitutional provision, the notion of personal dignity can act as a significant restraint on governmental action."[21]

In his exhaustive evaluation of dignity in the specific context of international human rights law, Professor Christopher McCrudden reviews cases from the

---

suffering from mental illness, courts 'must recognize the dignity and worth of such a person' with mental retardation or developmental disabilities"). For a relatively recent opinion (in an adequacy of counsel case involving a defendant with a severe mental disability), see State v. Rovin, 201 P. 3d 780, 787, ¶ 39 (Mont. 2009) (Nelson, J., concurring), criticizing the majority's reasoning in a case revoking a suspended sentence):

> While this approach may temporarily protect the public, it does little to treat the underlying cause of the individual's mental health problems; it does little to rehabilitate the individual so as to give him or her a chance to be a productive citizen; and it does little to protect the inviolable human dignity possessed by each of these individuals.

For an even more-recent opinion, see People v. Barrett, 281 P.3d 753, 144 Cal.Rptr.3d 661, 687 (2012) (Liu, J., concurring & dissenting):

> I conclude that there is no rational basis for denying Barrett—simply because she was alleged to be mentally retarded—the same advisement and the same dignity afforded by such an advisement to which other persons with mental disabilities are statutorily entitled when facing prolonged involuntary commitment.

17 *See, e.g.*, Arthur Chaskalson, *Dignity as a Constitutional Value: A South African Perspective*, 26 Am. U. Int'l L. Rev. 1377 (2011). For a helpful history, see Doron Schultziner, *Human Dignity in National Constitutions* (unpublished manuscript; on file with author). For a comparative analysis, see Doron Schultziner, *Human Dignity in a Cross Cultural Perspective* (unpublished manuscript; on file with author).

18 "At the individual level, the legal process upholds human dignity by allowing the criminal defendant to tell his own story." Katherine R. Kruse, *The Human Dignity of Clients*, 93 Cornell L. Rev. 1343, 1353 (2008), discussing David Luban, *Lawyers as Upholders of Human Dignity (When They Aren't Busy Assaulting It)*, in David Luban, Legal Ethics and Human Dignity 68–72 (2007).

19 "At the institutional level, the legal process upholds a criminal defendant's human dignity by allowing him to remain silent—to put the state to its proof of guilt beyond a reasonable doubt—and to argue any inferences that are consistent with innocence, even if the defendant (and his lawyer) know that these inferences are in fact false." Kruse, *supra* note 18, at 1353–54 discussing Luban, *supra* note 18, at 72–73.

20 Rao, *supra* note 15, at 219–20. *See also*, Kalb, *supra* note 15, at 1737–38:

> Giving content to "dignity" could increase the role it plays in informing a court's decisionmaking and, given its roots in international human rights law, advocates should refer courts back to this source for suggestions as to its development.

21 Kalb, *supra* note 15, at 1733.

International Court of Justice, the European Court of Human Rights, the European Court of Justice and the constitutional courts of many nations, and finds multiple categories of cases in which "dignity" is relied on as a basis for a court's judgment:

- cases involving prohibition of inhuman treatment, humiliation, or degradation by one person over another;[22]
- cases involving individual choice and the conditions for self-fulfillment, autonomy, and self-realization;
- cases involving protection of group identity and culture; and
- cases involving the creation of necessary conditions for individuals to have essential needs satisfied.[23]

The connection between these principles and the topics under discussion in this book should be clear. If a state intends to meet international human rights standards, it should guarantee, among other fundamental rights, the right to dignity in all aspects of the criminal trial process.[24] Dignity is a core component of restorative justice,[25] and of procedural justice.[26] Therapeutic jurisprudence emphasizes the treatment of participants in the legal process with dignity.[27] Dignity is the essence

---

22 On the connection between dignity and humiliation, see Daniel Statman, *Humiliation, Dignity and Self-Respect*, 13 Phil. Psychol. 523 (2000). The relationship between dignity and humiliation has developed into an important field of study. See http://humiliationstudies.org/index.php, and the Journal of Human Dignity and Humiliation Studies.

23 Christoper McCrudden, *Human Dignity and the Judicial Interpretation of Human Rights*, 19 Eur. J. Int'l L. 655, 686–94 (2008). On the multiple meanings of dignity in the context of court opinions, see Rex D. Glensy, *The Right to Dignity*, 43 Colum. Hum. Rts. L. Rev. 65 (2011).

24 *See* Rett R. Ludwikowski, *Fundamental Constitutional Rights in the New Constitutions of Eastern and Central Europe* 3 Cardozo J. Int'l & Comp. L. 73, 75 (1995).

25 *See* Mijha Butcher, *Using Mediation to Remedy Civil Rights Violations When the Defendant is Not an Intentional Perpetrator: The Problems of Unconscious Disparate Treatment and Unjustified Disparate Impacts*, 24 Hamline J. Pub. L. & Pol'y 225, 252 (2003) (restorative justice is a focus on the "restoration of human dignity"); David M. Lerman, *Restoring Dignity, Effecting Justice*, 26 Hum. Rts. Q. 20, 20–21 (Fall 1999) (describing successful restorative justice processes in several states). On restorative dignity, see Judith Baker, *Truth Commissions*, 51 U. Toronto L.J. 309, 321 (2001); *see generally* Joan W. Howarth, *Toward the Restorative Constitution: A Restorative Justice Critique of Anti-Gang Public Nuisance Injunctions*, 27 Hastings Const. L.Q. 717, 720 n.10 (2000) (citing research articles).

26 *See* Joseph B. Stulberg, *Mediation and Justice: What Standards Govern?*, 6 Cardozo J. Conflict Resol. 213, 227–28 (2005); Tom R. Tyler & E. Allan Lind, *Procedural Justice*, in Handbook of Justice Research in Law 65, 74–77 (Joseph Sanders & V. Lee Hamilton eds, 2001).

27 *See* Christina A. Zawisza & Adela Beckerman, *Two Heads Are Better Than One: The Case-Based Rationale for Dual Disciplinary Teaching in Child Advocacy Clinics*, 7

of the successful mental health court.[28] And one of the critical functions of counsel is to "protect the dignity and autonomy of a person on trial."[29]

Some cases scream out at us. Consider the trial in *Panetti v. Quarterman,*[30] the case that eventually led to the United States Supreme Court decision that a prisoner must possess a "rational understanding" of the reasons he is to be executed before the death penalty could be carried out.[31] Panetti, who had been convicted of capital murder in the slayings of his estranged wife's parents, had been hospitalized numerous times for serious psychiatric disorders.[32] Notwithstanding his "bizarre," scary" and "trance-like" behavior, he was found competent to stand trial and competent to waive counsel.[33] There can be no disputing Professor Richard Bonnie's conclusion about Panetti's trial:

FLA. COASTAL L. REV. 631, 643 (2006); David C. Yamada, *Human Dignity and American Employment Law*, 43 U. RICH. L. REV. 523 (2009).

28 Michael L. Perlin, *"There Are No Trials Inside the Gates of Eden": Mental Health Courts, the Convention on the Rights of Persons with Disabilities, Dignity, and the Promise of Therapeutic Jurisprudence*, in COERCIVE CARE: LAW AND POLICY (Bernadette McSherry & Ian Freckelton eds, 2013) (in press), relying on, inter alia, Norman Poythress et al., *Perceived Coercion and Procedural Justice in the Broward Mental Health Court*, 25 INT'L J. L. & PSYCHIATRY 517 (2002).

29 Jones v. Barnes, 463 U.S. 745, 759 (1983) (Brennan, J., dissenting). *See also, e.g.*, Philip Halpern, *Government Intrusion into the Attorney-Client Relationship: An Interest Analysis of Rights and Remedies*, 32 BUFF. L. REV. 127, 172 (1983) ("The right to counsel embraces two separate interests: reliable and fair determinations in criminal proceedings, and treatment of defendants with dignity and respect regardless of the effect on the outcome of criminal proceedings.").

30 551 U.S. 930 (2007). This issue is discussed in depth *infra* Chapter 8.

31 *Id.* at 956–58.

32 *Panetti*, 551 U.S. at 936.

33 *Id.*; *see generally* Michael L. Perlin, *"Good and Bad, I Defined These Terms, Quite Clear No Doubt Somehow": Neuroimaging and Competency to be Executed after Panetti*, 28 BEHAV. SCI. & L. 621 (2010).While representing himself, Panetti wore a purple cowboy costume, rambled incoherently, gestured threateningly at jurors, went into trances, nodded off, and tried to subpoena people like Jesus Christ and John F. Kennedy. See Rebecca J. Covarubias, *Lives in Defense Counsel's Hands: The Problems and Responsibilities of Defense Counsel Representing Mentally Ill or Mentally Retarded Capital Defendants*, 11 SCHOLAR 413, 463–64 nn.292–93 (2009), relying upon Todd J. Gillman & Diane Jennings, *Justices Block Execution of Texas Killer: Death for Schizophrenic Is Cruel and Unusual, Supreme Court Rules*, DALLAS MORNING NEWS, June 29, 2007, at A12, and Ralph Blumenthal, *Insanity Issue Lingers as Texas Execution Is Set*, N.Y. TIMES, Feb. 4, 2004, at A12. The Supreme Court eventually vacated Panetti's conviction, and established new rules for determining the competency of a severely mentally ill defendant to be executed. *See generally* PERLIN, *supra* note 2, at 69–84, and *infra* Chapter.8.

> Courts trivialize mental illness, disserve the important principle of autonomy … and compromise the dignity of the law when they allow defendants as disturbed as Panetti to represent themselves in criminal trials.[34]

Although one of the basic tenets of the criminal justice system is that "the trial of an incompetent defendant would undercut the dignity and decorum of the criminal justice system,"[35] it is clear that *many* such defendants are regularly tried, both *pro se*[36]and when represented by counsel.[37] Nothing has transpired in the past 20 years to cause us to question the wisdom of Benjamin Vernia's observation: "The pathetic spectacle of the trial of an incompetent defendant diminishes society's respect for the dignity of the criminal justice process."[38]

Similar issues arise in the context of a decision to enter an insanity plea:

> The decisions addressed by this article offer a perfect example of the difficulty of such a method of categorization: the decision whether to present evidence

---

34 Richard Bonnie, *Panetti v. Quarterman: Mental Illness, The Death Penalty, and Human Dignity*, 5 Ohio St. J. Crim. L. 257, 262 (2007). *See also* Jennifer W. Corinis, *A Reasoned Standard for Competency to Waive Counsel after Godinez v. Moran*, 80 B.U. L. Rev. 265, 288 (2000) ("To achieve the fundamental fairness, dignity, and integrity for which a legitimate system of criminal justice must strive, however, we cannot allow mentally disabled defendants to use the courts as instruments of self-destruction") (written seven years before the *Panetti* decision).

35 Paula Siuta Eichner, *Cooper v. Oklahoma and the Fundamental Right Not to Be Tried While Incompetent*, 24 New Eng. J. on Crim. & Civ. Confinement 511, 518 (1998), citing Bruce J. Winick, *Restructuring Competency to Stand Trial*, 32 UCLA L. Rev. 921, 952 (1985).

36 *See, e.g.*, Michael L. Perlin, *"Dignity Was the First to Leave":* Godinez v. Moran, *Colin Ferguson, and the Trial of Mentally Disabled Criminal Defendants*, 14 Behav. Sci. & L. 61 (1996); Bonnie, *supra* note 34.

37 *See, e.g.*, Josephine Ross, *Autonomy Versus a Client's Best Interests: The Defense Lawyer's Dilemma When Mentally Ill Clients Seek to Control Their Defense,* 35 Am. Crim. L. Rev. 1343, 1347 (1998) (some defendants, in spite of being found competent, "are incompetent to make decisions in their cases"), as discussed in Sara Longtain, *The Twilight of Competency and Mental Illness: A Conciliatory Conception of Competency and Insanity,* 43 Hous. L. Rev. 1563, 1564 (2007). *See also* United States v. Sermon, 228 F. Supp. 972, 978 (W.D. Mo. 1964). (defendant with severe memory loss, although very limited in ability to assist attorney, still found competent); United States v. MacDonald, 43 Fed. App'x 330 (10th Cir. 2002) (defendant found competent despite "occasional delusional verbalizations"); Burt v. Uchtman, 422 F.3d 557 (7th Cir. 2005) (defendant in capital case allowed to proceed after expressing difficulty communicating with attorney, testing at borderline IQ and having documented neurological impairments); Woods v. State, 994 S.W.2d 32 (Mo. Ct. App. 1999) (defendant allowed to proceed to trial despite ongoing delusions and a suicide attempt on the first day of trial).

38 Benjamin Vernia, *The Burden of Proving Competence to Stand Trial: Due Process at the Limits of Adversarial Justice*, 45 Vand. L. Rev. 199, 201 (1992).

> of mental illness and/or assert a mental health defense can be characterized as a strategic decision regarding the optimal means to defend a case, but in most cases such a decision also fundamentally implicates the client's objectives and personal dignity.[39]

IV. Conclusion

In short, dignity inquiries permeate the criminal justice system, especially as the concept applies to persons with mental disabilities. In the subsequent chapters in this book, I will seek to contextualize the issues that I discussed in the earlier portions of this chapter—adequacy of counsel, international human rights, mental health courts and alternative jurisprudences—with what we know about the significance of dignity in an effort to examine how the criminal justice process can better provide justice in cases of defendants with mental disabilities.

---

39 Martin Sabelli & Stacey Leyton, *Train Wrecks and Freeway Crashes: An Argument for Fairness and Against Self Representation in the Criminal Justice System*, 91 J. Crim. L. & Criminology 161, 182–83 (2000).

PART III
The Substantive Areas

Chapter 8
Competencies

I. **Introduction**

Although far more public and media attention is focused on cases involving insanity defense pleas and verdicts, the incompetency-to-stand-trial status is numerically far more significant in the administration of criminal justice. In this chapter, I will focus first on the state of the law of criminal competencies, as it applies to (1) standing trial, (2) waiving counsel and pleading guilty, and (3) the execution of a death row defendant with serious mental disabilities. I will then consider these substantive law developments in the context of the four factors that I discussed in Chapter 2—sanism, pretextuality, heuristics and "ordinary common sense"—and will evaluate them in the context of the five perspectives I discussed in Chapter 3: adequacy of counsel, international human rights developments, mental health courts, alternative jurisprudences, and the role of dignity. I will repeat this approach in the two following chapters, dealing with the insanity defense and sentencing.

II. Incompetency to Stand Trial

A. Substantive Standards[1]

1. Historical background

Few principles are as firmly embedded in Anglo-American criminal jurisprudence as the doctrine that an "incompetent" defendant may not be put to trial.[2] The

---

1 This section is largely adapted from 4 Michael L. Perlin, Mental Disability Law: Civil and Criminal, §8A-2.1 to 2.3, at 2–41 (2d ed. 2002), and Michael L. Perlin, *Competency to Stand Trial,* in Crime and Mental Illness: A Guide to Courtroom Practice 23 (Robert Sadoff & Frank Dattillio eds, 2008).

2 The incompetency-to-stand-trial determination has always been a numerically significant one. *See, e.g.*, Henry Steadman, Beating a Rap? Defendants Found Incompetent to Stand Trial 4 (1979) (approximately 9,000 defendants adjudicated incompetent yearly; 36,000 potentially incompetent defendants evaluated). For other empirical surveys, *see* sources cited in Bruce Winick, *Restructuring Competency to Stand Trial,* 32 UCLA L. Rev. 921, 922–23 (1985); *see generally* Gary Melton, et al., Psychological Evaluations for the Courts: A Handbook for Mental Health Professionals and Lawyers (2d ed. 1997). Professor Winick has characterized the costs of competency evaluations as "staggering." Winick, *supra* at 928. The numerical significance of incompetency determinations contrasts sharply with the remarkably few insanity defense cases adjudicated yearly. *See, e.g.*, Joseph

doctrine is traditionally traced to mid-seventeenth-century England,[3] with commentators generally focusing on: (1) the incompetent defendant's inability to aid in his defense;[4] (2) the parallels to the historic ban on trials *in absentia*;[5] and (3) the parallels to the problems raised by defendants who refused to plead to the charges entered against them.[6]

The primary purpose of the rule was, under all theories, to "safeguard the accuracy of adjudication,"[7] and, as early as 1899, a federal court of appeals held that it was "not 'due process of law' to subject an insane person (sic) to trial upon an indictment involving liberty or life."[8] Contemporaneously, a state supreme court suggested, "[i]t would be inhumane, and to a certain extent a denial of a trial on the merits, to require one who has been disabled by the act of God from intelligently making his defense to plead or to be tried for his life or liberty."[9]

Thus, it became black letter law that the "trial and conviction of a person mentally and physically incapable of making a defense violates certain immutable principles of justice which inhere in the very idea of a free government."[10] *First*, an incompetent defendant might alone have exculpatory information that he is incapable of transmitting to counsel.[11] *Second*, to try an incompetent defendant

---

Rodriguez, Michael L. Perlin & Laura M. LeWinn, *The Insanity Defense under Siege: Legislative Assaults and Legal Rejoinders*, 14 Rutgers L.J. 397, 401 (1983) (of 32,500 criminal cases studied in 1982, insanity defense raised in only 50, and was successful in only 15). *See also* Myths and Realities: A Report of the National Commission on the Insanity Defense 16 (1983) (paraphrasing testimony by Dr. Alan Stone that insanity defense is "a pock mark on the nose of justice, while the patient is dying of congestive heart failure").

3 *See* Bruce Winick & Terry DeMeo, *Competency to Stand Trial in Florida*, 35 U. Miami L. Rev. 31, 32 n.2 (1980); James Fife, *Restarting Criminal Proceedings after Restoration of Defendant's Competence*, 27 T. Jefferson L. Rev. 93, 96 n.9 (2004); Gianni Pirelli, William H. Gottdiener & Patricia A. Zapf, *A Meta-Analytic Review of Competency to Stand Trial Research*, 17 Psychol. Pub. Pol'y & L. 1 (2011). Professor Slovenko has suggested that, historically, the incompetency plea emerged as a means by which to "undercut the [death] penalty." Ralph Slovenko, *The Developing Law on Competency to Stand Trial,* 5 J. Psychiatry & L. 165, 178 (1977).

4 *See, e.g.*, 4 Blackstone, Commentaries 24 (9th ed. 1783); Hale, The History of the Pleas of the Crown 34 (1847).

5 *See, e.g.*, People v. Berling, 251 P.2d 1017 (Cal. App. 1953).

6 Until the late eighteenth century, if the court concluded that a defendant was remaining "mute of malice," it could order him subjected to the practice of *peine forte et dure,* the placing of increasingly heavy weights on the defendant's chest to "press" him for an answer. *See, e.g.*, Slovenko, *supra* note 3, at 168–69. *See also* Winick, *supra* note 2, at 952. This practice was abolished in 1772.

7 Note, *The Identification of Incompetent Defendants: Separating Those Unfit for Adversary Combat from Those Who Are Fit*, 66 Ky. L.J. 666, 668 (1978).

8 Youtsey v. United States, 97 F. 937, 941 (6th Cir. 1989).

9 Jordan v. State, 135 S.W. 327, 328 (Tenn. 1911).

10 Sanders v. Allen, 100 F. 2d 717, 720 (D.C. Cir. 1938).

11 *See, e.g.*, United States v. Chisolm, 149 F. 284, 287 (S.D. Ala. 1906).

has been likened to permitting an adversary contest "in which the defendant, like a small boy being beaten by a bully, is unable to dodge or return the blows."[12] *Third*, it has been suggested that the trial of an incompetent transforms the adversary process "from a reasoned interaction between an individual and his community" into "an invective against an insensible object."[13] *Fourth*, "it seems essential to the philosophy of punishment that the defendant knows why he is being punished, and such comprehension is to a great extent dependent on involvement with the trial itself."[14] Such actions were decried over three centuries ago by Lord Coke as "a miserable spectacle, both against law, and of extreme inhumanity and cruelty, and can be no example to others."[15]

American courts quickly adopted the common-law test for assessing competency to stand trial: "Does the mental impairment of the prisoner's mind, if there such be, whatever it is, disable him 'from fairly presenting his defense, whatever it may be, and make it unjust to go on with the trial at this time, or is he feigning to be in that condition'?."[16] To answer this question, courts considered whether the defendant was "capable of properly appreciating his peril and of rationally assisting in his defense."[17]

2. The Supreme Court standard

This standard—accepted by virtually every jurisdiction either on statutory or case law bases[18] —was slightly modified by the US Supreme Court in *Dusky v. United States*,[19] where the Court asked whether the defendant "has sufficient present ability to consult with his lawyer with a reasonable degree of rational understanding—and whether he has a rational as well as a factual understanding of the proceedings against him."[20] This emphasis on rationality extended earlier doctrine as to the requisite level of a defendant's "understanding"; under *Dusky*, he must also be able to "appraise and assess the proceedings."[21] Certain states and

---

12 *See, e.g.*, Frith's Case, 22 How. State Trials 307, 318 (1790).

13 Note, *Incompetency to Stand Trial*, 81 HARV. L. REV. 454, 458 (1967–68).

14 *Id.*

15 3 COKE, INSTITUTES 6 (1644). *See* Nobles v. Georgia, 168 U.S. 398 (1897).

16 *Chisolm*, 149 F. at 298.

17 United States v. Boylen, 41 F. Supp. 724, 725 (D. Or. 1941).

18 See Note, *supra* note 7, at 671–72 & *id.* at nn.27–29.

19 362 U.S. 402 (1960). Although *Dusky* established the test only for federal cases, several circuits and state supreme courts adopted it as also setting out minimal *constitutional* standards. See Note, supra note 7, at 674 n.35.

20 *Dusky*, 362 U.S. at 402.

21 Note, *supra* note 7, at 672. *See, e.g.*, People v. Swallow, 301 N.Y.S. 2d 798, 803 (Sup. Ct. 1969) (word "understanding" requires "some *depth* of understanding, not merely surface knowledge of the proceedings") (emphasis added). On the question of whether competency to stand trial standards should vary as to the seriousness of the underlying charge, *see* Alec Buchanan, *Competency to Stand Trial and the Seriousness of the Charge*, 34 J. AM. ACAD. PSYCHIATRY & L. 458 (2006).

professional associations have endorsed more elaborate and specific tests;[22] yet, *Dusky* is still perceived as the national standard.[23]

Dusky—which was commonly seen as confusing and "less than helpful"[24]—was supplemented by *Drope v. Missouri*[25] to require that the defendant be able to "assist in his defense."[26] Ruled the *Drope* court:

> [E]vidence of a defendant's irrational behavior, his demeanor at trial, and any prior medical opinion on competence to stand trial are all relevant in determining whether further inquiry is required, but that even one of these factors standing alone may, in some circumstances, be sufficient. There are, of course, no fixed or immutable signs which invariably indicate the need for further inquiry to determine fitness to proceed; the question is often a difficult one in which a wide range of manifestations and subtle nuances are implicated. That they are difficult to evaluate is suggested by the varying opinions trained psychiatrists can entertain on the same facts.[27]

Subsequently, a New York court listed six factors to be considered in determinations of incompetency:

> [W]hether the defendant: (1) is oriented as to time and place; (2) is able to perceive, recall, and relate; (3) has an understanding of the process of the trial and the roles of judge, jury, prosecutor and defense attorney; (4) can establish a working relationship with his attorney; (5) has sufficient intelligence and judgment to listen to the advice of counsel and, based on that advice, appreciate (without necessarily adopting) the fact that one course of conduct may be more beneficial to him than another; and (6) is sufficiently stable to enable him to withstand the stresses of the trial without suffering a serious prolonged or permanent breakdown.[28]

---

22 *See* Gerald Bennett, *A Guided Tour Through Selected ABA Standards Relating to Incompetence to Stand Trial*, 53 Geo. Wash. L. Rev. 375, 377–78 (1985) (discussing N.J. Stat. Ann. §2C:4-4 (West 1981); Wieter v. Settle, 193 F. Supp. 318, 321–22 (W.D. Mo. 1961); State v. Guatney, 299 N.W.2d 538, 545 (Neb. 1980) (Krivosha, C.J., concurring).

23 Debra Whitcomb & Ronald Brandt, Competency to Stand Trial 1 (1985). *But compare*, Grant Morris et al., *Competency on Trial on Trial*, 4 Hous. J. Health L. & Pol'y 193(2004) (on the significant differences in tests in some states).

24 Bennett, *supra* note 22, at 376.

25 420 U.S. 162 (1975).

26 *Id.* at 171.

27 *Id.* at 180.

28 People v. Picozzi, 482 N.Y.S. 2d 335, 337 (A.D. 1984), *appeal den.,* 64 N.Y.2d 1137(1985).

To be able to assist counsel, a defendant should have the ability to communicate,[29] the capacity to reason "from a simple premise to a simple conclusion,"[30] the ability to "recall and relate facts concerning his actions,"[31] and the ability "to comprehend instructions and advice, and make decisions based on well-explained alternatives."[32] Several courts have also considered whether a defendant is particularly susceptible to deterioration during the course of a trial.[33] Factors to be considered include "the defendant's tendency towards violence, the presence and extent of acute psychosis, suicidal depression, regressive withdrawal, and organic deterioration."[34]

Formulaic standards, however, do not end the inquiries. Dr. Loren Roth and his colleagues have suggested, for instance, that the search for a single test of competency "is a search for a Holy Grail";[35] on the other hand, Professor Robert Burt has speculated that "the conflicting motives provoked by the spectre of mental illness—solicitude and fear—appear to have induced state paralysis [in dealing with mental incompetency to stand trial]."[36] These two observations focus attention on the dual problems to be considered in assessing any competency to stand trial question:

> [T]he difficulties inherent in the phraseology outlining the elements of the test and, as with most other areas in which law interacts with psychiatry, the realization that hidden areas of motivation and unconscious impulses are usually far more significant than what appears on the surface.[37]

B. Procedural Standards[38]

It is axiomatic that the conviction of an accused person who is mentally incompetent violates due process, as was stated in *Pate v. Robinson.*[39] In addition, if there is

29 Peter Silten & Richard Tullis, *Mental Competency in Criminal Proceedings*, 28 Hastings. L.J. 1053, 1062 (1977).

30 *Id.* at 1064.

31 Allen Wilkinson & Arthur Roberts, *Defendant's Competency to Stand Trial*, 40 P.O.F.2d 171, 187 (1974).

32 *Id.* at 187.

33 *See, e.g.*, Hamm v. Jabe, 706 F.2d 765 (6th Cir. 1983); United States v. Mooney, 123 F. Supp. 2d 442 (N.D. Ill. 2000); United States v. Messervey, 317 F. 3d 457 (5th Cir. 2002) (same). *See also* People v. Vallen, 488 N.Y.S.2d 994, 995 (Cty. Ct. 1985).

34 Wilkinson & Roberts, *supra* note 31, at 187.

35 Loren Roth et al., *Tests of Competency to Consent to Treatment*, 134 Am. J. Psychiatry 279, 289 (1977).

36 Robert Burt, *Of Mad Dogs and Scientists: The Perils of the Criminal-Insane*, 123 U. Pa. L. Rev. 258, 276 (1974).

37 Michael L. Perlin, *Psychiatric Testimony in a Criminal Law Setting*, 3 Bull. Am. Acad. Psychiatry & L. 143, 147–48 (1975).

38 This section is partially adapted from 4 Perlin, *supra* note 1, § 8A-2.3.

39 383 U.S. 375, 385 (1966).

a "bona fide doubt" as to the defendant's competence,[40] the trial judge must raise the issue *sua sponte*[41] and weigh it at a "suitable hearing"[42] safeguarded with procedures adequate to "permit a trier of fact reasonably to assess an accused's competency against prevailing medical and legal standards."[43] Once such a hearing is ordered, the proceedings must be stayed.[44] The mere submission of *ex parte* letters by examining physicians cannot take the place of such a hearing.[45]

Other courts have couched this test in terms of whether the doubt as to a defendant's competency is "substantial,"[46] "sufficient,"[47] or "clear[] and unequivocal[],"[48] or "real and substantial,"[49] or "to positively, unequivocally, and

40 *See, e.g.*, United States v. Hollis, 569 F.2d 199, 205 n.8 (D.C. Cir. 1977); State v. Spivey, 319 A.2d 461, 469 (N.J. 1974). *See also, e.g.*, United States v. Davis, 365 F.2d 251, 254–55 (6th Cir. 1966) (obligation to order hearing rests on trial judge if court "is on notice that something is amiss"). This is rephrased as "reasonable grounds to doubt" in, inter alia, State v. Saddler, 549 So. 2d 1236, *reh'g denied*, 552 So. 2d 376 (La. 1989); *see also, e.g.*, People v. Vernon, 805 N.E.2d 1222 (Ill. App. 2004), *appeal denied*, 824 N.E.2d 290 (Ill. 2004); People v. Tursiois, 811 N.E.2d 1213 (Ill. App. 2004), *appeal denied*, 823 N.E.2d 977 (Ill. 2004); Davis v. Woodford, 384 F.3d 628 (9th Cir. 2004), *cert. dismissed sub. nom.* Davis v. Brown, 545 U.S. 1165 (2005) (judge based decision on interactions with defendant when deeming defendant competent).

41 *Pate*, 383 U.S. at 378; People v. Bannister, 728 N.Y.S.2d 164 (2001) (same); United States v. Messervey, 317 F.3d 457 (5th Cir. 2002) (same); State v. McCarthy, 101 P.3d 288 (Mo. 2004).

42 *E.g.*, United States v. Masthers, 539 F. 2d 721, 725 (D.C. Cir. 1976); *see also* People v. Meyers, 817 N.E.2d 173 (Ill. App. 2004) (discussions between defense counsel and trial court did not substitute for hearing on defendant's fitness to stand trial); People v. Smith, 818 N.E.2d 419 (Ill. App. 2004), *appeal denied*, 829 N.E.2d 793 (Ill. 2005) (once trial court had expressly raised, *sua sponte*, bona fide doubt as to defendant's fitness to stand trial, it was constitutionally required to hold fitness hearing; failure to so do constituted reversible error).

43 *See* Holmes v. King, 709 F.2d 965, 967 (5th Cir. 1983) (quoting Fulford v. Maggio, 692 F.2d 354, 361 (5th Cir. 1982), *rev'd on other grounds*, 462 U.S. 111 (1983)).

44 *See* State v. Calais, 615 So. 2d 4 (La. App. 1993), *writ denied*, 617 So. 2d 1180 (La. 1993).

45 *E.g.*, Gibson v. State, 474 So. 2d 1183 (Fla. 1985).

46 *See generally* Acosta v. Turner, 666 F.2d 949, 954 (5th Cir. 1982); Spencer v. Zant, 715 F.2d 1562, 1567 (11th Cir. 1983), *rev'd on other grounds*, 781 F.2d 1458 (11th Cir. 1986) (*en banc*).

47 *E.g.*, State v. Bartlett, 935 P.2d 1114, 1118 (Mont. 1997), *reh'g denied* (1997); Porter v. Horn, 276 F. Supp. 2d 278 (E.D. Pa 2003) (insufficient indicia of incompetence to warrant a *sua sponte* hearing); McDaniel v. State, 98 S.W.3d 704 (Tex. Crim. App. 2003) (motion asserting that there was an "issue" as to competency and requesting an expert was insufficient to warrant either a competency inquiry or a jury competency hearing).

48 *See* Grissom v. Wainwright, 494 F.2d 30, 32 (5th Cir. 1974).

49 Carriger v. Stewart, 95 F. 3d 755, 763 (9th Cir. 1996), *reh'g en banc granted*, 106 F.3d 1415 (9th Cir.), *vacated on other grounds*, 132 F.3d 463 (9th Cir. 1997), *cert. denied*, 523 U.S. 1133 (1998).

clearly generate a real, substantial and legitimate doubt,"[50] so as to determine whether there is a "reasonable doubt" as to whether the defendant is not fit to stand trial.[51]

There need not be "a full-blown competency hearing every time there is the slimmest evidence of incompetency."[52] Under the federal statutory scheme, for example, a motion to determine competency can be denied "only if the trial judge correctly determines that the motion is frivolous, is not in good faith, or does not set forth the grounds for believing that the accused may be incompetent."[53] As one federal court has phrased the issue, "*Pate* does not require that a trial judge be an omniscient psychiatrist, but that he act reasonably on the objective facts before him."[54]

The fact that a defendant is psychotic does not mean that he is necessarily incompetent to stand trial. Thus, courts have found, variously, that defendants with the following conditions were not necessarily incompetent to stand trial:

- the presence of severe mental illness,[55]
- a cumulative history of neurological and physiological ailments,[56]
- a history of hospitalization,[57]
- a finding of dangerousness,[58]

---

50 Nguyen v. Reynolds, 131 F.3d 1340, 1346 (10th Cir. 1997), *cert. denied*, 525 U.S. 852(1998), *stay denied*, 162 F.3d 600 (1998).

51 Pedrero v. Wainwright, 590 F. 2d 1383, 1388 (5th Cir. 1979), *cert. denied*, 444 U.S. 943 (1979).

52 Curry v. Estelle, 531 F. 2d 766. 768 (5th Cir. 1976).

53 United States v. Bradshaw, 690 F.2d 704, 712 (9th Cir. 1982), *cert. denied*, 463 U.S. 1210 (1983).

54 Reese v. Wainwright, 600 F. 2d 1085, 1092 (5th Cir. 1979), *cert. denied*, 444 U.S. 983 (1979).

55 United States *ex rel.* Cyburt v. Rowe, 638 F.2d 1100, 1103 (7th Cir. 1981).

56 *See* United States v. Sermon, 228 F. Supp. 972, 977 (W.D. Mo. 1964) (fact that defendant was suffering from: (1) chronic brain syndrome, secondary to cerebral arteriosclerosis, (2) arteriosclerotic heart disease, (3) cataracts, (4) osteoarthritis, (5) obesity, and (6) diabetes mellitus did not render him incompetent to stand trial); *see also* State v. Young, 780 P.2d 1233, 1237 (Utah 1989) (defendant suffered from "nervous difficulties"); State v. Caudill, 789 S.W.2d 213 (Mo. Ct. App. 1990) (defendant had history of manic-depressive illness); People v. Ross, 586 N.Y.S.2d 75, 76 (A.D. 1992), *appeal denied,* 589 N.Y.S.2d 861 (1992) (defendant suffered from personality disorder, periods of depression and "may have been hospitalized on prior occasions"); United States v. Burns, 811 F. Supp. 408, 416 (E.D. Wis. 1993), *aff'd*, 37 F.3d 276 (7th Cir. 1994), *cert. denied*, 515 U.S. 1149 (1995) ("alleged nervous breakdown … and subsequent psychiatric treatment").

57 People v. Dominique, 408 N.E.2d 280, 285, 288–89 (Ill. App. 1980); People v. Fowler, 583 N.E.2d 686 (Ill. App. 1991) (defendant had been involuntarily committed); People v. Wheeler, 672 N.Y.S.2d 155 (A.D. 1998) (same).

58 *Dominique*, 408 N.E. 2d 280 at 288–89.

- a suicide attempt,[59]
- borderline intelligence,[60]
- a finding that the defendant requires psychological treatment,[61]
- "bizarre, volatile, and irrational behavior,"[62]
- organic brain dysfunction,[63]
- a record of having received medication for "nerves and depression,"[64]
- "minor defects" in a defendant's cognitive abilities,[65]
- "diagnosed schizophrenic,"[66]
- a history of paranoid schizophrenia,[67]
- having a history of drug-induced psychosis[68]
- having unusual or fanatical religious beliefs,[69]
- having a severe physical pain or disability which affects cognitive functioning,[70] or
- having a past record of "aberrational acts."[71]

Also, a significant body of case law has developed holding that an "insane" person may nevertheless be competent to stand trial.[72] On the other hand, a defendant

---

59 People v. George, 636 N.E.2d 682 (Ill. App. 1994), *appeal denied*, 631 N.E.2d 713 (Ill. 1994), *cert. denied*, 512 U.S. 1241 (1994).

60 United States v. Murphy, 107 F. 3d 1199, 1203 (6th Cir. 1997).

61 People v. McMillen, 666 N.E. 2d 812, 814 (Ill. App. 1996).

62 Medina v. Singletary, 59 F. 3d 1095, 1107 (11th Cir. 1995), *cert. den.*, 517 U.S. 1247 (1996).

63 United States v. Housh, 89 F. Supp. 2d 1227, 1229–30 (D. Kan. 2000).

64 State v. Mercado, 787 S.W. 2d 848, 852 (Mo. App. 1990).

65 United States v. Liberatore, 846 F. Supp. 569, 577 (N.D. Ohio 1994).

66 State v. Martin, 485 S.E. 2d 352 (N.C. App. 1997).

67 United States v. Calek, 48 F. Supp. 2d 919 (D. Neb. 1999).

68 Welcome v. Ramirez-Palmer, 2002 U.S. Dist. LEXIS 12451 (N.D. Cal. 2002) (*habeas* relief denied where petitioner asserted in post-conviction proceedings that he was incompetent to stand trial, but where paranoid hallucinations occurred as the result of drug use four months prior to trial and there was no evidence that petitioner lacked competency during trial).

69 Ryan v. Clarke, 281 F. Supp. 2d 1008 (D. Nebraska 2003) (defendant was not incompetent to stand trial despite having fanatical religious beliefs, including belief that Yaweh was directing all decisions about the trial); United States v. James, 328 F.3d 953 (7th Cir. 2003) (defendant's beliefs as an adherent to the Moorish Science Temple, which included attempting to charge a fee every time his name was used, did not require further *sua sponte* competency evaluation).

70 People v. Avila, 11 Cal. Rptr. 3d 894 (App. 2004), *review denied*, 2004 Cal. LEXIS 5877 (2004) (chronic back condition and severe, painful headache did not prevent defendant from assisting in his defense).

71 *See*, *e.g.*, State v. Messenheimer, 817 S.W.2d 273 (Mo. App. 1991) (defendant had engaged in "abnormal behavior").

72 *See* Note, *supra* note 7, at 677 n.47 (citing cases).

must have "a modicum of intelligence" so as to assist counsel,[73] and must be able to "comprehend his own predicament."[74] The Washington Supreme Court has summarized the court's responsibility in this manner:

> The trial judge may make his [competency] determination from many things, including the defendant's appearance, demeanor, conduct, personal and family history, past behavior, medical and psychiatric reports and the statements of counsel.[75]

Thus, in individual cases, courts have focused on evidence that showed a defendant's professed inability to communicate intelligently and assist counsel to be volitional,[76] on the significance of a defendant's refusal to consult with court-appointed counsel,[77] on the significance of conflicts in the expert testimony,[78] and on the "coheren[ce]" of the defendant's responses to the court.[79]

One court has held that a defendant who "induced" his incompetency by refusing food and water for four days forfeited his right to be competent while tried. The defendant, Cayce Collins Moore, had been convicted of capital murder. Having previously been found competent to stand trial, he attempted suicide during trial. After being hospitalized and returned to jail for the resumption of trial, he began refusing food and water and on the fourth day was found unconscious in his cell. He later sought *habeas* relief on his claim that he was tried while incompetent. At his post-conviction hearing, lay witnesses testified that during trial he was weak, disoriented and unresponsive to his attorneys. An expert testified to major depression, but stated that the incompetency was caused by the dehydration and hunger strike in combination with the depression. The Eleventh Circuit found that his claim was not procedurally barred, but affirmed the conviction, concluding that it was not an unreasonable application of Supreme Court precedent for the state court to find that, by self-inducing incompetency, the

---

73 *See* Commonwealth v. Blackstone, 472 N.E.2d 1370, 1372 (Mass. App. 1985) ("modicum of rational understanding" is flexible enough concept to accommodate case of defendant whose refusal to plead not guilty by reason of insanity is indicative of "grievous detachment from reality"). *See, e.g.*, Noland v. Dixon, 831 F. Supp. 490 (W.D.N.C. 1993) (counsel regarded consultation with defendant as "useless"), *vacated on other grounds*, 53 F.3d 328 (4th Cir. 1995).

74 People v. Jordan, 364 N.Y.S. 2d 474, 477 (1974). *See also* Bundy v. Dugger, 850 F.2d 1402 (11th Cir. 1988), *cert. denied*, 488 U.S. 1034 (1989); Nowitzke v. State, 572 So. 2d 1346 (Fla. 1990).

75 State v. Johnson, 527 P. 2d 1310, 1312 (Wash 1974) (quoting State v. Dodd, 70 Wash. 2d 513, 424 P.2d 302, 303, *cert. denied*, 387 U.S. 948 (1967)).

76 United States v. Turner, 602 F. Supp. 1295, 1311–13 (S.D.N.Y. 1985).

77 United States v. Pederson, 784 F. 2d 1462, 1464–65 (9th Cir. 1986).

78 Strickland v. Francis, 738 F. 2d 1542, 1551–56 (11th Cir. 1984).

79 State v. Bailey, 627 N.E. 2d 1078, 1084 (Ohio App. 1992), *appeal dismissed as improvidently granted*, 624 N.E. 2d 1062 (Ohio 1994).

defendant had forfeited his right to be competent while tried. The court analogized this defendant to defendants who forfeit their right to be physically present by engaging in disruptive behavior. While acknowledging that it is unsettled as to whether this is the rule in capital cases, the court held that it was not unreasonable to conclude that the defendant intentionally absented himself from trial by self-inducing incompetency and forfeiting his right to be competent.[80]

C. The Accuracy of Competency Assessments

Professor Grant Morris and his colleagues have published data that calls into question one of the baseline assumptions of the entire competency to stand trial process: that clinicians' evaluations of competency are, in fact, reliable. In their article, *Competency to Stand Trial on Trial*, Morris and two forensic psychiatrists report on research they conducted reviewing how forensic experts implement the legal requirement that a criminal defendant must be competent to stand trial.[81] Using two vignettes—one of a defendant whose thinking is impaired, but his pre-trial behavior is normal; the other of a defendant whose pre-trial behavior is impaired, but her thinking is not—they found that, in the case of the first vignette, the experts split almost evenly.[82] About half considered the hypothetical defendant competent to stand trial, while the other half did not. In the second, although there was greater agreement, the divergence of expert opinions was still found to be troubling. The data, in their view, raised a "fundamental question" of whether experts really are experts.[83]

In his analysis of the Morris article, Professor John LaFond notes:

> The authors then analyze comments about the two vignettes made by individual evaluators. Some comments about the first vignette suggest that the evaluators too often "played lawyer" in reaching their conclusions, and may need to know about how the clients interacted with their attorney and what the legal defense might be to make a conduct a thorough evaluation. Comments about the second vignette suggest, among other things, that evaluators gave undue weight to the diagnosis and its severity in reaching their conclusion. Others took treatment needs into account. Simply put, experts infuse their own normative preferences and interpretations of legal standards when determining whether mentally ill defendants are competent to stand trial.[84]

---

80 *See* Moore v. Campell, 344 F.3d 1313 (11th Cir. 2003).

81 Morris et al., *supra* note 23, at 200.

82 *Id.* at 214.

83 *Id.* at 237.

84 John LaFond, *Foreword: Health Law in the Criminal Justice System*, 4 Hous. J. Health L. & Pol'y 181, 185–86 (2004).

In writing about these findings, I have said this:[85]

> What is the significance of these astounding findings? Let me suggest a few possibilities:
>
> 1. We have always accepted as conventional wisdom the fact there is high inter-rater concordance in the assessment of what should be a much more difficult evaluation: whether a defendant is insane (meaning, is he not responsible for his acts because of mental illness which led him to, variously, not know right from wrong, or be able to appreciate the nature or quality of his act). It would be reasonable to expect greater ambiguity on insanity questions because of several factors: (a) the ambiguity of the tests, (b) the political context of insanity defense evaluations, (c) the greater publicity attached to these cases, and (d) the ultimate implications of the ultimate finding. Yet most studies have demonstrated unfailingly that the rate of agreement in these cases is remarkably high—often approaching 90%. The contrast is startling.
> 2. The competency-to-stand-trial test is often seen as an "easy" or "minimalist" one.[86] Only, it is commonly argued, the most "out of it" criminal defendants will be found IST, in large part because the competency test demands so little. What then to do with the utterly contrary findings in this survey? In the years since Bernard Diamond exposed the fallacy of the "impartial expert,"[87] scholars, for the most part have avoided the "dirty little question" that was at the core of Diamond's writings in this area: Is there such a thing as a "neutral" or "objective" expert witness? I have always thought that this was a vastly under-discussed question, and perhaps, this article will reinvigorate that debate.[88]

III. Competency to Plead Guilty[89]

Prior to 1993, there were two distinct lines of competency to plead guilty cases: those that held that the standard for competency to plead guilty was the same as the standard for competency to stand trial, and those that held that the standard for

---

85 Michael L. Perlin, *"Everything's a Little Upside Down, as a Matter of Fact, the Wheels Have Stopped": The Fraudulence of the Incompetency Evaluation Process*, 4 Hous. J. Health L. & Pol'y 239, 244–45 (2004).

86 *See* Michael L. Perlin, *"Life Is In Mirrors, Death Disappears": Giving Life to* Atkins, 33 N. Mex. L. Rev. 315, 334 (2003).

87 Bernard L. Diamond, *The Fallacy of the Impartial Expert*, 3 Archives Crim. Psychodynamics 221, 223 (1959).

88 Perlin, *supra* note 85, at 244–45. *See generally* Michael L. Perlin, *"They're An Illusion To Me Now": Forensic Ethics, Sanism and Pretextuality*, in Psychology, Crime and Law: Bridging the Gap 239 (David Canter & Rita Zukauskien eds, 2008).

89 *See* 4 Perlin, *supra* note 1, §§ 8B-2 to 8B-2.3, at 101–10.

pleading guilty was a more stringent one.[90] In 1993, the Supreme Court resolved this dispute by holding, in *Godinez v. Moran*,[91] that a unitary standard was constitutionally appropriate.[92] Subsequently, the Supreme Court modified *Godinez* significantly, in *Indiana v. Edwards*,[93] holding that a state can limit defendant's self-representation at trial by insisting on representation by counsel if defendant lacks capacity to conduct trial defense unless so represented.[94]

In *Godinez*, the Supreme Court, per Justice Thomas, rejected the notion that competence to plead guilty must be measured by a higher (or even different) standard from that used in incompetency to stand trial cases.[95] It reasoned that a defendant who was found competent to stand trial would have to make a variety of decisions requiring choices: whether to testify, whether to seek a jury trial, whether to cross-examine his accusers, and, in some cases, whether to raise an affirmative defense.[96] While the decision to plead guilty is a "profound one," "it is no more complicated than the sum total of decisions that a defendant may be called upon to make during the course of a trial."[97] Finally, the court reaffirmed that any waiver of constitutional rights must be "knowing and voluntary."[98]It concluded on this point:

> Requiring that a criminal defendant be competent has a modest aim: It seeks to ensure that he has the capacity to understand the proceedings and to assist counsel. While psychiatrists and scholars may find it useful to classify the various kinds and degrees of competence, and while States are free to adopt competency standards that are more elaborate than the *Dusky* formulation, the Due Process Clause does not impose these additional requirements.[99]

Justices Kennedy and Scalia concurred, noting their concern with those aspects of the opinion that compared the decisions made by a defendant who pleads guilty with those made by one who goes to trial, and expressing their "serious doubts" that there would be a heightened competency standard under the Due Process Clause if these decisions were *not* equivalent.[100] Justice Blackmun dissented (for himself and Justice Stevens), focusing squarely on what he saw as the likelyhood that Moran's decision to plead guilty was the product of "medication and mental

---

90 *See id.* § 8B-2, at 101.

91 509 U.S. 389 (1993).

92 *Id.* at 398–403. *See* 4 Perlin, *supra* note 1, §8B-2.2, at 105–08.

93 554 U.S. 164 (2008).

94 *See generally* Michael L. Perlin & Heather Ellis Cucolo, Mental Disability Law: Civil and Criminal § 8B-3.1c(1), at 44–51 (2012 Cum. Supp.), discussing *Edwards* in this context.

95 *Godinez*, 509 U.S. at 390.

96 *Id.* at 398.

97 *Id.*

98 *Godinez*, 509 U.S. at 390.

99 *Id.* at 403.

100 *Id.*

illness."[101] He reviewed the expert testimony as to the defendant's state of depression, a colloquy between the defendant and the trial judge in which the court was informed that the defendant was being given medication, the trial judge's failure to inquire further and discover the psychoactive properties of the drugs in question, the defendant's subsequent testimony as to the "numbing" effect of the drugs, and the "mechanical character" and "ambiguity" of the defendant's answers to the court's questions at the plea stage.[102]

On the question of the multiple meanings of competency, Justice Blackmun added:

> [T]he majority cannot isolate the term "competent" and apply it in a vacuum, divorced from its specific context. A person who is "competent" to play basketball is not thereby "competent" to play the violin. The majority's monolithic approach to competency is true to neither life nor the law. Competency for one purpose does not necessarily translate to competency for another purpose.[103]

He concluded:

> To try, convict and punish one so helpless to defend himself contravenes fundamental principles of fairness and impugns the integrity of our criminal justice system. I cannot condone the decision to accept, without further inquiry, the self-destructive "choice" of a person who was so deeply medicated and who might well have been severely mentally ill.[104]

Justice Blackmun's dissent in *Godinez* is a powerful document that speaks simultaneously to the empirical realities of the criminal trial process, the impact of

---

101 *Id.* at 410,

102 *Id.* at 410–11. *See also id.* at 411 ("such drugs often possess side effects that may 'compromise the right of a medicated criminal defendant to receive a fair trial … by rendering him unable or unwilling to assist counsel'," quoting Riggins v. Nevada, 504 U.S. 127, 142 (1992) (Kennedy, J., concurring)).

103 *Godinez*, 509 U.S. at 413, citing Richard Bonnie, *The Competence of Criminal Defendant: A Theoretical Reformulation*, 10 Behav. Sci. & L. 291, 299 (1992); Ronald Roesch & Stephen Golding, Competency to Stand Trial 10–13 (1980).

104 *Godinez*, 509 U.S. at 414. On remand, the Ninth Circuit affirmed the trial court's denial of Moran's *habeas* petition, finding that his guilty plea entry was voluntary and intelligent. Moran v. Godinez, 40 F.3d 1567 (9th Cir.), *amended on denial of reh'g*, 57 F.3d 690 (9th Cir. 1994), *but see id.* at 1577 (Pregerson, J., dissenting). In a subsequent opinion, the Ninth Circuit found that a reasonable trial judge should have entertained a good faith doubt as to the defendant's competence during his change-of-plea hearing, and that the failure to hold a competency hearing was a due process violation, but also found that this violation was cured by a retrospective competency hearing, and that the defendant's waivers were voluntary and intelligent. Moran v. Godinez, 57 F.3d 690 (9th Cir. 1995), *but see id.* at 700 (Pregerson, J., dissenting).

mental illness and medication on a defendant's capacity for reasoned choice, and perhaps most importantly, the role of pretextuality in the incompetency to stand trial process.[105] He rejects the formulistic approach of Justice Thomas's majority opinion, weighs the pertinent social science evidence, and demonstrates how the trial record reflects the "ambiguity" of the controlling colloquy between counsel and the trial judge.

IV. Competency to Waive Counsel[106]

A significant amount of case law has developed over the question of the level of competency required for a defendant to waive representation by counsel. Since the US Supreme Court's ruling in *Faretta v. California*,[107] that a defendant has a federal constitutional right to represent himself if he voluntarily elects to do so, courts have focused on the question of whether a defendant has "the mental capacity to waive the right to counsel with a realization of the probable risks and consequences of his action."[108] To meet such a standard, it is not necessary that the defendant be technically competent to represent himself,[109] but only that he be "free of mental disorder which would so impair his free will that his decision to waive counsel would not be voluntary."[110] In fact, neither bizarre statements and actions,[111] mere eccentric behavior,[112] nor a finding that the defendant had been diagnosed as a paranoid schizophrenic,[113] have been found in specific cases to be enough to establish lack of capacity to represent oneself.[114] On the other hand, waiver of counsel should be "carefully scrutinized,"[115] and the record must reflect that "the accused was offered counsel and knowingly and intelligently refused the offer."[116]

105 *See* 4 Perlin, *supra* note 1, §§ 8C-1 *et. seq.*

106 *See id.*, §§ 8B-3.1 to 8B-3.1b.

107 422 U.S. 806, 835 (1975).

108 *See, e.g.*, People v. Clark, 213 Cal. Rptr. 837, 840 (App. 1985).

109 *Id.* at 840.

110 Curry v. Superior Court of Fresno County, 141 Cal. Rptr. 884, 888 (App. 1977).

111 People v. Miller, 167 Cal, Rptr. 816, 880 (App. 1980).

112 *Curry*, 141 Cal. Rptr. at 888.

113 State v. Evans, 610 P. 2d 34 (Ariz. 1980).

114 *Clark*, 213 Cal. Rptr. at 841. *See also, e.g.*, People v. Powell, 180 Cal. App. 3d 469, 225 Cal. Rptr. 703 (1986) (not abuse of discretion for court to find, after *Faretta* inquiry, that defendant had capacity to waive counsel in post-insanity acquittal commitment hearing); *see also* State v. Drobel, 815 P.2d 724 (Utah App. 1991), *cert. denied*, 836 P. 2d 1383 (Utah 1991).

115 People v. Kessler, 447 N.E. 2d 495, 499 (Ill. App. 1983), citing People v. Heral, 342 N.E.2d 34 (Ill. 1976).

116 *Kessler*, 447 N.E. 2d at 499 (citing People v. Williams, 96 Ill. App. 3d 519, 421 N.E.2d 551 (1981)); *see also* People v. Moore, 159 Ill. App. 3d 850, 513 N.E.2d 24, *appeal denied*, 117 Ill. 2d 550, 517 N.E.2d 1092 (1987); Cerkella v. Florida, 588 So. 2d 1058 (Fla. Dist. App. 1991).

In a searching decision, a New Jersey intermediate appellate court has considered the full range of underlying issues:

> Without the guiding hand of counsel, a defendant may lose his freedom because he does not know how to establish his innocence. … Trained counsel is also necessary to vindicate fundamental rights that receive protection from rules of procedure and exclusionary principles. … Where the doctrine supporting these rights "has any complexities the untrained defendant is in no position to defend himself."…
>
> These considerations militate strongly in favor of exercising great caution in determining whether a proposed waiver of counsel satisfies constitutional standards. Within the context of the potential pitfalls of self-representation, it has been said "the court must make certain by direct inquiry on the record that defendant is aware of 'the nature of the charges, the statutory offenses included with them, the range of allowable punishments thereunder, possible defenses to the charges and circumstances in mitigation thereof, and all other facts essential to a broad understanding of the whole matter'."[117]

The court is required to conduct "more than a routine inquiry when making that determination."[118] Thus, at least several courts had found than the standard for self-representation is a higher one than the standard for competency to stand trial,[119] since "literacy and a basic understanding over and above the competence to stand trial may be required."[120]As the Wisconsin Supreme Court has observed:

> Surely a defendant who, while mentally competent to be tried, is simply incapable of effective communication or, because of less than average intellectual powers, is unable to attain the minimal understanding necessary to present a defense, is not to be allowed "to go to jail under his own banner."…[121]

---

117 State v. Slattery, 571 A. 2d 1314, 1320–21 (N.J. App. Div. 1990) (citations omitted) (defendant functioned at "low average" range of intelligence).

118 *Kessler*, 447 N.E. 2d at 499 (citing People v. Feliciano, 93 Ill. App. 3d 642, 417 N.E.2d 824 (1981)). *See also*, *e.g.*, United States v. Purnett, 910 F.2d 51 (2d Cir. 1990) (defendant entitled to new trial where trial court accepted waiver of counsel before making determination of defendant's competency).

119 *See*, *e.g.*, United States *ex rel.* Konigsberg v. Vincent, 526 F.2d 131 (2d Cir. 1975); State v. Kolocotronis, 73 Wash. 2d 92, 436 P.2d 774 (1968); Pickens v. State, 292 N.W.2d 601 (Wis. 1980); State v. Harding, 670 P.2d 383, 391 (Ariz. 1983). *See also* Johnson v. State, 507 A.2d 1134, 1141 (Md. App. 1986) (finding of competency to stand trial does not automatically lead to a conclusion that an accused is also competent to waive right to counsel). *Pickens* was cited with approval in State v. Mott, 784 P.2d 278, 284 (Ariz. 1989).

120 *Pickens*, 292 N.W.2d at 611 (citing *Faretta*, 422 U.S. at 835).

121 *Pickens*, 292 N.W.2d at 611 (quoting United States v. Denno, 348 F.2d 12, 15 (2d Cir. 1965)). *See also* Powell, 225 Cal. Rptr. at 711–12. *But see* State v. Williams, 621 P.2d 423, 427 (Kan. 1980) (trial court not required to hold further hearings as to defendant's

In *Godinez v. Moran*, the Supreme Court ruled that, under federal constitutional law, the standard for waiving counsel is the same as for being found competent to stand trial.[122] It found there was "no reason" to believe that the decision to waive counsel requires an "appreciably higher level of mental functioning than the decision to waive other constitutional right."[123] It rejected the defendant's arguments that a self-representing defendant must have "greater powers of comprehension, judgment and reason, than would be necessary to stand trial with the aid of an attorney,"[124] concluding that this rested on a "flawed premise: the competence that is required of a defendant seeking to waive his right to counsel is the competence to *waive the right*, not the competence to represent himself."[125] Relying on its decision in *Faretta,* it found that a defendant's ability to represent himself "has no bearing upon his competence to choose self-representation."[126] Justice Blackmun dissented,[127] concluding on this point:

> A finding that a defendant is competent to stand trial establishes only that he is capable of aiding his attorney in making the critical decisions required at trial or in plea negotiations. The reliability or even relevance of such a finding vanishes when its basic premise—that counsel will be present—ceases to exist. The question is no longer whether the defendant can proceed with an attorney but whether he can proceed alone and uncounselled.[128]

The Supreme Court returned to the question of self-representation in *Indiana v. Edwards*,[129] holding that the Constitution permits states to insist upon representation by counsel for those who are competent enough to stand trial but who still suffer

---

continued competency to represent himself after he had broken a door and window subsequent to beginning of trial).

122 509 U.S. at 398.

123 *Id.*

124 *Id.*, citing Silten & Tullis, *supra* note 29, at 1068.

125 *Godinez*, 509 U.S. at 399 (emphasis in original).

126 *Id.*

127 At least one federal judge has endorsed Justice Blackmun's "thoughtful dissent," *see* Gov't of Virgin Islands v. Charles, 72 F.3d 401, 411 (3d Cir. 1995) (Lewis, J., concurring), concluding:

> That this result [allowing for the waiver of counsel in case of "unstable" defendant "prone to paranoid delusions," see id.] is constitutionally permissible is deeply disturbing and ultimately "impugns the integrity of our criminal justice system." *Godinez*, 509 U.S. at 417 (Blackmun J., dissenting).

Id. at 413. *And see id.* at 411:

> This case presents us with a window through which to view the real-world effects of [*Godinez*], and it is not a pretty sight.

128 *Godinez*, 509 U.S. at 411–12.

129 554 U.S. 164 (2008).

from severe mental illness to the point where they are not competent to conduct trial proceedings by themselves. Although the Court took pains to assert that *Godinez v. Moran* "does not answer" the question posed in *Edwards*[130] (although it "bears certain similarities" to it),[131] at the least, *Edwards* carves out an important exception to that decision.

Edwards had been charged with attempted murder, battery with a deadly weapon, criminal recklessness and theft—all charges emanating from his attempts to steal a pair of shoes from an Indiana department store.[132] At his first competency hearing, Edwards was found incompetent to stand trial, but at a second hearing—some 19 months later—the trial judge found that, while Edwards "suffered from mental illness," he was "competent to assist his attorneys in his defense and stand trial for the charged crimes."[133]

Seven months later but still before trial, Edwards' counsel sought yet another psychiatric evaluation of his client, and another competency hearing was held. At that time, Edwards' counsel presented further psychiatric and neuropsychological evidence showing that Edwards was suffering from serious thinking difficulties and delusions. A testifying psychiatrist reported that Edwards could understand the charges against him, but he was "unable to cooperate with his attorney in his defense because of his schizophrenic illness"; "[h]is delusions and his marked difficulties in thinking make it impossible for him to cooperate with his attorney." Subsequently, "the court concluded that Edwards was not then competent to stand trial and ordered his recommitment to the state hospital."[134]

About eight months after his commitment (nearly six years after Edwards' arrest), the hospital reported that Edwards' condition had again become competent to stand trial, and a year. after that, the trial began. Just before trial, Edwards asked to represent himself, and asked for a continuance, which, he said, he needed in order to proceed *pro se*.[135] The court refused, and Edwards proceeded to trial represented by counsel. The jury convicted him of criminal recklessness and theft but failed to reach a verdict on the charges of attempted murder and battery.[136]

When the State announced that it was going to retry Edwards on the charges on which the initial jury was hung (attempted murder and battery), Edwards again asked the court to permit him to represent himself.[137] Referring to the lengthy record of psychiatric reports, the trial court noted that Edwards still suffered from schizophrenia and concluded that "[w]ith these findings, he's competent to stand

---

130 *Id.* at 173.
131 *Id.* at 172.
132 *Id.* at 167.
133 *Id.* at 168.
134 *Id.*
135 *Id*, at 168–69.
136 *Id.* at 169.
137 *Id.*

trial but I'm not going to find he's competent to defend himself."[138] Edwards was then represented by appointed counsel at his retrial, and was convicted by a jury on both counts.[139]

He appealed to Indiana's intermediate appellate court, arguing that the trial court's refusal to permit him to represent himself at his retrial deprived him of his constitutional right of self-representation, citing *Faretta v. California*.[140] The court agreed and ordered a new trial. On further appeal, the Indiana Supreme Court found that "[t]he record in this case presents a substantial basis to agree with the trial court,"[141] but it nonetheless affirmed the intermediate appellate court on the belief that this Court's precedents (*Faretta* and *Godinez*) required the State to allow Edwards to represent himself.[142] The Supreme Court then granted the State's petition for *certiorari*.

The Court vacated and remanded. After re-articulating the holdings of *Dusky* and *Drope*,[143] it considered the significance of *Faretta*, and concluded that that case did not answer the question posed in *Edwards* because *Faretta* "did not consider the question of mental competency,"[144] noting that other post-*Faretta* cases made it clear that "the right of self-representation is not absolute."[145]

It then characterized *Godinez* as presenting "a question closer to that at issue here," referring to Moran (the criminal defendant in the *Godinez* case) as being "borderline-competent."[146] It then, however, distinguished *Godinez* on the grounds that, because that case involved a *guilty plea*,[147] the only question to be considered was the defendant's ability to *waive* the right, as compared to the case before it that sought to measure "the defendant's ability to conduct trial proceedings."[148] It thus concluded that "the very matters that we did not consider in *Godinez* are directly before us."[149]

The Court then posed the question: "We ask whether the Constitution permits a State to limit that defendant's self-representation right by insisting upon representation by counsel at trial—on the ground that the defendant lacks the mental capacity to conduct his trial defense unless represented."[150] It answered this question in the affirmative. First, it stressed that the competency cases—*Dusky* and *Drope*—set out a standard that focused upon a defendant's "present ability to

138 *Id.*
139 *Id.*
140 *Id.*
141 *Id.*, quoting Edwards v. State, 866 N.E.2d 252, 260 (Ind. 2007).
142 *Id.*, quoting Edwards v. State, 866 N.E.2d 252, 260 (Ind. 2007).
143 *Edwards*, 554 U.S. at 170.
144 *Id.* at 171.
145 *Id.*
146 *Id.*
147 *Id.* at 173.
148 *Id.*
149 *Id.*
150 *Id.* at 174.

consult with his lawyer," and a "capacity ... to consult with counsel," and an ability "to assist [counsel] in preparing his defense."[151] Second, it "caution[ed] against the use of a single mental competency standard for deciding both (1) whether a defendant who is represented by counsel can proceed to trial and (2) whether a defendant who goes to trial must be permitted to represent himself."[152] Here it turned to behavioral science and to concepts of procedural justice in explaining its rationale:

> Mental illness itself is not a unitary concept. It varies in degree. It can vary over time. It interferes with an individual's functioning at different times in different ways. The history of this case ... illustrates the complexity of the problem. In certain instances an individual may well be able to satisfy *Dusky*'s mental competence standard, for he will be able to work with counsel at trial, yet at the same time he may be unable to carry out the basic tasks needed to present his own defense without the help of counsel.[153]

Next, it looked at dignitarian concerns,[154] relying on *McKaskle v. Wiggins*[155] for the proposition that "'Dignity' and 'autonomy'" of the individual "underlie [the] self-representation right,"[156] and underscoring that, in the case of a defendant with an "uncertain mental state, the spectacle that could well result from his self-representation at trial is at least as likely to prove humiliating as ennobling."[157] Not only, it found, must proceedings *be* fair, they must "*appear* fair to all who observe them,"[158] quoting from an amicus brief's report on a psychiatrist's reaction to observing a defendant—who, although satisfying the *Dusky* standard, was still mentally ill—attempting to conduct his own trial: "[H]ow in the world can our legal system allow an insane man to defend himself?".[159]

---

151 *Id.*

152 *Id.* at 175.

153 *Id.*, citing Norman Poythress et al, Adjudicative Competence: The MacArthur Studies 103 (2002) ("Within each domain of adjudicative competence (competence to assist counsel; decisional competence) the data indicate that understanding, reasoning, and appreciation [of the charges against a defendant] are separable and somewhat independent aspects of functionallegal ability").

154 *See generally* Michael L. Perlin, *"Dignity Was the First to Leave": Godinez v. Moran, Colin Ferguson, and the Trial of Mentally Disabled Criminal Defendants*, 14 Behav. Sci. & L. 61 (1996).

155 465 U.S. 168 (1984) (appointment of standby counsel over self-represented defendant's objection is permissible).

156 *Edwards*, 554 U.S. at 176.

157 *Id.*

158 *Id.* at 177.

159 *Id.* at 177.

In short, the Court found that *Dusky* alone (while helpful) was not a sufficient protective standard,[160] and that "the Constitution permits judges to take realistic account of the particular defendant's mental capacities by asking whether a defendant who seeks to conduct his own defense at trial is mentally competent to do so."[161] In other words, "the Constitution permits States to insist upon representation by counsel for those competent enough to stand trial under *Dusky* but who still suffer from severe mental illness to the point where they are not competent to conduct trial proceedings by themselves."[162] Importantly, it rejected the state's request to directly overrule *Faretta*, pointing out that empirical research has revealed that that decision has led to, statistically, an insignificant number of unfair trials.[163]

Justice Scalia dissented (for himself and Justice Thomas), taking the position that:

> The Court today concludes that a State may nonetheless strip a mentally ill defendant of the right to represent himself when that would be fairer. In my view the Constitution does not permit a State to substitute its own perception of fairness for the defendant's right to make his own case before the jury—a specific right long understood as essential to a fair trial.[164]

In his eyes, "[t]he only circumstance in which we have permitted the State to deprive a defendant of this trial right is the one under which we have allowed the State to deny *other* such rights: when it is necessary to enable the trial to proceed in an orderly fashion."[165] He rejected the majority's view of the "dignity" issue in this manner:

> While there is little doubt that preserving individual "dignity" (to which the Court refers), is paramount among those purposes, there is equally little doubt that the loss of "dignity" the right is designed to prevent is *not* the defendant's making a fool of himself by presenting an amateurish or even incoherent defense. Rather, the dignity at issue is the supreme human dignity of being master of one's fate rather than a ward of the State—the dignity of individual choice.[166]

160 *Id.*

161 *Id.*

162 *Id.* at 178.

163 *Id.* at 178–79, citing Erica Hashimoto, *Defending the Right of Self-Representation: An Empirical Look at the Pro Se Felony Defendant*, 85 N.C.L. Rev. 423, 427, 447, 448 (2007) (of the small number of defendants who chose to proceed *pro se*—"roughly 0.3% to 0.5%" of the total, state felony defendants in particular, "appear to have achieved higher felony acquittal rates than their represented counterparts in that they were less likely to have been convicted of felonies").

164 *Id.* at 180.

165 *Id.* at 180.

166 *Id.* at 186.

Here, he specifically took issue with the "appearance of fairness" argument made by the majority:

> A further purpose that the Court finds is advanced by denial of the right of self-representation is the purpose of assuring that trials "appear fair to all who observe them.". ... To my knowledge we have never denied a defendant a right simply on the ground that it would make his trial appear less "fair" to outside observers, and I would not inaugurate that principle here.[167]

Finally, he suggested that the majority's opinion demonstrated bias towards persons with mental illness:

> In singling out mentally ill defendants for this treatment, the Court's opinion does not even have the questionable virtue of being politically correct. At a time when all society is trying to mainstream the mentally impaired, the Court permits them to be deprived of a basic constitutional right—for their own good.[168]

Edwards will likely cause all trial courts to consider what steps need be taken in cases involving the trials of defendants who, although competent for *Dusky*'s bare-bones purposes, suffer from serious mental illnesses. There are at least four important points relevant to the inquiries addressed in this volume:

- Although it goes out of its way to suggest that it is deciding matters "that [it] did not consider in *Godinez*,"[169] it is fairly clear that *Edwards* does modify and limit *Godinez* (which suggested that the *only* question to consider was the minimalistic one posed in *Dusky*).[170]
- In doing so, it also implicitly rejects the unitary standard that *Godinez* had established for all aspects of the criminal trial, and explicitly recognizes that mental illness is not an all-or-nothing dyadic concept (mentally ill/not

---

167 *Id.* at 187.

168 *Id.* at 189.

169 *Id.* at 173.

170 See Perlin, *supra* note 154; Michael L. Perlin, *Beyond Dusky and Godinez: Competency Before and After Trial*, 21 Behav. Sci. & L. 297 (2003), and Perlin, *supra* note 86, at 343:

> The *Godinez* holding may lead to a potentially absurd scenario where a defendant with a history of mental illness or who is mentally retarded may be found competent to stand trial if he is found to have some ability to assist counsel in some way, and later may be allowed to remove counsel and represent himself. The trial of Colin Ferguson [see Perlin, *supra* note 154] "graphically symbolizes the dangerous implications of courts using *Godinez*'s low standard of competency." (Footnotes omitted)

mentally ill),[171] a concept that is frequently endorsed by trial courts and by jurors.[172] Here it implicitly concedes the correctness of Justice Blackmun's dissent in *Godinez*, distinguishing competency-to-play-basketball from competency-to-play-the-violin.[173]

- Its focus on dignity and the perceptions of justice are, perhaps, the Supreme Court's first implicit endorsement of important principles of therapeutic jurisprudence in a criminal procedure context.[174]
- Justice Scalia's dissent—suggesting that the majority view is *sanist* (as the decision "permits [defendants with mental disabilities] to be deprived of a basic constitutional right for their own good")[175]—opens up a question that has not been paid that much attention in the post-*Godinez* years. Is it more sanist to deprive persons with mental disabilities of a right that all other citizens have (that of self-representation) or to allow such persons to represent themselves in trials that may be nothing more than charades?[176]

Since the decision in *Edwards,* many courts have grappled with the case's limits: at what point can a trial judge override a putatively mentally ill criminal defendant's desires to self-represent?[177] The New Jersey Appellate Division drew the dividing line clearly in *State v. McNeil:*

> We are satisfied that a trial judge in New Jersey may, consistent with *Edwards* and the State Constitution, deny a defendant the right of self-representation when the record sustains a finding, made for specific reasons, that a mentally ill defendant is competent to stand trial but cannot knowingly and intelligently waive his right to counsel without being deprived of a fair trial. We recognize that the federal competency standards may not be as protective of a defendant as New Jersey's, but we see no dramatic or substantive differences for purposes of *Edwards*. We urge, however, that a defendant must be mentally ill and not merely difficult to handle or disruptive to be deprived of the right of self-representation.[178]

---

171 *Edwards*, 554 U.S. at 165 ("Mental illness itself is not a unitary concept. It varies in degree. It can vary over time.").

172 *See, e.g.*, Michael L. Perlin, *"The Executioner's Face Is Always Well-Hidden": The Role of Counsel and the Courts in Determining Who Dies*, 41 N.Y.L. Sch. L. Rev. 201, 228 (1996) ("'enormous pressures' will often be placed on defense counsel to play into the hands of these myths and paint an exaggerated picture of a 'totally crazy' defendant to assuage jurors whose 'ordinary common sense' demands an all-or-nothing representation of mental illness") (footnotes omitted).

173 *Godinez*, 509 U.S. at 413 (Blackmun, J., dissenting).

174 *See supra* Chapter 6.

175 *Edwards*, 554 U.S. at 189.

176 *See generally*, Perlin, *supra* note 154.

177 See Perlin & Cucolo, *supra* note 94, §8B-3.1c(2), at 51–53.

178 State v. McNeil, 963 A.2d 358, 366 (N.J. App. Div. 2009), *certification denied*, 970 A.2d 1047 (N.J. 2009).For other cases following *Edwards*, *see*, *e.g.*, Dove v. State,

Other courts have distinguished *Edwards* in cases where the defendant's mental illness was not seen as "severe,"[179] and where the defendant had been found competent to proceed *pro se*.[180] Yet others have remanded in light of *Edwards* to determine whether a defendant was "sufficiently capable" of self-representation.[181] One court has distinguished *Edwards* in a case involving a defendant's competency to accept a plea offer, noting that that issue was not before the *Edwards* court.[182]

V. Competency to be Executed: The Question of Medication[183]

A. Introduction

The question of whether a defendant facing execution can be involuntarily medicated so as to make him competent to be executed has been the topic of strenuous and pointed debate among academic and forensic psychiatrists for decades.[184] In 1996, Drs. Alfred Freedman and Abraham Halpern laid down the gauntlet:

2010 U.S. Dist. LEXIS 4668 (D.N.J. Jan. 20, 2010); United States v. McMahill, 2009 U.S. Dist. LEXIS 118950 (W.D. Pa. Dec. 22, 2009).

179 *E.g.*, United States v. Berry, 565 F.3d 385 (7th Cir. 2009); *see also* Jones v. Steele, 660 F. Supp. 2d 1059 (E.D. Mo. 2009). For a pointed example, see United States v. Johnson, 610 F.3d 1138, 1144, 1147 (9th Cir. 2010):

> The behavior of the defendants during the trial in this case, while occasionally wacky, was not disruptive or defiant. … [T]hey did not exhibit a blatant disregard for courtroom rules or protocol and did not make it impossible for the court to administer fair proceedings. In fact, they made opening statements, closing arguments, cross-examined witnesses, argued jury instructions, and testified on their own behalf. … They were examined by a psychiatrist and found to be fine. In the absence of any mental illness or uncontrollable behavior, they had the right to present their unorthodox defenses and argue their theories to the bitter end.

180 *E.g.*, United States v. Arenburg, 2008 U.S. Dist. LEXIS 60318 (W.D.N.Y. Aug. 7, 2008); United States v. Schiff, 2010 U.S. App. LEXIS 11971 (9th Cir. June 11, 2010).

181 *E.g.*, State v. Connor, 973 A.2d 627 (Conn. 2009).

182 United States v. Mendez-Sanchez, 563 F.3d 935 (9th Cir. 2009).

183 This section is partially adapted from Michael L. Perlin, Mental Disability and the Death Penalty: The Shame of the States 85-92 (2013).

184 *Compare, e.g.,* Alfred Freedman & Abraham Halpern, *The Erosion of Ethics and Morality in Medicine: Physician Participation in Legal Executions in the United States*, 41 N.Y. L. Sch. L. Rev. 169 (1996), to Robert T.M. Phillips, *The Psychiatrist as Evaluator: Conflicts and Conscience*, 41 N.Y. L. Sch. L. Rev. 189 (1996), and *compare, e.g.*, Melissa McDonnell & Robert Phillips, *Physicians Should Treat Mentally Ill Death Row Inmates, Even if Treatment Is Refused*, 38 J. L. Med. & Ethics 774 (2010), to Howard Zonana, *Physicians Must Honor Refusal of Treatment to Restore Competency by Non-Dangerous Inmates on Death Row*, 38 J. L. Med. & Ethics 764 (2010). Noted Dr. Phillips in 1996, "In the past decade, nothing has sparked more intense debate among psychiatrists than

> The rationale that physicians should assist in the administration of justice, insofar as capital punishment is concerned, is frighteningly reminiscent of how German physicians justified their involvement in the torture and killing of thousands of innocent human beings and carried out the Nazi programs of sterilization and "euthanasia" by murdering countless children and adults.[185]

In contrast, Dr. Robert Phillips argued:

> While many hold strong opinions about the propriety of involvement of a psychiatrist that may lead to execution, there is no ethical barrier to testifying at the pre-trial, trial, or sentencing phase in a capital case. Despite the heavy reliance on psychiatric testimony, the psychiatrist is neither the judge nor the executioner.[186]

Other psychiatrists remain ambivalent and freely share their ambivalence. In the words of Dr. Julie Cantor:

> Though the *Singleton* case[187] has ended, its legacy is a paradox. I believe in the arguments set forth here. I believe that psychiatrists have an ethical duty to medicate prisoners in clinical situations like that of Charles Singleton. I believe that psychotic inmates deserve treatment, the kind of care that they would get in the outside world, and that psychiatrists should not deny that treatment because the inmate may become competent for execution. But that does not mean that I would have cheered at Singleton's execution, nor would I dance on his grave. The reasons that death penalty opponents cite are convincing—killing

---

their role in capital sentencing proceedings." Phillips, *supra* at 189, and *see id.* n.1 (listing references).

185 Freedman & Halpern, *supra* note 184, at 187. For a discussion of the positions of professional and medical organizations on this issue, see Kursten B. Hensl, *Restored to Health to Be Put to Death: Reconciling the Legal and Ethical Dilemmas of Medicating to Execute in Singleton v. Norris*, 49 Vill. L. Rev. 291, 327–28 (2004); Kacie McCoy Daugherty, *Synthetic Sanity: The Ethics and Legality of Using Psychotropic Medications to Render Death Row Inmates Competent for Execution*, 17 J. Contemp. Health L. & Pol'y 715, 730–32 (2001).

186 Phillips, *supra* note 184, at 193–94. Compare Hensl, *supra* note 185, at 323 (characterizing psychiatric involvement in this process as "treating to kill"). *See also, e.g.*, Mental Health America, *Position Statement 54: Death Penalty and People with Mental Illness*, accessible at http://nhma.org/go/position-statements/54 (accessed May 22, 2012) ("MHA is opposed to the practice of having a psychiatrist or other mental health professional treat a person in order to restore competency solely to permit the state to execute that person, and MHA opposes the practice of medicating defendants involuntarily in order to make them competent either to stand trial or to be executed.").

187 See *infra* text accompanying notes 218–33, discussing Singleton v. Norris, 992 S.W.2d 768 (Ark. 1999), and subsequent litigation in that case.

> Singleton will not bring back his victim; execution may not deter future killers; a life sentence is cheaper than the requisite appeals by orders of magnitude; given a different lawyer/skin color/jurisdiction, the outcome would have been different; and so on. To even the most callous observer, the inconsistencies in the punishment and the innocents exonerated from death rows around the country makes capital punishment seem "irrational, arbitrary, and unfair." Still, I would have treated Charles Singleton. And yet I remain troubled by the pointlessness of his crime and uneasy with the manner of his death.[188]

B. Case Law Development

In the aftermath of *Ford v. Wainwright*[189] (and eventually *Panetti v. Quarterman*),[190] this separate-but-related policy issue demands resolution. As new developments in psychiatry and psychotropic medication have enabled the state to render death row inmates competent for execution,[191] an issue self-evidently never contemplated at the time of the drafting of the Eighth Amendment, the question of the legality, morality and ethics of the use of such medications to "make competent" a defendant so as to allow an execution to proceed now confronts the courts.[192]

The Supreme Court had, over two decades ago, granted *certiorari* in *Perry v. Louisiana*[193] (presenting this precise question), thus making it appear that this gap would be resolved. However, the Court declined to rule on the merits, remanding the case, instead, to the Louisiana Supreme Court for reconsideration[194] in light of its then-contemporaneous decision in *Washington v. Harper*.[195]

---

188 Julie Cantor, *Of Pills and Needles: Involuntarily Medicating the Psychotic Inmate When Execution Looms*, 2 IND. HEALTH L. REV. 117, 169–70 (2005).

189 477 U.S. 399 (1986). *See* 4 PERLIN, *supra* note 1, § 12-4.1c, at 527–39.

190 551 U.S. 930 (2007). *See* PERLIN & CUCOLO, *supra* note 94, § 12-4.1f, at 143–49.

191 On refusal of medication generally, see 4 PERLIN, *supra* note 1, §§ 12-4.1 to 1e; 2 PERLIN, *supra* note 1, §§ 3B-1 *et seq.* (2d ed. 1999). On prisoners' right to refuse medication, see *id.*, § 3B-8.2; *see generally* Washington v. Harper, 494 U.S. 210 (1990). *See* MICHAEL L. PERLIN ET AL., COMPETENCE IN THE LAW: FROM LEGAL THEORY TO CLINICAL APPLICATION, 148–66 (2008).

192 *See, e.g.*, Michaela P. Sewall, *Pushing Execution over the Constitutional Line: Forcible Medication of Condemned Inmates and the Eighth and Fourteenth Amendments*, 51 B.C. L. REV. 1279, 1281 (2010). On the "little guidance" provided by the Model Rules, the Restatement, and the common law to attorney representing a defendant in these circumstances, see Michael D. Grabo & Michael Sapoznikow, *Current Development Note, The Ethical Dilemma of Involuntary Medication in Death Penalty Cases*, 15 GEO. J. LEGAL ETHICS 795, 808 (2002).

193 494 U.S. 1015 (1990).

194 498 U.S. 38 (1990), *reh'g denied*, 498 U.S. 1075 (1991).

195 494 U.S. 210 (1990).

Perry had been charged with the murder of five family members, including his parents.[196] After he was found competent to stand trial, Perry withdrew his previously entered not-guilty-by-reason-of-insanity plea (over counsel's advice) and entered a not-guilty plea.[197] He was convicted and sentenced to death.[198] On appeal, the Louisiana Supreme Court affirmed both his conviction and death sentence, but ordered an adversarial hearing on his present competence to be executed.[199]

At that competency hearing, the four expert witnesses agreed that Perry was psychotic, and that his condition improved when he was properly medicated.[200] Two of the witnesses found that he would be competent to be executed if he were to receive medication; a third, who did not believe Perry understood the purpose of his sentence, was not sure if the medication would make him competent; the fourth remained unconvinced that the defendant understood that he had really committed the murders in question.[201]

Following this hearing, the trial court, after it had received new reports from the prison hospital, ordered two of the experts to reexamine the defendant.[202] At this hearing (held five months after the initial hearing), testimony was adduced that Perry was now aware of the reason he was to be executed.[203]

The trial court then found that Perry was competent to be executed, adopting Justice Powell's definition of competence from the *Ford* opinion.[204] It further found that any due process right to refuse medication that Perry might have had was outweighed by two compelling state interests: the provision of proper psychiatric care, and carrying out a valid death penalty.[205] It thus ordered that Perry be medicated—by force if necessary—so that he would remain competent to be executed.[206] The Louisiana Supreme Court declined to review this order.[207]

---

196 State v. Perry, 502 So. 2d 543, 546 (La. 1986), State v. Perry, 502 So. 2d 543, 546 (La. 1986), *cert. denied*, 484 U.S. 872, *reh'g denied*, 484 U.S. 992 (1987).

197 *Id.* at 547.

198 *Id.* at 545. Following his conviction, Perry was treated on several occasions in the prison's psychiatric unit, where he received an antipsychotic drug (Haldol). L. Anita Richardson, *Involuntary Medication on Death Row: Is It Cruel and Unusual?*, 1990–91 ABA Preview 18 (Sept. 28, 1990).

199 Perry, 502 So. 2d at 563–64.

200 Perry v. Louisiana, No. 89-5120 (May 24, 1990) Perry v. Louisiana, No. 89-5120 (May 24, 1990), Petitioner's Brief on Merits, J.A. 126–49 (Petitioner's Brief).

201 *Id.*

202 *Id.*

203 *Id.*

204 See *Ford*, 477 U.S. at 522 (Powell, J., concurring), discussed in 4 Perlin, *supra* note 1, §12-4.1c, at 534.

205 Petitioner's Brief, *supra* note 200.

206 *Id.*

207 State v. Perry, 543 So. 2d 487 (La.). State v. Perry, 543 So. 2d 487 (La.), *reh'g denied*, 545 So. 2d 1049 (1989).

The United States Supreme Court subsequently granted *certiorari* to resolve, inter alia, the question of whether the Eighth Amendment prohibits states from forcibly medicating death row inmates for the purpose of making them competent to be executed.[208] However, as noted above, instead of deciding the case on the merits, the Court ultimately vacated and remanded[209] to the Louisiana Supreme Court for further reconsideration in light of its decision in *Washington v. Harper*.[210]

It is unclear why the Supreme Court chose to deal with *Perry* in this manner. It may be that the justices, after considering the case, felt that the only issue presented was that of forcible medication, finding the execution consequences irrelevant, and that they thus felt it was essential for the state court to consider, after *Harper*, whether the difference in long-term harm in a case such as *Perry* (his execution) outweighed the state's interests in involuntarily medicating him.[211] It may also be that, since one of the justices—Justice Souter—did not participate in *Perry*,[212] the court felt the issue was too important to decide without the benefit of a full court.

On remand, the Louisiana Supreme Court found, under state constitutional law,[213] that the state was prohibited from medicating Perry to make him competent to be executed.[214] Concluded the court:

> For centuries no jurisdiction has approved the execution of the insane. The state's attempt to circumvent this well-settled prohibition by forcibly medicating an insane prisoner with antipsychotic drugs violates his rights under our state constitution. … First, it violates his right to privacy or personhood. Such involuntary medication requires the unjustified invasion of his brain and body with discomforting, potentially dangerous and painful drugs, the seizure of control of his mind and thoughts, and the usurpation of his right to make decisions regarding his health or medical treatment. Furthermore, implementation of the state's plan to medicate forcibly and execute the insane prisoner would constitute cruel, excessive and unusual punishment. This particular application of the death penalty fails to measurably contribute to the social goals of capital punishment. Carrying out this punitive scheme would add severity and indignity to the

---

208 Perry v. Louisiana, 494 U.S. 1015 (1990).

209 498 U.S. 38 (1990), *reh'g denied*, 498 U.S. 1075 (1991).

210 494 U.S. 210; *see* 2 Perlin, *supra* note 1, §3B-8.2 (convicted prisoners' right to refuse treatment). Interestingly, the Supreme Court had decided *Harper* about one week prior to its decision to grant *certiorari* in *Perry*.

211 *Supreme Court Sidesteps Issue of Restoring Inmates' Competency to Allow Execution*, PSYCHIATRIC NEWS (Dec. 21, 1990), at 6 (quoting Dr. Paul Appelbaum).

212 See 498 U.S. at 1075.

213 A state can always provide more rights to a criminal defendant under its constitution than are afforded to the defendant under the US constitution, but can never afford fewer. *See, e.g.*, ERWIN CHEMERINSKY ET AL., FEDERAL JURISDICTION § 10.5, at 707 (4th ed. 2003) ("State constitutions can provide more rights than exist under the United States Constitution, but the state court must make it clear that the decision is based on the state constitution").

214 State v. Perry, 610 So. 2d 746 (La. 1992).

> prisoner's punishment beyond that required for the mere extinguishment of life. This type of punitive treatment system is not accepted anywhere in contemporary society and is apt to be administered erroneously, arbitrarily or capriciously.[215]

This decision was not re-appealed to the Supreme Court (presumably, because of its state constitutional law basis).

While the Supreme Court's disposition of *Perry* did not clarify the underlying issues,[216] it appeared inevitable that this question would arise again in the future, thus giving the Court, if it so chose, a second chance to weigh the competing values. Yet this never happened, and the only relevant developments were in the lower federal courts and the state courts.[217] By way of examples, the South Carolina Supreme Court relied upon the Louisiana Supreme Court's decision in *Perry* to support its conclusion that medicating a defendant to make him competent to be executed would violate the South Carolina *state* constitution.[218] On the other hand, in *Singleton v. Norris*,[219] the Arkansas Supreme Court ruled that the state had the burden to administer antipsychotic medication as long as a prisoner was alive and was a potential danger either to himself or to others, and that the collateral effect of the involuntary medication—rendering him competent to understand the nature and reason for his execution—did not violate due process. The Supreme Court subsequently denied *certiorari*.[220]

---

215 *Id.* at 747–48.

216 On the right of defendants awaiting trial or at trial to refuse the involuntary administration of antipsychotic medication, see Riggins v. Nevada, 504 U.S. 127 (1992), discussed in 2 PERLIN, *supra* note 1, § 3B-8.3. On the right of incompetent-to-stand-trial defendants to refuse the involuntary administration of antipsychotic medication designed to make them competent to stand trial, see Sell v. United States, 539 U.S. 166 (2003) (holding that defendant has qualified right to refuse to take antipsychotic drugs prescribed solely to render him competent to stand trial; medication over objection is permissible where court finds treatment medically appropriate, substantially unlikely to have side effects that may undermine the fairness of the trial, and, taking account of less intrusive alternatives, necessary significantly to further important governmental trial-related interest); *see generally* Michael L. Perlin, "*And My Best Friend, My Doctor / Won't Even Say What It Is I've Got": The Role and Significance of Counsel in Right to Refuse Treatment Cases*, 42 SAN DIEGO L. REV. 735, 736 (2005).

217 The following section draws on PERLIN & CUCOLO, *supra* note 94, § 12-4.3, at 166–69, and Michael L. Perlin, *"Insanity Is Smashing Up Against My Soul": Panetti v. Quarterman and Questions That Won't Go Away* (2008), accessible at http://papers.ssrn.com/sol3/papers.cfm?abstract_id=1130890.

218 Singleton v. State, 437 S.E.2d 53, 60 – 62 (S.C. 1993).

219 992 S.W.2d 768 (Ark. 1999).

220 *See* 528 U.S. 1084 (2000). The *Singleton* decision from Arkansas is criticized in Kelly Gabos, *The Perils of Singleton v. Norris: Ethics and Beyond*, 32 AM. J. L. & MED. 117 (2006).

Later, in the *Singleton* litigation, Singleton filed a petition for a writ of *habeas corpus* seeking a stay of execution. Denial of the writ was affirmed by the Eighth Circuit, which held that neither due process nor the Eighth Amendment prevented the state from executing an inmate who has regained competency as the result of forced medication that is part of "appropriate medical care."[221]

Turning to the substantive question, the Court noted that it was guided by both *Harper* and *Ford* and that its task was to weigh the state's interest in carrying out a lawfully imposed sentence against Singleton's interest in refusing medication. The Court found that Singleton "prefers to take the medication rather than be in an unmedicated and psychotic state" and that he suffered no substantial side effects.[222] It held that as a result, the state's interest in carrying out its lawfully imposed sentence was the "superior one."[223] The Court went on to note that Singleton had proposed no less intrusive means of ensuring his competence and never argued that he was not competent with the medication—other than to put forth what the Court termed his "artificial competence theory."[224]

The Court then turned to what it deemed the "core of the dispute" namely "whether the antipsychotic medication is medically appropriate for Singleton's treatment."[225] The Court found Singleton to have "implicitly conceded" that the treatment was in his short-term medical interest.[226] In addressing his central claims, the Court reasoned,

> Singleton's argument regarding his long-term medical interest boils down to an assertion that execution is not in his medical interest. Eligibility for execution is the only unwanted consequence of the medication. The due process interests in life and liberty that Singleton asserts have been foreclosed by the lawfully imposed sentence of execution and the *Harper* procedure. In the circumstances presented in this case, the best medical interests of the prisoner must be determined without regard to whether there is a pending date of execution. … Thus, we hold that the mandatory medication regime, valid under the pendency of a stay of execution, does not become unconstitutional under *Harper* when an execution date is set.[227]

The Court also rejected Singleton's claim, based on *State v. Perry*, that the Eighth Amendment prohibited execution of one who is made "artificially competent":

221 319 F.3d 1018 (8th Cir. 2003), *cert denied*, 540 U.S. 832 (2003).
222 319 F.3d at 1025.
223 *Id.*
224 *Id.*
225 *Id.*
226 *Id.* at 1026.
227 *Id.*

> Closely related to his due process argument, Singleton also claims that the Eighth Amendment forbids the execution of a prisoner who is "artificially competent." Singleton relies principally on a case construing an analogous provision in the Louisiana Constitution. *State v. Perry*, 610 So. 2d 746 (La. 1992). … We note, however, that the *Perry* court accepted the view of "best medical interests" that we have rejected. 610 So. 2d at 766. The court also found Perry's medication was ordered solely for purposes of punishment and not for legitimate reasons of prison security or medical need. 610 So. 2d at 757. We decline to undertake a difficult and unnecessary inquiry into the State's motives in circumstance [*sic*] where it has a duty to provide medical care.[228]

Citing *Estelle v. Gamble*,[229] for the proposition that the government has an obligation to provide medical care to those whom it incarcerates, the Court reasoned that "any additional motive or effect is irrelevant." It concluded,

> *Ford* prohibits only the execution of a prisoner who is unaware of the punishment he is about to receive and why he is to receive it. A State does not violate the Eighth Amendment as interpreted by Ford when it executes a prisoner who became incompetent during his long stay on death row but who subsequently regained competency through appropriate medical care.[230]

In a dissenting opinion, Judge Heaney stated,

> I believe that to execute a man who is severely deranged without treatment, and arguably incompetent when treated, is the pinnacle of what Justice Marshall called "the barbarity of exacting mindless vengeance."[231]

Judge Heaney went on to cite facts from the record that indicated that even in a *medicated* state, Singleton appeared not to fully or rationally comprehend death or the nature of his sentence. After noting examples of Singleton's beliefs regarding death, including the belief that his victim was not truly dead and that a person can be executed by correctional officers and then have his breathing "started up again" by judges, he turned to a discussion of "synthetic" sanity:

> Singleton's case is exemplary of the unpredictable result antipsychotic treatment has on mentally ill prisoners. … Based on the medical history in this case, I am left with no alternative but to conclude that drug-induced sanity is not the same as true sanity. Singleton is not "cured"; his insanity is merely muted, at times, by the powerful drugs he is forced to take. Underneath this mask of stability, he

228 *Id.* at 1027.

229 429 U.S. 97, 103 (1976).

230 *Singleton*, 319 F.3d at 1030, citing *Estelle*, 429 U.S. at 103.

231 *Id.*, citing Ford. v. Wainwright, 477 U.S. 399, 410 (1986).

> remains insane. *Ford*'s prohibition on executing the insane should apply with no less force to Singleton than to untreated prisoners.[232]

Finally, noting the impact of the majority's ruling not only on mentally ill prisoners but on the integrity of the medical profession, the dissent concluded,

> I would hold that the State may continue to medicate Singleton, voluntarily or involuntarily, if it is necessary to protect him or others and is in his best medical interest, but it may not execute him. I continue to believe that the appropriate remedy is for the district court to enter a permanent stay of execution.[233]

Cases that followed Singleton were inconclusive, and absolutely no coherent jurisprudential threads could be drawn from them.[234] The next important development in this area of the law came several years later when, in *Panetti v. Dretke*,[235] the Fifth Circuit found that a medicated defendant was competent to

232 *Id.* at 1034.

233 *Id.* at 1037. The US Supreme Court denied *certiorari*, *see* 540 U.S. 832 (2003), and after more than 20 years on death row, Singleton was executed in January of 2004. *Singleton* is sharply criticized in Stephanie Zwein, *Executing the Insane: A Look at Death Penalty Schemes in Arkansas, Georgia and Texas*, 12 Suffolk J. Trial & App. Advocacy 93 (2007), Hensl, *supra* note 185, and in Rebecca A. Miller-Rice, *The "Insane" Contradiction of Singleton v. Norris: Forced Medication in a Death Row Inmate's Medical Interest Which Happens to Facilitate His Execution*, 22 U. Ark. Little Rock L. Rev. 659 (2000). *But see* Dominic Rupprecht, *Compelling Choice: Forcibly Medicating Death Row Inmates to Determine Whether They Wish to Pursue Collateral Relief*, 114 Penn St. L. Rev. 333 (2009) (supporting *Singleton*'s rationale).

234 For a somewhat muddled decision involving an attempted challenge to ad hoc procedures in Texas for determining competency to be executed, see Kemp v. Cockrell, 2003 U.S. Dist. LEXIS 8736 (N.D. Tex. 2003) (due process claims were procedurally barred, petitioner had no right to counsel or *Ake* expert assistance and issue of competency to be executed was not ripe because no execution date was pending). For pre-*Panetti* commentary, *see, e.g.*, Howard Zonana, *Competency to Be Executed and Forced Medication: Singleton v. Norris*, 31 J. Amer. Acad. Psychiatry & L. 372 (2003); Gabos, *supra* note 220; Gregory Dolin, *A Healer or an Executioner? The Proper Role of a Psychiatrist in a Criminal Justice System*, 17 J. L. & Health 169 (2002); Cantor, *supra* note 188; Angela Kimber, *Psychotic Journeys of the Green Mile*, 22 T.M. Cooley L. Rev. 27 (2005).

235 448 F.3d 815 (5th Cir. 2006), *rev'd sub. nom.* Panetti v. Quarterman, 551 U.S. 930 (2007). On why Panetti's trial was "truly a judicial farce, and a mockery of self-representation," see Richard J. Bonnie, *Panetti v. Quarterman: Mental Illness, the Death Penalty, and Human Dignity*, 5 Ohio St. J. Crim. L. 257, 261 (2007) (quoting Scott Monroe, Panetti's standby counsel). Panetti was found competent while taking antipsychotic medication, which he stopped taking shortly prior to trial, and did not resume; Panetti represented himself in this unmedicated condition. 551 U.S. at 936–37. On remand, the *habeas* court again denied Panetti's claim, finding he was competent to be executed, concluding that his delusions "do not prevent his rational understanding of the causal connection between those murders and

be executed. There, it affirmed a decision of the district court that had found that the defendant suffered from schizoaffective disorder, and had a "delusional belief system in which he viewed himself as being persecuted for his religious activities and beliefs," believing that the state is "in league with the forces of evil to prevent him from preaching the Gospel." Nonetheless, as the defendant was aware that he was to be executed, that he had committed the murders for which he was convicted and sentenced to death, and that the "State's stated reason for executing him is that he committed two murders," the district court held that Panetti was competent to be executed.[236] The Supreme Court subsequently granted *certiorari*[237] and ultimately reversed, holding that the defendant was denied the constitutional procedures to which he was entitled under *Ford*.[238] The decision, however, did not discuss the issue of involuntary medication, so this question remains unresolved.[239]

---

his death sentence, and he in fact has such an understanding." Panetti v. Quarterman, 2008 WL 2338498, *36 (W.D. Tex. 2008). The court recognized that Panetti "was mentally ill when he committed his crime and continues to be mentally ill today, *id.* at *37, but nonetheless determined that he "has both a factual and rational understanding of his crime, his impending death, and the causal retributive connection between the two. Therefore, if any mentally ill person is competent to be executed for his crimes, this record establishes it is Scott Panetti." *Id. See, e.g.*, Lyn Entzeroth, *The Challenge and Dilemma of Charting a Course to Constitutionally Protect the Severely Mentally Ill Capital Defendant from the Death Penalty*, 44 Akron L. Rev. 529, 557 n. 152 (2011). Panetti appealed the decision to the Fifth Circuit Court of Appeals; however, before it issued an opinion, the Fifth Circuit stayed and abated the proceedings so that Panetti could return to the state court to raise a claim, based on the Supreme Court's then-recently issued decision in Indiana v. Edwards, 554 U.S. 164 (2008), establishing limits on the right to self-representation. *See* Panetti v. Quarterman, No. 08-70015 (5th Cir., Dec. 17, 2008). That claim was dismissed, *see ex parte*, *Panetti*, WR-37, 145-02 (Tex. Crim. App. 2009), and Panetti subsequently sought, and was granted, a motion to stay and abate until the *Edwards* claim could be resolved on appeal. *See* Panetti v. Thaler, 2010 WL 2640336 (W.D. Tex. 2010). Panetti's *Edwards* application was subsequently rejected, over dissent, in state court, *see ex parte*, *Panetti*, 326 S.W.3d 615 (Tex. Crim. App. 2010), *cert. denied*, 131 S. Ct. 3027 (2011). Panetti's subsequent *habeas corpus* petition was rejected because (1) *Edwards* did not retroactively apply to collateral attacks, and (2) because Panetti was found not incompetent to represent himself under *Edwards*. Panetti v. Thaler, 2012 WL 290115 (W.D. Tex. 2012). *See generally* Christopher Seeds, *The Afterlife of* Ford *and* Panetti*: Execution Competence and the Capacity to Assist Counsel*, 53 St. Louis U. L. J. 309 (2009), *and see* Jonathan Greenberg, *For Every Action There Is a Reaction: The Procedural Pushback against* Panetti v. Quarterman, 49 Am. Crim. L. Rev. 227, 228 (2012) ("the case law governing death row competency proceedings is so skeletal as to give lower courts almost unfettered discretion in determining which inmates will ultimately be executed.").

236 *Id.* at 817.

237 Panetti v. Quarterman, 549 U.S. 1106 (2007).

238 Panetti v. Quarterman, 551 U.S. 930 (2007).

239 On why the Supreme Court should not have "evaded" this issue, see Holland Sergent, *Can Death Row Inmates Just Say No?: The Forced Administration of Drugs to*

Few of the cases in this cohort pay particular attention to the trilogy of US Supreme Court cases that deal with involuntary medication in cases involving convicted prisoners, competent defendants pleading the insanity defense, or incompetent defendants whom the state seeks to medicate so as to make them competent to stand trial.[240] Professor Lyn Entzeroth, in writing about this trilogy in this context, suggests that "forcible administration of antipsychotic medication [to make one competent to be executed] seems at the very least inconsistent with the principles of *Harper*, *Riggins*, and even *Sell*."[241]

I have written extensively elsewhere about the relationship between sanism, pretextuality, and the right to refuse treatment.[242] In a cohort of civil cases, I found that "the data suggests that, in many jurisdictions, such counsel is woefully inadequate—disinterested, uninformed, roleless, and often hostile."[243] Certainly, in death penalty cases—where counsel's inadequacy is often the norm[244]—the likelihood that applications for involuntary medication will be met with vigorous advocacy is negligible.

Render Inmates Competent for Execution in the United States and Texas, 35 Tex. Tech. L. Rev. 1299, 1323 (2004).

240 See Washington v. Harper, 494 U.S. 210, 236 (1990) (holding that the right to be free of medication must be balanced against the state's duty to treat inmates with mental illness and run a safe prison); Riggins v. Nevada, 504 U.S. 127, 129 (1992) (reversing conviction because trial court enforced administration of antipsychotic drugs during defendant's trial at which he relied on the insanity defense); Sell v. United States, 539 U.S. 166, 179 (2003) (holding that a defendant has qualified right to refuse to take antipsychotic drugs prescribed solely to render him competent to stand trial; medication over objection is permissible where court finds treatment medically appropriate, substantially unlikely to have side effects that may undermine the fairness of the trial, and, taking account of less intrusive alternatives, necessary significantly to further important governmental trial-related interests). But compare e.g., Amir Vonsover, *No Reason for Exemption: Singleton v. Norris and Involuntary Medication of Mentally Ill Capital Murderers for the Purpose of Execution*, 7 U. Pa. J. Const. L. 311 (2004), discussing the potential application of these three cases, and concluding, *id.* at 339, that the involuntary administration of medication to incompetent defendants "comport[s] with the law of *Sell*" and "furthers the retributive and deterrent goals of capital punishment"; Brent W. Stricker, *Seeking an Answer: Questioning the Validity of Forcible Medication to Ensure Mental Competency of Those Condemned to Die*, 32 McGeorge L. Rev. 317, 339 – 40 (2000), reading Harper to allow involuntary medication in such circumstances.

241 *See* Lyn Entzeroth, *The Illusion of Sanity: The Constitutional and Moral Danger of Medicating Condemned Prisoners in Order to Execute Them*, 76 Tenn. L. Rev. 641, 658 (2009).

242 *See, e.g.*, Michael L. Perlin, The Hidden Prejudice: Mental Disability on Trial 125–56 (2000); Michael L. Perlin & Deborah A. Dorfman, *Is It More Than "Dodging Lions and Wastin' Time"?: Adequacy of Counsel, Questions of Competence, and the Judicial Process in Individual Right to Refuse Treatment Cases*, 2 Psychol. Pub. Pol'y & L. 114, 120 (1996); Perlin, *supra* note 216.

243 Perlin, *supra* note 216, at 738.

244 *See* Perlin, *supra* note 183, at 123–38.

C. Conclusion

It is virtually impossible to reconcile the conflicting positions. A student commentator thus concludes,

> A prisoner allowed to refuse anti-psychotic drugs is a prisoner forever trapped in madness. He must be isolated and shunned by prison officials and staff for their own safety. He will be a constant danger to himself. This result ignores the state's affirmative duty of care and may harm the prisoner in ways that cannot be contemplated by sane persons. One wonders how the Constitution could tolerate this extreme example of individualism despite an obligation of care.[245]

On the other hand, in a recent article on the ethical issues that face physicians who medicate death row inmates, Dr. Howard Zonana concludes this way:

> As a species we are too good at rationalizing what we are doing or decided to do in the past. A little known example from World War II is the story of Japan's Unit 731 and Hisato Yoshimura ("the scientific devil"). Here are examples of physicians poisoning prisoners with cyanide and potassium chloride, performing vivisection, and deliberately inoculating prisoners with deadly pathogens. Hundreds of Japanese physicians took part in such murders. Their rationale, according to surviving physicians, was that the prisoners were condemned to die regardless, but this way their deaths would contribute useful knowledge. We have good ethical guidelines, and we need to follow them.[246]

Professor Bruce Arrigo and a colleague have approached this question from the perspective of therapeutic jurisprudence,[247] and have concluded that involuntarily medicating death row prisoners to make them competent to be executed violates therapeutic jurisprudence principles both from the perspectives of the effects such drugging has on medical personnel engaged in administering the drugs, and from the effects it has on the inmate being medicated.[248] Further, Professor Bruce Winick underscores how the use of therapists as an adjunct to capital punishment

245 Stricker, *supra* note 240, at 340. See also, Dolin, *supra* note 234, at 214 ("the mere prospect of execution does not make psychiatric help unethical, any more than the fact of incarceration makes such help unethical").

246 Zonana, *supra* note 184, at 773.

247 See *supra* Chapter 6.

248 Bruce A. Arrigo & Jeffrey J. Tasca, *Right to Refuse Treatment, Competency to be Executed, and Therapeutic Jurisprudence: Toward a Systematic Analysis*, 23 Law & Psychol. Rev. 1, 43–47 (1999), relying upon, inter alia, Bruce Winick, The Right to Refuse Mental Health Treatment (1997), and Bruce Winick, *The Jurisprudence of Therapeutic Jurisprudence*, 3 Psychol. Pub. Pol'y & L. 184, 185–90 (1997).

may "undermine their roles as healers,"[249] speculating that medicating prisoners to make them competent to be executed could "drive many ethical and sensitive practitioners from the field or deter them from entering it."[250] I believe that these positions and Dr. Zonana's position are, by far, the more persuasive in this inquiry.

VI. Four Overarching Factors

A. Sanism

Sanism and pretextuality affect incompetency to stand trial jurisprudence in at least four critical ways: (1) courts resolutely adhere to the conviction that defendants regularly malinger and feign incompetency; (2) courts stubbornly refuse to understand the distinction between incompetency to stand trial and insanity, even though the two statuses involve different concepts, different standards, and different points on the "time line"; (3) courts misunderstand the relationship between incompetency and subsequent commitment, and fail to consider the lack of a necessary connection between post-determination institutionalization and appropriate treatment; and (4) courts regularly accept patently inadequate expert testimony in incompetency to stand trial cases.[251]

1. Fear of faking

Malingering by defendants with mental disabilities is statistically rare.[252] Research reveals that defendants attempt feigning in less than eight percent of all competency to stand trial inquiries.[253] Yet, in deciding incompetency to stand trial cases, courts continue to focus, in some cases almost obsessively, on testimony that raises the

---

249 Bruce Winick, *Competency to Be Executed: A Therapeutic Jurisprudence Perspective*, 10 Behav. Sci. & L. 317, 332 (1992).

250 *Id.* at 334.

251 See Michael L. Perlin, *Pretexts and Mental Disability Law: The Case of Competency*, 47 U. Miami L. Rev. 625, 678 (1993).

252 Michael L. Perlin, *Unpacking the Myths: The Symbolism Mythology of Insanity Defense Jurisprudence*, 40 Case W. Res. L. Rev. 599, 715–16 nn.556–58 (1989–90) (citing sources); *see also, e.g.*, David Schretlen & Hal Arkowitz, *A Psychological Test Battery to Detect Prison Inmates who Fake Insanity or Mental Retardation*, 8 Behav. Sci. & L. 75, 75 (1990) ("92–95% of subjects were correctly classified as either faking or not faking").

253 Dewey G. Cornell & Gary L. Hawk, *Clinical Presentation of Malingerers Diagnosed by Experienced Forensic Psychologists*, 13 Law & Hum. Behav. 375, 380–83 (1989). On the potential role of racial bias in such determinations, see *id.* at 382 (clinicians may over-diagnose malingering in black defendants). *See also, e.g.*, R. Michael Bagby et al., *Detection of Dissimulation with the New Generation of Objective Personality Measures*, 8 Behav. Sci. & L. 93 (1990); Richard Rogers et al., *The SIRS as a Measure of Malingering: A Validation Study with a Correctional Sample*, 8 Behav. Sci. & L. 85 (1990); Orest E. Wasyliw et al., *The Detection of Malingering in Criminal Forensic Groups: MMPI Validity*

specter of malingering.[254] The fear of such deception has "permeated the American legal system for over a century,"[255] despite the complete lack of evidence that such feigning "has ever been a remotely significant problem of criminal procedure."[256] This fear is a further manifestation of judicial sanism.

2. Conflation of standards

Trial courts continue to blur the distinction between incompetency to stand trial and insanity.[257] They confuse these concepts despite countless appellate admonitions as to the differences between the two states,[258] and despite different substantive standards, different behavioral criteria and obvious temporal differences.[259] Courts

Scales, 52 J. Personality Assessment 321 (1988). More recent research is discussed in Pirelli, Gottdiener & Zapf, *supra* note 3.

254 *See, e.g.*, Cowan v. State, 579 So. 2d 13, 15 (Ala. Crim. App. 1990); Farinas v. State, 569 So. 2d 425, 432 (Fla. 1990) (Grimes, J., dissenting); State v. Sharkey, 821 S.W.2d 544, 546 (Mo. Ct. App. 1991); People v. Perkins, 562 N.Y.S.2d 244, 245 (N.Y. App. Div. 1990); State v. Evans, 586 N.E.2d 1042, 1054 (Ohio 1992), *cert. denied*, 506 U.S. 886 (1992); Blacklock v. State, 820 S.W.2d 882, 884–85 (Tex. Ct. App. 1991); State v. Drobel, 815 P.2d 724, 727–28 (Utah Ct. App. 1991); Rogers v. State, 2012 WL 3776675 (Tenn. Crim. App. 2012); State v. Todd, 2012 WL 2150859 (Tenn. Crim. App. 2012); U.S. v. Derisma, 2011 WL 3878367 (M.D. Fla. 2011); State v. Smith, 2011 WL 5517646 (Tenn. Crim. App. 2012). In People v. Weeks, 960 N.E.2d 570 (Ill. App. 2011), the defendant was taken off medication to test whether he was malingering. *See* Perlin, *supra* note 85, at 250.

255 Michael L. Perlin, *The Supreme Court, the Mentally Disabled Criminal Defendant, and Symbolic Values: Random Decisions, Hidden Rationales, or Doctrinal Abyss*?, 29 Ariz. L. Rev. 1, 98 (1987).

256 Perlin, *supra* note 252, at 714; Perlin, *supra* note 85, at 250 ("[C]ourts resolutely adhere to the conviction that defendants regularly malinger and feign incompetency …"). See e.g., . Smart v. Harrington, 2011 WL 4726156 (N.D. Cal. 2011); Samuels v. Hernandez, 2009 WL 2730502 (C.D. Cal. 2009); Marrero v. Horn, 2008 WL 3833382 (W.D. Pa. 2008).

257 See 4 Perlin, *supra* note 1, § 8A-2.1, at 4 n.11 (citing sources).

258 *See, e.g.*, United States v. McEachern, 465 F.2d 833, 836 (5th Cir. 1972) ("we note the possible confusion caused by [the trial court's] use of the term 'insane' when the relevant inquiry is competence to stand trial"), *cert. denied*, 409 U.S. 1043 (1972); State v. Spivey, 319 A.2d 461, 470 (N.J. 1974) ("[t]he Court must be careful to distinguish between insanity and incapacity to stand trial"); Aponte v. State, 153 A.2d 665, 669–70 (N.J. 1959); see also Commonwealth v. Musolino, 467 A.2d 605 (Pa. Super. 1983) (trial court's instructions to jury confused competency at time of trial and defendant's insanity defense); Legrand v. United States, 570 A.2d 786 (D.C. 1990) (court's plea discussion with defendant confused competency and insanity when addressing current mental states). The error is often deemed harmless. *See, e.g.*, Buttrum v. Black, 721 F. Supp. 1268, 1295 (N.D. Ga. 1989), *aff'd*, 908 F.2d 695 (11th Cir. 1990).

259 *See, e.g.*, United States v. Santos, 131 F.3d 16, 20 (1st Cir. 1997) (insanity and competency to stand trial are independent determinations) United States v. Gold, 790 F.2d 235, 238 (2d Cir. 1986) (insanity and competency to stand trial are independent determinations); United States v. Williams, 998 F.2d 258, 264 n.15 (5th Cir. 1993) (insanity and competency to stand trial are independent determinations). For the purpose of inquiry

often ask defendants and experts irrelevant and meaningless questions that bear no relationship to the ultimate question to be decided by the court.[260]

While much of the judicial confusion may stem from experts' confusion about the two terms,[261] it is clear that attorneys, trial judges, forensic witnesses and other testifying mental health professionals equally misunderstand the core concepts.[262] The fact that this state of affairs continues, with little or no remediation, suggests that its perpetuation continues to meet sanist aims.[263]

3. Misunderstanding of incompetency commitments

Empirical studies demonstrate that trial judges misunderstand the relationship between a finding of incompetency to stand trial and subsequent hospital commitment. In a statewide study conducted four years after the Supreme Court's decision in *Jackson v. Indiana*,[264] almost one-half of all judges polled believed that commitment of incompetent criminal defendants to forensic hospitals should be automatic without regard to the severity of the underlying criminal offense or

---

regarding competency to stand trial, the relevant time is the time of the trial; for inquiry regarding insanity, the relevant time is the time of the crime. *See generally* State v. Ortiz, 492 P.2d 397 (Ariz. 1972).

260 *See, e.g.*, Richard Arens, Insanity Defense 78–79 (1974) (reproducing transcripts of competency hearings in which the judge merely asked defendants the date, the names of the President and Vice President, and the Washington Senators' (baseball team) standing in the American League); *see also* Michael L. Perlin, *Psychodynamics and the Insanity Defense: "Ordinary Common Sense" and Heuristic Reasoning*, 69 Neb. L. Rev. 3, 24 n.95 (1990) (discussing Arens, *supra*); Norman G. Poythress, *Mental Health Expert Testimony: Current Problems*, 5 J. Psychiatry & L. 201, 218 (1977) (reporting on a case in which the court asked the forensic psychologist who had administered the MMPI test to the defendant, "Do you believe in free will?" and "Do you believe in God?").

261 *See* Whitcomb & Brandt, *supra* note 23, at 2; George E. Dix & Norman G. Poythress, *Propriety of Medical Dominance of Forensic Mental Health Practice: The Empirical Evidence*, 23 Ariz. L. Rev. 961, 972–74 (1981); David B. Wexler et al., *The Administration of Psychiatric Justice: Theory and Practice in Arizona*, 13 Ariz. L. Rev. 1, 64–65 (1971); Carl R. Vann & Fred Morganroth, *Psychiatrists and the Competence to Stand Trial*, 42 U. Det. L. Rev. 75, 84 (1964); Helene R. Banks, *Immediate Appeal of Pretrial Commitment Orders: "It's Now or Never,"* 55 Fordham L. Rev. 785, 786 n.8 (1987).

262 William H. Erickson et al., *Competence to Stand Trial*, in ABA Criminal Justice Mental Health Standards 157, 159 (1989). For an example of counsel's misunderstanding, see Kirk v. State, 308 S.E.2d 592, 598 (Ga. Ct. App. 1983) (counsel mistakenly asked for incompetency to stand trial charge in insanity case), *aff'd*, 311 S.E.2d 821 (Ga. 1984).

263 Misstatements of the appropriate standard continue. *See* Lafferty v. Cook, 949 F.2d 1546, 1554 (10th Cir. 1991) (record revealed "unambiguously that the state trial court's evaluation of [defendant's] competency was infected by a misperception of the legal requirements set out in *Dusky*"), *cert. denied*, 504 U.S. 911 (1992).

264 406 U.S. 715, 731, 738 (1972) (incompetent criminal defendants cannot automatically be indefinitely housed in maximum security forensic facilities if it is not likely that they will regain their competency to stand trial within the foreseeable future).

to the defendant's present dangerousness.[265] A more recent national study of trial judges revealed that such hospitalization was the judicial intervention of choice in nearly 90% of all cases.[266] Even in states that expressly sanction outpatient commitment as an alternative in criminal incompetency cases, judges remain reluctant to employ this mechanism due to their fear that the patient might become violent in an outpatient setting.[267]

Unfortunately, there is no necessary correlation between such institutionalization and appropriate treatment. The starkest case is that of Theon Jackson, the appellant in *Jackson v. Indiana*.[268] Jackson was a deaf mute individual with mental retardation, incapable of reading, writing or communicating in any way except through a limited knowledge of sign language. He was indicted on two counts of robbery, both apparently involving purse snatching.[269] Notwithstanding testimony at his competency hearing that it was unlikely that Jackson could ever learn to read, write, or use sign language proficiently, and that it would be impossible for him to learn minimal communication skills in an Indiana state institution,[270] the trial court committed Jackson indefinitely to a state hospital "until such time as the state should certify to the court that 'the *defendant is sane*'."[271]

Although the Supreme Court held in favor of Jackson, striking down such commitments as tantamount to life sentences without trial,[272] the underlying problem has not been fully ameliorated. Forty years after the decision in *Jackson,* almost one-half of the states have not implemented its holding, and pre-*Jackson* problems "still persisted."[273] The commitment of defendants in incompetency

---

265 Ronald Roesch & Stephen Golding, *Legal and Judicial Interpretation of Competency to Stand Trial Statutes and Procedures*, 16 CRIMINOLOGY 420, 423–24 (1978). Compare Jodi L. Viljoen et al., *An Examination of the Relationship Between Competency to Stand Trial, Competency to Waive Interrogation Rights, and Psychopathology*, 26 LAW & HUM. BEHAV. 481 (2002) (most defendants with psychotic disorders evidenced no significant impairment in their capacity to stand trial).

266 Ingo Keilitz & J. Rudy Martin, *Criminal Defendants With Trial Disabilities: The Theory and Practice of Competency Assistance* 84 (unpublished manuscript) cited in Perlin, *supra* note 251, at 671 n.231.

267 Ann L. Hester, *State v. Gravette: Is There Justice for Incompetent Defendants in North Carolina?*, 69 N.C. L. REV. 1484, 1497 (1991).

268 406 U.S. 715 (1972). *See generally* 4 PERLIN, *supra* note 1, §§ 8A-5 to 8A-5.3, at 65–74.

269 Jackson, 406 U.S. at 717.

270 *Id.* at 718–19.

271 *Id.* at 719 (emphasis added).

272 *Id.* at 731–38.

273 Winick, *supra* note 2, at 941; *see also* Ellen C. Wertlieb, *Individuals With Disabilities in the Criminal Justice System: A Review of the Literature*, 18 CRIM. JUST. & BEHAV. 332, 336 (1991). Winick's research has been updated in Grant Morris & J. Reid Meloy, *Out of Mind? Out of Sight: The Uncivil Commitment of Permanently Incompetent Criminal Defendants*, 27 U.C. DAVIS L. REV. 1, 8 (1993) (a decade after Winick published

to stand trial cases to forensic hospitals often triggers a "shuttle" mechanism. Defendants are treated (usually with antipsychotic drugs),[274] temporarily stabilized, returned to court, found competent, and jailed to await trial. At this point, many "destabilize" and become incompetent once again.[275] This endless cycle has been well documented,[276] but courts have been remarkably, and uniformly, silent in their sanist non-responses.

4. Acceptance of inadequate testimony

Finally, courts regularly accept inadequate testimony in incompetency to stand trial cases.[277] For example, in *State v. Pruitt*, the sole expert witness testified in

---

his article, *Jackson* remained "ignored [and] circumvented"), in Michael L. Perlin, *"For the Misdemeanor Outlaw": The Impact of the ADA on the Institutionalization of Criminal Defendants with Mental Disabilities*, 52 ALABAMA L. REV. 193, 204 (2000) (Perlin, *Misdemeanor Outlaw*) ("more than half the states allow for the indefinite commitment of incompetent-to-stand-trial defendants, in spite of *Jackson*'s specific language outlawing this practice), and in Andrew R. Kaufman, Bruce B. Way & Enrico Suardi, *Forty Years After Jackson v. Indiana: States' Compliance with "Reasonable Period of Time" Ruling*, 40 J. AM. ACAD. PSYCHIATRY & L. 261 (20112) (most states out of compliance with *Jackson*). I discuss the significance of the earlier findings in Michael L. Perlin, *Fatal Assumption: A Critical Evaluation of the Role of Counsel in Mental Disability Cases*, 16 LAW & HUM. BEHAV. 39, 47–48 (1992). *Cf.* State v. Werner, 796 P.2d 610, 613 (N.M. Ct. App. 1990) (it was not error to treat dangerous patients committed pursuant to *Jackson* differently from civil patients).

274 *See* 4 PERLIN, *supra* note 1, §§ 8A-4.2 to 8A-4.2d, at 51–60, and PERLIN & CUCOLO, *supra* note 94, § 8A-4.2c(1), discussing Sell v. United States, 539 U.S. 166 (2003) (holding that defendant has qualified right to refuse to take antipsychotic drugs prescribed solely to render him competent to stand trial; medication over objection is permissible where court finds treatment medically appropriate, substantially unlikely to have side effects that may undermine the fairness of the trial, and, taking account of less intrusive alternatives, necessary significantly to further important governmental trial-related interest).

275 Hester, *supra* note 267, at 1498; *see* Bruce J. Winick, *Incompetency to Stand Trial: An Assessment of Costs and Benefits, and a Proposal for Reform*, 39 RUTGERS L. REV. 243, 248–49 (1987); Winick, *supra* note 2, at 934.

276 *See, e.g.*, Wertlieb, *supra* note 273, at 337 (discussing United States v. Juarez, 540 F. Supp. 1288 (W.D. Tex. 1982) (mentally retarded, incompetent-to-stand-trial defendant was not treated for over three years due to jurisdictional dispute between state and federal institutions).

277 WHITCOMB & BRANDT, *supra* note 23, at 2 (experts' reports are often "empty and meaningless"). For a review of such deficiencies, *see id.* at 1 (reporting on findings in Ingo Keilitz, *Mental Health Examination in Criminal Justice Settings: Organization, Administration, and Program Evaluation* (Sept. 1981) (unpublished manuscript, on file with the National Center for State Courts) (courts often fail to provide reasons for evaluation requests and fail to screen out unwarranted evaluation requests; no agreement exists between the justice and mental health systems as to the purpose of evaluation; and the evaluation report is frequently delayed at great length)).

conclusory terms that the defendant "suffered no mental disease or defect; and he understood the respective roles of the cast of characters at the trial, and the nature of the charges against him," yet "never indicated ... what the defendant actually understood."[278] Although the appellate court reversed Pruitt's conviction on other grounds, a majority of the court was satisfied that this testimony was a sufficient basis for a competency finding.[279] In *Hensley v. State*, the court found no abuse of discretion on the issue of incompetency to stand trial where the defendant was able to deny the crime and name the alleged victim, despite the uncontested fact that the defendant's "testimony and actions at the competency hearing were not generally meaningful."[280] In *People v. Lopez*, the appellate court held that the trial court's decision not to conduct a competency hearing was not error, notwithstanding defendant's history of hospitalization, attempted suicide, drug overdose, use of prescribed psychotropic medications, and suicidal thoughts.[281] These and other similar cases[282] suggest that the most minimal testimony will satisfy courts in such incompetency to stand trial inquiries.

Professor E. Lea Johnston's observations about sanism in the specific context of competency to stand trial issues fairly summarize this entire state of affairs:

> Sanism may manifest in a general tendency to distrust decisions of persons with mental illness and in assumptions that individuals who exercise their right to counsel are "crazy" and incapable of sufficiently autonomous decisionmaking. Beyond an attorney's biases, an attorney's self-interest may also militate against recognizing the values and interests of his client.[283]

---

278 480 N.E.2d 499, 504 (Ohio Ct. App. 1984). The witness also admitted that while he had been aware that the defendant was evaluated by mental health professionals at a V.A. hospital, he did not have copies of those records and that, depending on the content of those records, his opinion might have been different. *Id.*

279 *Id.* at 509 (Markus, J., concurring); *id.* (Nahra, J., concurring).

280 575 N.E.2d 1053, 1055 (Ind. App. Ct. 1991).

281 People v Lopez, 576 N.E.2d 246, 248–9 (Ill. App. Ct. 1991).

282 *See, e.g.*, United States v. Prince, 938 F.2d 1092,1093–95 (10th Cir.), *cert. denied*, 502 U.S. 961 (1991) (finding no abuse of discretion in trial court's refusal to hold a second competency hearing where defendant exposed himself and urinated in courtroom); Rollins v. Leonardo, 938 F.2d 380, 382 (2d Cir. 1991), *cert. denied*, 502 U.S. 1062 (1992) (defendant was an escapee from a psychiatric hospital at the time that he was tried for the offense); United States v. Caicedo, 937 F.2d 1227, 1232 (7th Cir. 1991) (although trial counsel stated that he did not know if the defendant "could cooperate with him in the preparation of his defense, he [stated that defendant] was '*perfectly competent*'") (emphasis in original).

283 E. Lea Johnston, *Representational Competence: Defining the Limits of the Right to Self-Representation at a Trial*, 86 Notre Dame L. Rev, 523, 536 (2011).

B. Pretextuality

There is little question that competency evaluations are used as a "back door" to hospitals to secure mental health treatment for individuals who are not otherwise committable.[284] The fact that 90% of the evaluations done at a forensic center in Alabama offered no information about defendants' "appreciation" or "reasoning" abilities[285] suggests that the evaluations are, in large measure, pretextual.

Several years ago, in discussing the research reported on by Professor Grant Morris and his colleagues,[286] I charged that the entire incompetency evaluation system was pretextual. I believe that what I wrote then holds just as true today:

> The Morris article reveals the extent to which pretextuality dominates the incompetency-to-stand-trial system. First, the entire system—implicitly and explicitly—assumes that the defendant committed the predicate criminal act with which he is charged. Although there is nothing in the invocation of the incompetency status that at all concedes factual guilt (as opposed to the entry of a not-guilty-by-reason-of-insanity plea that concedes the commission of the underlying criminal act),[287] it is assumed by all that the defendant did, in fact, commit the crime.
>
> When I was a public defender, I represented in individual cases well over 200 criminal defendants who had been found—at some point—incompetent to stand trial. In not a single case did the prosecutor, the judge, or the forensic evaluator even acknowledge the possibility that the defendant might have been "factually innocent" of the underlying charge. This is a topic that is rarely, if ever, addressed in the case law or the legal or behavioral literature, but I am convinced that it is one that must be taken seriously if we are going to carefully and comprehensively examine this question.[288]
>
> In fact, the research shows that "expert" evaluations frequently rely not on the examiners' experience or knowledge but on the facts of the criminal act

---

284 *See, e.g.*, Gwen A. Levitt et al., *Civil Commitment Outcomes of Incompetent Defendants*, 38 J. Am. Acad. Psychiatry & L. 349, 349 (2010).

285 Patricia A. Zapf et al., *Have the Courts Abdicated Their Responsibility for Determination of Competency to Stand Trial to Clinicians?*, 4 J. Forensic Psychol. Prac. 27 (2004).

286 *See* Morris et al, *supra* note 23.

287 *See* Jones v. United States, 463 U.S. 354, 363 (1983) ("A verdict of not guilty by reason of insanity establishes two facts: (i) the defendant committed an act that constitutes a criminal offense, and (ii) he committed the act because of mental illness.").

288 *See* Perlin, *Misdemeanor Outlaw*, *supra* note 273, at 206–07 :

> Consider this easy hypothetical. A defendant is charged with crime and is, in fact, factually innocent. Walking to the courthouse for the initial bail hearing, he is hit on the head by a cinder block from ongoing courthouse construction, causing severe organic brain damage. He will be found—most likely—incompetent to stand trial, but such finding in no way should allow us to assume that he is factually "guilty" of the underlying charge.

charged.[289] In one study, the "only variable" that distinguished those determined to be dangerous from those determined not to be dangerous was the alleged crime: "The more serious the alleged crime, the more likely that the psychiatrist would find the defendant dangerous."[290]

Second, the paper notes the Supreme Court's fact-not-in-evidence assumption that, in competency-to-stand-trial determinations, defense counsel "will often have the best-informed view of the defendant's ability to participate in his defense,"[291] and then observes that counsel "typically does not testify in the incompetency hearing."[292] The empirical data is even more dramatic than that. In a recent paper, Professor Randy Otto and his colleagues reported on data that revealed that, in a study of 674 juvenile incompetency cases (the subset where one might reasonably expect counsel would be more involved than in other cases), not a single defense counsel testified at the juvenile's competency hearing.[293] This pretext is just as glaring.

***

Fourth, the responses reveal an inappropriate fusing on the part of some of the experts between their evaluative role and their (non-existent) treating role.[294] One respondent thus answered: "She [the subject of the vignette] appears to need medication. I would lean toward unfit with greater period of observation as an inpatient."[295] The inappropriateness of this sort of response was first noted over thirty years ago,[296] and remarkably, it still appears to be flourishing. Again, it is the rankest sort of pretext to invoke or adapt the competency evaluation process to serve as a vehicle for treatment needs.

---

289 Perlin, *supra* note 251, at 663.

290 *Id.* (quoting Joseph J. Cocozza & Henry J. Steadman, *The Failure of Psychiatric Predictions of Dangerousness: Clear and Convincing Evidence*, 29 RUTGERS L. REV. 1084, 1096 (1976)).

291 Medina v. California, 505 U.S. 437, 450 (1992).

292 Morris et al., *supra* note 23 at 199.

293 Randy Otto, "Evaluations of Juveniles' Competence to Proceed," paper presented to the American Academy of Psychiatry and Law, Newport Beach, CA, October 24, 2002; *see also* Annette Christy et al., *Juveniles Evaluated Incompetent to Proceed: Characteristics and Quality of Mental Health Professionals' Evaluation*, 35 PROF. PSYCHOL.: RES. & PRAC. 380 (2004) (of the 1357 evaluations generated in the 674 cases, only 33 reported on an interview by the examining psychologist of the juvenile's lawyer).

294 Morris et al., *supra* note 23, at 222–23.

295 *Id.* at 222.

296 Now forty. *See* ARTHUR MATTHEWS, MENTAL DISABILITY AND THE CRIMINAL LAW 134 (1970) (noting the competency process is frequently invoked to effect hospitalization that might not otherwise be possible under the state's civil commitment statute); see also Winick, *supra* note 2, at 933.

Fifth, some of the responders simply rejected the significance of the difference between the two incompetency tests used in the study; "I'm not impressed with the standards …. really being different," wrote one.[297] Again, there is nothing new here:

> [A]fter considering Ontario's amended mental health law aimed at making involuntary civil commitment standards more stringent, a prominent local psychiatrist argued that the new law had little empirical weight: 'Doctors will continue to certify those whom they really believe should be certified; they will merely learn a new language.'"[298]

What is depressing is that this behavior continues, unabated, after more than thirty years.[299]

Sixth, the article reveals that, in spite of the impressive array of new competency assessment instruments now available to evaluators, "the overwhelming majority of psychiatrists and psychologists do not use psychological tests in assessing a defendant's competency."[300] This refusal to use such tools (e.g., the MacArthur Competence Assessment Tool—Criminal Adjudication) reflects, again, a pretextual turn on the part of experts who presumably feel that their expertise enables them to make such determinations without the assistance of "standardized and nationally norm-referenced clinical measure[s]."[301]

Finally, the respondents consistently failed to differentiate between forensic and clinical issues,[302] and it is this error that in many ways best demonstrates the pretextuality that is at play here. The answers of "numerous" respondents "clearly suggested" that clinical questions concerning the presence of mental illness, psychosis and amenability to treatment were determinative of their final (putatively) forensic conclusion. The overt—perhaps defiant—call on the part of the respondents to willfully ignore the legal standard and to superimpose

---

297 Morris et al., *supra* note 23, at 224.

298 Perlin, *supra* note 251, at 645 (quoting William O. McCormick, *Involuntary Commitment in Ontario: Some Barriers to the Provision of Proper Care*, 124 CAN. MED. ASS'N J. 715, 717 (1981)).

299 *See generally* William H. Fisher & Thomas Grisso, *Commentary: Civil Commitment Statutes – 40 Years of Circumvention*, 38 J. AM. ACAD. PSYCHIATRY L. 365 (2010).

300 Morris et al., *supra* note 23, at 234 (relying, inter alia, upon Randy Borum & Thomas Grisso, *Psychological Test Use in Criminal Forensic Evaluations*, 26 PROF. PSYCHOLOGY: RES. & PRAC. 465, 468 (1995) (11% of psychiatrists and 36% of psychologists regularly used such tests)).

301 Morris et al., *supra* note 23, at 233 (quoting Patricia Zapf & Jodi Viljoen, *Issues and Considerations Regarding the Use of Assessment Instruments in the Evaluation of Competency to Stand Trial*, 21 BEHAV. SCI. & L. 351, 359 (2003)).

302 *Id.* at 237.

> their own moralistic sense of how the case should be resolved tells us that this pretextual system is far more corrupt than any of us had known.[303]

C. Heuristics

The relationship between the use of heuristics and errors in the incompetency assessment process have been well known for decades.[304] The pretexts of the forensic mental health system are reflected both in the testimony of forensic experts and in the decisions of legislators and fact-finders. Experts frequently testify in accordance with their own self-referential concepts of "morality" and openly subvert statutory and case law criteria that articulate functional standards as prerequisites for an incompetency to stand trial finding.[305] Often this testimony is further warped by a heuristic bias. Expert witnesses—like the rest of us—succumb to the seductive allure of simplifying cognitive devices in their thinking, and employ such heuristic gambits as the vividness effect or attribution theory in their testimony.[306]

Some years ago, in discussing the incompetency case *United States v. Charters*,[307] I noted how the Fourth Circuit's *en banc* decision reflected inappropriate heuristic thinking in a variety of contexts, "including availability, typification, the myth of particularistic proofs, and the vividness effect" in its characterization of witness testimony, and pointed out how its attempts to simplify

---

303 Perlin, *supra* note 85, at 246–49.

304 *See* Perlin, *supra* note 251, at 663–64

305 *See, e.g.* People v. Doan, 366 N.W.2d 593, 598 (Mich. App. 1985), *app'l den.* (1985) (expert testified that defendant was "out in left field" and went "bananas").

306 Michael L. Perlin, *"Half-Wracked Prejudice Leaped Forth": Sanism, Pretextuality, and Why and How Mental Disability Law Developed As It Did*, 10 J. CONTEMP. LEG. ISS. 3, 18 (1999); see also, in the context of medicating incompetent defendants against their will, Michael L. Perlin, *Are Courts Competent to Decide Questions of Competency? Stripping the Facade From United States v. Charters*, 38 U. KAN. L. REV. 957, 966 (1990):

> By its language, its use of heuristic reasoning, its retreat into its conception of "ordinary common sense," and its reliance on myth, the court backpedals from the issue that remains at the core of the right-to-refuse-treatment inquiry. This issue is the competency of the institutionalized mentally disabled to retain autonomy in the most basic decision making that affects their mental and physical health and their potential length of stay in the institution. Until this aspect of the court's decision receives serious attention, it is impossible to understand why right-to-refuse-treatment litigation has developed as it has and why the debate over the right remains so contentious.

307 United States v. Charters, 829 F.2d 479, 483 (4th Cir. 1987), *on reh'g*, 863 F.2d 302 (4th Cir. 1988) (*en banc*), *cert. denied*, 494 U.S. 1016 (1990) (permitting the government to involuntarily medicate a defendant who was incompetent to stand trial). *Charters* preceded the Supreme Court decision of Sell v. United States, 539 U.S. 166 (2003), discussed *supra* note 216.

the complex questions involved in such medication decision-making "further reflects the pernicious effect of the heuristic of attribution theory."[308] *Charters* was far from an atypical decision, and the similar misuse of heuristics continue to poison the incompetency-to-stand-trial inquiry.

D. OCS

Courts and legislatures regularly base decisions upon perceptions about ordinary common sense and mental illness. OCS should not be applied to incompetency to stand trial jurisprudence, as human behavior is very often *opposite* to what OCS would suggest. The reliance on such propositions by legal decision-makers is risky behavior.[309] Careful research studies have found that judges, attorneys, legislators and mental health professionals all inappropriately employ irrelevant, stereotypical negative information in coming to conclusions on the related question of a mentally disabled criminal defendant's dangerousness.[310] Consider the trial judge's response to National Center for State Courts' survey that indicated that, "in his mind, defendants who were incompetent to stand trial could have communicated with and understood their attorneys 'if they [had] only wanted'."[311]

In short, unwitting reliance on OCS is a hidden animator of criminal justice decision-making. In the incompetency to stand trial context, it creates a "fraudulen[t], … gravely distorted and deeply flawed" incompetency process.[312]

IV. Five Perspectives

A. Counsel

As I have already discussed, counsel in many cases involving presumptively incompetent-to-stand-trial defendants is woefully incompetent.[313] When the defendant is represented, counsel is charged with helping the court assess the defendant's ability to participate appropriately.[314] Of course, it is by no means clear

---

308 Perlin, *supra* note 306, at 986–87.

309 Perlin, *supra* note 260, at 28.

310 Margaret A. Jackson, *The Clinical Assessment and Prediction of Violent Behavior: Toward a Scientific Analysis*, 16 Crim. Just. & Behav. 114, 125–26 (1989).

311 Michael L. Perlin, *"Baby, Look Inside Your Mirror": The Legal Profession's Willful and Sanist Blindness to Lawyers with Mental Disabilities*, 69 U. Pitt. L. Rev. 589, 600 n. 70 (2008), citing Keri Gould et al, *Criminal Defendants With Trial Disabilities: The Theory and Practice of Competency Assistance* 68 (unpublished manuscript).

312 Perlin, *supra* note 85, at 252–53.

313 See *supra* Chapter 3.

314 Anne Bowen Poulin, *Strengthening the Criminal Defendant's Right to Counsel*, 28 Cardozo L. Rev. 1213, 1281 (2006), and see *id*. n. 294 (discussing relevant cases).

that this happens in all cases.[315] One confounding issue may be the fact that the lawyer (as well as the judge and society at large) "may well have different goals, values, and priorities than the defendant."[316]

It is nearly three decades since Strickland was decided, yet the issues of incompetent counsel in incompetency cases still plagues the courts. Consider these recent examples:

In *Deere v. Cullen*,[317] a California federal court granted *habeas corpus* relief to a death-row petitioner who had pled guilty, ruling that counsel's failure to request a hearing into his competency to stand trial and to plead guilty was objectively unreasonable under *Strickland*, where counsel insisted to the court that the petitioner was competent, despite his questionable mental state.

In *Massachusetts v. A.B.*,[318] a state appellate court ordered a new trial for a defendant charged with assault and battery, holding that counsel was ineffective for failing to seek a competency hearing where the defendant was diagnosed with paranoid schizophrenia, had a 10-year history of intermittent hospitalization and medication noncompliance, and had previously been found incompetent with no clear finding of restoration to competency.[319]

In short, counsel's adequacy in competency matters cannot be presumed, and lack of adequacy—whether a *Strickland* violation is formally found or not—makes it less likely that the proceeding will be one that adheres to dignity values.

B. International Human Rights[320]

In the international arena, there is a strong argument that "the prohibition on execution of the insane is a customary norm of international human rights law."[321]

---

315 *See e.g.*, Chichakly v. United States, 926 F.2d 624, 632 (7th Cir. 1991) (competency hearing was not required, despite defendant's claim that psychiatric medication affected his mental and emotional state, when counsel did not request a hearing and assured court that medication did not affect defendant's ability to understand the charges). On the interplay between medication and competency, see *supra* Part V.

316 Johnston, *supra* note 283, at 535. Although Professor Johnston specifies "court appointed attorney[s]" in her conclusion, I see no reason to separate them out from retained counsel.

317 713 F.Supp.2d 1011 (C.D. Cal. 2010).

318 887 N.E.2d 1107 (Mass. Ct. App. 2008).

319 The defendant's history included five confinements at Bridgewater State Hospital and Taunton State Hospital, where he was diagnosed with paranoid schizophrenia and found to have a significant history of medication noncompliance resulting in psychotic decompensations and violence. *Id.* at 1109.

320 *See infra* Chapter 9 for a discussion of relevance of the Convention on the Rights of Persons with Disabilities to the populations in question.

321 William A. Schabas, *International Norms on Execution of the Insane and the Mentally Retarded*, 4 Crim. L.F. 95, 114 (1993).

Certainly, the same prohibition must apply to defendants who are not competent to stand trial.

Certainly, the Convention on the Rights of Persons with Disabilities potentially offers great protections to defendants who are incompetent to stand trial.[322] Consider just of the many potentially applicable sections: the right to access to support "in exercising legal capacity,"[323] "equal recognition before the law,"[324] and the right to "liberty and security of the person."[325] A system that deprives putatively incompetent persons to access to effective counsel,[326] that countenances facially illegal stays in maximum-security forensic facilities,[327] and that presumes factual guilt[328] falls far short of what is required by international human rights law.

C. Mental Health Courts

Much more attention has been paid in the scholarly literature to the relationship between the incompetency status and mental health courts.[329] Judges Anne Harper and Michael Finkle argue that a significant advantage of a mental health court is that the question of competency to stand trial can be addressed in a single court with a potentially accelerated process. In such circumstances, if a defendant presents competency issues, the referring court sends the case to the mental health court.[330]

Alison Redlich raises a difficult question in this context that relates to inquiries about therapeutic jurisprudence,[331] asking "from a purely clinical (and nonlegal) standpoint, are considerations of competence to consent to MHCs even salient in

---

322 *See generally*, *infra* Chapter 9, for a discussion of the impact of the Convention on insanity-pleaders.

323 Convention on the Rights of Persons with Disabilities, Jan. 24, 2007, 2515 U.N.T.S. 3, 46 I.L.M. 443 (CRPD), Article 12.

324 *Id.*

325 *Id.*, Article 15.

326 *See supra* text accompanying notes 313–19.

327 *See, e.g.*, Perlin, *Midemeanor Outlaw*, *supra* note 273.

328 *See supra* text accompanying note 288.

See also Lisa Kim Anh Nguyen, *In Defense of Sell: Involuntary Medication and the Permanently Incompetent Criminal Defendant*, 2005 U. Chi. Legal F. 597, 622 ("incompetency bears a stigma of guilt").

329 *See, e.g.*, Allison D. Redlich et al., *Enrollment in Mental Health Courts: Voluntariness, Knowingness, and Adjudicative Competence*, 34 Law & Hum. Behav. 91 (2010); Ronda Cress, J. Neil Grindstaff & Elizabeth Malloy, *Mental Health Courts and Title II of the ADA: Accessibility to State Court Systems for Individuals with Mental Disabilities and the Need for Diversion*, 25 St. Louis U. Pub. L. Rev. 307 (2006).

330 Anne Harper & Michael Finkle, *Mental Health Courts: Judicial Leadership and Effective Court Intervention*, 51 Judges' J. 4, 8 (Spring 2012).

331 See *infra* text accompanying notes 337–42.

therapeutic jurisprudence settings?"[332] She asks of less adversarial settings such as mental health courts, "does it matter if potential clients do not fully comprehend the contract into which they are being asked to enter?"[333] This question has not been answered satisfactorily in the seven years since Redlich posed it.[334]

These are not the only mental health court issues that demand TJ-related consideration. The overarching issues of effectiveness (with regard to recidivism reduction)[335] and the statutory limitations on eligibility (in terms of the seriousness of the underlying criminal offense)[336] also both raise profound TJ implications.

D. Alternative Jurisprudences

1. Therapeutic jurisprudence

Therapeutic jurisprudence inquiries need begin at the moment of arraignment.[337] Again, mental health court judges Anne Harper and Michael Finkle argue persuasively that there are significant TJ benefits to competency screenings in mental health courts. Such screenings, in their experience, allow intake screeners to offer voluntary social services, including the provision of housing, to potentially incompetent defendants, and maximize the possibility of out-of-custody evaluations (as much as two-thirds of the entire criminal caseload).[338] From a different perspective, Professor Mae Quinn questions the therapeutic jurisprudential implications of the question of trial competence being raised by the prosecutor or the judge, rather than by defendant or his lawyer.[339]

On the other hand, cases such as *Godinez v. Moran*[340] that countenance self-representation by criminal defendants with serious mental disabilities fly in the

---

332 Alison Redlich, *Voluntary, but Knowing and Intelligent? Comprehension in Mental Health Courts*, 11 Psychol. Pub. Pol'y & L. 605, 616 (2005).

333 *Id.*

334 *See also* E. Lea Johnston, *Theorizing Mental Health Courts*, 89 Wash. U. L. Rev. 519, 524–25 (2012), raising the same question.

335 *See, e.g.*, John Cummings, *The Cost of Crazy: How Therapeutic Jurisprudence and Mental Health Courts Lower Incarceration Costs, Reduce Recidivism, and Improve Public Safety*, 56 Loy. L. Rev. 279, 306 (2010).

336 *See, e.g.*, Johnston, *supra* note 334, at 521,

337 Keri A. Gould, *A Therapeutic Jurisprudence Analysis of Competency Evaluation Requests: The Defense Attorney's Dilemma*, 18 Int'l J. L. & Psychiatry 83, 99–100 (1995).

338 Harper & Finkle, *supra* note 330, at 8.

339 Mae Quinn, *Reconceptualizing Competence: An Appeal*, 66 Wash. & Lee L. Rev. 259, 311 (2009). On the question of the TJ implications of the role of the forensic psychologist in the incompetency evaluation proceeding, see Astrid Birgden & Tony Ward, *Pragmatic Psychology through a Therapeutic Jurisprudence Lens*, 9 Psychol. Pub. Pol'y & L. 334, 348 (2003).

340 509 U.S. 389 (1993).

face of therapeutic jurisprudence principles.[341] And there has been no resolution of the dilemma posed by Justice Scalia's dissent in *Indiana v. Edwards*:[342] is it more or less sanist to allow a seriously mentally disabled person to represent himself than to insist on counsel? These issues must be considered carefully in the context of the range of other issues discussed in this volume.

2. Procedural justice

Consider the procedural justice implications of the case discussed in the prior section on the question of the right of a defendant with mental disabilities to represent himself at trial. If the resulting trial is a sham, then procedural justice is not present. Professor John Blume and a colleague make this point clearly: "Sham trials involving severely mentally ill *pro se* defendants cannot be squared with the criminal justice system's normative values of reliability and fairness."[343] Certainly, there are significant procedural justice issues to consider here.

With regard to incompetency to stand trial *procedures*, LeRoy Kondo has considered the procedural justice implications of *Medina v. California*, the Supreme Court decision upholding the constitutionality of statutes that place the burden of proof on a defendant who is asserting incompetency,[344] and notes how this may make "ensuring procedural justice may be more problematic."[345] On this point, Bruce Winick explicitly notes how the *Medina* court's approach "threatens to freeze procedural practices in a nineteenth-century mold, preventing

---

341 See Perlin, *supra* note 172, at 235–36, discussing this issue broadly in the context of death penalty cases:

> If *Godinez* causes more severely mentally disabled defendants to be tried in life-or-death cases without the aid of counsel, what will the impact be on penal settings (especially death row settings) if there is a significant influx of additional mentally ill prisoners? Even if considered from the perspective of victims, there are therapeutic jurisprudence issues. Representatives of victims' rights organizations have testified before an ABA Task Force that adequate representation at all stages of the death penalty trial and appellate process was in the best interests of their constituencies.

342 554 U.S. 164 (2008).

343 John Blume & Morgan Clark, *"Unwell": Indiana v. Edwards and the Fate of Mentally Ill Pro Se Defendants*, 21 Cornell J.L. & Pub. Pol'y 151, 173 (2011). *See, e.g.*, Hartman v. States, 918 A.2d 1138, 1139-40 (Del. Super. Ct. 2007) (denying defendant's request to proceed *pro se* because of the court's independent interest in the integrity, efficiency, and fairness of the trial, and so that the trial not become a "sham," "charade," or "public disgrace").

344 505 U.S. 437, 446 (1992). *See generally* 4 Perlin, *supra* note 1, § 8A-3.1b, at 28–32.

345 LeRoy Kondo, *Advocacy of the Establishment of Mental Health Specialty Courts in the Provision of Therapeutic Justice for Mentally Ill Offenders*, 28 Am. J. Crim. L. 255, 294 (2001).

the progressive evolution of procedural justice."[346] Procedural justice should be a fertile field for further research in this area, especially in the context of the issue of the extent to which incompetent defendants retain a right to refuse medication intended to make them competent to stand trial.[347]

3. Restorative justice

In a recent thoughtful piece, Professor Thomas Hafemeister and his colleagues consider the application of competency concepts to restorative justice (RJ). They conclude that offenders with a mental disorder should have the functional ability to participate in RJ proceedings, and if their mental disorder "may significantly impair their factual or rational understanding of the proceedings or their ability to communicate with the parties involved, or may result in the offender being disruptive or threatening," a mental health screening may be necessary "to determine whether they are capable of participating in the restorative justice proceeding." In such instances, the presumption should be that offenders are capable of so participating.[348] Similarly, the authors point out, *voluntary* participation is a key to the success of RJ interventions, and "coercion is generally antithetical to the principles of procedural justice and oftentimes counterproductive with this population."[349] There is certainly ambivalence among both criminal defense lawyers and prosecutors about the RJ enterprise. The concern raised by defense counsel—that RJ conferencing may limit lawyer-client contact[350] and may draw

346 Bruce Winick, *Presumptions and Burdens of Proof in Determining Competency to Stand Trial: An Analysis of Medina v. California and the Supreme Court's New Due Process Methodology in Criminal Cases*, 47 U. Miami L. Rev. 817, 836 (1993).

347 *See* Sell v. United States, 539 U.S. 166 (2003), discussed *supra* note 216. By way of example, Riittakerttu Kaltiala-Heino and her colleagues have found generally that generally that patients who initially felt coerced were less likely to take medications, use mental health services, and show improvement in symptoms. Riittakerttu Kaltiala-Heino et al., *Impact of Coercion on Treatment Outcome*, 20 Int'l J.L. & Psychiatry 311, 320 (1997).

348 Thomas L. Hafemeister, Sharon G. Garner & Veronica E. Bath, *Forging Links and Renewing Ties: Applying the Principles of Restorative and Procedural Justice to Better Respond to Criminal Offenders with a Mental Disorder*, 60 Buff. L. Rev. 147, 209–10 (2012). On the barriers raised in RJ proceedings by the requirement that an offender disclose his mental disorder, *see id.* at 213–14 ("some offenders choose to remain silent about their condition because they are embarrassed or because they fear they may be stigmatized by this disclosure and suffer adverse consequences as a result"), citing, inter alia, Kevin Dew et al., *"It Puts Things Out of Your Control": Fear of Consequences as a Barrier to Patient Disclosure of Mental Health Issues to General Practitioners*, 29 Soc. Health & Illness 1059, 1059 (2007).

349 Hafemeister, Garner & Bath, *supra* note 348, at 211.

350 *See, e.g.*, Robert F. Cochran, Jr., *The Criminal Defense Attorney: Roadblock or Bridge to Restorative Justice*, 14 J. L. & Religion 211 (1999). *Compare, e.g.*, Douglas B. Ammar, *Forgiveness and the Law - A Redemptive Opportunity*, 27 Fordham Urb. L. J. 1583 (2000) (discussing restorative criminal defense practice).

inappropriately on a civil alternative dispute resolution model[351]—is a legitimate one, and needs to be addressed carefully by RJ advocates. The prosecutorial objection—that restorative justice is "soft on crime"[352]—is, to be charitable, banal, and deserves no serious attention. But the concerns raised by defense counsel do need to be addressed.

E. Dignity

One of the bedrock principles of competency to stand trial law is the way that competency is meant to preserve the moral dignity of the trial process.[353] The integrity of the adversarial system requires that courts not adjudicate incompetent

351 *See, e.g.*, JOHN BRAITHWAITE, RESTORATIVE JUSTICE AND RESPONSIVE REGULATION 249 (2002) (ADR and RJ "could not be philosophically further apart"). *Compare* Frederick W. Gay, *Restorative Justice and the Prosecutor*, 27 FORDHAM URB. L.J. 1651 (2000) (advocating for restorative justice by prosecutors); David M. Lerman, *Forgiveness in the Criminal Justice System: If It Belongs, Then Why is It so Hard To Find?*, 27 FORDHAM URB. L.J. 1663 (2000) (same).

352 Bruce P. Archibald, *Coordinating Canada's Restorative and Inclusionary Models of Criminal Justice: The Legal Profession and the Exercise of Discretion under a Reflexive Rule of Law*, 9 CAN. CRIM. L. REV. 215, 249 (2005).

353 *See* Richard J. Bonnie, *The Competency of Criminal Defendants: Beyond Dusky and Drope*, 47 U. MIAMI L. REV. 539, 551 (1993) (proceeding against incompetent defendants "offends the moral dignity of the [judicial] process because it treats the defendant not as an accountable person, but as an object of the state's effort to carry out its promises"); C. Lee Harrington, *Mental Competence and End-Of-Life Decision Making: Death Row Volunteering and Euthanasia*, 29 J. HEALTH POL. POL'Y & L. 1109, 1111 (2004) (same); *see also* Stephen G. Morse, *Mental Disorder and Criminal Law*, 101 J. CRIM. L. & CRIMINOL. 885, 910–11 (2011) ("that it violates the dignity of our criminal process to try to convict a defendant who does not really understand what is happening or is unable to help himself avoid conviction"). However, Professor Bonnie's formulation has been characterized as neither "a proper or sufficient measure of representational competence," in E. Lea Johnston, *Setting the Standard: A Critique of Bonnie's Competency Standard, and the Potential of Problem-Solving Theory for Self-Representation at Trial*, 43 U.C. DAVIS L. REV. 1605, 1626 (2010), discussing the "greater array of problem-solving abilities" a *pro se* defendant will need to manage a criminal trial. Professor Amy Dillard would expand the moral dignity definition even further: "The moral dignity issue is at the heart of every competency determination and must be the overarching concern for the trial judge who is charged with making the determination." J. Amy Dillard, *Madness Alone Punishes the Madman: The Search for Moral Dignity in the Court's Competency Doctrine as Applied in Capital Cases*, 79 TENN. L. REV. 461, 476 n. 87 (2012).

For an earlier (and prescient) similar formulation, see Alan R. Felthous, *Competency to Waive Counsel: A Step Beyond Competency to Stand Trial*, 7 J. PSYCHIATRY & L. 471, 474 (1979).

defendants.[354] Without competency, the judicial process becomes "communal attack" on a helpless being,[355] or an "invective against an insensible object."[356] There are two dimensions to this—both actual dignity and the *appearance* of dignity—"that drive … the competency doctrine."[357]

Dignity is destroyed in the case of the trial of an incompetent defendant who is "incapable of exercising the autonomy and self-determination expected of criminal defendants who must make crucial decisions."[358] In this context, the preservation of the competency doctrine "thus ensures public respect and confidence in the judicial process and legal system."[359] If, as the late Professor Bruce Winick argued, accurate criminal adjudication serves a "societal interest in the reliability of the criminal process,"[360] then the competency standards must be enforced to insure a dignified process.[361] Consider, again,[362] the *pro se* trial of Scott Panetti[363] in which the defendant "was acting out a role of an attorney as a facet of the mental illness, not a rational decision to represent himself at trial."[364] Cases such as this have led Professor Amy Dillard to recommend that, for those who are deemed marginally competent during the competency assessment, moral dignity should demand that the court determine executional competence before the trial begins."[365]

---

354 Brian G. Sellers & Bruce A. Arrigo, *Adolescent Transfer, Developmental Maturity, and Adjudicative Competence: An Ethical and Justice Policy Inquiry*, 99 J. Crim. L. & Criminology 435, 451 (2009).

355 Morris et al., *supra* note 23, at 202.

356 Sara Longtain, *The Twilight of Competency and Mental Illness: A Conciliatory Conception of Competency and Insanity*, 43 Hous. L. Rev. 1563, 1570 (2007), quoting Note, *supra* note 13, at 458.

357 Dillard, *supra* note 353, at 477.

358 Morse, *supra* note 353, at 911.

359 Megan Fulcher, *Compelling Mentally Incompetent Persons to Arbitrate Claims: Why Dusky and Drope Should Apply*, 27 Ohio St. J. on Disp. Resol. 683, 686–87 (2012).

360 Bruce J. Winick, *Reforming Incompetency to Stand Trial and Plead Guilty: A Restated Proposal and a Response to Professor Bonnie*, 85 J. Crim. L. & Criminology 571, 575–76 (1995).

361 Beyond the scope of this work is a dilemma raised by Professor Winick in this context: "Many criminal defendants who are *not* mentally ill may lack a meaningful understanding of the nature of criminal prosecution." Winick, *supra* note 360, at 579 (emphasis added), quoting Bruce J. Winick, *Restructuring Competency to Stand Trial*, 32 UCLA L. Rev. 921, 971 (1985).

362 *See supra* text accompanying notes 235–39.

363 *See* Panetti v. Quarterman, 551 U.S. 930 (2007); *see generally* Michael L. Perlin, *"Good and Bad, I Defined These Terms, Quite Clear No Doubt Somehow": Neuroimaging and Competency to Be Executed After Panetti*, 28 Behav. Sci. & L. 671 (2010); Perlin, *supra* note 183, 85-92.

364 Bonnie, *supra* note 235, at 261, quoting Sellk Affadvit, Joint Appendix, Panetti v. Quarterman, 551 U.S. 930 (No. 06-6407).

365 Dillard, *supra* note 353, at 487.

There are often complex conflicts between dignity values and autonomy values in this specific area. By way of example, in *Thompson v. Wainwright*,[366] the defendant alleged ineffective assistance of counsel, arguing in part that his trial attorney was incompetent in failing to investigate and present mitigating evidence.[367] Although the attorney believed his client was a person with a mental disability, he did not investigate his childhood, family life, school records or service records, specifically because, at the time of trial, his client had directed him not to conduct the investigation.[368] The Eleventh Circuit found that to be ineffective assistance of counsel, because the lawyer's client's mental condition "prevents him from exercising proper judgment."[369] The reader should not be lulled into thinking that the *Thompson* case reflects daily practice.[370] Also, on the merits, the evidence is clear that large numbers of currently psychotic defendants are still found competent to stand trial.[371] The trial of such defendants also serves to sever the retributive function of the criminal justice process.[372]

Another dilemma is raised by Professor Mae Quinn. She articulates some of the downsides of a policy that expands the universe of defendants found to be incompetent to stand trial:

> Again, in keeping with client-centered principles, whatever remedies defense counsel seek should be as consistent as possible with the role and discernable goals of the client, and should not work to disclose client confidences or defense strategy. It is also important that remedies not be used for punitive purposes and that reforms do not make a bad situation even worse for impaired defendants.[373]

---

366 787 F.2d 1447 (11th Cir. 1986).

367 *Id.* At 1450.

368 *Id.* at 1451. The court ultimately found that defendant had suffered no prejudice. *Id.* at 1453–54.

369 The significance of the *Thompson* case is discussed in Poulin, *supra* note 314, at 1244 n.133.

370 *See, e.g.*, United States v. Hartman, 2012 WL 2384380 (10th Cir. 2012) (no *Strickland* error where counsel failed to introduce medical records that might have triggered competency hearing); Gregory v. Com., 2012 WL 1957406 (Ky. App. 2012) (failure to request competency hearing no basis for *Strickland* claim); compare Comstock v. Lawler, 2011 WL 6425335, *2 (E.D. Pa. 2011) (counsel's failure to request competency hearing can constitute *Strickland* violation "if there are sufficient indicia of incompetence to give objectively reasonable counsel reason to doubt the defendant's competency, and there is a reasonable probability that the defendant would have been found incompetent to stand trial had the issue been raised and fully considered," quoting Taylor v. Horn, 504 F.3d 416, 438 (3d Cir. 2007).

371 Erica Hashimoto, *Resurrecting Autonomy: The Criminal Defendant's Right to Control the Case*, 90 B.U. L. Rev. 1147, 1186 (2010).

372 Christopher Seeds, *The Afterlife of Ford and Panetti: Execution Competence and the Capacity to Assist Counsel*, 53 St. Louis U. L.J. 309, 317 (2009).

373 Quinn, *supra* note 339, at 310–11.

The issues related to dignity become more pointed in cases that occupy the murky space between *Godinez* and *Edwards*. According to Professor Neomi Rao, the Court in *Edwards* walked a fine balancing line: It "wished to avoid humiliation for Edwards, but also to prevent loss of dignity to the criminal process."[374] It is clear that *Edwards* places some limitations on autonomy, and for those who find autonomy to be the sole bedrock principle that supports dignity, that would suggest that *Edwards* robs defendants of some quantum of dignity.[375] I believe that this is wrong, and believe that the state *may* "limit an individual's choices when it determines that this will be in his best interest and will prevent degradation and embarrassment."[376] I believe, as I wrote in the wake of the *Godinez* decision, that allowing defendants with severe mental illness to represent themselves robs both them—and the entire process[377]—of the dignity demanded by the constitution.[378]

V. Conclusion

Professor Erica Hashimoto concludes her comprehensive study of the right of criminal defendants to control the path of litigation in their cases by noting, "there may be legitimate reason for concern regarding the way in which seriously

374 Neomi Rao, *Three Concepts of Dignity in Constitutional Law*, 86 Notre Dame L. Rev. 183, 230 (2011).

375 See Indiana v. Edwards, 554 U.S. 164, 186–87 (2008) (Scalia, J., dissenting), as quoted in this context in Neomi Rao, *American Dignity and Healthcare Reform*, 35 Harv. J.L. & Pub. Pol'y 171, 176–77 (2012):

> [T]he loss of "dignity" the [Sixth Amendment] right is designed to prevent is not the defendant's making a fool of himself by presenting an amateurish or even incoherent defense. Rather, the dignity at issue is the supreme human dignity of being master of one's fate rather than a ward of the State--the dignity of individual choice.

376 Rao, *supra* note 374, at 230.

377 On the significance of public attitudes in this cluster of cases, see Jona Goldschmidt, *Autonomy and "Gray-Area" Pro Se Defendants: Ensuring Competence to Guarantee Freedom*, 6 NW J. L. & Soc. Pol'y 130 (2011); *see also*, Faretta v. California, 422 U.S. 806, 839–40 (1975) (Burger, C.J., dissenting) (majority decision, allowing for *pro se* representation in most criminal cases would likely hurt public confidence in the courts). Professor Grant Morris points out that "the dignity of the criminal process would be undermined by the *spectacle* of an incompetent defendant's trial." Grant Morris, *Mental Disorder and the Civil/Criminal Distinction*, 41 San Diego L. Rev. 1177, 1181 n. 22 (2004) (emphasis added). See also, Dillard, *supra* note 353, at 477, quoting in part, Note, *supra* note 13, at 458:

> Apparent fairness furthers a societal interest; if the defendant acts bizarrely or disrupts the normal courtroom proceedings, "[t]he adjudication loses its character as a reasoned interaction between an individual and his community."

378 *See generally* Perlin, *supra* note 154.

mentally ill defendants are processed through the criminal justice system."[379] Her focus is on the competency to proceed *pro se*, but I think her insights are equally applicable to competency considerations. The entire system remains riddled with sanism and pretextuality, and decision-making bears the badges of heuristics and OCS.

We must take seriously each of the perspectives that I discuss in this volume if we are to bring the needed measure of dignity to this process.

379 Hashimoto, *supra* note 371, at 1186.

Chapter 9
The Insanity Defense

I. The Significance of the Insanity Defense Plea

A. Introduction[1]

Although the insanity defense is numerically insignificant, it remains profoundly important to the criminal justice system as the focal point of the ongoing debate on the relationship between legal responsibility, free will, mental illness and punishment.[2] The insanity defense has substantially survived in spite of persistent philosophical and political criticism. Its history reflects a balance and tension between changes in attitudes toward developments in psychiatry and psychology and changes in attitudes toward criminal justice, incapacitation, and the desire to punish.[3] Probably no other area of criminal law and procedure reflects a jurisprudence that is so driven by myths as that of the insanity defense. Insanity defense issues have concerned the courts and legislative bodies for hundreds (perhaps thousands) of years.[4]

As the various tests have developed—*M'Naghten*, irresistible impulse; *Durham*, the test proposed in the American Law Institute's Model Penal Code (ALI-MPC); the federal Insanity Defense Reform Act,[5]—and as efforts are made to limit the scope and use of the defense, either by use of a "guilty but mentally ill" verdict[6] or by outright abolition,[7] it is clear that the symbolic values of the insanity defense must be considered carefully at all times.[8]

---

1 This section is partially adapted from Michael L. Perlin, *Criminal Responsibility, Defenses, and Standards*, in 1 Encyclopedia of Psychology and Law 161 (Brian Cutler ed., 2008).

2 *See generally* Michael L. Perlin, The Jurisprudence of the Insanity Defense (1994).

3 *See generally* Michael L. Perlin, *"The Borderline Which Separated You From Me": The Insanity Defense, the Authoritarian Spirit, the Fear of Faking, and the Culture of Punishment,* 82 Iowa L. Rev. 1375 (1997).

4 *See generally* 4 Michael L. Perlin, Mental Disability Law: Civil and Criminal, § 9A-2, at 139–45 (2d ed. 2002).

5 See *id.* at §§ 9A-3 to 9A.3.7, at 245–79.

6 *Id.*, § 9A-6, at 229–35; Perlin, *supra* note 2, at 133–38.

7 *See generally* Michael L. Perlin, *Psychodynamics and the Insanity Defense: "Ordinary Common Sense" and Heuristic Reasoning*, 69 Neb. L. Rev. 3, 8–12 (1990).

8 *See generally* Michael L. Perlin, *Unpacking the Myths: The Symbolism Mythology of Insanity Defense Jurisprudence*, 40 Case W. Res. L. Rev. 599 (1989–90).

No area of our legal system has engendered a more intense level of debate than the role of the insanity defense in the criminal justice process. On the one hand, this difficult subject is seen as a reflection of the fundamental moral principles of the criminal law, resting on beliefs about human rationality, deterrability (i.e., whether the punishment of a person whose profound mental illness leads him to commit what would otherwise be a criminal act would serve as a deterrent to others), and free will, and as a bulwark of the law's moorings of condemnation for moral failure.[9] On the other hand, it is castigated by a former attorney general of the United States as the major stumbling block in the restoration of "the effectiveness of Federal law enforcement" and as tilting the "balance between the forces of law and the forces of lawlessness."[10] Yet the percentage of insanity defenses pled is small (at the most 1%), the percentage of those that are successful is smaller (one-quarter of 1%), and the percentage of those successful in *contested* cases is minuscule (one-tenth of one-quarter of 1%).[11]

Notwithstanding the defense's relative *numerical insignificance*, it touches—philosophically, culturally, and psychologically—on our ultimate social values and beliefs; it is rooted in moral principles of excuse that are accepted in both ordinary human interaction and criminal law; and it continues to serve as a surrogate for resolution of the most profound issues in criminal justice.[12] Although the defense has been significantly narrowed in many jurisdictions in the past nearly 30 years[13]—a condition intensified by the verdict in the John Hinckley case (which involved the attempted assassination of President Ronald Reagan)[14] as well as several other unpopular or "wrong" jury verdicts in cases involving sensationalized crimes or public figure victims—reports of its demise are, to a great extent, exaggerated and, in spite of public outrage, and the doctrine has remained alive in most jurisdictions.[15]

B. History

The insanity defense has been a major component of the Anglo-American common law for more than 700 years. Rooted in Talmudic, Greek and Roman history, its

---

9 *See* John Monahan, *Abolish the Insanity Defense-Not Yet*, 26 RUTGERS L. REV. 719, 731 (1973); *see generally* 4 PERLIN, *supra* note 4, § 9A-2, at 140–41.

10 Michael L. Perlin, *The Things We Do For Love: John Hinckley's Trial and the Future of the Insanity Defense in the Federal Courts* (Book Review of LINCOLN CAPLAN, THE INSANITY DEFENSE AND THE TRIAL OF JOHN W. HINCKLEY, JR. (1984)), 30 N.Y. L. SCH. L. REV. 857, 865 n.43 (1985); *see generally* S. Rep. No. 225, 98th Cong., 1st Sess. 2 (1983), reprinted in 1984 U.S. CODE CONG. & AD. NEWS, 3182, 3184–85.

11 Perlin, *supra* note 8, at 648–51.

12 Ingo Keilitz, *Researching and Reforming the Insanity Defense*, 39 RUTGERS L.REV. 289, 322 (1987).

13 PERLIN, *supra* note 2, at 96–100; 4 PERLIN, *supra* note 4, §§ 9C-5 to 9C-7, at 338–50.

14 PERLIN, *supra* note 2, at 333–48.

15 4 PERLIN, *supra* note 4, § 9C-8, at 351–52.

forerunners actually can be traced back to more than 3,000 years.[16] The sixth-century Code of Justinian explicitly recognized that the insane were not responsible for their acts.[17] By the ninth century, the "Dooms of Alfred" (a code of laws compiled by Alfred the Great) acknowledged that an impaired individual—who could not acknowledge or confess his offenses—was absolved from personally making restitution. In pre-Norman England, the law similarly shifted reparations responsibility in the event that a "man fall out of his senses or wits … and kill someone."[18]

The defense's "modern" roots can be traced at least as far back as 1505, the first recorded jury verdict of insanity, but it is clear that even prior to that case, juries considered "acquittal to be the appropriate result" in certain insanity defense cases.[19] Furthermore, William Lambarde's late-sixteenth-century text on criminal responsibility (*The Eirenarcha*) suggested that the insanity defense was already well settled in England,[20] and Sir Edward Coke's 1628 treatise, *Institutes of the Laws of England*, gave the law the familiar maxim that the "madman is only punished by his madness."[21]

1. Early developments

In the early eighteenth century, English judges began the process of attempting to define for juries that condition of the mind that would excuse, as a matter of law, otherwise criminal behavior.[22] In *Rex v. Arnold*,[23] the first of the historically significant insanity defense trials, Judge Tracy charged the jury in the following manner:

> That is the question, whether this man hath the use of his reason and sense? If he … could not distinguish between good and evil, and did not know what he did … he could not be guilty of any offence against any law whatsoever. … On the other side … it is not every kind of frantic humour or something unaccountable in a man's actions, that points him out to be such a madman as is to be exempted from punishment: *it must be a man that is totally deprived of his understanding and memory, and doth not know what he is doing, no more than an infant, than a brute, or a wild beast, such a one is never the object of punishment.*[24]

16 *Id.* § 9A-2, at 143, citing Barbara Weiner, *Not Guilty by Reason of Insanity – A Sane Approach*, 56 Chicago-Kent L. Rev. 1057, 1058 (1980).

17 *Id*, at 144, citing Weiner, *supra* note 16, at 1058.

18 *Id.*, citing Jonas Robitscher & Andrew Ky Haynes, *In Defense of the Insanity Defense*, 31 Emory L.J. 9, 10 n.2 (1982).

19 Robitscher & Haynes, *supra* note 18, at 12 n.10.

20 *See* Rita James Simon & David E. Aaronson, The Insanity Defense—A Critical Assessment of the Law and Policy in the Post Hinckley Era 10 (1988).

21 2 Coke, Institutes of the Laws of England 247a–247b (1853).

22 4 Perlin, *supra* note 4, § 9A-3.1, at 146.

23 16 How. St. Tr. 694 (1724).

24 *Id.* at 765 (emphasis added).

The law of criminal responsibility evolved further in 1800, in the case of James Hadfield, which envisioned insanity in the following manner:

> That a man could know right from wrong, could understand the nature of the act he was about to commit, could manifest a clear design and foresight and cunning in planning and executing it, but if his mental condition produced or was the cause of a criminal act he should not be held legally responsible for it.[25]

This trend toward a more liberal defense continued in the case of *Regina v. Oxford*, which concerned the attempted assassination of Queen Victoria, in which the jury charge combined portions of what would later be known as the "irresistible impulse" test and the "product" test.[26]

2. M'Naghten case

The most significant case in the history of the insanity defense in England (and perhaps in all common-law jurisdictions) arose out of the shooting by Daniel M'Naghten of Edward Drummond, the secretary of the man he mistook for his intended victim, Prime Minister Robert Peel (as with all the other cases already discussed, the victim was a major political figure).[27] Enraged by the jury's insanity verdict, Queen Victoria questioned why the law was of no avail, since "everybody is morally convinced that [the] malefactor … [was] perfectly conscious and aware of what he did,"[28] and demanded that the legislature "lay down the rule" so as to protect the public "from the wrath of madmen who they feared could now kill with impunity."[29] In response to the Queen's demand, the House of Lords asked the Supreme Court of Judicature to answer five questions regarding the insanity law; the judges' answers to two of these five became the *M'Naghten* test :

> The jurors ought to be told in all cases that every man is presumed to be sane, and to possess a sufficient degree of reason to be responsible for his crimes, until the contrary be proved to their satisfaction; and that to establish a defence on the

---

25 Hadfield's Case, 27 How. St. Tr. 1281 (K.B. 1800).

26 Regina v. Oxford, 173 Eng. Rep. 941 (N.P. 1840).

27 4 PERLIN, *supra* note 4, § 9A-3.2, at 149.

28 *Id.* at 150, quoting see RICHARD MORAN, KNOWING RIGHT FROM WRONG: THE INSANITY DEFENSE OF DANIEL MCNAUGHTAN 20 (1981).

29 MORAN, *supra* note 28, at 19. This language has been regularly repeated. *See* Russell Covey, *Criminal Madness: Cultural Iconography and Insanity*, 61 STAN. L. REV. 1375, 1408 (2009) (quoting District of Columbia prosecutor in Durham v. U.S., 214 F. 2d 862, 866 (D.C. Cir. 1954)—see *infra* text accompanying notes 39–44—speculating on what would happen if defendant (who had been charged with housebreaking) were to be found not guilty by reason of insanity ("if that man committed a murder next week then it is my responsibility"); PERLIN, *supra* note 2, at 24 (discussing then-Assistant US Attorney Rudolph Giuliani's false testimony at the hearings on the Insanity Defense Reform Act that the insanity defense allowed defendants to "get away with murder" in "many, many … cases").

> ground of insanity, it must be clearly proved that, at the time of the committing of the act, the party accused was labouring under such a defect of reason, from disease of the mind, as not to know the nature and quality of the act he was doing; or, if he did know it, that he did not know he was doing what was wrong.[30]

There are three main features of this formulation: First, it is predicated on proof that the defendant was suffering from a "defect of reason, from disease of the mind." From the time of *M'Naghten* until today some finding of "mental disease or defect" has been a necessary predicate for the insanity defense. Second, once such a "disease" is shown, the inquiry focuses on what the defendant was able to "know." That is, the interest of the law under this test is in the ability of the defendant to "know" certain things. It is for this reason that the inquiry is sometimes referred to as a "cognitive" formula. Third, the *M'Naghten* test focuses on two things the defendant must be able to "know" to be guilty of a crime. One is "the nature and quality" of the act that was committed. The other is that the act "was wrong." In both instances, the question is whether the defendant was "capable" of knowing these things, that is, whether the mental illness had robbed the defendant of the capacity to know what "normal" people are able to know about their behavior. The idea, in sum, is that people who are unable to know the nature of their conduct or who are unable to know that their conduct is wrong are not proper subjects for criminal punishment. In commonsense terms, such persons should not be regarded as morally responsible for their behavior.[31]

This test has been severely criticized as rigid and inflexible, based on outmoded views of the human psyche, of little relation to the truths of mental life, reflecting antiquated and outworn medical and ethical concepts. Furthermore, the use of language such as "know" and "wrong" has been criticized as "ambiguous, obscure, unintelligible and too narrow."[32] Professor Donald Hermann and a colleague have argued, by way of example, that the cognitive aspect of one's personality cannot be seen as the sole determinant of one's subsequent behavior (and the basis of one's ultimate criminal guilt) because the psyche is an integrated entity.[33] Critics also maintain that the narrow scope of the expert testimony required by the *M'Naghten* test deprives the jury of a complete picture of the psychological profile of the defendant as the test ignores issues of affect and control.[34]

---

30 M'Naghten's Case, 8 Eng. Rep. 718, 722 (H.L. 1843).

31 4 Perlin, *supra* note 4, § 9A-3.2, at 151, quoting Peter W. Low, John Calvin Jeffries, Jr., & Richard J. Bonnie, The Trial of John W. Hinckley, Jr.: A Case Study in the Insanity Defense 11 (1986).

32 4 Perlin, *supra* note 4, § 9A-3.2, at 152, quoting Donald H.J. Hermann & Yvonne S. Sor, *Convicting or Confining? Alternative Directions in Insanity Law Reform: Guilty But Mentally Ill Versus New Rules for Release of Insanity Acquittees*, 1983 BYU L. Rev. 499, 512.

33 Perlin, *supra* note 2, at 82.

34 Hermann & Sor, *supra* note 32, at 512–13.

Nevertheless, American courts readily adopted the *M'Naghten* formulation and codified it as the standard test, with little modification, in virtually all jurisdictions until the middle of the twentieth century.[35]

3. Irresistible impulse

In a partial response to criticisms of the *M'Naghten* test, several courts developed an alternative test that later became known as the "irresistible impulse" test, adapted from a test first formulated in 1883 by Lord Stephen:

> If it is not, it ought to be the law of England that no act is a crime if the person who does it is at the time. … prevented either by defective mental power or by any disease affecting his mind from controlling his own conduct, unless the absence of the power of control has been produced by his own default.[36]

This rule allowed for the acquittal of a defendant if his mental disorder caused him to experience an "irresistible and uncontrollable impulse to commit the offense, even if he remained able to understand the nature of the offense and its wrongfulness."[37] It was based, in the words of Abraham Goldstein, one of the leading legal scholars on the history of the insanity defense, on four assumptions:

> First, that there are mental diseases which impair volition or self-control, even while cognition remains relatively unimpaired; second, that the use of *M'Naghten* alone results in findings that persons suffering from such diseases are not insane; third, that the law should make the insanity defense available to persons who are unable to control their actions, just as it does to those who fit *M'Naghten;* fourth, no matter how broadly *M'Naghten* is construed, there will remain areas of serious disorder which it will not reach.[38]

At its high-water mark, this test had been adopted in 18 jurisdictions, but today, far fewer states follow its teachings.

4. The "product test"

Charles Doe, a mid-nineteenth-century New Hampshire State Supreme Court judge, first crafted what became known as the "product test": "If the [crime] was the offspring or product of mental disease in the defendant, he was not guilty by reason

35 4 PERLIN, *supra* note 4, §§ 9A-3.2, at 153–53.

36 JAMES FITZJAMES STEPHEN, A HISTORY OF THE CRIMINAL LAW OF ENGLAND 168 (1883).

37 4 PERLIN, *supra* note 4, §§ 9A-3.3, at 156, quoting George Dix, *Criminal Responsibility and Mental Impairment in American Criminal Law: Responses to the Hinckley Acquittal in Historical Perspective*, in 1 LAW AND MENTAL HEALTH: INTERNATIONAL PERSPECTIVES 1, 7 (David N. Weisstub ed., 1986).

38 ABRAHAM S. GOLDSTEIN, THE INSANITY DEFENSE 67 (1967).

of insanity."[39] This test first entered the legal public's consciousness in 1954, when it was adopted by the District of Columbia in *Durham v. United States*,[40] rejecting both the *M'Naghten* and the irresistible impulse tests as based on "an entirely obsolete and misleading conception of the nature of insanity," one that ignored the reality that "the science of psychiatry now recognizes that a man is an integrated personality and that reason, which is only one element in that personality, is not the sole determinant of his conduct,"[41] and that a far broader test would be appropriate.

Durham held that an accused would not be criminally responsible if his "unlawful act was the product of mental disease or mental defect."[42] This test would provide for the broadest range of psychiatric expert testimony, "unbound by narrow or psychologically inapposite legal questions."[43] The case was the first modern, major break from the *M'Naghten* approach and created a feeling of intellectual and legal ferment. It was adopted, however, in fewer than a handful of jurisdictions, and became the topic of fairly rigorous criticism: that it allegedly failed to provide helpful guidelines to the jury and was—at its core—a "nonrule," providing the jury with no standard by which to judge the evidence; that it misidentified the moral issue of responsibility with the scientific issues of diagnosis and causation; and that it was too heavily dependent on expertise, leading to the usurpation of jury decision-making by psychiatrists.[44] Within a few years after the *Durham* decision, the court began to modify and—ultimately—dismantle it, culminating in its decision in *United States v. Brawner*,[45] the most important of the many federal cases that had rejected *M'Naghten* and adopted instead the ALI-MPC test.

5. American Law Institute's Model Penal Code test

In an effort to avoid the major criticisms of *M'Naghten*, the irresistible impulse test, and *Durham*, the ALI couched the substantive insanity defense standard of the MPC, using language that focused on volitional issues as well as on cognitive ones.[46] According to the ALI-MPC standard, a defendant is not responsible for his criminal conduct if, as a result of mental disease or defect, he "lacks substantial capacity either to appreciate the criminality of his conduct or to conform his conduct to the requirements of law."[47] Under this formulation, the term mental

39 State v. Pike, 49 N.H. 399, 342 (1870).

40 214 F. 2d 862 (D.C. Cir. 1954), *overruled* in United States v. Brawner, 471 F. 2d 969, 981 (D.C. Cir. 1972).

41 *Durham*, 214 F. 2d at 871.

42 *Id. at* 874–75.

43 Barbara Weiner, *Mental Disability and Criminal Law*, in Samuel Jan Brakel, John Parry & Barbara A. Weiner, The Mentally Disabled and the Law 693, 710 (3d. ed. 1985).

44 4 Perlin, *supra* note 4, § 9A-3.4, at 160, citing Hermann & Sor, *supra* note 32, at 520.

45 471 F. 2d 969, 973 (D.C. Cir. 1972).

46 4 Perlin, *supra* note 4, §§ 9A-3.5, at 160, citing Hermann & Sor, *supra* note 32, at 521–22.

47 Model Penal Code, § 4.01(1).

disease or defect specifically excluded "an abnormality manifested only by repeated criminal or otherwise antisocial conduct."[48]

Although the ALI-MPC test was rooted in the *M'Naghten* standard, there were several significant differences. First, its use of the word *substantial* was meant to respond to case law developments that had required a showing of total impairment for exculpation from criminal responsibility.[49] Second, the substitution of the word *appreciate* for the word *know* showed that a sane offender must be emotionally as well as intellectually aware of the significance of his or her conduct and that mere intellectual awareness that the conduct is wrongful when divorced from an appreciation or understanding of the moral or legal import of behavior can have little significance.[50] Third, by using a broader language of mental impairment than had *M'Naghten,* the test captured both the cognitive and affective aspects of impaired mental understanding.[51] Fourth, its substitution in the final proposed official draft of the word *wrongfulness* for *criminality* reflected the position that the insanity defense dealt with an impaired *moral* sense rather than an impaired sense of *legal* wrong.[52]

Although there were some immediate criticisms of the ALI-MPC test, principally due to the attempt to bar "psychopaths" or "sociopaths" from successfully using the defense,[53] the test was generally applauded as encouraging adjudication based on reality and the practical experience of psychiatrists by recognizing that both the volitional and the cognitive processes of an individual may be impaired.[54] The test was subsequently adopted by more than half of the states and, in some form, by all but one of the federal circuits.[55] Perhaps most significant, the District of Columbia Court of Appeals, in overruling its "product" test of *Durham v. United States* in *United States v. Brawner*, adopted the ALI-MPC test.[56]

6. Insanity Defense Reform Act

Slightly more than a decade after *Brawner*, in the wake of John Hinckley's failed attempt to assassinate US President Ronald Reagan,[57] Congress enacted the federal Insanity Defense Reform Act.[58] This law had the effect of returning the insanity

48 *Id.*, § 4.01(2).

49 GOLDSTEIN, *supra* note 38, at 87.

50 United States v. Freeman, 357 F. 2d 606, 623 (2d Cir. 1966).

51 Hermann & Sor, *supra* note 32, at 522.

52 *Id. See also* Henry Weihofen, *Capacity to Appreciate "Wrongfulness" or "Criminality" Under the A.L.I.-Model Penal Code Test of Mental Responsibility*, 58 J. CRIM. L, CRIMINOLOGY & POLICE SCI. 27 (1967).

53 GOLDSTEIN, *supra* note 38, at 88.

54 Weiner, *supra* note 43, at 712.

55 *See* 4 PERLIN, *supra* note 4, § 9A-3.5, at 162 n.183 (collecting cases).

56 471 F. 2d 969 (D.C. Cir. 1972). *See* Heathcote W. Wales, *The Rise, the Fall, and the Resurrection of the Medical Model*, 63 GEO . L.J. 87, 103 (1974).

57 *See* Perlin, *supra* note 10.

58 *See* 4 PERLIN, *supra* note 4, § 9C-5, at 338–39. This Act was a reform compromise that followed the inability of the Reagan Administration to succeed in having the defense

defense in federal jurisdictions to *status quo ante* 1843: the year of *M'Naghten*.[59] The bill changed the federal law in several material ways:

1. It shifted the burden of proof to defendants, by a quantum of clear and convincing evidence.
2. It articulated, for the first time, a substantive insanity test, adopting a more restrictive version of *M'Naghten*, thus discarding the ALI-MPC test previously in place in all federal circuits.
3. It established strict procedures for the hospitalization and release of defendants found not guilty by reason of insanity.
4. It severely limited the scope of expert testimony in insanity cases.[60]

7. "Guilty but mentally ill"

Perhaps the most significant development in substantive insanity defense formulations in the past 25 years has been the adoption in more than a dozen jurisdictions of the hybrid "guilty but mentally ill" (GBMI) verdict.[61] It received its initial impetus in Michigan, as a reflection of legislative dissatisfaction with and public outcry over a state Supreme Court decision that had prohibited automatic commitment of insanity acquittees.[62] There, legislation was enacted that provided for a GBMI verdict—as an alternative to the not guilty by reason of insanity (NGRI) verdict—if the following were found by the trier of fact beyond a reasonable doubt:

1. that the defendant is guilty of an offense,
2. that the defendant was mentally ill at the time of the commission of the offense,
3. that the defendant was not legally insane at the time of the commission of the offense.[63]

The rationale for the passage of the GBMI legislation was that the implementation of such a verdict would decrease the number of persons acquitted by reason of insanity and ensure treatment of those who were GBMI within a correctional

abolished. *See* Covey, *supra* note 29, at 1418, and *see* Perlin, *supra* note 3, at 1382:

> The Reagan Administration originally called loudly for the abolition of the insanity defense. However, in the face of a nearly-unified front presented by most of the relevant professional organizations and trade associations, it quietly dropped its call for abolition and supported the IDRA as a reform compromise. This quiet change in position ensured that the symbolic call for abolition would be the lasting public image.

59 Perlin, *supra* note 3, at 1382.

60 4 Perlin, *supra* note 4, § 9C-5, at 340–41.

61 *Id.*, § 9A-3.7, at 169.

62 *Id.*, citing People v. McQuillan, 221 N.W.2d 569 (1974).

63 Mich. Stat. Ann. § 768.36.

setting.[64] It was conceived that once a defendant were to be found GBMI, he or she would be evaluated on entry to the correctional system and provided appropriate mental health services either on an inpatient basis as part of a definite prison term or, in specific cases, as a parolee or as an element of probation.[65]

This model was followed—in large part—in most of the other states that have adopted the GBMI test.[66] Most academic analyses have been far more critical, rejecting it as conceptually flawed and procedurally problematic and as not only superfluous but also dangerous.[67] By way of example, in practice, the GBMI defendant is not ensured treatment beyond that available to other offenders.[68] Thus, Professor Christopher Slobogin (one of the leading current scholars in this area of the law) suggests, it is "not only misleading but dangerous to characterize the [GBMI] verdict either as a humane advance in the treatment of mentally ill offenders or as a more effective way of identifying offenders in need of treatment."[69] The GBMI verdict, he concludes, is "a verdict in name only."[70]

C. Insanity Defense Myths

The empirical research has revealed that at least half a dozen myths about the insanity defense, which have arisen and been regularly perpetuated, are all disproven by the facts. The research shows that the insanity defense opens only a small window of nonculpability, that defendants found that NGRI does not "beat the rap," and, perhaps most important, that the tenacity of these misbeliefs in the face of contrary data is profound.[71]

Myth 1: The insanity defense is overused. All empirical analyses have been consistent: the public, legal profession and, specifically, legislators dramatically and grossly overestimate both the frequency and the success rate of the insanity plea.[72] This error undoubtedly is abetted by media distortions in presenting information on persons with mental illness charged with crimes.[73]

Myth 2: The use of the insanity defense is limited to murder cases. In one jurisdiction where the data have been closely studied, slightly less than one third

64 *See* Ames Robey, *Guilty But Mentally Ill*, 6 Bull. Am. Acad. Psychiatry & L. 374, 379–80 (1978).

65 Weiner, *supra* note 43, at 715.

66 4 Perlin, *supra* note 4, § 9A-3.7, at 171.

67 Joseph Rodriguez, Michael L. Perlin & Laura M. LeWinn, *The Insanity Defense Under Siege: Legislative Assaults and Legal Rejoinders*, 14 Rutgers L.J. 397, 431 (1983).

68 Bradley McGraw et al., *The "Guilty But Mentally Ill" Plea and Verdict: Current State of the Knowledge*, 30 Vill. L. Rev. 117, 187 (1985).

69 Christopher Slobogin, *The Guilty But Mentally Ill Verdict: An Idea Whose Time Should Not Have Come*, 53 Geo. Wash. L. Rev. 494, 515 (1985).

70 *Id.*

71 Perlin, *supra* note 2, at 229–32.

72 4 Perlin, *supra* note 4, § 9C-3.1 at 331.

73 *Id.* at 332.

of the successful insanity pleas entered over an eight-year period were reached in cases involving a victim's death.[74] Furthermore, individuals who plead insanity in murder cases are no more successful in being found NGRI than persons charged with other crimes.[75]

Myth 3: There is no risk to the defendant who pleads insanity. Defendants who asserted an insanity defense at trial and who were ultimately found guilty of their charges served significantly longer sentences than defendants tried on similar charges but did not assert the insanity defense.[76] The same ratio is found when exclusively homicide cases are considered.[77]

Myth 4: NGRI acquittees are quickly released from custody. Of all the individuals found NGRI over an eight-year period in one jurisdiction, only 15% had been released from all restraints, 35% remained in institutional custody, and 47% were under partial court restraint following conditional release.[78]

Myth 5: NGRI acquittees spend much less time in custody than do defendants convicted of the same offenses. Contrary to this myth, NGRI acquittees actually spend almost double the amount of time that defendants convicted of similar charges spend in prison settings and often face a lifetime of post-release judicial oversight.[79]

Myth 6: Criminal defendants who plead insanity are usually faking. This is perhaps the oldest of the insanity defense myths and is one that has bedeviled American jurisprudence since the mid nineteenth century.[80] Of 141 individuals found NGRI in one jurisdiction over an eight-year period, there was no dispute that 115 diagnosed with schizophrenia (including 38 of the 46 cases involving a victim's death), and in only three cases was the diagnostician unable to specify the nature of the patient's mental illness.[81]

D. Abolition and Limitation Proposals

In the past two decades, state legislatures in Idaho, Montana, Kansas, and Utah have abolished the insanity defense, and in those jurisdictions, state supreme courts have subsequently held that abolition of the defense did not violate due process.[82] Arizona stopped barely short of abolishing the insanity defense by creating a "guilty except insane" verdict that eliminates the "nature and quality of

74 *Id.*, § 9C-3.2, at 332.

75 *Id.*

76 Rodriguez, Perlin & LeWinn, *supra* note 67, at 401–02.

77 4 PERLIN, *supra* note 4, § 9C-3.3, at 333.

78 *Id.*, § 9C-3.4, at 333.

79 *Id.*, § 9C-3.5, at 334.

80 *See* Michael L. Perlin, *"Life Is In Mirrors, Death Disappears": Giving Life to Atkins*, 33 N. MEX. L. REV. 315, 321 (2003), quoting ISAAC RAY, A TREATISE ON THE MEDICAL JURISPRUDENCE OF INSANITY § 247, at 243 (Winfred Overholser ed., 1962 edition).

81 4 PERLIN, *supra* note 4, § 9C-3.6, at 335–36, citing Rodriguez, Perlin & LeWinn, *supra* note 67, at 404. See *supra* note 58.

82 4 PERLIN, *supra* note 4, § 9A-6, at 229–35.

the act" prong from the *M'Naghten* test.[83] In one instance (Nevada), such abolition was struck as unconstitutional in *Finger v. State*,[84] with the majority of the sharply divided court finding that legal insanity was a "fundamental principle" entitled to due process protections.[85]

The court reasoned as follows:

> Mens rea is a fundamental aspect of criminal law. Thus it follows that the concept of legal insanity, that a person is not culpable for a criminal act because he or she cannot form the necessary mens rea, is also a fundamental principle.[86]

The US Supreme Court subsequently addressed questions raised in Arizona's new insanity defense formulation: Whether due process prohibits Arizona's use of an insanity test stated solely in terms of the capacity to tell whether an act charged as a crime was right or wrong; and whether Arizona violates due process in restricting consideration of defense evidence of mental illness and incapacity to its bearing on a claim of insanity, thus eliminating its significance directly on the issue of the mental element of the crime charged (*mens rea*).[87] In both instances, the Court held there was no violation of due process.[88]

II. Four Factors

A. Sanism

Our insanity jurisprudence is riddled with examples of sanism. Think of some of these myths that permeate case law, statutes and practice:[89]

- reliance on a fixed vision of popular, concrete, visual images of "craziness",[90]
- an obsessive fear of feigned mental states,[91]

---

83 Ariz. Rev. Stat. § 13–502(A).

84 27 P. 3d 66 (Nev. 2001).

85 *Id.* at 80.

86 *Id.*

87 Clark v. Arizona, 548 U.S. 735 (2006).

88 *See generally* Michael L. Perlin & Heather E. Cucolo, Mental Disability Law: Civil and Criminal, § 9A-3.8, at 68–82 (2012 Cum. Supp.).

89 *See generally* Michael L. Perlin, *"For the Misdemeanor Outlaw": The Impact of the ADA on the Institutionalization of Criminal Defendants with Mental Disabilities*, 52 Ala. L. Rev. 193, 234–35 (2000).

90 *See, e.g.*, Michael L. Perlin, *On Sanism,* 46 SMU L. Rev. 373, 402 (1992); *see generally* Wainwright v. Greenfield, 474 U.S. 284, 297 (1986) (Rehnquist, J., concurring); State v. Clayton, 656 S.W.2d 344, 350–51 (Tenn. 1983).

91 *See, e.g.*, Perlin, *supra* note 90, at 402; *see generally* Lynch v. Overholser, 369 U.S. 705, 715 (1962); United States v. Brown, 478 F.2d 606, 611 (D.C. Cir. 1973), *as*

- sanctioning of the death penalty in the case of defendants with mental retardation *in spite of* Supreme Court caselaw banning that practice,[92] some defendants who are "substantially mentally impaired," or defendants who have been found guilty but mentally ill (GBMI),[93]
- the incessant confusion and conflation of substantive mental status tests,[94] and
- the regularity of sanist appeals by prosecutors in insanity defense summations, arguing that insanity defenses are easily faked, that insanity acquittees are often immediately released, and that expert witnesses are readily duped.[95]

Valid and reliable research has confirmed the role of sanism in insanity defense attitudes,[96] reflecting the ways that jurors demonstrate "irrational brutality, prejudice, hostility, and hatred toward insanity pleaders."[97] Until we come to grips with this virulence, it is futile to expect any significant ameliorative change.

B. Pretextuality

Indeed, all aspects of the judicial decision-making process embody pretextuality. The fear that defendants will fake the insanity defense to escape punishment continues to paralyze the legal system in spite of an impressive array of empirical evidence that reveals (1) the minuscule number of such cases, (2) the ease with which trained clinicians are usually able to catch malingering in such cases, (3) the inverse greater likelihood that defendants, even at grave peril to their life, will be more likely to try to convince examiners that they're "not crazy," (4) the high risk in pleading the insanity defense (leading to statistically significant greater prison terms meted out to unsuccessful insanity pleaders), and (5) that most successful insanity pleaders remain in maximum security facilities for a far greater length of

---

discussed in Peter Margulies, *The Pandemonium Between the Mad and the Acquittees After* Jones v. United States, 36 Rutgers L. Rev. 793, 806–07 n.85 (1984).

92 *See* Atkins v. Virginia, 536 U.S. 304 (2002), *see generally* Michael L. Perlin, Mental Disability and the Death Penalty: The Shame of the States 45-68 (2013).

93 Perlin, *supra* note 3, at 1422.

94 *See* Perlin, *supra* note 90, at 403; *see generally* Buttrum v. Black, 721 F. Supp. 1268, 1295 (N.D. Ga. 1989), *aff'd*, 908 F.2d 695 (11th Cir. 1990).

95 Michael L. Perlin, *"The Executioner's Face Is Always Well-Hidden": The Role of Counsel and the Courts in Determining Who Dies*, 41 N.Y.L. Sch. L. Rev. 201, 228 (1996); *see, e.g.*, People v. Camden, 578 N.E.2d 1211, 1223 (Ill. 1991); People v. Aliwoli, 606 N.E.2d 347, 353–54 (Ill. App. Ct. 1992).

96 Christian Breheny et al., *Gender Matters in the Insanity Defense*, 31 Law & Psychol. Rev. 93 (2007).

97 Michael L. Perlin, *"His Brain Has Been Mismanaged with Great Skill": How Will Jurors Respond to Neuroimaging Testimony in Insanity Defense Cases?*, 42 Akron L. Rev. 885, 900 (2009), quoting Perlin, *supra* note 2, at 317.

time than they would have had they been convicted on the underlying criminal indictment. In short, pretextuality dominates insanity defense decision-making. The inability of judges to disregard public opinion and inquire into whether defendants have had fair trials is both the root and the cause of pretextuality in insanity defense jurisprudence.[98]

C. Heuristics

We cannot understand the insanity defense unless we look at it through the cognitive psychology construct of "heuristics," that is, the way that we seek to simplify information-processing tasks by privileging the vivid, negative, accessible anecdote, and by subordinating the factual, the logical, the statistical, the rational.[99] Over 20 years ago, in an article specifically considering the impact of heuristic thinking on insanity defense policy, I wrote what I believe is just as accurate today:

> Public perceptions of the insanity defense comprise a prime exhibit in the case against the soundness of human cognition and inference. Heuristics and biases influence public perceptions, combining to produce invidious scenarios which doggedly resist rational correction. For example, insanity defense defenders attempt to use statistics to rebut empirical myths about how often the defense is used; scientific studies to demonstrate that "responsibility" is a valid, externally verifiable term, and that certain insanity-pleading defendants are simply different from "normal" defendants; and principles of moral philosophy to "prove" that responsibility and causation questions are legitimate ones for moral and legal inquiry.
>
> In contrast, President Reagan, who was the victim of an insanity-pleader, was able to stir public opinion against the defense, in large part, because he used a case-specific style that relied on concrete, vivid and emotion-arousing anecdotes. Such a technique is instinctively more accessible to the fact-finder than relying on "boring" empirical studies, and philosophical debates. It is no surprise that counterdemands by empiricists that change be based on scientific evidence rather than emotionalism receive scant attention.
>
> Insanity defense decisionmaking is a uniquely fertile field in which the distortive vividness effect can operate, and in which the legal system's poor mechanisms of coping with systematic errors in intuitive judgment made by heuristic information processors become especially troubling. The chasm between perception and reality on the question of the frequency of use of the insanity defense, its success rate, and the appropriateness of its success rate reflect these effects.[100]

98 Perlin, *supra* note 3, at 1423; Perlin *supra* note 89, at 236–37.

99 Perlin, *supra* note 3, at 1378; *see generally* Perlin, *supra* note 7, at 12–22.

100 Perlin, *supra* note 7, at 20–21.

D. OCS

OCS should not be applied to insanity defense law jurisprudence, where human behavior is very often *opposite* to what OCS would suggest.[101] Not only is OCS prereflexive and self-evident, it is also susceptible to precisely the type of idiosyncratic, reactive decision making that has traditionally typified insanity defense legislation and litigation.[102]

Again, as I wrote some 22 years ago:

> Empirical investigations similarly corroborate the inappropriate application of OCS to insanity defense decisionmaking. Studies demonstrate that judges "unconsciously express public feelings ... reflect[ing] the community's attitudes and biases because they are 'close' to the community."' Others show that virtually no members of the public can actually articulate what the substantive insanity defense test is. Still others illustrate that the public is seriously misinformed about both the "extensiveness and consequences" of an insanity defense plea and that the public explicitly and consistently rejects any such defense substantively broader than the "wild beast" test. These realities may lead into yet one more trap. While judges and attorneys are accustomed to weighing and interpreting several factors at once, the conflict that arises from the attorney's fear that a jury will reject, or will be less impressed by, explanations that require complex analysis and a lengthy explanation may lead to important distortions of forensic testimony.[103]

III. Five Perspectives

A. Counsel

The cases are wildly inconsistent on the duties of counsel in potential insanity defense cases involving defendants with serious mental disabilities.[104] In some, counsel has been held not to be ineffective where defendant would not allow counsel to pursue insanity defense;[105] in others, it has been held that counsel's presentation of insanity defense over defendant's objection violated defendant's constitutional

101 *Id.* at 28. See Michael L. Perlin, *"And I See Through Your Brain": Access To Experts, Competency To Consent, And The Impact Of Antipsychotic Medications In Neuroimaging Cases In The Criminal Trial Process*, 2009 Stanford Technol. L. J. 1, *24 ("insanity defense cases are so often so utterly dissonant with jurors' flawed … OCS").

102 Perlin, *supra* note 3, at 1420.

103 Perlin, *supra* note 7, at 25, quoting, in part, Richard Arens & Jackwell Susman, *Judges, Jury Charges, and Insanity*, 13 How. L.J. 1, 34 n.43 (1966).

104 *See generally* Anne Bowen Poulin, *Strengthening the Criminal Defendant's Right to Counsel*, 28 Cardozo L. Rev. 1213, 1245 n.134 (2006) (discussing cases).

105 Alvord v. Wainwright, 725 F.2d 1282, 1289 (11th Cir. 1984).

rights;[106] in others that the trial court did not abuse its discretion when it failed to impose insanity defense on a defendant;[107] in others, that counsel's admitted failure to raise an insanity defense required an evidentiary hearing on *Strickland* issues.[108]

Although most recent cases considering the issue in the context of whether the client has a Sixth Amendment ineffective assistance claim when counsel overrides a client's decision about the insanity defense have held that the client controls the decision,[109]other empirical research has reported, based on a survey of state attorneys general, that the insanity defense can be raised over the defendant's objection or without the defendant's knowledge in 17 states.[110] In at least one jurisdiction, there is statutory authorization for counsel to raise an insanity defense over the defendant's objection where the court finds raising the insanity defense "necessary for a just determination of the charge against the defendant."[111] This, of course, is problematic as the entry of an insanity plea is a concession that the defendant factually committed the crime.[112] To allow the state to *force* the defendant to concede this appears to be a per se violation of the defendant's right to dignity.

B. International Human Rights

Among other goals, the UN safeguards aim to exempt from the death penalty those who are or have become "insane." A 1989 revision of one of these safeguards expanded this exemption to include people "suffering from mental retardation or extremely limited mental competence, whether at the sentencing stage or at execution."[113] The European Union (EU) has specifically spoken out against

---

106 Jacobs v. Commonwealth, 870 S.W.2d 412 (Ky. 1994); Treece v. State, 547 A.2d 1054, 1062 (Md. 1988).

107 United States v. Marble, 940 F.2d 1543, 1548 (D.C. Cir. 1991).

108 Cotto v. State, 89 So.3d 1025 (Fla. App. 2012). *See generally supra* Chapter 3.

109 *See* Christopher Slobogin & Amy Mashburn, *The Criminal Defense Lawyer's Fiduciary Duty to Clients with Mental Disability*, 68 Fordham L. Rev. 1581, 1630 n.227 (2000), *discussing* Jacobs v. Commonwealth, 870 S.W.2d 412, 418 (Ky. 1994), and Treece v. State, 547 A.2d 1054, 1062 (Md. 1988).

110 Robert D. Miller et al., *Forcing the Insanity Defense on Unwilling Defendants: Best Interests and the Dignity of the Law*, 24 J. Psychol. & L. 487, 504 (1996). *See, discussing this issue*, Slobogin & Mashburn, *supra* note 109, at 1630.

111 Hendricks v. State, 10 P.3d 1231, 1236 (Colo. 2000).

112 *See* Jones v. United States, 463 U.S. 354, 363 (1983) ("a verdict of not guilty by reason of insanity establishes two facts: (i) the defendant committed an act that constitutes a criminal offense, and (ii) he committed the act because of mental illness.").

113 Liliana Lyra Jubilut, *Death Penalty and Mental Illness: The Challenge of Reconciling Human Rights, Criminal Law, and Psychiatric Standards*, 6 Seattle J. for Soc. Just. 353, 365 (2007), citing U.N. Econ. & Soc. Council [ECOSOC], *Safeguards Guaranteeing Protection of the Rights of those Facing the Death Penalty*, U.N. Doc. RES/1984/50 (May 25, 1984), and G.A. Res. 39/118, U.N. Doc. A/RES/30/118 (Dec. 14, 1984). *See also* Roger Hood, The Death Penalty: A World-Wide Perspective 85 (2d ed. 1996).

inflicting the death penalty on any person with a serious mental illness.[114] Again, the argument can persuasively be made that customary international law prohibits the execution of prisoners who are "insane."

Lack of adequate counsel in insanity cases and the omnipresence of sanism and pretextuality in the trial process underscore the need for all participants in the system to take seriously international human rights standards if there is to be a dignified criminal trial process.

The Convention on the Rights of Persons with Disabilities provides persons with disabilities with the rights to, among others:

- equality before the law without discrimination;
- right to life, liberty and security of the person;
- equal recognition before the law and legal capacity;
- freedom from torture, from exploitation, violence and abuse;
- right to respect physical and mental integrity;
- freedom of movement and nationality;
- respect for inherent dignity and individual autonomy, including the freedom to make one's own choices and the independence of persons; and
- non-discrimination.[115]

It goes without saying that insanity defense pleaders are regularly denied virtually all of these rights on an ongoing basis in all American jurisdictions.[116] It is necessary to start taking seriously how the operationalization of the insanity defense violates international human rights law precepts.[117]

---

114 European Union, Delegation of the European Commission to the United States, EU Policy on the Death Penalty, Letter to Governor of Georgia (Feb. 2002), available at http://www.eurunion.org/legislat/DeathPenalty/WilliamsGAGovLett.htm, cited in Laurie Izutsu, *Applying Atkins v. Virginia to Capital Defendants with Severe Mental Illness*, 70 Brook. L. Rev. 995, 1010 n.99 (2005).

115 *See* Michael L. Perlin, International Human Rights and Mental Disability Law: When the Silenced Are Heard 143–58(2011).

116 *See generally* Perlin, *supra* note 2.

117 Beyond the scope of this book are the interrelationships between the insanity defense and the international criminal justice system. *See, e.g.*, Olaoluwa Olusanya, *Excuse and Mitigation under International Criminal Law: Redrawing Conceptual Boundaries*, 13 New Crim. L. Rev. 23, 36 (2010) (arguing that the insanity defense and diminished responsibility doctrine "compromise the integrity of the international criminal justice system by masking the role of state propaganda in the commission of international crimes"); *but compare* Jennifer L. Larkin, *The Insanity Defense Founded on Ethnic Oppression: Defending the Accused in the International Criminal Tribunal for the Former Yugoslavia*, 21 N.Y.L. Sch. J. Int'l &. Comp. L. 91, 92 (2001) (evidence of an ethnically oppressive environment could be used to establish insanity). *See generally* Robert Cryer et al., An Introduction to International Criminal Law and Procedure 331–33 (2007).

C. Mental Health Courts

It is especially important to consider the impact of sanist myths here in the context of this population. The "fear of feigning"[118] may lead prosecutors assigned to mental health courts to reject applications on behalf of defendants who, they believe, are faking as "an easy way to escape punishment."[119] If defendants who have pled insanity in the past are barred from entering mental health court programs,[120] the value of such programs will be seriously limited.[121]

Professor Jennifer Bard reminds us that "violent crimes make up only a small percentage of insanity pleas," in support of her position that "the idea of mental health courts is a positive step towards recognizing that a person can be impaired by mental illness without being totally disabled by it."[122] Given the stunning gap

---

118 *See* Perlin, *supra* note 8, at 604.

119 Michael L. Perlin, The Hidden Prejudice: Mental Disability on Trial 230–33 (2000). *See* LeRoy Kondo, *Advocacy of the Establishment of Mental Health Specialty Courts in the Provision of Therapeutic Justice for Mentally Ill Offenders*, 28 Am. J. Crim. L. 255, 298 n. 255 (2001), citing David Schretlen & Hal Arkowitz, *A Psychological Test Battery to Detect Prison Inmates Who Fake Insanity or Mental Retardation*, 8 Behav. Sci. & L. 75 (1990) (reporting that some studies reveal that medical experts correctly classify 92–95% of all persons as either faking or not faking.)

120 Joseph Cormier, *Providing Those with Mental Illness Full and Fair Treatment: Legislative Considerations in the Post-Clark Era*, 47 Am. Crim. L. Rev. 129, 139 (2010):

> For an individual with schizophrenia who is not diverted to a mental health court, the insanity defense is the only remaining option by which individuals with schizophrenia are able to avoid the harsh conditions of prison and potentially receive treatment necessary for the productive reintegration into society.

Of course, the insanity defense is rarely pled and even less rarely successful. *See* Michael L. Perlin, *"She Breaks Just Like a Little Girl" : Neonaticide, the Insanity Defense, and the Irrelevance of "Ordinary Common Sense,"* 10 Wm. & Mary J. Women & L. 1, 18–19 (2003), citing Perlin, *supra* note 2, at 107–09:

> The uncontradicted (indeed, uncontradictable) evidence that: (1) the insanity defense is rarely successful, (2) a failed insanity defense translates into significantly longer prison sentences than those imposed on otherwise-like defendants for like crimes (3) a successful insanity defense translates into longer terms of institutionalization in maximum security confinement (albeit in a forensic "hospital" rather than in a prison).

121 *Compare* Carmen Cirincione, *Revisiting the Insanity Defense: Contested of Consensus?*, 24 Bull. Am. Acad. Psychiatry & Law 165, 166 (1996). (setting up mental health courts to divert less dangerous offenders from the prison system seen as element of insanity defense reform).

122 Jennifer S. Bard, *Re-arranging Deck Chairs on the Titanic: Why the Incarceration of Individuals with Serious Mental Illness Violates Public Health, Ethical, and Constitutional Principles and Therefore Cannot Be Made Right by Piecemeal Changes to the Insanity Defense*, 5 Hous. J. Health L. & Pol'y 1, 42 (2005), relying in part on John

between the percentage of prison inmates with serious mental disabilities[123]and the miniscule number of successful insanity pleas,[124] it is clear that this is a universe to which we must pay serious attention.

D. Alternative Jurisprudences

1. Therapeutic jurisprudence

I have written extensively about the relationship between therapeutic jurisprudence and the insanity defense. In 1994, in a book-length treatment of the insanity defense, I urged policy makers "to weigh the therapeutic potential of the different policy choices that are presented at each of [the] points" of the insanity defense system in order to make that system "coherent."[125] In the course of the sub-chapter that I devoted to this question, I considered a range of insanity defense policy issues:

- Is a non-responsibility verdict therapeutic?
- Does the substantive standard matter?
- Do procedural rules matter?
- Should post-acquittal commitment procedures track the traditional involuntary civil commitment model, or is a separate, more restrictive means of determining commitment appropriate?
- Once institutionalized, how should insanity acquittees be treated?, and
- How should insanity acquittees be monitored in community settings?[126]

In the same book, I also noted that "Lawyers representing [mentally disabled criminal defendants] often ignore potential mental status defenses, or, in some cases, contradictorily, seek to have the insanity defense imposed on their client

---

Q. LaFond & Mary L. Durham, *Cognitive Dissonance: Have Insanity Defense and Civil Commitment Reforms Made a Difference?*, 39 Vill. L. Rev. 71, 93–94 (1994).

123 *See*, *e.g.*, Doris J. James & Lauren E. Glaze, Bureau of Justice Statistics, U.S. Dep't of Justice, Mental Health Problems of Prison and Jail Inmates 3 (2006), available at http:// bjs.ojp.usdoj.gov/index.cfm?ty=pbdetail&iid=789 (56% of state inmates and 45% of federal inmates have mental health problems); Kondo, *supra* note 119, at 271 n. 84 (10–30% of all inmates have "serious" mental disabilities).

124 Less than a fraction of one percent. *See* Perlin, *supra* note 2, at 108.

125 *Id.* at 419.

126 *Id.* at 429–36. I then noted that there remained a "menu" of other issues that needed to be considered from a TJ perspective: "the procedural due process requirements needed at the recommitment process, the right of defendants to refuse to enter an insanity plea, the impact of a failed insanity plea on a subsequent sentence, the impact of a successful plea on other legal statutes, and the systemic ways that counsel is assigned to potential insanity pleaders." *Id.* at 436–37.

over his objections. Such lawyers often succumb to sanist stereotypes and are compliant co-conspirators in pretextual court decisions."[127]

I also stressed:

> [W]e must rigorously apply therapeutic jurisprudence principles to each aspect of the insanity defense. We need to take what we learn from therapeutic jurisprudence to strip away sanist behavior, pretextual reasoning and teleological decision making from the insanity defense process. This would enable us to confront the pretextual use of social science data in an open and meaningful way.[128]

In a more recent article,[129] I raised these TJ dilemmas for the lawyer representing a client with an arguable insanity defense:

- What are the TJ implications of counseling a defendant to plead, or not to plead, the insanity defense?[130]
- Can a defendant who pleads NGRI ever, truly, "take responsibility?"[131]
- Does the fact that the insanity-pleading defendant must concede that he committed the actus reus distort the ongoing lawyer–client relationship?[132]
- To what extent do the ample bodies of case law construing the "ineffectiveness assistance of counsel" standard established by the US Supreme Court in *Strickland v. Washington*[133] even consider the implications of TJ lawyering?[134]

---

127 *Id.* at 437 n.106, citing, in part, Michael L. Perlin, *On "Sanism,"* 46 SMU L. REV. 373, 404–06 (1992).

128 *Id.* at 443.

129 Michael L. Perlin, *"Too Stubborn to Ever Be Governed by Enforced Insanity": Some Therapeutic Jurisprudence Dilemmas in the Representation of Criminal Defendants in Incompetency and Insanity Cases*, 33 INT'L J.L. & PSYCHIATRY 475 (2010).

130 *See, e.g.*, Richard J. Bonnie et al., *Decision-Making in Criminal Defense: An Empirical Study of Insanity Pleas and the Impact of Doubted Client Competence*, 87 J. CRIM. L. & CRIMINOLOGY 48 (1996).

131 *See* Michael L. Perlin & Keri K. Gould, *Rashomon and the Criminal Law: Mental Disability and the Federal Sentencing Guidelines*, 22 AM. J. CRIM. L. 431, 449 (1995):

> The entry of the insanity plea has been seen as evidence of a failure to demonstrate contrition (presumably because the plea entry denied legal responsibility for the offense), and that lack of contrition has been seen as a failure to accept responsibility, thus bringing the defendant out of the ambit of another Guideline … which provides for a downward departure if the defendant "clearly demonstrates a recognition and affirmative acceptance of personal responsibility for his criminal conduct."

132 *See* Jones v. United States, 463 U.S. 354, 363 (1983), discussed *supra* note 113.

133 466 U.S. 668, 689 (1984) ("whether counsel's conduct so undermined the proper function of the adversarial process that the trial court cannot be relied on as having produced a just result"). See *supra* Chapter 3.

134 *See* 4 PERLIN, *supra* note 4, § 8A-4.3, at 60–65 (adequacy of counsel in IST proceedings), and § 9A-7, at 235–41 (adequacy of counsel in insanity cases); § 12-3.6,

- To what extent does the pervasiveness of sanism make it obligatory for lawyers in such cases to educate jurors about both sanism and why sanism may be driving their decision-making, and to what extent should lawyers in such cases embark on this educational process using TJ principles?[135]

Subsequently, in the same article, I set out some conversations that a TJ-minded lawyer might have with her putative insanity-pleading client:

- "That was you at the time of the crime, but you're better now."
- "Let's understand that if we raise the defense, you are likely to hear lots of testimony about how out of it you were then. But that doesn't mean you can't control yourself now or later, or understand what conduct is wrong."
- "If we succeed on this defense, it will lessen your hospital commitment if you see yourself as better and in control, and not as continuing to be ill and irresponsible."
- "If we proceed in this manner (and the defense is successful), there may be an uphill battle for you all the way to convince hospital authorities that you have a right to 'have a voice' in your treatment regimen. How can we make it most likely that this will happen?"[136]
- "Are you aware that, when you plead 'not guilty by reason of insanity', you are conceding that you committed the underlying physical act?"[137]

---

at 505–10 (adequacy of counsel in death penalty cases involving defendants with mental disabilities) (discussing case law), and PERLIN & CUCOLO, *supra* NOTE 88, § 8A-4.3, at 28–30; § 9A-7, at 91–93; § 12-3.6, at 137–40 (updating cases).

135 On the sanism of jurors in general, *see* Michael L. Perlin, *The Sanist Lives of Jurors in Death Penalty Cases: The Puzzling Role of "Mitigating" Mental Disability Evidence*, 8 NOTRE DAME J.L., ETHICS & PUB. POL'Y 239, 256–59 (1994); *see also* Perlin, *supra*, note 80, at 335, quoting Denis Keyes et al., *Mitigating Mental Retardation in Capital Cases: Finding the "Invisible" Defendant,* 22 MENTAL & PHYSICAL DISABILITY L. REP. 529, 536 (1998) (stating that "the defense lawyer must educate the jury about mental retardation, its various presentations, and the distinct difference between mental retardation and mental illness").

136 On the anti-therapeutic nature of the post-NGRI acquittal commitment system in general, see Jana R. McCreary, *Not Guilty ... Until Recommitment: The Misuse of Evidence of the Underlying Crime In NGRI Recommitment Hearings*, 2009 UTAH L. REV. 1253, 1257 (current system turns "therapeutic system for persons with mental illness into nothing more than incarceration").

137 *Jones*, 463 U.S. at 363. I discuss the implications of this decision in this context in Michael L. Perlin, *"Everything's a Little Upside Down, As a Matter of Fact the Wheels Have Stopped": The Fraudulence of the Incompetency Evaluation Process*, 4 HOUSTON J. HEALTH L. & POL'Y 239, 246 (2004). For a thorough examination of all the adverse consequences that may flow from the entry of an NGRI plea, see Justine A. Dunlap, *What's Competence Got to Do with It: The Right Not to be Acquitted by Reason of Insanity*, 50 OKLA. L. REV. 495, 507–14 (1997). If a defendant does not understand the full range of these consequences, an important question can be raised as to whether the entry of this plea is truly "voluntary." I discuss these conversations in Perlin, *supra* note 129.

This sample, I think, reflects dialogues that must be begun if criminal representation in these cases is to be non-sanist and is to accord with TJ principles, and if the criminal defense lawyer is ever to become, in David Wexler's words a "change agent."[138]

There are other important approaches to consider. Ira Packer has written about the innovative system developed in Massachusetts in connection with the court clinic that he has supervised, in cases involving defendants charged with minor crimes who are competent to stand trial but most likely meet the criteria of an insanity finding. In such cases, an arrangement is made for the defendant to admit to facts sufficient to warrant a finding of guilty:[139]

> This disposition is reached through negotiation between defense counsel and the prosecutor in consultation with the court clinic personnel. An admission to sufficient facts results in the defendant being assigned probation surety, which entails the defendant agreeing to abide by certain conditions imposed by the court (such as compliance with mental health treatment, or abstinence from substance abuse) for a set period of time. If the individual complies with these conditions, the case will be dismissed at the end of the period. If not, the case will go to trial where the insanity defense will be contested. The defense usually agrees to this arrangement because there is no guarantee that an insanity defense would succeed and even if the insanity defense is successful, the defendant may be committed to a psychiatric hospital for a period of time longer than the possible criminal sentence.] This latter alternative is possible because a person acquitted because of insanity may be indefinitely committed as long as he or she continues to meet civil commitment criteria The prosecution generally agrees to this arrangement because it provides for public safety (by gaining the defendant's cooperation with treatment), and the prosecution also has no guarantee about the outcome of the trial.[140]

According to Packer, this procedure comports with TJ because if "increase[es] the defendant's sense of control over the treatment decision, the likelihood of compliance and positive outcome is potentially increased, [and this] mechanism is also consistent with protecting public safety since it allows for some monitoring of the defendant's behavior in the community."[141] Further, he asserts that an argument can also be made from a rights-oriented perspective that this disposition is likely to

---

138 David B. Wexler, *Therapeutic Jurisprudence and the Rehabilitative Role of the Criminal Defense Lawyer*, 17 St. Thomas L. Rev. 743, 747–48 (2005).

139 Ira Packer, *The Court Clinic System in Massachusetts: A Therapeutic Approach Vs. a Rights-Oriented Approach,* 20 New Eng. J. on Crim. & Civ. Confinement 291, 296–97 (1994).

140 *Id.* at 297.

141 *Id.*

be in the defendant's best interest as a means of allowing the defendant to "avoid the stigma of an insanity finding by agreeing to this disposition."[142]

This approach raises intriguing therapeutic jurisprudence questions about the use (and avoidance) of the insanity defense in pretrial plea-bargaining,[143] and is one that I believe is worthy of far greater scrutiny.[144]

There are other perspectives to consider as well. An Israeli public defender has sensitively and thoughtfully posed the question of the TJ consequences of entering an insanity plea on behalf of a client charged with a minor offense who, if convicted, might have faced only a fine or a minor term of imprisonment.[145] This is a critical question as the research demonstrates that, in the case of misdemeanors and lesser felonies, defendants who "successfully" plead insanity generally serve nine times as long in a maximum security facility than they would have served had they been convicted. [146] It is a question that the TJ-sensitive defense lawyer must ask herself.

2. Procedural justice

Consider first the plight of defendants on whose behalf insanity pleas were entered, but who never knew that this was being done.[147] Could there be an example of a greater deprivation of procedural justice anywhere in the criminal trial system?

Just as judicial procedural decisions about the incompetency status may make "ensuring procedural justice may be more problematic,"[148] so has legislation shifting the burden of proof in insanity defense cases, or abolishing the defense in its entirety similarly made procedural justice a less attainable goal in cases

---

142 *Id.* at 298.

143 Michael L. Perlin, *Therapeutic Jurisprudence: Understanding the Sanist and Pretextual Bases of Mental Disability Law*, 20 New Eng. J. on Crim. & Civ. Confinement 369, 380 n.79 (1994).

144 On the relationship between therapeutic jurisprudence and the criminal trial process in general (a relationship that self-evidently encompasses multiple issues related to plea bargaining), see David B. Wexler, *New Wine in New Bottles: The Need to Sketch a Therapeutic Jurisprudence "Code" of Proposed Criminal Processes and Practices*, in Therapeutic Jurisprudence and Problem-Solving Justice (Jane Donoghue ed., 2013) (in press).

145 Oran Alyagon Darr, *TJ and Zealous Advocacy: Tension and Opportunity*, in Rehabilitating Lawyers: Principles of Therapeutic Jurisprudence for Criminal Law Practice 162, 164 (David B. Wexler ed., 2008).

146 Perlin, *supra* note 89, at 210.

147 *See, e.g.*, Dunlap, *supra* note 147, at 508–10; *see, e.g.*, State v. Mikulic, No. 70269 (Ohio Ct. App. Dec. 12, 1996), discussed in *Criminal Responsibility*, 21 Mental & Physical Disability L. Rep. 170, 173 (1997) (robbery defendant did not enter a knowing, voluntary, and intelligent guilty plea because he had not received correct information about the insanity defense).

148 Kondo, *supra* note 119, at 294, discussed *supra* Chapter 8, at text accompanying notes 344–45.

involving this cohort of defendants.[149] Beyond this, virtually no attention is ever paid to the question of whether insanity-pleading defendants feel that the court procedures to which they are subjected are "fair."[150]

There is an important "flip side" to this. Professors Tom Tyler and Robert J. Boeckmann point out that the public—inaccurately—believes that the courts let too many criminals off due to "legal technicalities" such as the insanity defense. Since people who feel that the procedures they are dealing with are unfair, they react to those procedures by judging the favorability of their outcomes, and thus may be evaluating procedural protections in outcome terms because they regard current legal protections as basically unfair "legal technicalities," that is, as unfair procedures.[151]

3. Restorative justice

From a very different perspective, Tina Ikpa points out perceptively that "restorative justice recognizes the need to help the offender heal from any harms that might have 'contributed to their offending behavior.'"[152] Noting that the assertion of the insanity defense is one of the few moments in the criminal justice system in which there is an inquiry as to "what might be driving an offender to commit the actions he does," she notes that RJ would expand on that limited inquiry, bringing about as it does, "an awareness of the limits and negative byproducts of punishment."[153]

149 *Id.*

150 Compare Jose E. Alvarez, *Rush to Closure: Lessons of the Tadic Judgment*, 96 MICH. L. REV. 2031, 2102 (1998), discussing JOHN W. THIBAUT & LAURENS WALKER, PROCEDURAL JUSTICE: A PSYCHOLOGICAL ANALYSIS 67–116 (1975), in the context of litigants' process satisfaction in international criminal courts.

151 Tom R. Tyler & Robert J. Boeckmann, *Three Strikes and You Are Out, but Why? The Psychology of Public Support for Punishing Rule Breakers*, 31 LAW & SOC'Y REV. 237, 259 (1997), citing, inter alia, E. ALLAN LIND & TOM R. TYLER, THE SOCIAL PSYCHOLOGY OF PROCEDURAL JUSTICE (1988). *See also*, Robert J. Boeckmann & Tom R. Tyler, *Commonsense Justice and Inclusion within the Moral Community: When Do People Receive Procedural Protections from Others?*, 3 PSYCHOL. PUB. POL'Y & L. 362, 363 (1997):

> The argument that legal procedures are abused by criminals is more broadly reflected in the argument that criminals go free as a result of legal "technicalities," such as the use of the insanity defense, the exclusion of illegally obtained evidence, and other "misuses" of legal procedures. Given the widespread public view that criminals unfairly benefit from legal procedures (it is not surprising that a second, but less widely noted, manifestation of punitiveness is the desire to deny or limit procedural rights to those accused of crimes.

152 Tina Ipka, *Balancing Restorative Justice Principles and Due Process Rights in Order to Reform the Criminal Justice System*, 24 WASH. U. J.L. & POL'Y 301, 304 n.12 (2007), quoting HOWARD ZEHR, THE LITTLE BOOK OF RESTORATIVE JUSTICE 17 (2002).

153 Ipka, *supra* note 154, at 304 n.12, quoting ZEHR, *supra* note 154, at 16.

Interestingly, restorative justice is part of the insanity defense fabric elsewhere. Just prior to the submission of this manuscript, Anders Breivek—who killed 77 people in Norway in 2011 at the Norwegian Labor Party's summer youth camp—was sentenced to 21 years in prison, a sentence that could be extended "indefinitely" if he were to be deemed a threat to society.[154] The court rejected the prosecution's arguments that Breivik was insane,[155] and imposed the sentence following testimony from victims' families, explicitly in accordance with restorative justice mandates.[156] As an op-ed column posted on the New York Times website explained:

> By affirming the humanity of each victim, the court tried to satisfy a traumatized society's thirst for truth and justice without denying the defendant's right to a fair hearing.
>
> The Breivik trial thus sought to provide a measure of restorative justice within the normal criminal court system. [The trial aimed] for acknowledgment of the human suffering caused by the atrocities.

***

154 *Norwegian Killer Ruled Sane, Given 21 Year Term*, KLAMATH FALLS (OR.) HERALD & NEWS (Aug. 25, 2012). It is considered "unlikely" that the defendant will ever be released from prison. *See* Mark Lewis & Sarah Lyall, *Norway Mass Killer Gets the Maximum: 21 Years*, NEW YORK TIMES (Aug. 25, 2012), accessible at 2012 WLNR 18043708.

155 See *Prosecutors in Norway Call for Breivik Insanity Verdict*, BBC NEWS EUROPE (June 21 2012), accessible at http://www.bbc.co.uk/news/world-europe-18530670.

156 *See* Toril Moi & David L. Paletz, *In Norway, a New Model for Justice*, accessible at http://www.nytimes.com/2012/08/23/opinion/at-breivik-trial-a-chance-for-norway-to-heal.html?_r=2&nl=opinion&emc=tya2_20120824:

> Before the trial began, the court named 174 lawyers, paid by the state, to protect the interests of the victims and their families during the criminal investigation and the trial. …
>
> The court also allotted time to testimony from survivors, some with horrific injuries. We attended the trial during their testimonies, and to listen to the story of their pain and their efforts to continue their lives was indescribably moving. The effect was not just to establish in detail exactly what happened in Oslo and on Utoya, but to remind us that behind each number there is a human being.
>
> On the last day of the trial, after summations by the prosecution and the defense, the court allowed five representatives of victims' families and friends to express their loss. Some of them did so with such eloquence and power that the otherwise restrained audience (mostly victims and their families) applauded.

> The Breivik trial provides an example of the opposite point of view: that full acknowledgment of the truth of human suffering can have healing effects, for the victims and their families, and for a whole nation. That, even more than the verdict itself, should be the lasting legacy of this horrific event in Norway's history.[157]

Of course, any strategy to humanize the insanity defense process is likely to be met with great opposition and hostility. Insanity pleaders are, of course, one of the most "despised" cohorts of individuals in society.[158] The Norway approach would, most likely, be flatly rejected by legislators and by voters as appearing impossibly "soft on crime."[159] But, I believe, it is only through initiatives such as RJ that we can achieve what we must: an expansion of dignity in the criminal justice system.

E. Dignity

One of the most important dignity considerations here is whether an insanity defense can be imposed on a defendant who does not wish to present it, as the entry of the plea is a concession that the defendant committed the act in question.[160] It should be self-evident that legally coercing a defendant to admit to the commission of the *actus reus*—over his objection or without even informing him of what is being done—robs the defendant and the entire criminal justice process of dignity.

---

157 *Id.*

158 Successful insanity defendants have traditionally been perceived as perhaps the "most despised" and most "morally repugnant" group of individuals in society. See Deborah C. Scott et. al., *Monitoring Insanity Acquittees: Connecticut's Psychiatric Security Review Board*, 41 Hosp. & Community Psychiatry 980, 982 (1990). See also Perlin, *supra* note 3, at 1379. At this point in time, it is likely that this cohort has been replaced by sexually violent predators as the "most despised." See e.g., Heather Ellis Cucolo & Michael L. Perlin, *Preventing Sex-Offender Recidivism through Therapeutic Jurisprudence Approaches and Specialized Community Integration*, -- Temple Political & Civil Rts. L. Rev.– (2013) (in press); Heather Ellis Cucolo & Michael L. Perlin, *"They're Planting Stories In the Press": The Impact of Media Distortions on Sex Offender Law and Policy,* -- Denver U. Crim. L. Rev. – (2013) (in press).

159 *See* Insanity Def. Work Group, Am. Psychiatric Ass'n, *APA Statement on the Insanity Defense*, 140 Am. J. Psychiatry 681, 682 (1983) ("During the last ten years, interest in abolishing or modifying the insanity defense has been renewed because of several factors. Public officials, speaking for a growing conservative consensus and a public understandably disturbed by the failures of the entire criminal justice system, have championed the cause that the insanity defense is one more indication that the country is 'soft on crime'"), as quoted in Michael Corrado, *The Case for a Purely Volitional Insanity Defense*, 42 Tex. Tech L. Rev. 481, 481 n.1 (2009).

160 *See* Jones v. United States, 463 U.S. 354, 363 (1983), discussed in this context *supra* note 112, as discussed in Perlin, *supra* note 97, at 899 n. 92.

In considering this issue, the Nevada Supreme Court found forcefully that a defendant had the absolute right to prohibit defense counsel from interposing an insanity defense over his objections,[161] noting that the "*social stigmatization* that may attach to an assertion or adjudication of insanity also weighs in favor of leaving the final decision of whether to assert an insanity defense to the competent defendant and not to counsel."[162] This reasoning, according to Christopher Johnson, reflects the attitude that "a uniquely serious insult to a defendant's dignity attaches to the insanity defense."[163]

As noted above, in a "sizeable minority"[164] of jurisdictions, the court can impose the insanity defense over a defendant's objections.[165] Dr. Robert Miller, the author of the empirical study that disclosed this information, subsequently stressed:

> Those courts that have approved of these practices have often held that the "dignity of the law" does not permit an insane defendant to be found guilty. The dignity of defendants and their competent decisions count for little against the law itself.[166]

There is yet another side to this complex dilemma: to what extent do persons with mental disabilities have the right to the "dignity of risk,"[167] the ability to assume personal responsibility for their lives and bear the consequences of their

---

161 People v. Johnson, 17 P. 3d 1008 (Nevada 2001).

162 *Id.* at 1015 (emphasis added).

163 Christopher Johnson, *The Law's Hard Choice: Self-Inflicted Injustice or Lawyer-Inflicted Indignity*, 93 Ky. L.J. 39, 107–08 (2004–05). Johnson takes exception with the uniqueness of this stigma, arguing that "no greater social stigma attaches to mental illness than to criminal conviction and incarceration, especially where the charged crime is serious and the term of incarceration lengthy," *id.* at 108, a position with which I disagree. *See, e.g.*, Laura Reider, *Toward a New Test for The Insanity Defense: Incorporating the Discoveries Of Neuroscience into Moral and Legal Theories*, 46 UCLA L. Rev. 289, 341 (1998) ("An expanded insanity defense does not seek to diminish human dignity; rather, it simply endeavors to acknowledge reality by recognizing that individuals do not share the same capacities and abilities"). On the classical Szaszian position that no insanity plea can be "humanitarian, because it diminishes personal responsibility and thus impairs human dignity," see Robitscher & Haynes, *supra* note 18, at 39–40, discussing Thomas Szasz, Ideology and Insanity 111(1970). I discuss the libertarian attack on the insanity defense in Perlin, *supra* note 2, at 134–35 n.275.

164 Slobogin & Mashburn, *supra* note 109, at 1630.

165 See *supra* text accompanying note 110.

166 Robert D. Miller, *Patient Responsibilities: The Other Side of the Coin*, 17 T.M. Cooley L. Rev. 91, 118 (2000).

167 See Elizabeth Nevins-Saunders, *Not Guilty as Charged: The Myth of Mens Rea for Defendants with Mental Retardation*, 45 U.C. Davis L. Rev. 1419, 1474 n. 260 (2012), quoting Robert Perske, *The Dignity of Risk*, reprinted in Wolf Wolfensberger, The Principle of Normalization in Human Services 194, 194–95 (1972) (advocating

choices?[168] And to what extent does that guarantee them total autonomy in insanity defense decision-making? If a defendant is competent to stand trial—and to enter an insanity plea, he must be[169]—it makes no sense to say that the state can impose an insanity plea when it cannot force a defendant to plead self-defense, alibi, justification, or other accepted criminal defenses. To coerce a defendant into entering such a plea is to demean his dignity.

IV. Conclusion

Some years ago, I wrote:

> [W]e must rigorously apply therapeutic jurisprudence principles to each aspect of the insanity defense. We need to take what we learn from therapeutic jurisprudence to strip away sanist behavior, pretextual reasoning and teleological decision making from the insanity defense process. This would enable us to confront the pretextual use of social science data in an open and meaningful way.[170]

But we have not done this. We accept an insanity defense system that is sanist, pretextual and teleological, a system that rests on the shaky underpinnings of heuristic reasoning and a false OCS (ordinary common sense). And this acceptance may ultimately doom to failure any attempt to reconstitute insanity defense policy, even when examined through the lens of therapeutic jurisprudence.

Why is this? I believe that our refusal to care about or think about the objective realities that I have been discussing, and our dogged, banal reliance on sanist myths and pretextual reasoning is made far easier by both phenomena that I discussed earlier: our authoritarian spirit, and our culture of punishment. These phenomena allow us—encourage us—to wilfully blind ourselves to behavioral, scientific, cultural and empirical realities, They do this to preserve the illusion of a "borderline" between "you and me". The evanescence of this borderline becomes, in the end, the reason why, after centuries, our insanity defense jurisprudence continues to operate as it always has—out of consciousness.[171]

---

opportunities for people with mental retardation to take risks commensurate with their functioning).

168 Robert W. Pratt, *Whither the Disability Rights Movement?* 109 MICH. L. REV. 1103, 1104 (2011).

169 *See e.g.*, Coolbroth v. District Court, 766 P.2d 670, 671-73 (Colo. 1988), the Colorado Supreme Court struck down a statute permitting a trial of an incompetent defendant on the issue of insanity only. See generally, 4 PERLIN, *supra* note 1, § 8B-3.3f, at 123.

170 PERLIN, *supra* note 2, at 443; see also, Perlin, *supra* note 97, at 913.

171 Perlin, *supra* note 3, at 1425–26.

Chapter 10
Sentencing

I. **Introduction**

There is an extensive body of literature on incompetency status, on the insanity defense, and on the impact of mental disability on death penalty decision-making.[1] But there has been far less written about the impact of mental disability on the sentencing process.[2] Intuitively, this is surprising, as the percentage of sentenced defendants with some sort of mental disability is significant.[3] But, for whatever reason, this issue appears to be beneath-the-radar for most scholars writing in this area.

In this section of this chapter, I will consider first the impact of the Federal Sentencing Guidelines on developments in this area of law, the significance of subsequent Supreme Court decisions and, finally, the impact of these cases on litigation involving defendants with serious mental disabilities.

---

1 See 4 MICHAEL L. PERLIN, MENTAL DISABILITY LAW, chapters 8, 9 & 12 (2d ed. 2002), and sources cited.

2 One of the very few mentions is in ANDREW VON HIRSCH, PAST OR FUTURE CRIMES: DESERVEDNESS AND DANGEROUSNESS IN THE SENTENCING OF CRIMINALS 71–73 (1985) (identifying, in an assessment of culpability, a range of factors including the actor's mental state, including both his motives and any significant mental disability, and the presence of mitigating or aggravating circumstances such as necessity or duress). I discuss these issues in 4 PERLIN, *supra* note 1, Chapter 11.

3 *See, e.g.*, Robin Wilson, *Mental Health and the Law*, 14 WASH. U. J.L. & POL'Y 315, 319 (2004) (as many as one-third of prisoners have mental disabilities). The percentage of prisoners in state high security or segregated units ranges from 23% to 50%. See SASHA ABRAMSKY & JAMIE FELLNER, HUMAN RIGHTS WATCH, ILL EQUIPPED: U.S. PRISONS AND OFFENDERS WITH MENTAL ILLNESS 147–49 (2003), *available at* http:// www.hrw.org/reports/2003/usa1003/usa1003.pdf, and Jamie Fellner, *A Corrections Quandry: Mental Illness and Prison Rules*, 41 HARV. C.R.-C.L. REV. 391 (2006); *see generally* Christina Canales, *Prisons: The New Mental Health System*, 44 CONN. L. REV. 1725 (2012).

II. Impact of the Federal Sentencing Guidelines: The Early Years[4]

In response to criticisms of indeterminate sentencing,[5] Congress[6] passed the 1984 Sentencing Reform Act,[7] in an attempt to bring about a measure of regularity and uniformity in federal sentencing procedures. Under this law, a Sentencing Commission was created[8] and mandated to promulgate Sentencing Guidelines in accordance with the Act.[9] The constitutionality of these Guidelines—a binding set of rules that courts must use in imposing sentences[10]—was initially upheld by the Supreme Court in *Mistretta v. United States.*[11]

Under the Guidelines, a sentencing court initially was allowed to depart from the prescribed ranges where "the defendant committed a non violent offense[12]

---

4 *See generally* Michael L. Perlin & Keri K. Gould, *Rashomon and the Criminal Law: Mental Disability and the Federal Sentencing Guidelines*, 22 Am. J. Crim. L. 431 (1995); Michael L. Perlin, The Hidden Prejudice: Mental Disability on Trial 245–58, 287–88 (2000); 4 Perlin, *supra* note 1, § 11-2.1, at 448–58.

5 *See* Mistretta v. United States, 488 U.S. 361 (1989) (discussing sentencing disparities).

6 Some states similarly adopted determinate sentencing laws. *See, e.g.*, State v. Allert, 815 P.2d 752 (Wash. 1991) (combination of depression, personality disorder and alcoholism did not justify exceptional sentence); State v. Sepulvado, 655 So. 2d 623 (La. App. 1995), *writ denied*, 662 So. 2d 465 (La. 1995) (upward departure not excessive). For a careful opinion considering the appropriate scope of discretion in such cases, see People v. Watters, 595 N.E.2d 1369 (Ill. App. 1992), *appeal denied*, 602 N.E.2d 473 (Ill. 1992). For a representative opinion from a *non-Guidelines* state, *see, e.g.*, State v. Chase in Winter, 534 N.W.2d 350 (S.D. 1995) (200 year sentence of mentally ill defendant not cruel and unusual punishment).

7 *See* 18 U.S.C. §§ 3551-3742 and 28 U.S.C. §§ 991-998 (1988). *See generally* Stephen J. Schulhofer, *Assessing the Federal Sentencing Process: The Problem Is Uniformity, Not Disparity*, 29 Am. Crim. L. Rev. 833 (1992).

8 *See* 28 U.S.C. § 991.

9 *See* 28 U.S.C. § 994(a)(1).

10 *See id.* Under the Act, a series of permissible sentencing ranges is created for each federal criminal offense. See 28 U.S.C. § 994(b)(2).

11 488 U.S. 361 (1989); *see generally* Ilene Nagel, *Structuring Sentencing Discretion: The New Federal Sentencing Guidelines*, 80 J. Crim. L. & Criminology 883 (1990); Deborah Young, *Fact-Finding at Federal Sentencing: Why the Guidelines Should Meet the Rules*, 79 Cornell L. Rev. 299 (1994); Frank Bowman, *The Quality of Mercy Must Be Restrained, and Other Lessons in Learning to Love the Federal Sentencing Guidelines*, 1996 Wis. L. Rev. 679 (1996); Ira Bloom, *The Aftermath of* Mistretta*: The Demonstrated Incompatibility of the United States Sentencing Commission and Separation of Powers Principles*, 24 Am. J. Crim. L. 1 (1996); Michael O'Hear, *Remorse, Cooperation, and the "Acceptance of Responsibility": The Structure, Implementation, and Reform of Section 3E1.1 of the Federal Sentencing Guidelines*, 91 Nw. U. L. Rev. 1507 (1997).

12 On the meaning of "non-violent offense," *see e.g.*, United States v. Shannon, 94 F.3d 1065 (7th Cir. 1996) (statutory rape not a crime of violence for purposes of the

while suffering from significantly reduced mental capacity[13] not resulting from voluntary use of drugs or other intoxicants."[14] In such cases, a lower sentence "may be warranted" to reflect the extent to which the reduced mental capacity contributed to the commission of the offense, as long as the defendant's criminal history "does not indicate a need for incarceration to protect the public."[15]

In April 1998, the Guidelines were amended to read:

> A sentence below the applicable guideline range may be warranted if the defendant committed the offense while suffering from a significantly reduced mental capacity. However, the court may not depart below the applicable guideline range if (1) the significantly reduced mental capacity was caused by the voluntary use of drugs or other intoxicants; (2) the facts and circumstances of the defendant's offense indicate a need to protect the public because the offense involved actual violence or a serious threat of violence, or (3) the defendant's

---

Guidelines); United States v. Clements, 144 F.3d 981 (6th Cir. 1998) (extortion "crime of violence" under terms of Guidelines).

13 On the question of whether a compulsive gambling disorder satisfies the Guidelines, see United States v. Katzenstein, 1991 WL 24386 (S.D.N.Y. 1991) (unless defendant could demonstrate that total rehabilitation had been achieved, it would be necessary for her to introduce evidence showing lack of correlation between compulsive gambling disorder and increased propensity for criminal activity); United States v. Rosen, 896 F.2d 789 (3d Cir.), *reh'g & reh'g en banc denied* (1990) (defendant's compulsive gambling did not warrant downward departure), *superseded by statute as stated in* United States v. Askari, 159 F.3d 774 (3rd Cir. 1998); United States v. Carucci, 33 F. Supp. 2d 302 (S.D.N.Y. 1999) (compulsive gambling did not warrant downward departure in case of stockbroker who had pled guilty to unlawful securities trading practices); *compare* United States v. Martinez, 978 F. Supp. 1442 (D.N.M. 1997) (downward departure appropriate in case of compulsive gambler convicted of robbery of illegal casino operating on Indian reservation). *See generally* Lawrence Lustberg, *Sentencing the Sick: Compulsive Gambling as the Basis for a Downward Departure Under the Federal Sentencing Guidelines*, 2 Seton Hall J. Sport L. 51 (1992). See *infra* text accompanying note 17 (gambling dependence statutorily eliminated as a potential grounds for dowanward departures).

14 United States Sentencing Commission Guidelines Manual § 5k2.13 (*Manual*). *See, e.g.*, United States v. Rybicki, 96 F.3d 754 (4th Cir. 1996) (alcoholism forbidden basis for downward sentencing departure); United States v. Webb, 134 F.3d 403 (D.C. Cir. 1998), *on remand*, 1998 WL 93052 (1998) (drug addiction could not form basis for downward departure); United States v. Hunter, 980 F. Supp. 1439 (M.D. Ala. 1997), *aff'd*, 172 F.3d 1307 (1999) (same).

15 *Manual, supra* note 14. *See generally* Kirk Houser, *Downward Departures: The Lower Envelope of the Federal Sentencing Guidelines,* 31 Duq. L. Rev. 361 (1993); Donald Wayne, *Chaotic Sentencing: Downward Departures Based on Extraordinary Family Circumstances,* 71 Wash. U. L.Q. 443 (1993). For relevant early cases, *see, e.g.*, United States v. Atkins, 116 F.3d 1366 (D.C. Cir. 1997), *cert. denied*, 522 U.S. 975 (1997); United States v. Mitchell, 113 F.3d 1528 (10th Cir. 1997), *reh'g denied* (1997), *cert. denied*, 522 U.S. 1063 (1998); United States v. Bradshaw, 1999 WL 1129601 (N.D. Ill. 1999).

> criminal history indicates a need to incarcerate the defendant or protect the public. If a departure is warranted, the extent of the departure should reflect the extent to which the reduced mental capacity contributed to the commission of the offense.[16]

and

> Addiction to gambling is not a reason for a downward departure.[17]

Relying on this new language, the Third Circuit found that its earlier decision in *United States v. Rosen* was thus superseded.[18]

The 1998 amendments also re-defined "reduced mental capacity" to include volitional as well as cognitive impairments. Under the amended Guidelines:

> "Significantly reduced mental capacity" means the defendant, although convicted, has a significantly impaired ability to (A) understand the wrongfulness of the behavior comprising the offense or to exercise the power of reason, or (B) control behavior that the defendant knows is wrongful.[19]

The Feeney Amendment—effective 2003—further limited the circumstances under which a court can depart from the range of sentences prescribed in the Guidelines. Among other restrictions, the amendment limits departures based on aberrant behavior and physical impairment.[20] The amendment also prohibited departures based on diminished capacity in cases involving crimes against children and sexual offenses. In general, the amendment prohibited departures based on factors that are not enumerated in the Guidelines or on combinations of factors that would not independently warrant a departure.[21]

Great discretion is vested in the trial courts in determining when a sentence reduction is appropriate under the Guidelines,[22] and decisions not to depart from

---

16 United States Sentencing Guidelines § 5k2.13 (amended 1998).

17 United States Sentencing Guidelines § 5h1.4 (amended 1998).

18 United States v. Askari, 159 F. 3d 774 (3d Cir. 1998), superseding United States v. Rosen, 896 F. 2d 789 (3d Cir. 1990), *reh'g & reh'g en banc denied* (3d Cir. 1990) (defendant's compulsive gambling did not warrant downward departure). *See supra* note 13.

19 United States Sentencing Guidelines § 5K2.13, comment (n.1) (amended 1998).

20 United States Sentencing Guidelines §§ 5K2.20, 5K2.22 (amended 2003).

21 18 U.S.C. § 3553 (b)(2) (amended 2003); United States Sentencing Guidelines § 5K2.0(b) (amended 2003).

22 *See, e.g.*, United States v. Yellow Earrings, 891 F.2d 650, 654-55 (8th Cir. 1989); United States v. White, 71 F.3d 920 (D.C. Cir. 1995); United States v. Organek, 65 F.3d 60 (6th Cir. 1995); United States v. Moreland, 119 F.3d 8 (9th Cir.), *cert. denied*, 522 U.S. 962 (1997); United States v. Volpe, 78 F. Supp. 2d 76 (E.D.N.Y. 1999), *aff'd in part & dismissed in part*, 224 F.3d 72 (2d Cir. 2000).

the Guidelines are generally not appealable.[23] Only where it appears that the District Court misunderstood its authority to reduce the defendant's sentence will appellate courts be willing to disturb sentencing determinations.[24]

In several cases, courts have invoked the Guidelines to reduce a defendant's sentence based on his reduced mental capacity.[25] In *United States v. Speight*,[26] for instance, the court found that a defendant (convicted of drug and firearm offenses) who suffered from schizophrenia and other emotional disturbances met all the criteria of the Guidelines, and that a sentence reduction was thus warranted.[27] In *United States v. Ruklick*,[28] the court emphasized that, under the Guidelines, it was not necessary to find that the defendant's reduced mental capacity amounted to

23 *See* United States v. Ghannam, 899 F.2d 327 (4th Cir. 1990); United States v. Follett, 905 F.2d 195 (8th Cir. 1990), *cert. denied*, 501 U.S. 1207 (1991); *compare id.* at 197 (Heaney, S.C.J., dissenting); United States v. Patterson, 15 F.3d 169 (11th Cir. 1994); United States v. Schechter, 13 F.3d 1117 (7th Cir. 1994); United States v. Turner, 7 F.3d 228 (4th Cir. 1993); United States v. Chigbo, 38 F.3d 543 (11th Cir. 1994), *cert. denied*, 516 U.S. 826 (1995); United States v. Estergard, 77 F.3d 491 (9th Cir. 1996); United States v. Nugent, 89 F.3d 836 (6th Cir. 1996), *cert. denied*, 519 U.S. 941 (1996); United States v. Wilson, 98 F.3d 646 (D.C. Cir. 1996); United States v. Walker, 104 F.3d 368 (10th Cir. 1996), *cert. denied*, 520 U.S. 1191 (1997); United States v. Hemling, 116 F.3d 1489 (10th Cir. 1997); United States v. Black, 116 F.3d 198 (7th Cir.), *cert. denied*, 522 U.S. 934 (1997); United States v. Mikaelian, 168 F.3d 380 (9th Cir.), *amended*, 180 F.3d 1091 (9th Cir. 1999); United States v. Watkins, 179 F.3d 489 (6th Cir. 1999); United States v. Steele, 178 F.3d 1230 (11th Cir. 1999), *cert. denied*, 528 U.S. 933 (1999); United States v. Romero, 210 F.3d 373 (6th Cir. 2000); United States v. Timbana, 222 F.3d 688 (9th Cir. 2000), *cert. denied*, 531 U.S. 1028 (2000).

24 *See, e.g.*, United States v. Ruklick, 919 F.2d 95 (8th Cir. 1990) (reversing trial court's refusal to depart from Guidelines in case where defendant had mental capacity of twelve-year-old). On the need for specific findings in Guideline decision-making, *see, e.g.*, United States v. Perkins, 963 F.2d 1523 (D.C. Cir. 1992); United States v. Zackson, 6 F.3d 911 (2d Cir. 1993).

25 *See also* United States v. Lara, 905 F.2d 599 (2d Cir. 1990) (upholding departure from Guidelines based on defendant's likely "extreme vulnerability" in a correctional facility); United States v. Cotto, 793 F. Supp. 64 (E.D.N.Y. 1992) (defendant's near retardation, vulnerability, efforts at rehabilitation and incompetence warranted downward departure); United States v. Cantu, 12 F.3d 1506 (9th Cir. 1993) (posttraumatic stress disorder is type of mental disorder that can support mental disability-based downward departure).

26 726 F. Supp. 861 (D.D.C. 1989).

27 *Id.* at 867–68. *See also* United States v. Adonis, 744 F. Supp. 336 (D.D.C. 1990); United States v. Glick, 946 F.2d 335 (4th Cir. 1991); United States v. Chambers, 885 F. Supp. 12 (D.D.C. 1995). *Compare* United States v. Doering, 909 F.2d 392 (9th Cir. 1990) (prohibiting *upward* departure where evidence reflected need for psychiatric care). For other cases involving defendants with other mental disabilities, *see e.g.*, United States v. Brown, 1997 WL 786643 (N.D. Ill. 1997) (severe depression and post-traumatic stress disorder); United States v. Follette, 990 F. Supp. 1172 (D. Neb. 1998) (bipolar disorder and post-traumatic stress disorder).

28 919 F. 2d 95 (9th Cir. 1990).

"but-for causation" in order to reduce a sentence, as long as his diminished mental capacity "comprised a contributing factor in the commission of the offense."[29] Other cases have found that the "precise degree" to which the defendant's mental illness contributed to his criminal activity need not be "pinpoint[ed] or quantif[ied],"[30] that a defendant's assertion of the insanity defense did not preclude a downward departure,[31] and that a defendant's post-arrest efforts at drug rehabilitation might warrant such a departure.[32]

On the other hand, determinations to *not* depart from the Guidelines have been upheld where:

- the underlying crime was violent, and where the defendant's violent criminal record raised the possibility that he would be a threat to public safety,[33] or likelihood of victimization if incarcerated,[34]
- the court did not find the defendant's disability so significant as to warrant such a reduction,[35]

---

29 *Id.* at 97–98; *see also* United States v. Fluehr, 1995 WL 37527 (E.D. Pa.), *amended by* 1995 WL 106878 (E.D. Pa. 1995), *aff'd*, 74 F.3d 1228 (3d Cir. 1995), *cert. denied*, 517 U.S. 1137 (1996); United States v. Leandre, 132 F.3d 796 (D.C. Cir.), *cert. denied*, 523 U.S. 1131 (1998); United States v. Perry, 173 F.3d 427 (4th Cir. 1999); United States v. McBroom, 124 F.3d 533 (3d Cir. 1997), *on remand*, United States v. McBroom, 991 F. Supp. 445 (D.N.J. 1998) (departures granted).

30 United States v. Royal, 902 F. Supp. 268, 272 (D.D.C. 1995).

31 United States v. Barnes, 46 F. 3d 33 (8th Cir. 1995).

32 United States v. Workman, 80 F. 3d 688 (2d Cir. 1996), *cert. denied*, 519 U.S. 938, 519 U.S. 955 (1996); United States v. Whitaker, 152 F.3d 1238 (10th Cir. 1998), *reh'g & reh'g en banc denied*, 162 F. 3d 1179 (11th Cir. 1998); United States v. Kane, 88 F. Supp. 2d 408 (E.D. Pa. 2000); United States v. McGee, 201 F.3d 1022 (8th Cir. 1999), *reh'g & reh'g en banc denied* (2000).

33 United States v. Wilson, 891 F.2d 293 (6th Cir. 1989) (Table) (full text available on WESTLAW), United States v. Braxton, 19 F.3d 1385 (11th Cir.), *cert. denied*, 513 U.S. 935 (1994); United States v. Lombardi, 5 F.3d 568 (1st Cir. 1993), *denial of post-conviction relief aff'd*, 48 F.3d 1211 (1st Cir. 1995); United States v. Marquez, 827 F. Supp. 205 (S.D.N.Y. 1993), *aff'd*, 41 F.3d 1502 (2d Cir. 1994); United States v. Salemi, 26 F.3d 1084 (11th Cir.), *cert. denied*, 513 U.S. 1032 (1994); United States v. Premachandra, 32 F.3d 346 (8th Cir. 1994), *denial of post-conviction relief aff'd*, 101 F.3d 68 (8th Cir. 1996); Halmos v. United States, 872 F. Supp. 762 (D. Haw. 1995); United States v. Jones, 48 F.3d 1222 (7th Cir. 1995); United States v. Dailey, 24 F.3d 1323 (11th Cir. 1994); United States v. Santos, 131 F.3d 16 (1st Cir. 1997); United States v. Moore-Bey, 981 F. Supp. 688 (D.D.C. 1997), *aff'd*, 159 F.3d 638 (1998), *cert. denied*, 522 U.S. 918 (1998); Norflett v. United States, 981 F. Supp. 718 (D. Mass. 1997).

34 United States v. Hamilton, 949 F.2d 190 (6th Cir. 1991); United States v. Lauzon, 938 F.2d 326 (1st Cir.), *cert. denied*, 502 U.S. 972 (1991); United States v. Fairman, 947 F.2d 1479 (11th Cir. 1991), *cert. denied*, 503 U.S. 947 (1992); United States v. Poff, 926 F.2d 588 (7th Cir.), *cert. denied*, 502 U.S. 827 (1991); United States v. Coates, 996 F.2d 939 (8th Cir. 1993).

35 United States v. Tucker, 986 F.2d 278 (8th Cir.), *cert. denied*, 510 U.S. 820 (1993); United States v. Benson, 7 F.3d 226 (4th Cir. 1993); *Fluehr, supra*; United States v. Sammoury,

- the defendant's behavior was not sufficiently aberrant,[36]
- the court did not find defendant's "extraordinary post-arrest efforts" at drug rehabilitation sufficient to warrant such a reduction,[37]
- there was no connection demonstrated between the defendant's diminished capacity and the commission of the crime,[38] or
- the court felt that the defendant did not take sufficient responsibility for his role in the criminal offenses in question.[39]

Courts have split on the impact of childhood abuse and neglect on a defendant,[40] and on the question of whether a defendant's "dangerous mental state" would make an *upward* departure appropriate,[41] with at least one appellate court vacating an upward departure sentence, and concluding that the appropriate mechanism for protecting the public in such a case was a commitment proceeding rather than an extended sentence.[42] Another court has rejected a request for a downward

---

74 F.3d 1341 (D.C. Cir. 1996); United States v. Jackson, 56 F.3d 959 (8th Cir. 1995); United States v. Johnson, 71 F.3d 539 (6th Cir. 1995), *cert. denied*, 517 U.S. 1113 (1996); United States v. Withers, 100 F.3d 1142 (4th Cir. 1996), *cert. denied*, 520 U.S. 1132 (1997).

36 Thompson v. United States, 2000 WL 821711 (N.D. Ill. 2000).

37 United States v. Zeigler, 1 F. 3d 1044 (10th Cir. 1993), *appeal after remand*, 39 F.3d 1058 (10th Cir. 1994); United States v. Williams, 37 F.3d 82 (2d Cir. 1994), *appeal after remand*, 65 F.3d 301 (2d Cir. 1995); United States v. Barton, 76 F.3d 499 (2d Cir. 1996).

38 United States v. Johnson, 49 F.3d 766 (D.C. Cir. 1995); United States v. White, 71 F.3d 920 (D.C. Cir. 1995); United States v. Shaoul, 1996 WL 120713 (S.D.N.Y.), *aff'd*, 104 F.3d 351 (2d Cir. 1996); United States v. Vasquez, 1997 WL 187315 (S.D.N.Y. 1997); United States v. Cyprowski, 173 F. 3d 426 (4th Cir. 1999), *cert. denied*, 527 U.S. 1030 (1999); United States v. Dyer, 216 F.3d 568 (7th Cir. 2000); United States v. Sassani, 139 F. 3d 895 (4th Cir. 1998), *cert. denied*, 525 U.S. 921 (1998); United States v. Barajas-Nunez, 91 F.3d 826 (6th Cir. 1996); *see also* United States v. Bissell, 954 F. Supp. 841 (D.N.J. 1996), *aff'd*, 142 F.3d 429 (3d Cir. 1998) (diminished mental capacity based on "personality flaw" that made defendant "placid, unquestioning and compliant" insufficient to require downward departure).

39 United States v. Haddad, 10 F. 3d 1252 (7th Cir. 1993); United States v. Amerson, 864 F. Supp. 458 (M.D. Pa. 1994); United States v. Gordon, 64 F.3d 281 (7th Cir. 1995), *cert. denied*, 516 U.S. 1062 (1996); United States v. Bhagavan, 911 F. Supp. 356 (N.D. Ind. 1995), *aff'd*, 116 F. 3d 189(7th Cir. 1997); United States v. Artim, 944 F. Supp. 363 (D.N.J. 1996).

40 *Compare* United States v. Ayers, 972 F. Supp. 1197 (N.D. Ill. 1997) (defendant entitled to downward departure), *with* United States v. Vela, 927 F.2d 197 (5th Cir. 1991), *cert. denied*, 502 U.S. 875 (1991) (defendant not entitled to such a departure); United States v. Rosa, 104 F. 3d 355 (2d Cir. 1996) (same); United States v. Rivera, 192 F.3d 81 (2d Cir. 1999), *cert. denied*, 528 U.S. 1129 (2000) (same).

41 United States v. Hines, 26 F. 3d 1469 (9th Cir. 1994), *appeal after remand*, 68 F.3d 481 (9th Cir. 1995) (remanding for further explanation by the trial court); *see also* United States v. Barnes, 125 F.3d 1287 (9th Cir. 1997) (upward departure appropriate).

42 United States v. Moses, 106 F. 3d 1273 (6th Cir. 1997), discussing availability of the commitment mechanism found in 18 U.S.C. § 4246.

departure based on the defendant's alleged susceptibility to undue influence by a co-defendant who emotionally and sexually abused her.[43]

III. Subsequent Supreme Court Developments

Later judicial developments have radically altered FSG practice. First, in *Blakely v. Washington*, the Supreme Court struck down the Washington state sentencing guidelines as unconstitutional.[44] In *Blakely*, the Supreme Court applied its earlier ruling in *Apprendi v. New Jersey*,[45] to hold that a defendant's Sixth amendment right to a jury trial was violated by a sentencing scheme that allowed a judge to impose a sentence above the statutory maximum based on facts neither admitted by the defendant nor found beyond a reasonable doubt by a jury.

Justice Scalia, writing for the majority, ruled that Washington's scheme as applied to *Blakely* ran afoul of the Court's ruling in *Apprendi*, which held that "other than the fact of a prior conviction, any fact that increases the penalty for a crime beyond the prescribed statutory maximum must be submitted to a jury and proved beyond a reasonable doubt."[46] The majority noted that it was not holding determinate sentencing per se unconstitutional,[47] and specifically, that the Federal Sentencing Guidelines were not before the Court.[48]

In its next term, a deeply divided Supreme Court ruled in *United States v. Booker* and *United States v. Fanfan*,[49] that the federal sentencing guidelines were subject to jury trial requirements of the Sixth Amendment, and that the Sixth Amendment's requirement that the jury find certain sentencing facts was incompatible with Federal Sentencing Act, thus requiring severance of the Act's provisions that had made guidelines "mandatory."[50] At least one commentator has read *Booker* to make it "incumbent upon judges to consider the physical or mental health of a defendant during the sentencing phase, where it ordinarily would not have been allowed pre-*Booker* when the Guidelines were mandatory,"[51]

In a thoughtful early analysis, John Parry, who believes that their impact on mental disability law will most likely be "limited,"[52] has observed:

43 United States v. Rouse, 168 F. 3d 1371 (D.C. Cir. 1999).

44 542 U.S. 296 (2004).

45 530 U.S. 466 (2000).

46 Blakely, 542 U.S at 301.

47 *Id.* at 309.

48 *Id.* at 305 n.9.

49 543 U.S. 220 (2005).

50 *Id.* at 245.

51 Natalie Hinton, *Curing the BOP Plague with Booker: Addressing Inadequate Medical Treatment in the Bureau of Prisons*, 41 J. Marshall L. Rev. 219, 228 (2007).

52 John Parry, *Summary U.S. Supreme Court Actions*. 29 Ment. & Phys. Dis. L. Rep. 137, 137 (2005).

> *Booker* and other recent cases—e.g., *Blakely; Apprendi; Ring*—create the impression that in sentencing matters juries are sacrosanct, or close to it. The good aspect for defendants is that they have a Sixth Amendment right to have juries decide sentencing matters. This gives defense lawyers an important constitutional card to play in defending their clients, which is particularly important when mitigating circumstances are to be presented.[53]

Continuing, Parry expressed concern that "this trend … helps fuel the misimpression that juries are somehow better suited to assessing expert evidence related to sentencing than are judges,"[54] adding that one of the "critical problems" in the criminal justice system for defendants with mental and other disabilities is that jurors are not particularly competent in dealing with complex expert evidence, and like many people in society, tend to have a bias against such defendants, who tend to be stigmatized by their disabilities." Parry continued "The notion that expert evidence regarding a person's mental status—which even in the best circumstances engenders considerable doubts in terms of its relevance and accuracy—can be made more relevant and accurate after being 'weighed' by a jury is not only naive but is also incredible."[55]

IV. Impact of *Booker*

Courts have slowly begun to consider the impact of *Booker* on cases involving defendants with mental disabilities.[56] In *United States v. Anderson*,[57] in the course of interpreting *Booker* in a case vacating defendant's sentence, the court specifically noted that the government "fail[ed] to account for the district court's consideration and discussion of Anderson's 'serious mental health issues,' presented in support

---

53 *Id.*

54 *Id.*

55 *Id.*

56 See *Developments in the Law, Booker, the Federal Sentencing Guidelines, and Violent Mentally Ill Offenders*, 121 HARV. L. REV. 1133 (2008). See also Jeffrey T. Ulmer & Michael T. Light, *The Stability of Case Processing and Sentencing Post-Booker*, 14 J. GENDER RACE & JUST. 143, 175 (2010), relying upon Paul Hofer, *United States v. Booker as a Natural Experiment: Using Empirical Research to Inform the Federal Sentencing Policy Debate*, 6 CRIMINOLOGY & PUB. POL'Y 433, 450 (2007):

> [P]revious employment, drug and alcohol dependence, age, family and community ties, and mental and emotional conditions are cited in a larger portion of cases after the Booker decision than they were before, which suggests that the Guideline commentary making these characteristics "not ordinarily relevant" is more frequently being disregarded by judges or given a more restricted reading.

57 452 F. 3d 87 (1st Cir. 2006).

of his request for a downward departure."[58] Elsewhere, courts have relied on *Booker* as authority for imposing non-guidelines sentences in cases of defendants seeking downward departures based on diminished mental capacities.[59]

V. Four Factors

A. Sanism

How is it possible that people should be punished more harshly because they were born with mental illness?[60] Cases decided under the Guidelines reflect a lack of understanding by federal judges of the meaning of mental disability and its role as a potential sentencing mitigator.[61] In sentencing decision-making, judges conceptualize mental disability as an "all or nothing" absolute construct, demand a showing of mental disability that approximates the amount needed for an exculpatory insanity defense, continue to not "get" distinctions between mental illness, insanity, and incompetency, repeat sanist myths about mentally disabled criminal defendants, and engage in pretextual decision-making.

The ominous spirit of Justice Scalia's partial dissent in *Penry v. Lynaugh*—castigating the majority for allowing an "outpouring … [of] unfocused sympathy"[62]—looms over many of these cases. Most of the few cases in which

58 *Id.* at 93.

59 United States v. Pallowick, 364 F. Supp. 2d 923, 926 (E.D. Wis. 2005) ("In the present case, defendant moved for a downward departure based on his diminished mental capacity and vulnerability to abuse in prison. However, this was before Booker made the guidelines advisory. … Consistent with [defendant's] argument, I concluded that a non-guideline sentence was appropriate"); United States v. MacKinnon, 401 F.3d 8 (1st Cir. 2005) (same); United States v. Jones, 352 F. Supp. 2d 22, 23–24 (D. Maine 2005) (sentence would have been impossible before Booker because neither mental and emotional conditions, diminished capacity, nor efforts toward rehabilitation would have entitled the defendant to a downward departure), as discussed in Susan R. Klein, *The Return of Federal Judicial Discretion in Criminal Sentencing*, 39 VAL. U. L. REV. 693, 726–27 (2005); *see also* United States v. Villanueva, 2007 WL 4410378, *3 (E.D. Wis. 2007) ("But if *Booker* means anything at all, it must mean that the court can give further weight to factors covered by the guidelines, and consider personal characteristics deemed disfavored or discouraged by the guidelines.").

60 J.C. Oleson, *Risk in Sentencing: Constitutionally Suspect Variables and Evidence-Based Sentencing*, 64 SMU L. REV. 1329, 1395 (2011).

61 *See* Perlin & Gould, *supra* note 4, at 452–55.

62 492 U.S. 302, 359–60 (1989) (Scalia, J., concurring in part & dissenting in part). The majority in *Penry* had concluded that evidence as to the defendant's mental retardation was relevant to his culpability and that, without such information, jurors could not express their "reasoned moral response" in determining the appropriateness of the death penalty. *Id.* at 321. I discuss *Penry* extensively in 4 PERLIN, *supra* note 1, § 12-3.3, at 493–500, and in Michael L. Perlin, *"The Executioner's Face Is Always Well-Hidden": The Role of Counsel and the Courts in Determining Who Dies*, 41 N.Y.L. SCH. L. REV. 201, 213–14 (1996).

mental disability is seen as a mitigator eerily track the fact pattern of the few situations in which jurors grudgingly sanction the use of the insanity defense: when a defendant—especially one who has previously sought counseling—commits a nonplanful crime.[63]

The attitudes expressed in these cases are frequently sanist. For example, in a Sixth Circuit case the court rejected the defendant's "suicidal tendencies" as a possible basis for a downward departure in an embezzlement case.[64] The court held that departure would never be permissible on this basis, because any consideration of such an argument would lead to "boilerplate" claims and force courts to "separate the wheat of valid claims from the chaff of disingenuous ones," a "path before which we give serious pause."[65] This argument tracks, nearly verbatim, the reasoning of the Fourth Circuit, which refused to grant a downward departure in the case of a defendant who had suffered severe childhood sexual abuse, referring to the "innumerable defendants" that could plead "unstable upbringing" as a potential departure grounds.[66]

Just as evidence of organic disorder appears more "real" to judges in insanity cases (than does evidence of psychological disability),[67] so does such evidence appear more "real" in Guidelines cases. In *United States v. Hamilton*,[68] the Sixth Circuit affirmed a trial court's refusal to enter a downward departure in the case of a defendant suffering a "major depressive episode," on the theory that the Commission was "talking about things such as a borderline mental intelligence capacity."[69] The court concluded that because the defendant was "able to absorb information in the usual way and to exercise the power of reason," he did not suffer from a "significantly reduced mental capacity."[70]

The District of Columbia Circuit has explicitly rejected the admission of expert testimony on an individual defendant's potential for successful rehabilitation on two grounds: Another defendant without access to such expert testimony might be able to make a similar case for leniency, and reliance on "scientific" predictions could transform sentencing hearings into an inappropriate "battle of experts."[71] But, as Professor Schulhofer notes in his critique of this case, a district court always has the capacity to appoint expert witnesses to aid a defendant at sentencing, an option made explicitly constitutional in a different context in *Ake v. Oklahoma*.[72]

---

63 Michael L. Perlin, *The Sanist Lives of Jurors in Death Penalty Cases: The Puzzling Role of "Mitigating" Mental Disability Evidence*, 8 Notre Dame J.L. Ethics & Pub. Pol'y 239, 245–49 (1994).

64 United States v. Harpst, 949 F.2d 860, 871 (6th Cir. 1991).

65 *Id.*

66 United States v. Daly, 883 F. 313, 319 (4th Cir. 1989).

67 Michael L. Perlin, The Jurisprudence of the Insanity Defense 252–58 (1994).

68 949 F.2d 190 (6th Cir. 1991). See *supra* note 34.

69 *Id.* at 193.

70 *Id.*

71 United States v. Harrington, 947 F.2d 956, 960 (D.C. Cir. 1991).

72 470 U.S. 68 (1985); *see also* Schulhofer, *supra* note 7, at 869 (discussing *Ake*).

Underlying many of the Guidelines cases is a powerful current of *blame*: The defendant succumbed to temptation by not resisting drugs or alcohol, by not overcoming childhood abuse, and so forth. This sense of blame mirrors courts' sanist impatience with mentally disabled criminal defendants in general, attributing their problems in the legal process to "weak character or poor resolve."[73] Thus, as noted earlier in this volume, we should not be surprised to learn that a trial judge, responding to a National Center for State Courts survey, indicated that incompetent-to-stand-trial defendants could have understood and communicated with their counsel and the court "if they [had] only wanted."[74] Again, one of the leading texts on white-collar crimes sentencing stresses:

> Judges consider[ ] two major concepts pertinent to individual attributes of the offender: blameworthiness and consequence. ... Certain characteristics of offenders relate to the culpability of or degree of blameworthiness of the particular defendant. Illustrations include mental competency. ...[75]

B. Pretextuality

In addition to the use of sanism, sentencing decisions are also often pretextual. There is no question that sentencing discourse is often pretextual, reflecting a system in which "stakeholders inconsistently advance varyingly deferential degrees of appellate review suspiciously consonant with the practical sentencing outcomes they desire."[76]

---

73 Michael L. Perlin, *Pretexts and Mental Disability Law: The Case of Competency*, 47 U. Miami L. Rev. 625, 670–710 (1993). *See generally* Bernard Weiner, *On Sin Versus Sickness: A Theory of Perceived Responsibility and Social Motivation*, 48 Am. Psychologist 957 (1993) (proposing conceptual system of social motivation to balance societal tendencies that tend to encourage punishment for those who demonstrate a "lack of effort" or are "responsible" for their failure); Michael L. Perlin, *"The Borderline Which Separated You From Me": The Insanity Defense, the Authoritarian Spirit, the Fear of Faking, and the Culture of Punishment*, 82 Iowa L. Rev. 1375, 1423 (1997) ("Because of sanism, society blames mentally ill individuals for their own plight").

74 Perlin, *supra* note 73, at 671 (quoting Keri A. Gould et al., *Criminal Defendants With Trial Disabilities: The Theory and Practice of Competency Assistance* 90 (1993) (unpublished manuscript)), discussed *supra* Chapter 8; see also Perlin, *supra* note 73, at 671 nn.230–31 (citing sources).

75 Stanton Wheeler et al, Sitting in Judgment: The Sentencing of White Collar Criminals 20–21 (1988).

76 Adam Shajnfeld, *The Eleventh Circuit's Selective Assault on Sentencing Discretion*, 65 U. Miami L. Rev. 1133, 1133 (2011), focusing on the decision in United States v. Irey, 612 F.3d 1160 (11th Cir. 2010) (*en banc*), a case, according to Shajnfeld, that is improperly based upon "misguided notions of culpability, mental illness, deterrence, the severity of supervised release, and obeisance to the Sentencing Guidelines." *See id.* at 1143, discussing the court's "morally impoverished conceptions of mental illness."

In the case of a chronically depressed, compulsive gambler under threats of violence to pay off his debts (apparently from organized crime figures), the Sixth Circuit justified its rejection of a downward departure on the grounds that the defendant could have "just said no." The court moralized: "He had the option of reporting the threats he received to the authorities, of course, but he chose instead to engage in serious violations of the law."[77]

Just as judges do not "get" the differences between the differing legal standards in insanity and incompetency to stand trial cases,[78] they similarly do not "get" the difference between either of these statuses and the degree of mental capacity needed to justify a downward departure under the Guidelines. For example, one trial court concluded (in reliance on the prosecutor's argument) that because the defendant, who was learning disabled, physically disabled, and of borderline intelligence, was competent to stand trial and responsible for his act (the distribution of LSD), he was therefore ineligible for a downward departure under the Guidelines.[79] This decision was affirmed by the First Circuit in an opinion "agree[ing with] and applaud[ing]" the trial judge's "thoughtful consideration" of the underlying issues.[80]

C. Heuristics

Judges are susceptible to cognitive illusions and biases.[81] We know that heuristics play a part in judicial sentencing decision-making.[82] The vividness effect has always had a powerful impact on all aspects of the criminal trial process as it affects persons with mental disabilities.[83] And the availability heuristic dominates

---

77 United States v. Hamilton, 949 F.2d 190, 193 (6th Cir. 1991). See *supra* note 34.

78 Perlin, *supra* note 67, at 679.

79 United States v. Lauzon, 938 F.2d 326, 332 (1st Cir. 1991). *Lauzon* is one of almost two dozen reported Guidelines cases involving defendants that were so-called "Deadheads," followers of the Grateful Dead rock group.

80 *Id.*

81 Chris Guthrie, Jeffery J. Rachlinski & Andrew J. Wistrich, *Inside the Judicial Mind*, 86 Cornell L. Rev. 777 (2001).

82 *Id.* at 794 (discussing the anchoring heuristic); *see also* Raymond J. McKoski, *Reestablishing Actual Impartiality as the Fundamental Value of Judicial Ethics: Lessons from "Big Judge Davis,"* 99 Ky. L.J. 259, 308 (2010–11) (same); *See* Birte Englich, Thomas Mussweiler & Fritzl Strack, *Playing Dice with Criminal Sentences: The Influence of Irrelevant Anchors on Experts' Judicial Decision Making*, 32 Personality & Soc. Psychol. Bull. 188 (2006). (anchoring and adjustment heuristics in sentencing).

83 *See, e.g.*, Peter Finn & Monique Sullivan, *Police Handling of the Mentally Ill: Sharing Responsibility With the Mental Health System*, 17 J. Crim. Just. 1, 4 (1989); Shari Seidman Diamond & Loretta J. Stalans, *The Myth of Judicial Leniency on Sentencing*, 7 Behav. Sci. & L. 73, 87–88 (1989) (vividness of media stories about particularly violent criminal offenses has a "disproportionate impact" on public perceptions about crime); Albert W. Alschuler, *"Close Enough for Government Work": The Exclusionary Rule After Leon*, 1984 Sup. Ct. Rev. 309, 347–48 (fear that application of exclusionary rule might potentially

all aspects of the sentencing process.[84] The attribution heuristic plays a major role in the sentencing process as well.[85] Interestingly, judges are more aware of biasing errors based on, for example, the hindsight bias and the representativeness heuristic as they affect legal decision-making on the part of *juries* but not how they affect themselves.[86] In short, distortive heuristic thinking has a profound impact on sentencing decisions, especially in cases involving defendants with serious mental disabilities. We must acknowledge this if there is to be any ameliorative change in the criminal justice system.

D. OCS

There is no question that courts and legislatures mistakenly use "ordinary common sense" to "generalize and wrongly stereotype persons with mental disorder in order to justify prejudiced decision making against them."[87] One of the greatest areas of OCS-caused dissonance emerges in cases involving mental illness ("If he had just tried harder, he really could have gotten better").[88] Such cases are "treasure troves

---

free "next year's Son of Sam" will overwhelm empirically based arguments in support of rule); Richard E. Nisbett et al., *Popular Induction: Information Is Not Necessarily Informative*, in JUDGMENT UNDER UNCERTAINTY: HEURISTICS AND BIASES 101, 113 (Daniel Kahneman et al. eds, 1982) (comparing "influenceability" by abstract and concrete information); Paul Slovic et al., *Facts Versus Fears: Understanding Perceived Risk*, in JUDGMENT UNDER UNCERTAINTY: HEURISTICS AND BIASES, *supra* at 463, 468; (impact of biased newspaper coverage on perceived risks in cases of various disaster scenarios); Loretta J. Stalans & Arthur J. Lurigio, *Law and Professionals' Beliefs About Crime and Criminal Sentences: A Need for Theory, Perhaps Schema Theory*, 17 CRIM. JUST. & BEHAV. 333 (1990) (lay persons rely disproportionately on unrepresentative impressions in forming beliefs about punishment and crime).

84 Rachel E. Barkow, *Federalism and the Politics of Sentencing*, 105 COLUM. L. REV. 1276, 1283–84, 1292–94 (2005).

85 Arthur J. Lurigio et al., *Understanding Judges' Sentencing Decisions: Attributions of Responsibility and Story Construction*, in APPLICATIONS OF HEURISTICS AND BIASES TO SOCIAL ISSUES 91 (Linda Heat et al. eds, 1994).

86 Jeffrey J. Rachlinski, *Heuristics and Biases in the Courts: Ignorance or Adaptation?*, 79 OR. L. REV. 61, 93 (2000).

87 Grant Morris, *The Evil That Men Do: Perverting Justice to Punish Perverts*, 2000 U. ILL. L. REV. 1199, 1201 n.13, *discussing* Michael L. Perlin, *"Half-Wracked Prejudice Leaped Forth": Sanism, Pretextuality, and Why and How Mental Disability Law Developed as It Did*, 10 J. CONTEMP. LEGAL ISSUES 3, 29 (1999).

88 *See, e.g.*, Michael L. Perlin, *The ADA and Persons with Mental Disabilities: Can Sanist Attitudes Be Undone?*, 8 J.L. & HEALTH 15, 31 n.90 (1993–94). *See also* J.M. Balkin, *The Rhetoric of Responsibility*, 76 VA. L. REV. 197, 238 (1990) ("Hinckley prosecutor suggested to jurors, 'if Hinckley had emotional problems, they were largely his own fault'"); State v. Duckworth, 496 So.2d 624, 635 (La. Ct. App. 1986) (holding that juror who felt defendant would be responsible for actions as long as he "wanted to do them" could not be excused for cause).

of self-righteousness, narrow thinking, and 'atrophied [ ] moral development.'"[89] In an article that I co-authored with Professor Keri Gould some 17 years ago, I had this to say about the impact of false OCS on this issue:

> The cases reported so far reflect no coherent reading of the Guidelines and no real understanding of the role of mental disability, short of an exculpating insanity defense, in criminal behavior. Federal judges are remarkably inconsistent in their reading of mental disability. The caselaw [] suggests that federal judges have not seriously considered the way mental disability should be assessed in sentencing decisions, and that random decisions generally reflect a judge's "ordinary common sensical read" of whether an individual defendant "really" could have overcome his disability.
>
> We contend that this is caused by several factors: (1) a lack of understanding on the part of federal judges and defense counsel as to the meaning of mental disability and its potential interrelationship with criminal behavior;
>
> ...
>
> (3) the structure of the insanity defense as an all-or-nothing alternative, causing many to believe that lesser evidence of mental disorder is simply an insufficient factor to consider in sentencing decisions.[90]

VI. Five Perspectives

A. Counsel

It is black-letter law that the right to counsel extends to the sentencing aspect of the criminal trial.[91] As in the other aspects of criminal procedure under consideration in this volume, courts are mixed on the role of counsel (and the standards of effectiveness of counsel) in cases in which there was a failure to produce relevant evidence at sentencing. Although the Supreme Court has held in *Williams v. Taylor*[92] that an attorney's actions "fell short of professional standards" when he failed adequately to prepare and introduce extensive mitigating evidence at the sentencing phase of a

---

89 Michael L. Perlin, "*She Breaks Just Like a Little Girl": Neonaticide, The Insanity Defense, and the Irrelevance of Ordinary Common Sense*, 10 Wm. & Mary J. Women & L. 1, 9 (2003) , quoting, in part, Michael L. Perlin, *Unpacking the Myths: The Symbolism Mythology of Insanity Defense Jurisprudence*, 40 Case W. Res. L. Rev. 599, 644 (1989–90).

90 Perlin & Gould, *supra* note 4, at 434.

91 *See, e.g.*, Glover v. United States, 531 U.S. 198, 203–04 (2001); Mempa v. Rhay, 389 U.S. 128, 136–37 (1967).

92 529 U.S. 362 (2000).

capital case,[93] other courts do not interpret *Williams* vigorously. By way of example, in *Vega v. Comm'r of Corr.*,[94] a state court held that holding that trial counsel's failure to present mitigating evidence of psychiatric report of defendant did not constitute deficient performance that prejudiced defendant.[95] Note that some scholars would impose a per se rule: "evidence of mental illness … *must* be presented to a trier of fact in order to guarantee the integrity of the criminal justice process."[96] Speaking with the promise of anonymity, a judge in Canada has thus stated:

> It's absolutely appalling what we get on sentencing. I think it's by far the most important work I do … get virtually no help from counsel with the rarest of exceptions … But, I swear these folks believe they're going to win every case and their clients are never going to plead guilty so why would they need to know anything about sentencing.[97]

What is critical here is that we are finally beginning to understand that defense lawyers must focus on "sentencing advocacy" as a means of protecting the "integrity" of the criminal trial system.[98] Counsel also must "get" that dealing with their criminal charges can be a highly emotional experience for most defendants. If the client's criminal case is related to mental illness, "confronting the existence of such a problem and coming to terms with the need to deal with it can produce considerable psychological distress."[99]

---

93 *Id.* at 395.

94 930 A.2d 75, 77–78 (Conn. App. Ct. 2007).

95 The court here reasoned that this was so because the psychiatric report that was in question could have reinforced the discretionary determination that a maximum sentence was necessary to protect the public. *Id.*

96 Martin Sabelli & Stacey Leyton, *Train Wrecks and Freeway Crashes: An Argument for Fairness and against Self Representation in the Criminal Justice System*, 91 J. Crim. L. & Criminology 161, 166 (2000).

97 Megan Stephens, *Lessons from the Front Lines in Canada's Restorative Justice Experiment: The Experience of Sentencing Judges*, 33 Queen's L.J. 19, 53 (2007). Elsewhere, Stephens characterizes the sentencing practice in Canada (where she practices law) as "a rather opaque process." *Id.* at 76.

98 Cait Clarke & James Neuhard, *"From Day One": Who's in Control as Problem Solving and Client-Centered Sentencing Take Center Stage?,* 29 N.Y.U. Rev. L. & Soc. Change 11, 48 (2004).

99 Bruce J. Winick, *Redefining the Role of the Criminal Defense Lawyer at Plea Bargaining and Sentencing: A Therapeutic Jurisprudence/Preventive Law Model*, 5 Psychol. Pub. Pol'y & L. 1034, 1041 (1999). *See also* Donald H. Stone, *Giving A Voice to the Silent Mentally Ill Client: An Empirical Study of the Role of Counsel in the Civil Commitment Hearing*, 70 UMKC L. Rev. 603; Natalie Wolf, *The Ethical Dilemmas Faced by Attorneys Representing the Mentally Ill in Civil Commitment Proceedings*, 6 Geo. J. Legal Ethics 163 (1992); *compare* State v. Soares, 916 P.2d 1233 (Hawaii App. 1996) (court recognizing the unique position of lawyers representing mentally ill clients), *overruled* in

B. International Human Rights

Certainly, the Supreme Court's decision in *Graham v. Florida*,[100] holding that sentencing juveniles who have not been convicted of homicide to life-without-parole violates the Eighth Amendment, referencing, as it did, the international consensus (informed by human rights law) against that practice, bespeaks, per Beth Caldwell, "a greater willingness to consider international human rights standards and practices when assessing sentencing practices within the United States."[101]

An examination of international human rights law reveals articulation of "evolving standards of decency" as revealed in "robust" interpretations of "claims of degrading treatment that violate … human dignity,"[102] in a variety of cases involving sentencing terms.[103] The Convention on the Rights of Persons with Disabilities[104]—mandating "[r]espect for inherent dignity"[105]—also is a potential source of rights in such cases for this population.

C. Mental Health Courts

"In mental health court … rehabilitation rather than punishment is the focus of sentencing."[106] Explicitly, one of the goals of mental health courts is to "begin to focus on the access to care instead of punishing mental health consumers with prison sentences for their illnesses,"[107] a goal that can best be met if there is "critical

State v. Janto, 986 P.2d 306 (Hawai'I 1999) (determination regarding a defendant's fitness to proceed will be reviewed for abuse of discretion).

100 130 S. Ct. 2011 (2011).

101 Beth Caldwell, Twenty-Five To Life for Adolescent Mistakes: Juvenile Strikes as Cruel and Unusual Punishment, 46 U.S.F. L. Rev. 581, 599 (2012). I explore this issue further in Michael L. Perlin, *"Yonder Stands Your Orphan with His Gun": The International Human Rights and Therapeutic Jurisprudence Implications of Juvenile Punishment Schemes*,– Texas Tech L. Rev. – (2013) (in press).

102 Eva S. Nilsen, *Decency, Dignity, and Desert: Restoring Ideals of Humane Punishment to Constitutional Discourse*, 41 U.C. Davis L. Rev. 111, 160 (2007). See *supra* Chapter 7.

103 *See id.*, discussing how international human rights standards forbid "capital punishment, life without parole for juveniles, life without parole for adults, mandatory rather than individualized sentencing, frequent use of segregation, and placing mentally ill lawbreakers in prisons rather than hospitals").

104 Convention on the Rights of Persons with Disabilities, Jan. 24, 2007, 2515 U.N.T.S. 3, 46 I.L.M. 443 (CRPD), Article 12.

105 *Id.*, Article 3. *See, e.g.*, Michael L. Perlin, *"Abandoned Love": The Impact Of Wyatt v. Stickney On The Intersection Between International Human Rights And Domestic Mental Disability Law*, 35 Law & Psychol. Rev. 121, 140 (2011).

106 Ronald Roesch & Kaitlyn McLachlan, *Book Review* of Richard D. Schneider, Hy Bloom, and Mark Heerema, Mental Health Courts: Decriminalizing the Mentally Ill (2007), 25 Windsor Rev. Legal & Soc. Issues 113, 114 (2008).

107 Bonnie Sultan, *The Insanity of Incarceration and the Maddening Reentry Process: A Call for Change and Justice for Males with Mental Illness in United States Prisons*, 13

leadership" on the part of the assigned judges.[108] The sentencing goals of mental health courts differ from those in traditional criminal courts: "To correct or heal the offender, who receives most services and benefits. Society is secondary; victim benefits to the extent that offender is rehabilitated."[109] Thus, mental health court treatment often allows defendants either the possibility of dismissal of charges or reduced sentencing,[110] in accordance with the articulated aim of mental health courts to aid in connecting offenders to community-based treatment and support services "that encourage recovery."[111]

D. Alternative Jurisprudences

1. Therapeutic jurisprudence

One of the basic premises of therapeutic jurisprudence is that "a rigid, inflexible sentencing scheme, especially one characterized by mandatory incarcerative penalties" is antitherapeutic.[112] Former Judge Michael King has underscored

---

Geo. J. Poverty L. & Pol'y 357, 382 (2006). *But compare* Shane Levesque, *Closing the Door: Mental Illness, The Criminal Justice System, and the Need for a Uniform Mental Health Policy*, 34 Nova L. Rev. 711, 727 (2010) ("the creation of a mental health court system that diverts a majority of mentally ill offenders out of prisons and jails is unlikely").

108 Roger K. Warren, *Evidence-Based Sentencing: The Application of Principles of Evidence-Based Practice to State Sentencing Practice and Policy*, 43 U.S.F. L. Rev. 585, 626 (2009).

109 Teresa W. Carns, Michael G. Hotchkin & Elaine M. Andrews, *Therapeutic Justice in Alaska's Courts*, 19 Alaska L. Rev. 1, 4(2002). Some defendants in mental health courts may forego sentencing entirely. *See* Nancy Wolff, Nicole Fabrikant & Steven Belenko, *Mental Health Courts and Their Selection Processes: Modeling Variation for Consistency*, 35 Law & Hum. Behav. 402, 403 (2011).

110 Joseph Cormier, *Providing Those with Mental Illness Full and Fair Treatment: Legislative Considerations in the Post-Clark Era*, 47 Am. Crim. L. Rev. 129, 139 (2010).

111 Kathryn C. Sammon, *Therapeutic Jurisprudence: An Examination of Problem-Solving Justice in New York*, 23 St. John's J.L. Comm. 923, 950 (2008).

112 David B. Wexler, *A Tripartite Framework for Incorporating Therapeutic Jurisprudence in Criminal Law Education, Research, and Practice*, in Rehabilitating Lawyers: Principles of Therapeutic Jurisprudence for Criminal Law Practice 11, 15 (David B. Wexler ed., 2008) (Rehabilitating Lawyers); *see also* David B. Wexler, *Therapeutic Jurisprudence and Family-Friendly Criminal Law Practice*, 17 Barry L. Rev. 7 (2011). On the relationship between TJ and the criminal court process in general, *see* Salmon Shomade, *Case Disposition in the Drug Court: Who Is the Most Central Actor?*, 31 Just. Sys. J. 74 (2010); Salmon Shomade, *Judging in Trial Courts: Cross-Fertilization of Therapeutic Jurisprudence Practices from Specialized Courts into Conventional Criminal Courts*, accessible at http://papers.ssrn.com/sol3/papers.cfm?abstract_id=1642379, published as Salmon Shomade, *Sentencing Patterns: Drug Court Judges Serving in Conventional Criminal Courts*, Judicature (2012).Beyond the scope of this book, but related directly to therapeutic jurisprudence values and principles, are the ways that persons with mental disabilities are disproportionately treated punitively and oppressively in prisons. *See*, *e.g.*, Brown v. Plata, 131 S. Ct. 1910 (2011); *see generally*

that a therapeutic jurisprudence approach towards criminal defense practice "is changing the dynamics of courtrooms, particularly in the context of sentencing."[113] The late Professor Bruce Winick has written extensively about the need for criminal defense lawyers to rethink their traditional roles at sentencing, and to infuse their work with a significant measure of therapeutic jurisprudence, urging them to seek judicial enforcement of "relapse prevention methods," involving the "fashioning of creative community alternatives."[114] In his lead article on this topic, Winick focused on the case of *United States v. Flowers*,[115] in which District Court Judge Jack Weinstein recognized "that sentencing judges enjoy broad discretion to postpone or defer sentencing in appropriate cases in order to allow the defendant to commence a rehabilitative program that, if successful, might provide the basis for a downward departure" from the Sentencing Guidelines.[116] Embracement of TJ principles, Winick continued, require new visions on the part of defense attorneys:

> Not only do these attorneys need to develop new skills, but they need to think of themselves in new ways.[117] They need to understand the vocabulary and techniques

---

Katherine Smith, *Lost Souls: Constitutional Implications for the Deficiencies in Treatment for Persons with Mental Illness in Custody*, 42 Golden Gate U. L. Rev. 497 (2012); Doris J. James & Lauren E. Glaze, *U.S. Dep't of Justice, Mental Health Problems of Prison and Jail Inmates* 1, 3 (2006), available at http:// bjs.ojp.usdoj.gov/content/pub/pdf/mhppji.pdf.

113 Michael King, *Therapeutic Jurisprudence, Criminal Law Practice, and the Plea of Guilty*, in Rehabilitating Lawyers, *supra* note 112, at 238.

114 Winick, *supra* note 99, at 1036.

115 983 F. Supp. 159 (E.D.N.Y. 1997).

116 Winick, *supra* note 99, at 1037, discussing *Flowers*, 983 F. Supp. at 163. On the multiple stages of the "construction of a TJ sentence," see Michael Crystal, *The Therapeutic Sentence: Chicken Soup for an Ailing Criminal Court*, in Rehabilitating Lawyers, *supra* note 112, at 183, 184. On the "value in welcoming the perspective of therapeutic jurisprudence in … sentencing advocacy," see Robert Ward, *Criminal Defense Practice and Therapeutic Jurisprudence: Zealous Advocacy through Zealous Counseling: Perspectives, Plans and Policy*, in Rehabilitating Lawyers, *supra* note 112, at 206, 207. Paul Marcus and Vicki Waye have pointed out other benefits of an individualized sentencing approach:

> The retention of judicial discretion enables the sentencing judge to take account of the offender's personal situation and the circumstances of the offending, encourages guilty pleas to appropriate charges, and enables a creative and customized sentence more likely to incorporate therapeutic or restorative elements.

Vicki Waye & Paul Marcus, *Australia and the United States: Two Common Criminal Justice Systems Uncommonly at Odds*, Part 2, 18 Tul. J. Int'l & Comp. L. 335, 399 (2010).

117 *See, e.g.*, Amy Ronner, *Dostoyevsky and the Therapeutic Jurisprudence Confession*, 40 J. Marshall L. Rev. 41, 52–53 (2006), citing David B. Wexler, *Therapeutic Jurisprudence And the Rehabilitative Role of the Criminal Defense Lawyer*, 17 St. Thomas L. Rev. 743, 753 (2005): "With respect to pleas and sentencing, a therapeutic jurisprudence criminal lawyer should be adept at assembling a rehabilitation-oriented packet to help secure a favorable plea arrangement or fair sentence."

> of these new rehabilitative approaches. They need to develop techniques for dealing with their clients about the issue of rehabilitation with a higher degree of psychological sensitivity. They need to understand that, whether they know it or not, they are functioning as therapeutic agents in their interactions with their clients, particularly in the plea and sentencing process. They need to recognize the opportunities that these new developments provide to offer new modes of assistance to their clients that can promote both their interests in maintaining their liberty and in achieving a higher degree of psychological well-being.[118]

2. Procedural justice

Scholars frequently consider the impact of procedural justice on sentencing decision-making.[119] There is no question that the research on the psychological effects of procedural justice suggests that defendants who are treated fairly at sentencing will have more respect for the law and legal authorities than defendants who are treated unfairly.[120] The sentencing process must "provide a mechanism that settles the conflict in a manner that induces community respect for the fairness of its processes as well as the reliability of its outcomes."[121] As procedural justice in sentencing can advance the "rehabilitation and crime-prevention ends of criminal law,"[122] it is especially important in cases involving defendants with mental disabilities.[123] To be sure, some judges treat the formalities surrounding plea

118 Winick, *supra* note 99, at 1038.

119 *See, e.g.*, Adam Lamparello, *Incorporating the Procedural Justice Model into Federal Sentencing Jurisprudence in the Aftermath of United States v. Booker: Establishing United States Sentencing Courts*, 4 N.Y.U. J.L. & Liberty 112 (2009) (Lamparello, *Procedural Justice Model*); Adam Lamparello, *Social Psychology, Legitimacy, and the Ethical Foundations of Judgment: Importing the Procedural Justice Model to Federal Sentencing Jurisprudence*, 38 Colum. Hum. Rts. L. Rev. 115 (2006); Thomas L. Hafemeister, Sharon G. Garner & Veronica E. Bath, *Forging Links and Renewing Ties: Applying the Principles of Restorative and Procedural Justice to Better Respond to Criminal Offenders with a Mental Disorder*, 60 Buff. L. Rev. 147 (2012).

120 Michael O'Hear, *Explaining Sentences*, 36 Fla. St. U. L. Rev. 459, 461 (2009). *See also* David Welsh, *Procedural Justice Post-9/11: The Effects of Procedurally Unfair Treatment of Detainees on Perceptions of Global Legitimacy*, 9 U. N.H. L. Rev. 261, 273 (2011), citing Jonathan D. Casper et al., *Procedural Justice in Felony Cases*, 22 L. & Soc. Rev. 483, 483 (1988) ("an exploration of procedural justice in felony cases revealed that defendants' evaluations of the judicial system did not depend exclusively on the favorability of sentencing").

121 Peter Arenella, *Rethinking the Functions of Criminal Procedure: The Warren and Burger Courts' Competing Ideologies*, 72 Geo. L.J. 185, 202 (1983).

122 Michael M. O'Hear, *Appellate Review of Sentence Explanations: Learning from the Wisconsin and Federal Experiences*, 93 Marq. L. Rev. 751, 754 (2009) (O'Hear, *Appellate Review*); *see also* Michael M. O'Hear, *Plea Bargaining and Procedural Justice*, 42 Ga. L. Rev. 407, 432–36 (2008) (O'Hear, *Plea Bargaining*).

123 It is also a way of insuring that "the defendant always retains his essential human dignity," O'Hear, *Appellate Review, supra* note 122, at 754.

acceptance and sentencing with "obvious disdain";[124] yet, it appears uncontestable that procedural justice values continue to grow in significance in the criminal justice system.[125]

3. Restorative justice:

As I discussed in Chapter 6, there has been some literature studying the impact of procedural justice on sentencing cases in general.[126] One of the signature aspects of restorative justice in this context is the use of sentencing circles. Such circles, designed to address the needs of victims, communities and offenders, offers a "space" through which those involved can "share experiences about the event and its impact in an effort to search for understanding and healing."[127] Explicitly, one of the objectives of such circles "is to restore harmony within the community."[128] Interestingly, in Canada, even judges who had been skeptical about this approach found it to be of value in cases involving aboriginal defendants,[129] another classically marginalized group.[130]

---

124 O'Hear, *Plea Bargaining,* supra note 122, at 460–61.

125 On how the importance of procedural justice grows as the stakes in the proceeding grow, see Tom R. Tyler, Why People Obey the Law 105 (1990).

126 The forerunner of this work is Marvin Frankel, Criminal Sentences: Law Without Order (1973). *See* Jonathan D. Casper et al., *Procedural Justice in Felony Cases*, 22 L. & Soc. Rev. 483, 483 (1988) (procedural justice in felony cases revealed that defendants' evaluations of the judicial system did not depend exclusively on the favorability of sentencing); *see also* Lamparello, *Procedural Justice Model*, *supra* note 119, at 118–19; Daniel Isaacs, *Baseline Framing in Sentencing*, 121 Yale L.J. 426 (2011); O'Hear, *Appellate Review,* supra note 122; Edna Erez, *Victim Voice, Impact Statements and Sentencing: Integrating Restorative Justice and Therapeutic Jurisprudence Principles in Adversarial Proceedings*, 40 Crim. L. Bull. 483 (2004). For contrasting views, see Chris Cuneen & Carolyn Hoyle, Debating Restorative Justice (2010).

127 Mara Schiff, *Models, Challenges, and the Promise of Restorative Conferencing Strategies*, in Restorative Justice & Criminal Justice: Competing or Reconcilable Paradigms 315, 322(Andrew von Hirsch et al. eds, 2003); *see also* Howard Zehr, The Little Book of Restorative Justice 50–51 (2002).

128 Rebecca Rexroad, *Reshaping the Sentencing Circle: Striking a Balance Between Restoration of Harmony and Punishment of Offenders in Indigenous Domestic Violence Cases*, 13 Sw. J. L. & Trade Am. 403, 409 (2007).

129 *See, e.g.*, Stephens, *supra* note 97, at 56. Accord: Sonny Lee Hodgin, *Elder Wisdom: Adopting Canadian and Australian Approaches to Prosecuting Indigenous Offenders*, 46 Val. U. L. Rev. 939, 987 (2012). While some may be skeptical about the ability of the bureaucratic federal government to adopt such a progressive approach to justice, sentencing circles in Canada and Minnesota and Australia's Indigenous sentencing courts are proof that such a system is more than feasible.

130 On marginalization in mental disability law, see Michael L. Perlin, *Competency, Deinstitutionalization, and Homelessness: A Story of Marginalization*, 28 Hous. L. Rev. 63 (1991); *see also* Laura E. Hortos, *Asylum Protection for the Mentally Disabled: How the Evolution of Rights for the Mentally Ill in the United States Created a "Social Group,"*

A primary step in integrating restorative justice into sentencing would be to authorize judges to impose what would be, in name, purpose, and content, "restorative sentences."[131] Restorative justice has brought an awareness of the limits and negative byproducts of punishment."[132] It may also be an important tool in reducing recidivism.[133] And studies have shown that "restorative justice practices—like circle sentencing—promote perceptions of systemic legitimacy and provide stakeholders a measure of 'process control.'"[134]

E. Dignity

One of the important commentaries on the FSG spoke directly to the dignity issue. According to Professor Kevin Cole, "A defendant's dignity is preserved when both the defendant and the judge perceive that the judge's treatment of the defendant is significantly controlled by law that focuses the judge on pertinent sentencing factors."[135] Similarly, Professor Michael O'Hear has invoked "the lens of the dignity paradigm," in arguing that "sentencing procedures ought to embody respect for the defendant as a member of a national community that is committed to ideals of individual liberty and status-equality."[136] In fact, dignity demands that mitigation evidence be presented at sentencing (in capital cases) even over the objections of the defendant.[137]

---

20 Conn. J. Int'l L. 155, 157 (2004) ("The history of the legal and social treatment of the mentally ill in this country reveals the discrimination and marginalization of a group who, today, struggles to gain equality and find equal footing in the eyes of society").

131 Lynn Branham, *Plowing in Hope: A Three-Part Framework for Incorporating Restorative Justice into Sentencing and Correctional Systems*, 38 Wm. Mitchell L. Rev. 1261, 1269 (2012).

132 Nancy Lucas, *Restitution, Rehabilitation, Prevention, and Transformation: Victim-Offender Mediation for First-Time Non-Violent Youthful Offenders*, 29 Hofstra L. Rev. 1365, 1371 (2001).

133 *Id.* at 1375.

134 Josh Bowers & Paul H. Robinson, *Perceptions of Fairness and Justice: The Shared Aims & Occasional Conflicts of Legitimacy and Moral Credibility*, 47 Wake Forest L. Rev. 211, 268 n.273 (2012).

135 Kevin Cole, *The Empty Idea of Sentencing Disparity*, 91 Nw. U. L. Rev. 1336, 1340 (1997).

136 Michael O'Hear, *The Original Intent of Uniformity in Federal Sentencing*, 74 U. Cin. L. Rev. 749, 804 (2006).

137 Daniel R. Williams, *Mitigation and the Capital Defendant Who Wants to Die: A Study in the Rhetoric of Autonomy and the Hidden Discourse of Collective Responsibility*, 57 Hastings L.J. 693, 726 (2006). *See generally* Valerie McClain, Elliot Atkins & Michael L. Perlin, *"Oh, Stop That Cursed Jury": The Role of the Forensic Psychologist in the Mitigation Phase of the Death Penalty Trial*, in Handbook Of Forensic Psychology (Mark Goldstein ed. 2013) (in press).

The forerunner theoretical baseline for this is Judge Marvin Frankel's trailblazing book, *Criminal Sentences: Law Without Order*.[138] Written nearly 40 years ago, this work is universally seen as "the book that helped launch the sentencing reform movement."[139] Although persons with mental disabilities are not directly mentioned in the following paragraph, Frankel's vision of dignity can certainly be expanded to apply to this population as well:

> There is dignity and security in the assurance that each of us—plain or beautiful, rich or poor, black, white, tall, curly, whatever— is promised treatment as a bland, fungible "equal" before the law.[140]

VII. Conclusion

We tend to ignore what happens to defendants with mental disabilities at the sentencing phase of a criminal trial, especially in cases that are not notorious or "headline material." Judges frequently ignore the impact of mental disability on the commission of criminal behavior as well as on the impact of mental disability on the prison life of sentenced defendants. The sanism and pretextuality that permeates the entire criminal trial process are especially pernicious here.

We need to confront these issues if we are ever to bring a serious measure of dignity to this aspect of the criminal trial process.

---

138 Frankel, *supra* note 126.

139 *See*, *e.g.*, Paul J. Hofer, *Immediate and Long-Term Effects of United States v. Booker: More Discretion, More Disparity, or Better Reasoned Sentences*? 38 Ariz. St. L.J. 425, 439 (2006); Kate Stith & José A. Cabranes, Fear of Judging: Sentencing Guidelines in the Federal Courts 106 (1998).

140 Frankel, *supra* note 126, at 11.

Chapter 11
Conclusion

I. Introduction

One of the questions that emerges again and again in the context of the issues explored in this book is how dignity can be maximized in the criminal process in all cases involving defendants with mental disabilities. Such maximization of dignity can only take place if we consciously take specific steps to minimize sanism and stigma and to eradicate pretextuality. That, I believe, is the first effort needed in this enterprise. Such an effort would create a system that is more fair, more dignified, and more humane. It would, not unimportantly, privilege both the "ethic of care" that is one of the hallmarks of therapeutic jurisprudence and the "ethic of justice" that is one of the hallmarks of restorative justice. It is impossible to disentangle sanism and pretextuality—"enforced by" the use of heuristics and "ordinary common sense"—from the ways that persons with mental disabilities are deprived of dignity in the criminal trial process. I believe, however, that if the perspectives that I focus on in this book are taken seriously, there is some hope of remediating the current situation

We thus need first to ask ourselves these questions:

- How can counsel roles be modified to enhance dignity?
- How can international human rights principles be drawn on to enhance dignity?
- To what extent can the expansion of mental health courts—ones modeled after the approach of Judge Ginger Lerner-Wren in Broward County, Florida (and others that operate similarly)—enhance dignity?
- How can alternative jurisprudences be embraced to enhance dignity?

After we consider these questions, we can then focus on the substantive questions addressed in this volume: How can the answers to these questions inform a strategy to privilege dignity values in the competency, insanity defense and sentencing processes? What follows are my recommendations as to how this can be done, in the context of the five perspectives discussed throughout this book.

II. The Four Perspectives and the Role of Dignity

A. Counsel

Dedicated, advocacy-focused counsel would give dignity to their clients—simply by the act of taking them seriously "as human beings"[1]—and would force courts to similarly provide more due process. One of the critical functions of counsel is to "protect the dignity and autonomy of a person on trial."[2] Counsel that supports and endorses the autonomy of their clients will best be able to do this.

Counsel must reject the sanist assumptions made by so many lawyers: that their clients are "incapable of sufficiently autonomous decisionaking."[3] My optimal solution—one that I recognize is not likely to happen at this point of time—would be a litigation strategy that would seek to drastically modify the *Strickland v. Washington*[4] standard. Such a solution would reject *Strickland*'s presumption of "reasonable professional assistance"[5] in cases involving defendants with serious mental disabilities, and would articulate, at the Supreme Court level, a new standard, imposing new stringent requirements on defense counsel in such cases, and drawing on the alternative vision of *in re K.G.F.*[6] Since I acknowledge that this is not likely to happen in the near future, my alternative strategies are these:

- A state-by-state strategy,[7] using *K.G.F.* as the model, seeking the articulation of an adequacy standard that acknowledges that "reasonable

1 Falter v. Veterans' Admin., 502 F. Supp. 1178, 1185 (D.N.J. 1980); *see* Michael L. Perlin & John Douard, *"Equality, I Spoke That Word/As If a Wedding Vow": Mental Disability Law and How We Treat Marginalized Persons*, 53 N.Y.L. Sch. L. Rev. 9, 10–11 (2008) (discussing the significance of this phrase in the development of mental disability law).

2 Jones v. Barnes, 463 U.S. 745, 759 (1983) (Brennan, J., dissenting). *See also, e.g.*, Philip Halpern, *Government Intrusion into the Attorney–Client Relationship: An Interest Analysis of Rights and Remedies*, 32 Buff. L. Rev. 127, 172 (1983) ("The right to counsel embraces two separate interests: reliable and fair determinations in criminal proceedings, and treatment of defendants with dignity and respect regardless of the effect on the outcome of criminal proceedings.").

3 *See* E. Lea Johnston, *Representational Competence: Defining the Limits of the Right to Self-Representation at Trial*, 86 Notre Dame L. Rev. 523, 536 (2011), discussing sanism as described in Michael L. Perlin, The Hidden Prejudice 21–24, 48–58 (2000).

4 466 U.S. 668 (1984).

5 *Id.* at 689.

6 29 P.3d 485 (Mont. 2001). *See* Michael L. Perlin, *"I Might Need a Good Lawyer, Could Be Your Funeral, My Trial": A Global Perspective on the Right to Counsel in Civil Commitment Cases, and Its Implications for Clinical Legal Education*, 28 Wash. U. J. L. & Soc'l Pol'y 241, 246–49 (2008).

7 State constitutional law has long been a remedy in cases involving individuals with severe mental disabilities. *See, e.g.*, Michael L. Perlin, *State Constitutions and Statutes as*

professional assistance"—the linchpin of the *Strickland* decision[8]—"cannot be presumed in a proceeding that routinely accepts—and even requires—an unreasonably low standard of legal assistance and generally disdains zealous, adversarial confrontation."[9] I have argued, in the context of involuntary civil commitment hearings, that *K.G.F.* provides an "easily transferable blueprint for courts that want to grapple with adequacy of counsel issues;"[10] I believe it is just as transferable in that cohort of criminal cases that deal with defendants with mental disabilities.

- The creation of specialized units within public defender offices to represent persons with serious mental disabilities, a parallel to the way many states have created such specialized units to do death penalty cases, in recognition that most criminal defense attorneys lacked the specialized experience necessary to render effective representation in death penalty cases.[11] In the same way, most defense attorneys lack the expertise to represent persons with mental disabilities,[12] and the creation of such units would help obviate many of the problems encountered on a daily basis.
- The development of serious training programs for public defenders and appointed counsel so as to avoid the likelihood of situations in which lawyers provided inadequate and ineffective counsel because they could not identify issues related to mental disabilities.[13] By way of example, the National Association of Criminal Defense Lawyers is providing training on the implications of *Padilla v. Kentucky*,[14] requiring defense counsel to

---

Sources of Rights for the Mentally Disabled: The Last Frontier?, 20 LOYOLA L.A. L. REV. 1249 (1987).

8 Perlin, *supra* note 6, at 247.

9 *In re* Mental Health of K.G.F., 29 P.3d 485, 492 (Mont. 2001). (citing Michael L. Perlin, *Fatal Assumption: A Critical Evaluation of the Role of Counsel in Mental Disability Cases*, 16 LAW & HUM. BEHAV. 39, 53–54 (1992) ("identifying the *Strickland* standard as 'sterile and perfunctory' where 'reasonably effective assistance' is objectively measured by the 'prevailing professional norms'")).

10 Michael L. Perlin, *"And My Best Friend, My Doctor / Won't Even Say What It Is I've Got": The Role and Significance of Counsel in Right to Refuse Treatment Cases*, 42 SAN DIEGO L. REV. 735, 741 (2005).

11 Andrew Hammel, *Discrimination and Death in Dallas: A Case Study in Systematic Racial Exclusion*, 3 TEX. F. ON C.L. & C.R. 187, 225 n.328 (1997), *and see* Louis D. Bilionis & Richard A. Rosen, *Lawyers, Arbitrariness, and the Eighth Amendment*, 75 TEX. L. REV. 1301, 1323 (1997). *See also id.* at 1322–26 (describing states' attempts to insure consistently high-quality representation in the defense of indigent capital clients).

12 *See generally* Perlin, *supra* note 6.

13 This will not be easy. A survey in Pennsylvania revealed that only 21% of that state's public defender offices provided criminal law training program for new attorneys, and 83% had no training budget. *See* Wallace J. Mlyniec, *In re Gault at 40: The Right to Counsel in Juvenile Court-A Promise Unfulfilled*, 44 CRIM. L. BULL. 371, 379–80 (2008).

14 130 U.S. 1473 (2010).

advise criminal defendants of the collateral immigration consequences of a guilty plea, including the collateral consequence of deportation.[15] Similar training could be provided on the issues discussed in this volume.
- The development of parallel training programs for prosecutors and judges.[16]

Of course, even if none of these reforms were to be adopted, the fallback position is this: If *Strickland v. Washington* were to be interpreted more robustly, that would lead to greater dignity. If defendants were to know that their lawyer needs to be more than a "warm body,"[17] they would more likely feel as if the trial was not a charade. Dedicated, trained, non-sanist counsel is essential at every stage of the criminal prosecution, and even more so in cases involving the population under consideration here.[18]

B. International Human Rights

The regular and on-going use of international human rights principles would force courts to consider seriously the worldwide consensus on how persons with mental disabilities are treated in the criminal trial process, and would "arm" lawyers with

15 Eric Beckemeier, *The Surprise Appearance of Padilla v. Kentucky: Practical Implications for Criminal Defense Attorneys and Possibilities for Expansion*, 80 UMKC L. Rev. 437, 459 (2011).

16 *Compare* Cynthia Jones, *Confronting Race in the Criminal Justice System*, 27 Crim. Just. 12, 16 (Summer 2012) (discussing program training judges to confront racial bias in the judicial system). On the need for all participants in the criminal justice system to undergo training, see Helena Alviar, *The Classroom and the Clinic: The Relationship Between Clinical Legal Education, Economic Development and Social Transformation*, 13 UCLA J. Int'l L. & Foreign Aff. 197, 212 (2008), quoting World Bank Legal Vice Presidency, Legal and Judicial Reform: Observations, Experiences, and Approach of the Legal Vice Presidency 41 (July 2002), available at http://www-wds.worldbank.org/external/default/WDSContentServer/WDSP/IB/2002/12/06/000094946_0211260401346/Rendered/PDF/multi0page.pdf:

> Appropriate training programs should be designed to enhance performance of the main actors of the legal system (Legislatures, Judiciary, Executive, the prosecutors, public defenders, the media, the legal profession, and the public at-large) and instil the values of impartiality, professionalism, competency, efficiency, and value of public service.

17 *See* Fred Cohen, *Law, Lawyers, and Poverty*, 43 Texas L. Rev. 1072, 1086 (1965), discussed *supra* Chapter 3.

18 In this book, I consider only competency, insanity and sentencing, but this just skims the surface of the need for counsel reform. By way of example, I confront this question in the specific case of the death penalty in Michael L. Perlin, Mental Disability and the Death Penalty: The Shame of the States (2013). On how counsel assigned to represent persons with mental disabilities is often sanist, see Michael L. Perlin, *"You Have Discussed Lepers and Crooks": Sanism in Clinical Teaching*, 9 Clinical L. Rev. 683, 694 (2003).

arguments to be used on their clients' behalf.[19] It is time that lawyers began to acknowledge the importance of international human rights law and its application to the populations discussed in this book.[20] Such arguments can and should be incorporated into all sorts of cases involving defendants with mental disabilities, not just death penalty cases. Violation of the right of this population to equal dignity is a violation of international human rights law.[21]

Lawyers representing this population should develop as part of their trial *and* appellate strategies arguments based on the United Nations' Convention on the Rights of Persons with Disabilities.[22] Two provisions of the Convention that demand attention and focus are Articles 12 and 13, mandating:

> States Parties shall take appropriate measures to provide access by persons with disabilities to the support they may require in exercising their legal capacity,[23]

and

> States Parties shall ensure effective access to justice for persons with disabilities on an equal basis with others, including through the provision of procedural and age appropriate accommodations, in order to facilitate their effective role as direct and indirect participants, including as witnesses, in all legal proceedings, including at investigative and other preliminary stages.[24]

Chapters 8–10 of this book offer multiple textbook examples of how this "access" is regularly denied persons with mental disabilities at many critical stages of the criminal trial process. A search of all reported criminal cases reveals, however, not a single one in which arguments based on *any* provision of the

---

19 *See* Michael L. Perlin, *The Death Penalty, International Human Rights Law, Mental Disability, and Therapeutic Jurisprudence* (paper presented at annual conference of the European Criminological Society, Bilbao, Spain, Sept. 2012) (on file with author).

20 *See generally* Michael L. Perlin, International Human Rights and Mental Disability Law: When the Silenced are Heard 159–67 (2011); Perlin, *supra* note 18, at 139–48.

21 *Compare* Barbara Frey & X. Kevin Zhao, *The Criminalization of Immigration and the International Norm of Non-Discrimination: Deportation and Detention in U.S. Immigration Law*, 29 Law & Ineq. 279, 279 (2011).

22 *See* Perlin, *supra* note 20, at 143–69; *see generally* Michael L. Perlin, *"A Change Is Gonna Come": The Implications of the United Nations Convention on the Rights of Persons with Disabilities for the Domestic Practice of Constitutional Mental Disability Law*, 29 No. Ill. U. L. Rev. 483 (2009).

23 CRPD, Article 12.

24 CRPD, Article 13. *See generally* Michael L. Perlin, *Promoting Social Change in Asia and the Pacific: The Need for a Disability Rights Tribunal to Give Life to the UN Convention on the Rights of Persons with Disabilities*, 44 Geo. Wash. Int'l L. Rev. 1, 22–23 (2012).

Convention were considered by any US court.[25] It is time that defense lawyers familiarized themselves with the Convention and incorporated its provisions into their "lawyering unconscious."[26] In a recent book, I asked, "to what extent will the CRPD be used as a vigorous advocacy tool to remediate" the ways that persons with mental disabilities are regularly "treated horribly in old and new institutions";[27] lawyers representing the populations discussed in this book must acknowledge this reality.

C. Mental Health Courts

The expanded use of dignity-providing mental health courts would allow for diversion of more of this cohort of defendants out of the criminal court process (and ultimately, out of destructive correctional facilities) into alternative placements where it is more likely they will be treated with at least a modicum of dignity.[28] Importantly, one of the leading mental health court judges in the nation has linked up the essentiality of dignity in the court process with the enforcement of international human rights obligations:

> The guiding principles and values articulated in the United Nations Convention on the Rights of Persons with Disabilities should be implemented and fully integrated into every mental health court process in order to ensure the promotion of dignity, civil rights and human rights.[29]

---

25 WESTLAW search of the ALLSTATES database for "Convention on the Rights of Persons with Disabilities" (searched on September 12, 2012). Compare Henry Dlugacz & Christopher Wimmer, *The Ethics of Representing Clients with Limited Competency in Guardianship Proceedings*, 4 St. Louis U. J. Health L. & Pol'y 331, 362–63 (2011), discussing *In re* Mark C.H., 906 N.Y.S.2d 419, 433 (Sur. 2010) (although the United States has not yet ratified the CRPD, "a state's obligations under it are controlled by the Vienna Convention of the Law of Treaties[,] which requires signatories 'to refrain from acts which would defeat [the Disability Convention's] object and purpose.'"). See also, Perlin, *supra* note 20, at 154–55; 221–22.

26 *See* Michael L. Perlin, *Stepping Outside the Box: Viewing Your Client in a Whole New Light*, 37 Cal. West. L. Rev. 65, 79 (2000).

27 Perlin, *supra* note 20, at 222, quoting, in part, Larry Gostin, *"Old" and "New" Institutions for Persons with Mental Illness: Treatment, Punishment, or preventive Confinement*, 122 Public Health 906, 912 (2008).

28 "The purpose of the mental health court is to insure that mentally ill people are treated with dignity and provided with the opportunity for treatment while at the same time protecting the public's safety" and "preventing criminalization of the mentally ill." See Stacey M. Faraci, *Slip Slidin' Away? Will our Nation's Mental Health Court Experiment Diminish the Rights of the Mentally Ill?*, 22 Quinnipiac L. Rev. 811, 824 (2004).

29 Ginger Lerner-Wren, *Mental Health Courts: Serving Justice and Promoting Recovery*, 19 Annals Health L. 577, 593 (2010).

The arbitrary limitation in some mental health courts cutting off eligibility for persons who are charged either with committing felonies or crimes of "violence"[30] self-evidently greatly limits the cohort of individuals who can be diverted to such courts. Absent any empirical justification for these limitations—and none has been offered[31]—it makes no sense to perpetuate these cut offs,[32] especially in the context of the vast discretion traditionally vested in prosecutors with regards to the charging process.[33]

To a great extent, prosecutors' decisions follow the initial judgments of police officers. But the near-boundless discretion vested in police decision-making makes this counterproductive. By way of example, consider the factual settings in the Supreme Court cases of *Addington v. Texas*,[34] and *Jones v. United States*.[35] Addington, who was subjected to the involuntary civil commitment process, had originally been apprehended following an alleged "assault by threat" on his mother.[36] Jones, for whom an insanity defense plea had been entered, had originally been apprehended after he allegedly attempted to shoplift a jacket in a downtown Washington, DC department store.[37] Addington's acts appear to have been more serious (and more "dangerous") than did Jones's; yet, for undisclosed, and unarticulated extra-judicial reasons, Addington was brought into the mental health system while Jones was

30 *See* Julie Grachek, *The Insanity Defense in the Twenty-First Century: How Recent United States Supreme Court Case Law Can Improve the System*, 81 Ind. L.J. 1479, 1495 (2006); Ursula Castellano, *Courting Compliance: Case Managers as "Double Agents" in the Mental Health Court*, 36 Law & Soc. Inquiry 484, 490 (2011). Misdemeanors are accepted by 87% of mental health courts responding to a recent survey; 77% of such courts accept non-violent felonies, and over one-third of the courts accept violent felonies. Julie B. Raines & Glenn T. Laws, *Mental Health Court Survey*, 45 Crim. L. Bull. 627, 630 (2009).

31 The rationale appears to be purely political: "Violent offenders have traditionally been excluded from mental health courts because of *public outcry* to the heinous nature of their crimes vis-a-vis the public's empathetic perception of mentally ill, nonviolent offenders." Jared Hodges & Brett Williams, *Courts*, 28 Ga. St. U. L. Rev. 293, 303 (2011) (emphasis added). Of course, not all felonies are remotely "heinous." *See infra* text accompanying note 37.

32 *See* Andrew Wasicek, *Mental Illness and Crime: Envisioning a Public Health Strategy and Reimaging Mental Health Courts*, 48 Crim. L. Bull. 106, 139(2012) ("Mental health courts should accept [cases of defendants charged with] violent felonies").

33 *See, e.g.*, Norman Abrams, *Internal Policy: Guiding the Exercise of Prosecutorial Discretion*, 19 UCLA L. Rev. 1, 2 (1971); Conor Clark & Austin Sarat, *Beyond Discretion: Prosecution, the Logic of Sovereignty, and the Limits of Law*, 33 Law & Soc. Inquiry 387, 389 (2008).

34 441 U.S. 418 (1979) (burden of proof in civil commitment case at least "clear and convincing evidence").

35 463 U.S. 354 (1983) (constitutionally acceptable to provide insanity acquittees with fewer procedural due process protections in a retention hearing than civil committees).

36 *Addington*, 441 U.S. at 420.

37 *Jones*, 463 U.S. at 359.

arrested and thus brought into the criminal justice system.[38] Notwithstanding the fact that Jones was charged with a felony (attempted petit larceny [shoplifting]), it makes no sense to suggest that this was the sort of "heinous" crime that would automatically disallow diversion to a mental health court.[39]

Scholars and practitioners who have written about mental health courts frequently stress the need for "creativity" in the use of such courts as a tool for enhancing the decision to divert a defendant from traditional criminal court.[40] In such courts, judges must seek to craft "creative judicial responses to offending conduct that address the root causes of that conduct in the hope that, in the end, the prevalence of such conduct will subside."[41] An expansion of these courts will best serve the population under consideration in this work. Consider here the thoughts of Gerald Nora, an Illinois state's attorney:

> The bottom line is that mental health courts are heroic efforts to bring some justice to a severely underserved population. It is society's failure, not the criminal justice system's failure, if these courts continue to be the brightest candles in the darkness we have imposed upon the mentally ill. We are prosecuting the mentally ill as criminals. And many mental health workers are prevented from doing their jobs unless they are partnered with lawyers, probation officers, and court orders. And our preferred patients are those who commit crimes. We let the law-abiding suffer alone.[42]

Nora's indictment is a powerful one: "If we persist in prosecuting mentally ill defendants in willful ignorance of their medical problems, our system will stand as an asylum whose keepers are as deluded as the inmates."[43] The expansion of mental

38 I discuss the implications of this in Michael L. Perlin, *"Half-Wracked Prejudice Leaped Forth": Sanism, Pretextuality, and Why and How Mental Disability Law Developed As It Did*, 10 J. Contemp. Leg. Iss. 3, 30 n.158 (1999).

39 *See id.* at 29–30: "Untrammeled discretion vested in police officers leads to inexplicable disjunctions in mental disability law developments."

40 *See, e.g.*, Cait Clarke & James Neuhard, *Making the Case: Therapeutic Jurisprudence and Problem Solving Practices Positively Impact Clients, Justice Systems and Communities They Serve*, 17 St. Thomas L. Rev. 781, 781 (2005) (on how "creative" advocacy can achieve diversion or alternatives to incarceration in this context); Sandra F. Cannon & Joseph Krake, *Mental Health Diversion Alternatives to Jail: Thirteen Pilot Programs Funded by ODMH in April 2000: Where Are They Now and What Have We Learned?* 32 Cap. U. L. Rev. 1021, 1027 (2004) ("Diversion programs that pool resources from different systems—mental health, substance abuse and criminal justice—and those that utilize creative strategies to approach housing and other treatment issues will undoubtedly fare the best").

41 Raymond H. Brescia, *Beyond Balls and Strikes: Towards a Problem-Solving Ethic in Foreclosure Proceedings*, 59 Case W. Res. L. Rev. 305, 315 (2009).

42 Gerald Nora, *Prosecutor as "Nurse Ratched"? Misusing Criminal Justice as Alternative Medicine*, 22 Crim. Just. 18, 22(Fall 2007).

43 *Id.*

health courts—following the models of Judge Wren,[44] Judge Matthew D'Emic,[45] Judge Michael Finkle,[46] and others[47]—is a major component in the prescription of dignity for this population, and, importantly, as a way to minimize sanism.[48]

D. Alternative Jurisprudences

The adoption of alternative jurisprudences would treat defendants more humanely, would better insure their "voice" and would make more likely that their decisionmaking in the criminal trial process was voluntary.[49]

1. Therapeutic Jurisprudence

The deployment of therapeutic jurisprudence would make it more likely that defendants would be satisfied with the outcome of court proceedings, and, in cases involving therapeutic intervention, this outcome satisfaction would lead to greater compliance and "success."[50] It would give richer textures to sentencing procedures, and would more likely bring about the sort of reconciliation that can only be positive for mental health purposes.[51]

---

44 *See* Wren, *supra* note 29.

45 *See* Matthew J. D'Emic, *The Promise of Mental Health Courts*, 22 CRIM. JUST. 24 (Fall 2007) (New York).

46 *See* Anne Harper & Michael Finkle, *Mental Health Courts: Judicial Leadership and Effective Court Intervention*, 51 JUDGES' J. 4 (Spring 2012) (Washington).

47 *E.g.*, Judge Stephanie Rhoades of Alaska; *see* Shauhin Talesh, *Mental Health Court Judges as Dynamic Risk Managers: A New Conceptualization of the Role of Judges*, 57 DEPAUL L. REV. 93, 115 (2007) (discussing Judge Rhoades).

48 *See* Sana Loue, *The Involuntary Civil Commitment of Mentally Ill Persons in the United States and Romania: A Comparative Analysis*, 23 J. LEGAL MED. 211, 235 n.120 (2002) (same) ("sanist biases may be reduced through the establishment of mental health courts, with a judiciary trained to be sensitive to such issues"), citing Elaine M. Andrews & Stephanie Rhoades, *Anchorage District Court Initiates Two New Programs: People with Disabilities Offered Alternatives in Judicial Proceeding*, 23 ALASKA BAR RAG 1 (May/June 1999). I discuss this proposition in Perlin, *supra* note 10, at 748.

49 *See generally* Amy D. Ronner, *The Learned-Helpless Lawyer: Clinical Legal Education and Therapeutic Jurisprudence as Antidotes to Bartleby Syndrome*, 24 TOURO L. REV. 601, 627 (2008) (describing the "three Vs": voice, validation and voluntariness). *See supra* pp. 82–83.

50 *See, e.g.*, Bernard P. Perlmutter, *George's Story: Voice and Transformation Through the Teaching and Practice of Therapeutic Jurisprudence in a Law School Child Advocacy Clinic*, 17 ST. THOMAS L. REV. 561, 596 (2005) ("Even when the hearing outcome is negative, people treated fairly, in good faith, and with respect, experience greater satisfaction with the result and are more likely to comply with the decision rendered by the court").

51 *See generally* Edna Erez, *Victim Voice, Impact Statements and Sentencing: Integrating Restorative Justice and Therapeutic Jurisprudence Principles in Adversarial Proceedings*, 40 CRIM. L. BULL. 483 (2004); *see, e.g.*, Bruce Winick, *Therapeutic Jurisprudence and the Role of Counsel in Litigation*, 37 CAL. W. L. REV. 105, 112–13 (2000), discussing how the application of TJ to the negotiation process helps "to achieve

We must also recognize that TJ perspectives in criminal procedure cannot be limited to the specific substantive questions that I address in this book. In a recent important essay, Professor David Wexler charges us to "examine the governing 'legal landscapes' (legal rules and legal procedures) in mainstream criminal courts to see how 'TJ-friendly'—or unfriendly—they may be."[52] If we take this challenge seriously—as we should and must— we will begin to incorporate TJ into *all* aspects of the criminal trial process, a decision that cannot help but benefit persons with mental disabilities at all stages of that process.

2. Procedural Justice

There is no disputing the fact that procedural justice principles apply to cases involving persons subject to civil commitment[53] and to criminal cases in general.[54] And we should be equally clear that it applies—or at least, it should apply—to matters involving determinations of incompetency,[55] insanity,[56] and sentencing in cases involving defendants with serious mental disabilities.[57]

Over a decade ago, I wrote about the moment when I realized how sanism dominated the legal process as it applied to persons with mental disabilities:

---

reconciliation. Exercising a degree of control and self-determination in significant aspects of one's life may be an important ingredient of psychological wellbeing.").

52 David B. Wexler, *New Wine in New Bottles: The Need to Sketch a Therapeutic Jurisprudence "Code" of Proposed Criminal Processes and Practices*, in THERAPEUTIC JURISPRUDENCE AND PROBLEM-SOLVING JUSTICE (Jane Donoghue, ed., 2013) (in press).

53 *See* Tom Tyler, *The Psychological Consequences of Judicial Procedures: Implications for Civil Commitment Hearings*, 46 SMU L. REV., 433, 443 (1992), as discussed in Michael L. Perlin & Deborah A. Dorfman, *"Is It More Than Dodging Lions and Wastin' Time"? Adequacy of Counsel, Questions of Competence, and the Judicial Process in Individual Right to Refuse Treatment Cases*, 2 PSYCHOLOGY, PUB. POL'Y & L.114, 119 (1996).

54 *See, e.g.*, Ronner, *supra* note 48, at 93–94 (when criminal defendants believe legal system has treated them with fairness, dignity, and respect, they are less likely to recidivate).

55 A decade ago, LeRoy Kondo pointed out that achieving procedural justice would be difficult in jurisdictions in which, the burden of proof to demonstrate incompetency was on the defendant. *See* LeRoy Kondo, *Advocacy of the Establishment of Mental Health Specialty Courts in the Provision of Therapeutic Justice for Mentally Ill Offenders*, 28 AM. J. CRIM. L. 255, 294–95 (2001). In 1992, the Supreme Court sanctioned this practice in Medina v. California, 505 U.S. 437 (1992). *See* Michael L. Perlin, *The Sanist Lives of Jurors in Death Penalty Cases: The Puzzling Role of Mitigating Mental Disability Evidence*, 8 NOTRE DAME J. L., ETHICS & PUB. POL. 239, 274 (1994) (criticizing Medina for its likely impact on death penalty cases involving defendants with serious mental disabilities).

56 *See* Kondo, *supra* note 55, at 294 (discussing jurisdictions in which the burden of proving an insanity defense was shifted to the defendant, or where the defense was abolished). *See* Michael L. Perlin, *Unpacking the Myths: The Symbolism Mythology of Insanity Defense Jurisprudence*, 40 CASE W. RES. L. REV. 599 (1989–90) (criticizing the abolition movement).

57 *See, e.g.*, Adam Lamparello, *Incorporating the Procedural Justice Model into Federal Sentencing Jurisprudence in the Aftermath of United States v. Booker: Establishing United States Sentencing Courts*, 4 N.Y.U. J.L. & LIBERTY 112 (2009).

> I remember, over twenty years ago, the moment when I read [Dr. Morton] Birnbaum's essay,[58] and how, immediately, something simply "clicked." At that point in time, I had already spent several years providing individual and class action representation to institutionalized persons with mental disabilities,[59] and I had grown accustomed to asides, snickers, and comments from judges, to "eyerolling" from my adversaries, to running monologue commentaries by bailiffs and court clerks (all about my clients' "oddness"). But I had never before consciously identified what Birnbaum had been writing about: that this was all sanist behavior on the part of the other participants in the mental disability law system.[60]

This sort of behavior is the antithesis of sort of procedural justice that must be the centerpiece of any morally coherent criminal justice system.

3. Restorative Justice

The use of restorative justice principles in cases involving these cohorts of defendants will both minimize the power of sanism (by combating stigma)[61] and increase dignity.[62] It has been said—accurately, I believe—that restorative justice is a focus on the "restoration of human dignity."[63] If restorative justice fulfills its mandate—that all individuals, including offenders "should be treated in a humane, egalitarian way that values their worth as human beings and respects their right to justice and dignity"[64]—then its application to the sorts of cases discussed here should be clear. If its core values of "healing rather than hurting, moral learning, community participation and community caring, respectful

---

58 The phrase "sanism" was most likely coined by Dr. Morton Birnbaum. See *supra* Chapter 2, note 9.

59 Much of this work was on behalf of individuals at the Vroom Building, then New Jersey's maximum security facility for the "criminally insane." *See* Perlin, *supra* note 38, at 7.

60 *Id.* at 9.

61 On how restorative justice can do this, see Jessica A. Focht-Perlberg, *Two Sides of One Coin – Repairing the Harm and Reducing Recidivism: A Case for Restorative Justice in Reentry in Minnesota and Beyond*, 31 Hamline J. Pub. L. & Pol'y 219, 251–52 (2009).

62 On how restorative justice can do this, see Thomas L. Hafemeister, Sharon G. Garner & Veronica E. Bath, *Forging Links and Renewing Ties: Applying the Principles of Restorative and Procedural Justice to Better Respond to Criminal Offenders with a Mental Disorder*, 60 Buff. L. Rev. 147, 197 (2012).

63 Mijha Butcher, *Using Mediation to Remedy Civil Rights Violations When the Defendant is Not an Intentional Perpetrator: The Problems of Unconscious Disparate Treatment and Unjustified Disparate Impacts*, 24 Hamline J. Pub. L. & Pol'y 225, 252 (2003); *see also*, Ric Simmons, *Private Criminal Justice*, 42 Wake Forest L. Rev. 911, 949 (2007) ("a major tenet of restorative justice is recognizing the humanity and dignity of all the participants").

64 Gerry Johnstone, Restorative Justice: Ideas, Values, Debates 11 (2002), as quoted in Angela Harris, *Heteropatriarchy Kills: Challenging Gender Violence in a Prison Nation*, 37 Wash. U. J.L. & Pol'y 13, 48 n.121 (2011).

dialogue, forgiveness, responsibility, apology, and making amends"[65] are to be effectuated in cases involving the population that is at the heart of this book, then it is necessary to keep focus on the pernicious power of sanism.

4. Combining the Alternative Jurisprudences

As stated flatly by Judge Juan Ramirez and Professor Amy Ronner, "the right to counsel is … the core of therapeutic jurisprudence."[66] If counsel representing persons with mental disabilities in criminal trials fails to meet the standards articulated in the Convention on the Rights of Persons with Disabilities—as well as constitutional minima—it strains credulity to argue that such a practice might comport with TJ principles. TJ is the perfect mechanism "to expose [the law's] pretextuality";[67] this pretextuality is clear in the context of the cases discussed in this volume. And, of course, TJ underpins the mental health court movement. Notes Judge Wren: "A core principle in the Broward County Mental Health Court, which is common to all existing U.S. specialty courts, is a strong commitment by the presiding judge to therapeutic jurisprudence."[68] In addition, we are now discovering significant and robust connections between TJ principles and international human rights principles as they relate to mental disability-law-specific questions.[69]

There is more. We know that "procedural justice is a key to the success of mental health courts,"[70] and that it is critical to the enforcement of international

65 John Braithwaite, *Restorative Justice: Assessing Optimistic and Pessimistic Accounts*, 25 Crime & Just. 1, 5 (1999). Braithwaite acknowledges that international human rights (see *supra* Chapter 4) are a "constraining value" on restorative justice. John Braithwaite, *Principles of Restorative Justice*, in Restorative Justice & Criminal Justice: Competing or Reconcilable Paradigms 1, 9 (Andrew von Hirsch et al eds, 2003). *Compare* Thomas Antowiak, *An Emerging Mandate for International Courts: Victim-Centered Remedies and Restorative Justice*, 47 Stan. J. Int'l L. 279 (2011). On how the restorative justice discourse must be "broaden[ed]" around the issue of international human rights, see Ann Skelton & Makubetse Sekhonyane, *Human Rights and Restorative Justice*, in Handbook of Restorative Justice 580, 591–93 (Gerry Johnstone & Daniel W. Van Ness, eds, 2007).

66 Juan Ramirez Jr. & Amy D. Ronner, *Voiceless Billy Budd: Melville's Tribute to the Sixth Amendment*, 41 Cal. Western L. Rev. 103, 119 (2004).

67 Michael L. Perlin, *"Things Have Changed": Looking at Non-Institutional Mental Disability Law through the Sanism Filter*, 46 N.Y. L. Sch. L. Rev. 535, 544 (2002–03).

68 Wren, *supra* note 29, at 590; *see also* http://www.nda.ie/cntmgmtnew.nsf/0/8B71583417C5138080257444003F95FC/$File/NDAConferenceLuncheonRemarkspresented%20byJudgeGingerLerner_Wren.htm (remarks by Judge Wren at National Disability Authority Conference (Ireland), October 2008); Broward's Mental Health Court, *A Community Creates Change and Leads a Nation* (June 2007).

69 Perlin, *supra* note 20, at 217.

70 Hafemeister, Garner & Bath, *supra* note 62, at 201–02. An important open question is whether participants in felony mental health courts perceive more or less coercion and more or less procedural justice than participants in misdemeanor mental health courts. *See* Carol Fisler, *Building Trust and Managing Risk: A Look at a Felony Mental Health Court*, 11 Psychol. Pub. Pol'y & L. 587, 602 (2005).

human rights law.[71] Moreover, "procedural justice hinges on access to and the assistance of counsel."[72] Restorative justice values also must be considered in the context of the other perspectives discussed here. Counsel must be able to apply these principles in the whole range of cases involving defendants with mental disabilities.[73] As noted by Professor Bruce Archibald, "Restorative justice initiatives can originate with defence counsel who identify the appropriate community resources, and present prosecutors with an attractive alternative in the process of plea discussions."[74] Beyond this, the evidence seems to suggest that offenders diverted to mental health courts "will similarly be amenable to restorative justice sessions."[75] And, to a great extent, restorative justice is a concept drawn from the international human rights context, as it "seeks to repair society through reconciliation, ultimately healing both victims and society itself."[76] Finally, Brian Sellers and Professor Bruce Arrigo consider TJ and RJ together, and conclude that the "collective effect" of these practices is "the cultivation of an integrity-based society," in which "the moral fiber of individuals is more fully embraced and the flourishing prospects for human justice are more completely realized."[77]

---

71 *See, e.g.*, Gates Garrity-Rokous & Raymond H. Brescia, *Procedural Justice and International Human Rights: Towards a Procedural Jurisprudence for Human Rights Tribunals*, 18 Yale J. Int'l L. 559 (1993), and *see id.* at 603:

> Increased access and broader due process protection by regional adjudicators can enhance the perceived legitimacy of a regional system among both its member states and their populations. Thus a procedural jurisprudence that emphasizes due process over political unity concerns will bolster the unity of the system in the long term.

72 Barry C. Feld, *Abolish the Juvenile Court: Youthfulness, Criminal Responsibility, and Sentencing Policy*, 88 J. Crim. L. & Criminology 68, 89 (1997).

73 *Compare* Kristen F. Grunewald & Priya Nath, *Defense-Based Victim Outreach: Restorative Justice in Capital Cases*, 15 Cap. Def. J. 315, 338 (2003) ("Counsel should provide the court with the victim liaison's specific goals and the means by which the liaison applies the principles of restorative justice to *capital cases*" (emphasis added).

74 Bruce P. Archibald, *The Politics of Prosecutorial Discretion: Institutional Structures and the Tensions Between Punitive and Restorative Paradigms of Justice*, 3 Can. Crim. L. Rev. 69, 90 (1998).

75 Hafemeister, Garner & Bath, *supra* note 62, at 220. *See generally* Randal B. Fritzler, *How One Misdemeanor Mental Health Court Incorporates Therapeutic Jurisprudence, Preventive Law, and Restorative Justice*, in Management and Administration of Correctional Health Care: Policy, Practice, Administration 17 (Jacqueline Moore ed., 2003).

76 Kaimipono David Wenger, *"Too Big to Remedy?" Rethinking Mass Restitution for Slavery and Jim Crow*, 44 Loyola L.A. L. Rev. 177, 227–28 (2010). *See generally* Daniel W. Van Ness, Restorative Justice and International Human Rights, in Restorative Justice: International Perspectives 17, 24 (Burt Galaway & Joe Hudson eds, 1996).

77 Brian G. Sellers & Bruce A. Arrigo, *Adolescent Transfer, Developmental Maturity, and Adjudicative Competence: An Ethical and Justice Policy Inquiry*, 99 J. Crim. L. & Criminology 435, 439 (2009).

As I discussed earlier, the connection between the core principle of dignity and the other topics under discussion here should be clear. The right to dignity in all aspects of the criminal trial process is mandated by international rights principles,[78] and dignity, similarly, is at the core of restorative justice,[79] procedural justice[80] and therapeutic jurisprudence;[81] it also is the key underpinning of mental health courts.[82]

So, how would embracing these concepts "play out" in the substantive aspects of criminal law and procedure under discussion in this book?

III. The Three Substantive Areas of the Criminal Law

A. Competencies

First, consider the application of TJ principles to the question of competency to stand trial. In a recent article,[83] I considered some of the dilemmas that a TJ-friendly defense lawyer might need to ponder in a case involving a client whose competence is in question:

---

78 *See* Rett R. Ludwikowski, *Fundamental Constitutional Rights in the New Constitutions of Eastern and Central Europe*, 3 CARDOZO J. INT'L & COMP. L. 73, 75 (1995).

79 *See* Butcher, *supra* note 63, at 252 (restorative justice is a focus on the "restoration of human dignity"); David M. Lerman, *Restoring Dignity, Effecting Justice*, 26 HUM. RTS. Q. 20, 20–21 (Fall 1999) (describing successful restorative justice processes in several states). On restorative dignity, see Judith Baker, *Truth Commissions*, 51 U. TORONTO L.J. 309, 321 (2001); *see generally* Joan W. Howarth, *Toward the Restorative Constitution: A Restorative Justice Critique of Anti-Gang Public Nuisance Injunctions*, 27 HASTINGS CONST. L.Q. 717, 720 n.10 (2000) (citing research articles).

80 *See* Joseph B. Stulberg, *Mediation and Justice: What Standards Govern?*, 6 CARDOZO J. CONFLICT RESOL. 213, 227–28 (2005); Tom R. Tyler & E. Allan Lind, *Procedural Justice*, in HANDBOOK OF JUSTICE RESEARCH IN LAW 65, 74–77 (Joseph Sanders & V. Lee Hamilton eds, 2001).

81 *See* Christina A. Zawisza & Adela Beckerman, *Two Heads Are Better Than One: The Case-Based Rationale for Dual Disciplinary Teaching in Child Advocacy Clinics*, 7 FLA. COASTAL L. REV. 631, 643 (2006); David C. Yamada, *Human Dignity and American Employment Law*, 43 U. RICH. L. REV. 523 (2009).

82 Michael L. Perlin, *"There Are No Trials Inside the Gates of Eden": Mental Health Courts, the Convention on the Rights of Persons with Disabilities, Dignity, and the Promise of Therapeutic Jurisprudence*, in COERCIVE CARE: LAW AND POLICY (Bernadette McSherry & Ian Freckelton eds. 2013) (in press), relying on, inter alia, Norman Poythress et al., *Perceived Coercion and Procedural Justice in the Broward Mental Health Court*, 25 INT'L J. L. & PSYCHIATRY 517 (2002).

83 Michael L. Perlin, *"Too Stubborn To Ever Be Governed By Enforced Insanity": Some Therapeutic Jurisprudence Dilemmas in the Representation of Criminal Defendants in Incompetency and Insanity Cases*, 33 INT'L J. L. & PSYCHIATRY 475 (2010).

- If a defendant is, in fact, incompetent to stand trial, that means that he does not have "sufficient present ability to consult with his lawyer with a reasonable degree of rational understanding" and or a "rational as well as factual understanding of the proceedings against him;"[84] how can TJ principles be invoked in such a case?
- If a defendant is initially found to be incompetent to stand trial, will the lawyer act as most lawyers and consider him to be de facto incompetent for the entire proceeding (as a significant percentage of lawyers do act for any client who is institutionalized)?[85]
- If a defendant is found to be incompetent to stand trial, will the lawyer assume that he is also guilty of the underlying criminal charge?[86]
- What are the issues that a lawyer must consider in addition to the client's mental state in assessing whether or not to invoke an incompetency determination?[87]
- What are the TJ implications for a case in which the incompetency status is not raised by the defendant, but, rather, by the prosecutor or the judge?[88]
- Are there times when TJ principles might mandate not raising the incompetency status (for example, in a case in which the maximum sentence to which the defendant is exposed is six months in a county workhouse but is in a jurisdiction in which IST defendants are regularly housed in maximum security forensic facilities for far longer periods of time than the maximum to which they could be sentenced)?[89]

---

84 Dusky v. United States, 362 U.S. 402, 402 (1960). *See* Michael L. Perlin, *For the Misdemeanor Outlaw: The Impact of the ADA on the Institutionalization of Criminal Defendants with Mental Disabilities*, 52 Alabama L. Rev. 193, 200 (2000) (criticizing Dusky as "confusing and less than helpful").

85 *See* Perlin, *supra* note 18, at 696–97 ("these lawyers treat their clients as 'patients that are sick'," quoting Bruce Arrigo, Punishing the Mentally Ill: A Critical Analysis of Law and Psychiatry 29–30 (2002)).

86 *See* Michael L. Perlin, *"Everything's a Little Upside Down, As a Matter of Fact the Wheels Have Stopped": The Fraudulence of the Incompetency Evaluation Process*, 4 Houston J. Health L. & Pol'y 239, 246 (2004) (on how invoking the incompetency status leads all to assume that the defendant is factually guilty of the underlying crime), and see *supra* p. 149.

See also *id.*, discussing hypothetical posed in Perlin, *supra* note 84, at 206–7.

87 *See, e.g.*, Paul A. Chernoff & William G. Schaffer, *Defending the Mentally Ill: Ethical Quicksand*, 10 Am. Crim. L. Rev. 505 (1972); Christopher Slobogin & Amy Mashburn, *The Criminal Defense Lawyer's Fiduciary Duty to Clients with Mental Disability*, 68 Fordham L. Rev. 1581 (2000).

88 *See* Perlin, *supra* note 84, at 198 n.33: "Also, unlike other criminal pleas, [the incompetency status] can be raised *sua sponte* by the court or the prosecutor." *See* Drope v. Missouri, 420 U.S. 162 (1975); 18 U.S.C. § 4241 (a) (1994); Hamm v. Jabe, 706 F.2d 765, 767 (6th Cir. 1983); United States v. Warren, 984 F.2d 325, 329 (9th Cir. 1993).

89 *See generally* Perlin, *supra* note 84, at 201–07. I pose a variant on this question in Michael L. Perlin, Mental Disability Law: Cases and Materials 753 (2d ed. 2005).

And there is more. If counsel assumes the guilt of her client about whom the incompetency status has been raised,[90] if she assumes that the entry of an incompetency status is a "victory,"[91] if she blinds herself to the reality that many of the defendants who are found to be incompetent will be consigned to maximum security hospitals for decades or even for life in cases involving minor offenses,[92] it is likely that dignity will never be attained.

Consideration of the perspectives raised here could end—or, at least, sharply limit—these practices. Competent counsel has an important role to play in this process; she needs to consider the implications of international human rights law and the potential for diversion to mental health court in a significant portion of these cases.

If the defendant is taken more seriously at the competency stage, procedural justice principles tell us that the "outcome" (in the broadest sense of that word) will be far better than if he is sanistly trivialized in pretextual court proceedings. The cleansing of stigma—a major focal point of restorative justice—is also a more likely outcome. Writing about the case of *Godniez v. Moran*[93] some years ago, I began the title of my article, "Dignity was the first to leave."[94] Dignity is sorely lacking in all aspects of the incompetency process.

Consider also other competency statuses. Often, we privilege autonomy only in cases of defendants with serious mental disabilities who wish to represent themselves, often pretextually insuring their conviction.[95] Justice Scalia's

---

90 *See* Perlin, *supra* note 86, at 246:

> Although there is nothing in the invocation of the incompetency status that at all concedes factual guilt (as opposed to the entry of a not-guilty-by-reason-of-insanity plea that concedes the commission of the underlying criminal act), it is assumed by all that the defendant did, in fact, commit the crime.

91 On how such victories may by "Pyrrhic," see S.D. Parwatikar et al., *The Detection of Malingered Amnesia in Accused Murderers*, 13 Bull. Am. Acad. Psychiatry & L. 97, 102–03 (1985).

92 *See generally* Perlin, *supra* note 84.

93 509 U.S. 389 (1993).

94 *See* Michael L. Perlin, *"Dignity Was the First to Leave": Godinez v. Moran, Colin Ferguson, and the Trial of Mentally Disabled Criminal Defendants*, 14 Behav. Sci. & L. 61 (1996).

95 *See id.* at 63:

> At the time, *Godinez* was seen as yet another Supreme Court criminal procedure victory for prosecutors, and as a means of insuring both more convictions and fewer appellate reversals of convictions. If all that was required was a finding that the defendant could meet the incompetency to stand trial test of *Dusky v. United States* (that the defendant had a "rational understanding of die proceedings") then it would be likely that more mentally ill-but-legally-competent defendants would plead guilty and would waive counsel. In both instances, more convictions—convictions now nearly impervious (on these grounds, at least) on appeal—would flow.

cynical dissent in *Indiana v. Edwards*,[96] while couched in purportedly non-sanist language, meretriciously advances sanist ends.[97] Similarly, we pretextually ignore Supreme Court doctrine in cases such as *Ford v. Wainwright*[98] and *Panetti v. Quarterman*.[99] Recall my earlier reference to the pathetic record of the Fifth Circuit in its across-the-board rejections of *Ford* claims in the years before *Panetti*.[100] Courts simply assume that a death row defendant is *not* sufficiently mentally disabled to bar execution.[101] And then consider the fact that, on remand, Panetti's writ of *habeas corpus* was denied because, in the view of the trial judge, Panetti had "both a factual and rational understanding of his crime, his impending death, and the causal retributive connection between the two,"[102] and then consider this against the tableau of the *Panetti* trial since memorialized in multiple law review articles.[103]

Again, dignity is totally missing from this picture.

B. Insanity

Think next about insanity. We regularly assume that any defendant who pleads insanity is presumptively dangerous.[104] We accept unthinkingly the regularity of sanist appeals by prosecutors in insanity defense summations, arguing that insanity defenses are easily faked,[105] that insanity acquittees are often immediately

96 554 U.S. 164 (2008) (state can limit defendant's self-representation at trial by insisting on representation by counsel if defendant lacks capacity to conduct trial defense unless so represented); *see generally* Michael L. Perlin & Heather Ellis Cucolo, Mental Disability Law: Civil and Criminal § 8B-3.1c(1), at 44–51 (2012 Cum. Supp.), discussing *Edwards* in this context.

97 *Id.* at 48.

98 477 U.S. 399 (1986).

99 551 U.S. 930 (2007).

100 *See supra* Chapter 8.

101 Perlin, *supra* note 18, Chapter 7. On Panetti's trial, see *supra* Chapter 7 at notes 28–32.

102 Panetti v. Quarterman, 2008 WL 2338498, *37 (W.D. Tex. 2008).

103 *See, e.g.*, Lyn Entzeroth, *The Challenge and Dilemma of Charting a Course to Constitutionally Protect the Severely Mentally Ill Capital Defendant from the Death Penalty*, 44 Akron L. Rev. 529, 557 n.152 (2011); Richard J. Bonnie, *Panetti v. Quarterman: Mental Illness, the Death Penalty, and Human Dignity*, 5 Ohio St. J. Crim. L. 257, 261 (2007); Christopher Seeds, *The Afterlife of Ford and Panetti: Execution Competence and the Capacity to Assist Counsel*, 53 St. Louis U. L. J. 309 (2009).

104 Indeed, this was the rationale of Jones v. United States, 463 U.S. 354 (1983), an attempted shoplifting case. I discuss this in this context in Perlin, *supra* note 84, at 194.

105 *See generally* Michael L. Perlin, *"The Borderline Which Separated You From Me": The Insanity Defense, the Authoritarian Spirit, the Fear of Faking, and the Culture of Punishment*, 82 Iowa L. Rev. 1375 (1997).

released,[106] and that expert witnesses in such cases are readily duped.[107] As in the case of the defendant who is potentially incompetent to stand trial, consider again the similar dilemmas facing the potential insanity pleader:

- What are the TJ implications of counseling a defendant to plead, or not to plead, the insanity defense?[108]
- Can a defendant who pleads NGRI ever, truly, "take responsibility?"[109]
- Does the fact that the insanity-pleading defendant must concede that he committed the actus reus distort the ongoing lawyer–client relationship?[110]
- To what extent do the ample bodies of case law in cases involving defendants with mental disabilities (including insanity defense cases) that construe the "ineffectiveness assistance of counsel" standard established by the US Supreme Court in *Strickland v. Washington*[111] even consider the implications of TJ lawyering?[112]
- To what extent does the pervasiveness of sanism make it obligatory for lawyers in such cases to educate jurors about both sanism and why sanism

---

106 *See* Michael L. Perlin, The Jurisprudence of the Insanity Defense 110–11 (1994).

107 *See* Michael L. Perlin, *"His Brain Has Been Mismanaged with Great Skill": How Will Jurors Respond to Neuroimaging Testimony in Insanity Defense Cases?*, 42 Akron L. Rev. 885, 900–01 (2009).

108 *See, e.g.*, Richard J. Bonnie et al., *Decision-Making in Criminal Defense: An Empirical Study of Insanity Pleas and the Impact of Doubted Client Competence*, 87 J. Crim. L. & Criminology 48 (1996). *See generally* Perlin, *supra* note 83, at 479–81. I refer to these same dilemmas extensively *supra* Chapter 9.

109 *See* Michael L. Perlin & Keri K. Gould, *Rashomon and the Criminal Law: Mental Disability and the Federal Sentencing Guidelines*, 22 Am. J. Crim. L. 431, 449 (1995):

> The entry of the insanity plea has been seen as evidence of a failure to demonstrate contrition (presumably because the plea entry denied legal responsibility for the offense), and that lack of contrition has been seen as a failure to accept responsibility, thus bringing the defendant out of the ambit of another Guideline, which provides for a downward departure if the defendant "clearly demonstrates a recognition and affirmative acceptance of personal responsibility for his criminal conduct."

110 *See* Jones v. United States, 463 U.S. 354, 363 (1983) ("a verdict of not guilty by reason of insanity establishes two facts: (i) the defendant committed an act that constitutes a criminal offense, and (ii) he committed the act because of mental illness.").

111 466 U.S. 668, 689 (1984) ("whether counsel's conduct so undermined the proper function of the adversarial process that the trial court cannot be relied on as having produced a just result").

112 *See* 4 Michael L. Perlin, Mental Disability Law: Civil and Criminal (2d ed. 2002), § 8A-4.3, at 60–65 (adequacy of counsel in IST proceedings), and § 9A-7, at 235–41 (adequacy of counsel in insanity cases) § 12-3.6, at 505–10 (adequacy of counsel in death penalty cases involving defendants with mental disabilities) (discussing case law).

> may be driving their decision-making in insanity defense cases, and to what extent should lawyers in such cases embark on this educational process using TJ principles?[113]

There are multiple TJ-related questions about the insanity defense that need to be answered: Is a nonresponsibility verdict therapeutic? Does the substantive standard really matter for TJ purposes? Do procedural rules matter for TJ purposes? Should post-acquittal commitment procedures track the traditional civil commitment model? Once institutionalized, how should insanity acquittees be treated? How should such acquittees be monitored in community settings?[114] To what extent have these dilemmas been meaningfully confronted by the criminal justice system?

In discussing the impact of sanism on the criminal justice system, John Parry focuses on its pernicious impact on judges and jurors: "Stigma affects the law in at least two interrelated ways: (1) negative effects on the liberty interests of the person with a mental disability, who is the subject of a legal proceeding, and (2) potential bias, due to sanism, that judges and other courtroom participants may demonstrate towards that person."[115] I believe that this same bias permeates the representation of all defendants in cases involving incompetency, insanity or sentencing issues.[116]

Sanism permeates the legal representation process both in cases in which mental capacity is a central issue and in those in which such capacity is a collateral question. Sanist lawyers (1) distrust their mentally disabled clients, (2) trivialize their complaints, (3) fail to forge authentic attorney–client relationships with such clients and reject their clients' potential contributions to case strategizing, and (4) take less seriously case outcomes that are adverse to their clients.[117]

In an earlier article about the right to refuse treatment in the civil commitment context, I said that "the failure to assign adequate counsel bespeaks sanism and pretextuality."[118] The problems are multiplied tenfold (at least) in criminal procedure cases in which defendants face the death penalty or lengthy prison

---

113 On the sanism of jurors in general, see Perlin, *supra* note 55, at 242; *see also*, Michael L. Perlin, *"Life Is In Mirrors, Death Disappears": Giving Life to Atkins*, 33 N. Mex. L. Rev. 315, 335 (2003), quoting Denis Keyes et al., *Mitigating Mental Retardation in Capital Cases: Finding the "Invisible" Defendant*, 22 Mental & Physical Disability L. Rep. 529, 536 (1998) (stating that "the defense lawyer must educate the jury about mental retardation, its various presentations, and the distinct difference between mental retardation and mental illness").

114 Perlin, *supra* note 3, at 288–301.

115 John Parry, *The Death Penalty and Persons with Mental Disabilities: A Lethal Dose of Stigma, Sanism, Fear of Violence, and Faulty Predictions of Dangerousness*, 29 Mental & Physical Disability L. Rep. 667 (2005).

116 I also believe it is an issue in death penalty cases. *See generally*, Perlin, *supra* note 18; see Parry, *supra* note 115, at 667 ("Nowhere is [the] prejudice [of sanism] more apparent than with capital punishment").

117 Perlin, *supra* note 18, at 695.

118 Perlin, *supra* note 10, at 750.

sentences. In this environment, it is easy to see how in death penalty cases, by way of example, inadequate counsel can lead evidence of mental illness that was ostensibly introduced for mitigating purposes[119] to be construed by judges as aggravating instead.[120] In one notorious Florida case, for example, a trial judge concluded that because of the defendant's mental disability (paranoid schizophrenia manifested by hallucinations in which he "saw" others in a "yellow haze"), "the only assurance society can receive that this man never again commits to another human being what he did to [the brutally murdered decedent] is that the ultimate sentence of death be imposed."[121] And of course "[j]udicial complicity in the assignment and performance of inadequate counsel evidences sanism."[122]

Pretextually and sanistly—relying on the vividness heuristic and false "ordinary common sense"—we close our eyes to the ways that defendants with legitimate insanity defenses are denied such defenses and are sent to prison, in spite of the fact that many in this cohort are not responsible for their actions.[123] Although largely beyond the scope of this book, we also close our eyes to the conditions of confinement faced by such defendants when they are successful in insanity pleas and are then sent to *de facto* prisons that masquerade as maximum security forensic hospitals.[124] Again, our insanity defense system provides neither procedural justice nor restorative justice, and it denies defendants the basic modicum of dignity to which they are constitutionally and morally entitled.

C. Sentencing

There are multiple relevant collateral questions to consider in the context of the sentencing of defendants with mental disabilities:

- What is the relationship between duress and diminished mental capacity in this context?
- Is there a right to a psychiatric evaluation prior to sentencing (and is there a right to funds for such an evaluation?
- What is the impact of intellectual disability on a defendant's gullibility and ability to be manipulated, thus leading to a plea (and ultimate sentence) in a case in which he may be factually innocent?
- How treatable is the defendant's mental disorder?

---

119 *See supra* chapter 4.

120 *See* Ellen F. Berkman, *Mental Illness as an Aggravating Circumstance in Capital Sentencing*, 89 Colum. L. Rev. 291, 299–300 (1989); Christopher Slobogin, Minding Justice: Laws That Deprive People with Mental Disabilities of Life and Liberty 90–96 (2006).

121 Miller v. State, 373 So. 2d 882, 885 (Fla. 1979) (vacating death sentence).

122 Perlin, *supra* note 10, at 751.

123 *See* Perlin, *supra* note 106, at 310 (on the "wrong verdict" phenomenon).

124 *Id.* at 110–11.

- To what extent is the trial judge likely to lengthen the sentence of a defendant he believes to be feigning mental disability?
- Should there be a relationship between the defendant's mental disability and the propriety of imposing consecutive sentences?[125]

We ignore the sentencing outcomes of defendants with serious mental disabilities, and pay little attention to the fates that befall them in prisons. The evidence is crystal-clear that downward departures are often not entered in cases of defendants with severe mental disabilities;[126] in fact, there is evidence of cases in which past insanity acquittals have been seen as aggravating circumstances worthy of *upward* departures.[127] This too subordinates dignity values.[128] And counsel needs to consider restorative justice issues at this juncture as well.[129]

In two papers that I have written with Astrid Birgden, an Australian forensic psychologist, we discuss the interconnectivity between international human rights law and therapeutic jurisprudence in the context of correctional law,[130] and argue that the adoption of human rights models "can assist therapeutic jurisprudence … develop a normative base,"[131] and that "therapeutic jurisprudence offers a

125 4 Perlin, *supra* note 112, § 11-2.1, at 456–58. On the question of factual innocence, see Perlin, *supra* note 18, at 5–9; Michael L. Perlin, *Mental Disability, Factual Innocence and the Death Penalty* (paper presented to the Asian Society of Criminology, Seoul, Korea, August 2012) (on file with author).

126 *See generally* Perlin & Gould, *supra* note 109.

127 *Id.* at 449 n.98, discussing United States v. Medved, 905 F.2d 935, 942 (6th Cir. 1990), and United States v. McKenley, 895 F.2d 184, 186 (4th Cir. 1990).

128 We must also consider the "dignity of risk," allowing persons with intellectual disabilities to take risks commensurate with their functioning, discussed *supra* Chapter 9, text accompanying note 167. *See* Robert Perske, *The Dignity of Risk*, reprinted in Wolf Wolfensberger, The Principle of Normalization in Human Services 194, 194–95 (1972) . Professor Elizabeth Nevins-Saunders argues that dignity will be enhanced if this population has the opportunity to "get [their] day in court and be treated as … accountable person[s]." Elizabeth Nevins-Saunders, *Not Guilty as Charged: The Myth of Mens Rea for Defendants with Mental Retardation*, 45 U.C. Davis L. Rev. 1419, 1474 (2012).

129 *See* Regina Austin, *Documentation, Documentary, and the Law: What Should Be Made of Victim Impact Videos?*, 31 Cardozo L. Rev. 979, 1009 (2010) ("Defense counsel should think of the sentencing phase of the trial, during which victim impact evidence and mitigation evidence are introduced, as the first step in a long process of rehabilitation and restorative justice").

130 *See* Astrid Birgden & Michael L. Perlin, *"Tolling for the Luckless, the Abandoned and Forsaked": Community Safety, Therapeutic Jurisprudence and International Human Rights Law As Applied to Prisoners and Detainees*, 13 Leg. & Criminol. Psychology 231 (2008) (*Tolling*); Astrid Birgden & Michael L. Perlin, *"Where The Home In The Valley Meets The Damp Dirty Prison": A Human Rights Perspective On Therapeutic Jurisprudence And The Role Of Forensic Psychologists In Correctional Settings*, 14 Aggression & Violent Behavior 256 (2009).

131 *Tolling*, *supra* note 130, at 235.

potentially redemptive solution" to the reality that prisoners and detainees with mental illness are frequently confined in prison and forensic facilities that "regularly and grossly violate international human rights standards."[132] This topic—the connection between these two sets of values—has not been the focus of much scholarly attention at all,[133] and I believe it is essential that we turn our immediate attention to it. Certainly, serious consideration of these issues would have the likely effect of making us think much more carefully about the ultimate outcome of any sentencing matter involving a defendant with a serious mental disability.

IV. Conclusion

The evidence is clear. If counsel takes her client seriously and takes her client's case seriously, dignity will be enhanced. If international human rights are taken seriously, dignity will be enhanced. If mental health courts follow the model created by Judge Wren, Judge D'Emic and others discussed here, dignity will be enhanced. If courts *and* counsel take alternative jurisprudential approaches seriously, dignity will be enhanced.

We know that sanism and pretextuality continue.[134] We know that the vividness heuristic and false "ordinary common sense"—fueled on media distortions—still control the public's view of the criminal trial process.[135] We know that counsel assigned to criminal defendants with mental disabilities all too often is "the

---

132 *Id.* at 240

133 *But see* Nicola Ferencz & James McGuire, *Mental Health Review Tribunals in the UK: Applying a Therapeutic Jurisprudence Perspective*, 37 Court Rev. 48 (Spring 2000); Tony Ward & Astrid Birgden, *Human Rights and Correctional Clinical Practice*, 12 Aggression & Violent Behav. 628 (2007); Bruce J. Winick, *Therapeutic Jurisprudence and the Treatment of People with Mental Illness in Eastern Europe: Construing International Human Rights Law*, 21 N.Y.L. Sch. J. Int'l & Comp. L. 537 (2002) (all discussing this intersection).

134 *See generally* William H. Fisher & Thomas Grisso, *Commentary: Civil Commitment Statutes—40 Years of Circumvention*, 38 J. Am. Acad. Psychiatry L. 365 (2010) (on pretextuality); Jennifer M. Poole et al., S*anism, "Mental Health," and Social Work/Education: A Review and Call to Action*, 1 Intersectionalities: Glob. J. Soc'l Work Anal., Res. Polity & Prac,. 20 (2012) (sanism).

135 *See, e.g.*, Eric Silver et al., *Demythologizing Inaccurate Perceptions of the Insanity Defense*, 18 Law & Hum. Behav. 63, 64 (1994) (researchers found that 86% of all print stories featuring former mental patients included a violent crime as its focus) *See also* Perlin, *supra* note 104, at 1407, (quoting Lisa Calvino, *Too Much Time*, Fresno Bee, Feb. 12, 1995, at B10):

> In the words of a thirteen-year-old. writing about the O.J.[Simpson] trial to the Fresno Bee: 'Of course, if he did do it, there's always the good old temporary insanity defense, a sure-fire way to bail out of just about any heinous crime, especially murder..

bottom of the barrel."[136] I titled this book "A prescription for dignity" because I believe that dignity is sorely missing from the entire criminal justice process in cases that involve defendants with mental disabilities. I hope I have made that point successfully. And, as I have stressed, I believe that a reformulation of what "adequacy of counsel" really means, that a deep consideration of human rights law, that an expansion of those mental health courts that take the mandate of "problem-solving court" seriously, and that adoption of the "alternative jurisprudences" I have discussed, when taken together, will best infuse the system with dignity. It is then, and only then, that we can effectively "strip the façade"[137] from the sanism that dominates this area of the law, that we can open our eyes to the dominance of pretextuality, that we can articulate responses to the cognitive-simplifying heuristics that control our discourse, and reject the false "ordinary common sense" that drives judicial and legislative decision-making in this area. Then, and only then, can we seriously talk about long-lasting and ameliorative reform in this most difficult and troubling area of law and policy, and, perhaps, again,[138] in the words of Professor Anthony Alfieri, finally "transform the criminal-justice system into a dignity-affirming institution."[139]

---

136 Victor Streib, *Would You Lie to Save Your Clien's Life? Ethics and Effectiveness in Defending against Death*, 42 Brandeis L.J. 405, 428 (2003/2004); *see generally* Stephen B. Bright, *Counsel for the Poor: The Death Sentence Nor for the Worst Crime but for the Worst Lawyer*, 103 Yale L.J. 1835 (1994).

137 *See, e.g.*, Michael L. Perlin, *Are Courts Competent to Decide Questions of Competency? Stripping the Facade From United States v. Charters*, 38 U. Kan. L. Rev. 957 (1990).

138 *See supra* Chapter 1, note 49.

139 Anthony V. Alfieri, *Jim Crow Ethics and the Defense of the Jena Six*, 94 Iowa L. Rev. 1651, 1689 (2009), discussing David Luban, Legal Ethics and Human Dignity 118 (2007).

Index